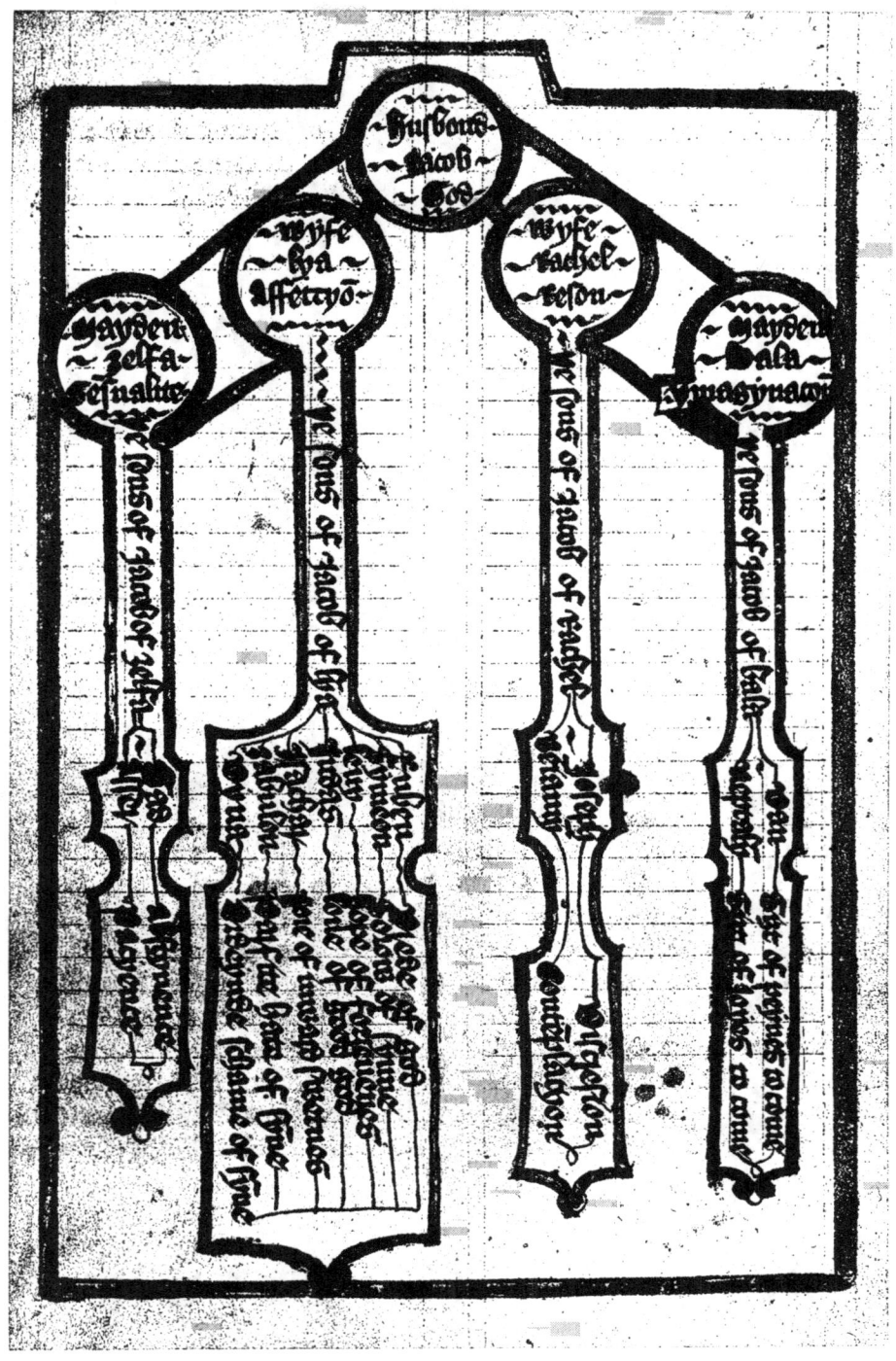

A Tretyse of þe Stodye of Wysdome þat Men
Clepen Beniamyn

MS. Harleian 674 (f. 112ª)

Deonise Hid Diuinite

AND OTHER
TREATISES ON CONTEMPLATIVE PRAYER
RELATED TO

The Cloud of Unknowing

A Tretyse of þe Stodye of Wysdome
þat Men Clepen Beniamyn

A Pistle of Preier

A Pistle of Discrecioun of Stirings

A Tretis of Discrescyon of Spirites

EDITED BY
PHYLLIS HODGSON

Published for
THE EARLY ENGLISH TEXT SOCIETY
by the
OXFORD UNIVERSITY PRESS
LONDON NEW YORK TORONTO

OXFORD

UNIVERSITY PRESS

Great Clarendon Street, Oxford OX2 6DP
United Kingdom

Oxford University Press is a department of the University of Oxford.
It furthers the University's objective of excellence in research, scholarship,
and education by publishing worldwide. Oxford is a registered trade mark of
Oxford University Press in the UK and in certain other countries

Published in the United States of America by Oxford University Press
198 Madison Avenue, New York, NY 10016, United States of America

British Library Cataloguing in Publication Data
Data available

Library of Congress Cataloging in Publication Data
Data available

Original Series, 231

ISBN 978-0-85-991946-3

TO THE MEMORY

OF

DOROTHY EVERETT

PREFACE

FIVE short treatises found together in two of the most important manuscripts of *The Cloud of Unknowing* have often been attributed to the same anonymous fourteenth-century writer. This edition of them has been prepared as the complement of the edition of *The Cloud of Unknowing and The Book of Privy Counselling* (E.E.T.S., o.s. No. 218, London, 1944) and follows the arrangement of the earlier publication, avoiding mere duplication by frequent reference. The Bibliography has not been repeated. *Hid Diuinite*, part of the heading of one treatise, has been adopted as a collective title for them all, since all of them are religious and mystical in content. Their order in the basic manuscript has been reversed, and here they are set according to their closeness to *The Cloud*. The aim of the apparatus is to establish and elucidate the text, to characterize the prose, to show how far the minor treatises are homogeneous in thought and expression, and to examine the extent of their affinity with *The Cloud*.

Though there is no question of common authorship, there is some justification for including the text of *A Ladder of Foure Ronges* in Appendix B. Many passages in the *Ladder* are similar in theme to parts of *The Cloud* group of treatises, and illustrate common teaching. Moreover, the *Ladder* shares the common inheritance of Latin rhetorical writings and earlier English prose; yet, by its difference from the treatises in just those features which are shown to be highly characteristic of their style, its evidence further supports the theory of single authorship for the group.

It is a pleasure to thank all those who have helped in the preparation of this edition, though obligations are too numerous for individual mention. Most of the work has been done at the British Museum, where through the courtesy of various authorities manuscripts have been deposited from Oxford, Cambridge, and Glasgow, on extended loan. The editor thanks the British Museum for permission to reproduce MS. Harleian 674 (f. 112ª) as frontispiece.

She gratefully acknowledges the kindness of the Librarians of Westminster School and Liverpool University in allowing her to consult their manuscripts; of Bristol City Reference Library, the Huntington Library, California, Mr. W. K. Richardson's private library in Boston, in arranging to send microfilms and rotographs; of Quarr Abbey in lending rare books. The expenses incurred have been partly met by a grant from the Central Research Fund of London University.

This edition completes a project begun some twenty years ago and often, of necessity, superseded by other tasks. In the late stages of preparation the editor has been greatly indebted to Dr. A. I. Doyle for reading the section on the Description of the Manuscripts and most generously suggesting the incorporation of some of the results of his own research, not yet published. Miss P. M. Kean and Dr. M. Day have given continual advice and assistance while the edition was at press; Miss M. Cardwell and Mr. S. S. Hussey have helped with the proof-reading. Among the many who have sustained her by encouragement and material aid the editor wishes especially to thank her father for summer months spent in typing, and Abbot Justin McCann for constructive criticism of the Introduction and Notes, and for the proposal that the text of *De Mystica Theologia* should be withdrawn from the latest edition of his modernized version of *The Cloud of Unknowing* and included in the present volume as Appendix A. Her indebtedness throughout to the late Miss Dorothy Everett is immeasurable and inexpressible.

PHYLLIS HODGSON

UNIVERSITY OF LONDON, BEDFORD COLLEGE

May 1955

In the present reprint, misprints have been corrected, but for technical reasons it has not been possible to incorporate fresh evidence on the vocabulary made available in the Middle English Dictionary. A full bibliography for the treatises of *Deonise Hid Diuinite* is to be found in the 1958 reprint of *The Cloud of Unknowing* (E.E.T.S., o.s. 218).

P. H.

March 1958

CONTENTS

INTRODUCTION

PART I. THE MANUSCRIPTS

A. Description of the Manuscripts

THE five treatises edited in this volume are found in the following manuscript collections:

1. *Deonise Hid Diuinite*
   British Museum. MS. Harleian 674.
   University Library, Cambridge. MS. Kk. vi. 26.

2. *A Tretyse of þe Stodye of Wysdome þat Men Clepen Beniamyn*
   British Museum. MSS. Harleian 674, 1022, 2373; Arundel 286.
   University Library, Cambridge. MSS. Ff. vi. 33, Ii. vi. 39, Kk. vi. 26.
   Hunterian Library, Glasgow University. MS. 258 (U. 4. 16).
   Westminster School Library, MS. 10 Top. 17.
   Also in the United States of America:
   Huntington Library, California. MS. 127.
   W. K. Richardson Library,* Boston, Mass. MS. 22.

3. *A Pistle of Preier*
   British Museum. MSS. Harleian 674, 2373.
   University Library, Cambridge. MSS. Ff. vi. 31, Kk. vi. 26.
   Bodleian Library, Oxford. MS. 576.
   Cohen Library, Liverpool University. MS. Ryl. F. 4. 10 (Harmsworth).

4. *A Pistle of Discrecioun of Stirings*
   British Museum. MSS. Harleian 674, 2373.
   University Library, Cambridge. MSS. Ff. vi. 31, Kk. vi. 26.

5. *A Tretis of Discrescyon of Spirites*
   British Museum. MSS. Harleian 674, 993, 2373.
   University Library, Cambridge. MSS. Ff. vi. 31, Kk. vi. 26.
   Bodleian Library, Oxford. MS. 576.
   Bristol City Reference Library. MS. 6.

* The Richardson MSS. now belong to Harvard University.

With the exception of *Deonise Hid Diuinite*, all these treatises are also to be found in Pepwell's early printed edition of 1521, copies* of which are extant in the British Museum and the library of Trinity College, Cambridge.

Many of these manuscripts have already been fully described in the edition of *The Cloud of Unknowing* and *The Book of Privy Counselling* (Early English Text Society publication, o.s. No. 218, London, 1944, 1958),† of which this present edition is intended to be the complement. To avoid unnecessary repetition, page references only‡ to the earlier descriptions will be given here. The following descriptions of the individual manuscripts are not always complete. Selection of detail has been made to give some idea of the format and the appearance of the text, to indicate with which works these pieces were commonly associated, and to show what evidence there is of the kind of people for whom they were transcribed and among whom they circulated.

British Museum Manuscripts

MS. Harleian 674 (Har[1])
   See *Cloud*, pp. ix–x.

MS. Harleian 2373§ (Har[2])
   See *Cloud*, pp. x–xi.

MS. Harleian 993‖ (Har[4])¶

Octavo; vellum; 38 leaves, $4\frac{1}{4} \times 6\frac{1}{4}$ in. +5 fly-leaves**; careful book-hand, probably mid fifteenth-century; vertical and horizontal rulings in faint ink; single columns of text, usually 17 lines to a page.

This manuscript consists of:
   f. 1ᵃ Walter Hilton's *A Treatise of Eight Chapters*.††

---

* See E. G. Duff, H. R. Plomer, A. W. Pollard, *Handlists of English Printers, 1501–1556* (London, 1913), vol. iv. A third copy mentioned here as belonging to the University Library of Louvain was destroyed by enemy action.

† This will be referred to henceforth as *Cloud*.

‡ Supplementary information may be added.

§ Those who incline to attribute *The Cloud* to Walter Hilton find their strongest support in the late fifteenth-century annotations of Greenhalgh here and in MS. Douce 262. See *Medium Ævum*, vol. xvi (1947), p. 41.

‖ Described in *A Catalogue of the Harleian MSS. in the British Museum* (London, 1808), vol. i, p. 501.   ¶ Har[3] is MS. Harleian 959. See *Cloud*, p. xi.

** On the second fly-leaf is written: 'thys boke is ssuster anne colvylle'. This may well have been the nun of that name of Syon Abbey in 1518. See G. J. Aungier, *The History and Antiquities of Syon Monastery* (1840), p. 81.

†† Edited in a modernized version by D. Jones, *Minor Works of Walter Hilton* (London, 1929).

ff. 24ᵃ–37ᵇ *The Treatise of Discretion of Spirits* (The first few lines are missing. The text begins 80/9: 'seiþ þe profete . . .'.)

f. 38ᵃ Colophon.*

MS. Harleian 1022† (Har⁵)

Quarto; partly parchment, partly paper; 99 leaves, 5½ × 8 in.; written in different hands, probably at different dates, containing various tracts, some in Latin, some in English. The Latin tracts include a set of *Narrationes Legendariae* and a *Tractatus de Utilitate Orationis Dominice*. The English pieces include:

f. 16ᵃ An imperfect text of Hilton's *Scale of Perfection*, Book I.

f. 47ᵃ Rolle's *Form of Living*.

f. 62ᵃ Rolle's *Encomium Nominis Iesu*, in English.

f. 64ᵃ A translation of chapter iii of the pseudo-Bonaventuran *Meditationes Vitae Christi*.‡

f. 66ᵃ Dan John of Gaysteke's (i.e. Gaytryge's) translation of Archbishop Thoresby's Catechism, in verse and dated 1357.

* 'This book was maad of þe goodis of robert holond for a comyn profite þat þat persoone þat haþ þis book committid to him of þe persoone þat haþ power to committe it. haue þe uss þerof þe terme of his lijf. preiynge for the soule of þe same Robert. And þat he þat haþ þe forseid vss of commissioun whanne he occupieþ it not: leene he it for a tyme to sum oþer persoone. Also þat persoone to whom it was committid for þe teerme of lijf. vndir þe forseid condiciouns deliuere it to a noþer persoone þe teerme of his lijf / And so be it deliuered & committid from persoone to persoone man or womman as longe as þe book enduriþ.'

'James Palmer owneth this Booke, yet without þe least intent to pray for þe soule of Robert Holland, being a wicked & simple custome, of sottishly ignorant Papistes.'

For a note on the 'common profit' manuscripts, see Jones, op. cit., pp. xi–xvi. Cf. Cambridge University Library MS. Ff. vi. 31 described below. Other manuscripts made 'for a common profit', to be passed from owner to owner until worn out, are Lambeth MS. 472, Douce MS. 25, Harleian MS. 2336. See H. E. Allen, *Writings Ascribed to Richard Rolle* (New York, 1927), pp. 176, 197. These manuscripts seem to be a closely related group, for personal interrelationship as well as textual and paleographical can be traced. According to Jones, p. xxxiii: 'A Robert Holland, shearman, died intestate in 1441, and . . . the administration of his goods was granted to one John Collopp of the parish of St. Michael in the Royal.'

This John Collopp was appointed to distribute alms for the executors of the famous Richard Whittington, and he may have been identical with the servant and executor of John Killum (?†1416). The colophon of Lambeth MS. 472 gives the information that 'this booke was maad of þe goodis of Jon Killum for a comyne profite' and was to 'be deliuered to Richard Colop Parchemanere of London' after his decease (Jones, p. xi).

† Described in *Catalogue of Harleian MSS.*, vol. i, pp. 510–11.

‡ Also in the Westminster MS. See below. Edited by C. Horstman, *Yorkshire Writers. Richard Rolle of Hampole* (London, 1895), vol. i, pp. 158-61.

f. 74ᵃ The translation of *Benjamin Minor*.*

MS. Arundel 286† (Ar)

Octavo; vellum; 191 leaves+1 fly-leaf; 5 × 8 in., several sections, written in at least two different fifteenth-century hands; single columns of text, 25–27 lines to a page. This manuscript contains:

f. 1ᵃ A treatise on the Passion, written for a woman.

f. 15ᵇ Part of the *Revelations of St. Brigit*—how reason shall be keeper of the soul.‡

f. 20ᵃ A treatise on Christian Warfare§ with appended discourses on the Incarnation, the Sacrament of the Altar, the Trinity.

f. 82ᵃ A translation of the *Epistola continens Viginti Quinque Memorialia*, attributed to St. Bonaventura.‖

f. 92ᵃ A translation of the *Meditatio XIII*,¶ usually ascribed to St. Anselm.

f. 100ᵃ A translation of the *De Duodecim Utilitatibus Tribulationis* of Petrus Blesensis,** sometimes attributed to Rolle.††

f. 115ᵃ A treatise on the life of the soul.

f. 129ᵃ Devout contemplations on the Hours, translated from St. Edmund Rich's *Speculum Ecclesie*.

f. 134ᵇ A treatise on Virginity.‡‡

f. 149ᵃ An exposition of the hymn 'Ave Maris Stella'.

f. 161ᵃ A translation of *Benjamin Minor* (no title, but with the ending 'Explicit de xij filiis Jacob').

f. 179ᵃ An exposition of the Decalogue.§§

---

* Horstman, op. cit., p. 157, suggests that the manuscript was compiled *c.* 1420–30, a few years earlier than the Thornton MS. The text of the translation of *Benjamin Minor* is written in an early fifteenth-century hand. Horstman, op. cit., pp. 3–49, 157–72, 186–91, edits part of the *Form of Living* from this manuscript, and all the other pieces except *The Scale* and the *Catechism*.

† Described in *Catalogue of Manuscripts in the British Museum*, N.S., vol. i. The Arundel Manuscripts (London, 1840), pp. 84–85.

‡ Also in MS. Harleian 6615, f. 253ᵃ.

§ Also in MS. Egerton 842, f. 247ᵃ.

‖ *S. Bonaventurae Opera Omnia* (Quaracchi, 1898), vol. viii, pp. 491–8.

¶ Migne, *Patrologia Latina*, t. clviii, c. 773. This work will henceforth be cited as *P.L.*

** Horstman, op. cit., vol. ii, pp. 45 ff., 389 ff., prints two Middle English translations of this very popular and widely distributed Latin work, the text of which is to be found in *P.L.*, t. ccvii, c. 989.

†† This is very unlikely. See Allen, op. cit., pp. 355–6.

‡‡ Also in the Westminster MS. See below.

§§ This appears to be the standard exposition. See W. N. Francis, *Book of Vices and Virtues*, E.E.T.S., o.s. No. 217 (London, 1942), appendix and introduction.

Pepwell's Printed Edition* (Pw)

Quarto, divided into seven parts, each with a title and woodcut illustration; 50 leaves, no pagination; 31 lines of text to a page; register from A to K in alternate fours and sixes; F irregularly signatured.

The treatises are in the following order and with the titles given below:

1. *A veray deuoute treatyse (named Benyamyn) of the myghtes & vertues of mannes soule | & of the way to true contemplacyon | compyled by a noble & famous doctoure a man of grete holynes & deuocyon | named Rycharde of saynt Vyctor.*

2. *Dyuers doctrynes deuoute & fruytfull | taken out of the lyfe of that gloryous vyrgyne | & spouse of our lorde Saynt Katheryn of Seenes. And fyrst those whiche our lorde taught & shewed to herselfe | and syth these whiche she taught and shewed vnto others.*

3. *A shorte treatyse of contemplacyon taught by our lorde Jhesu cryst | or taken out of the boke of Margery kempe ancresse of Lynne.*

4. *A deuoute treatyse called the Epystle of prayer.*

5. *A deuoute treatyse compyled by mayster Walter Hylton of the songe of aungelles.*

6. *A veray necessary Epystle of dyscrecyon in styrynges of the soule.*

7. *A deuoute treatyse of dyscernynge of spyrytes veray necessary for ghoostly lyuers.*

Cambridge University Library Manuscripts

MS. Ff. vi. 31† (CP)

Parchment; 164 leaves, $4 \times 5\frac{3}{4}$ in.; numbered (pt. i) 1–64, (pt. ii) 1–100; different cursive hands pt. i, pt. ii, ff. 43–end; pt. ii, ff. 1–42^b in book-hand, probably mid-fifteenth century; 18–23 lines to a page. This manuscript includes:

Pt. i

    f. 1^b *Propur Wille.*‡

    f. 11^a Treatise on the Seven Deadly Sins.§

* See *Handlists*, p. x, n.*, above. This edition was 'Imprynted at London in Poules chyrchyarde at the sygne of the Trynyte by Henry Pepwell. In the yere of our lorde god MCCCCCXXI, the XVI daye of Nouembre.' Pw is treated henceforth as a manuscript.

† Described in *A Catalogue of the Manuscripts Preserved in the Library of the University of Cambridge*, Cambridge, 1857, vol. ii, pp. 533–4.

‡ Also in Cambridge University Library MSS. Dd. v. 55, Ff. v. 40; edited by Horstman, op. cit., vol. i, pp. 173–5.

§ A fairly common treatise by the Carmelite, Richard Lavenham.

Pt. ii

ff. 1–42ᵇ Treatises on the reading of Scripture, the Sacraments, and on unfaithful priests.*

f. 43ᵃ *A Tretys of iij dyuers þouȝtes þt come ofte to men & ask to know to wiþstond hem* (*A Treatise of Discretion of Spirits*).

f. 53ᵃ *The Epistle of Discretion of Stirrings*, 'Here rede good reu (? le *cut away*).'

f. 68ᵃ *þis matere suyng techiþ how þou schalt dispose þee to preie* (*The Epistle of Prayer*).

f. 80ᵃ A treatise teaching 'vertuous besinesse, and to eschewe foly besinesse'.

f. 92ᵃ Translation of a treatise by Hugh of St. Victor, 'teching hou a man owiþ to haue him in alle temptacions'.

f. 98ᵇ Four Errors which 'letten þe verrey knowyng of holy Writt'.

f. 100 Colophon.†

MS. Ff. vi 33‡ (F)

Parchment; 142 numbered leaves+2 fly-leaves, 4½×6 in.; late fifteenth- or early sixteenth-century hand;§ average of 19 lines to a page. This manuscript contains:

f. 1ᵃ The translation of *Benjamin Minor*, here entitled *The boke of the xii patriarkys*.

f. 21ᵇ *Notable saynges of holy doctours of the vertue of holy prayer*.

f. 26ᵃ On the indulgences granted by Pope John XXII.

f. 26ᵇ A brief exposition of the Pater Noster.

f. 31ᵇ A 'more breve exposicioun' (of the Pater Noster); Ave and translation; Credo and translation, each phrase being attributed to one of the twelve apostles.

f. 33ᵇ Four requests of Our Lady to her son.‖

* These treatises are moderately Lollard in outlook. The first was edited by M. Deanesly, *The Lollard Bible* (Cambridge, 1920), pp. 445–56.

† 'This booke was made of þe goodis of John Collopp for a comyn profite. That þt persoone þt hath þis booke committid to him of þe persoone þt haþ powere to committe it: haue þe vse þerof þe teerme of his lijf. prayng for þe soule of þe seid John. And þt he þt haþ þe forseid vse of commyssioun whanne he occupieth it not: leene it for a tyme to sum oþer persoone. Also þat persoone to whom it was committid for þe teerme of lijf. vnder þe forseid condiciouns delyuere it to anoþer persoone þe teerme of his lijf. & so be it delyuered & committid fro persoone to persoone man or womman as longe as þe booke endurith.' See above, p. xi.

‡ Described in *Catalogue*, vol. ii, pp. 534–6.

§ A. I. Doyle in a forthcoming publication hopes to show that it is by the hand of William Darker of Sheen, who wrote a number of manuscripts in that period, both for Carthusian use and for Syon. From its contents this may well have been transcribed for the Brigittine nuns of Syon.

‖ Written for Queen Isabel of France. The same English version occurs in Pepys MS. 2125.

f. 37^b Nine Virtues (dated 1345).*
f. 38^b The Brigittine Rule.
f. 67^b Five Wiles of King Pharaoh.
f. 88^a The Augustinian Rule.†
f. 98^b On the direction of a man's life (7 chapters).
f. 114^a Message from our Saviour to the Pope.‡
f. 115^a Translation of the *Scala Claustralium* of Guigo II, with the heading *A ladder of foure ronges by the which men mowe wele clyme to heven*, and the running title of *The Laddyr of cloystrerys*.§
f. 138^a A translation of the Epistle of St. Machary.

MS. Ii. vi. 39 (Ii)
  See *Cloud*, p. xiii.
MS. Kk. vi. 26 (Kk)
  See *Cloud*, p. xiv.

Other Manuscripts

Bodleian Library MS. 576 (Bo)
  See *Cloud*, p. xvi.
Liverpool University, Cohen Library, MS. Ryl. F. 4. 10 (*Harmsworth*)
  Folio; vellum; 100 leaves + 2 fly-leaves, 7½ × 11 in.; late fifteenth-century book-hand; single columns of text; contemporary blind-stamped leather binding. This manuscript contains:

f. 1^a *The Chastising of God's Children.*
f. 42^b An anonymous treatise on Prayer beginning: 'Prayinge is a gracious gifte of oure lorde god. . . .'||
ff. 51^b–53^b Most of *The Epistle of Prayer* corresponding to 48/5–58/9 of the present text, and entitled in a late sixteenth- or early seventeenth-century hand: *A Treatise of Love or reverente affection by Walter Hilton as is supposed*.¶

* Three versions printed by Horstman, op. cit., vol. i, pp. 110 ff.; vol. ii, pp. 455–6. One English version is possibly a translation by Rolle of a work widely attributed, though probably erroneously, to Albertus Magnus. See Allen, op. cit., pp. 317–20.
† The same version as in St. Paul's Cathedral MS. WD. 24, which was made for Syon.
‡ Again from St. Brigit's *Revelations*, concerning the confirmation of her Rule.
§ Also in MS. Harleian 1706 in the British Museum and MS. Douce 322 in the Bodleian Library, Oxford. See Appendix B.
|| Part of the *Gracia Dei*, identified by Miss Allen, op. cit., pp. 286–7, printed by Horstman, op. cit., vol. i, pp. 295 ff.
¶ Though this text was fully collated with the other manuscripts in the preparation of the present edition, it was not found practicable to include

f. 54ᵃ Part of the table of *The Scale of Perfection*, followed by Book I of *The Scale*, with part of the last chapter missing.

Bristol City Reference Library, MS. 6* (Br)

Octavo; vellum; 140 leaves, 6×9 in.; dated 1502;† single columns of text; average of 30 lines to a page.

This manuscript contains a collection of treatises on tribulation, almsgiving (a Latin version of the Nine Virtues noted in F), the diversities of temptations,‡ rules for the hermitical life, expositions of difficult words in the Missal and the Sarum sequences, &c.

ff. 127ᵇ–133ᵇ *The Treatise of Discretion of Spirits*, with the title: *A Profytable ynformacyon techyng a man to knowe the kynd of spyrytys whych ben good and whych not.*

Glasgow University, Hunterian Library MS. 258 (U. 4. 16)§ (G)

Vellum; 12 leaves+2 paper fly-leaves, 7¼×10¼ in.; from the numbering, 167–190, this appears to have been part of a larger manuscript;∥ single columns of text in a careful late fifteenth-century hand; an average of 31 lines to a page; apart from some doggerel lines in a different hand, this manuscript contains only the translation of *Benjamin Minor*, entitled here *Studium Sapiencie*.

Westminster School MS.¶ (W)

Octavo; vellum; 230 leaves, 5¼×7¾ in., unnumbered; regular early to mid fifteenth-century court-hand; single columns of text; average of 24 lines to a page; contemporary binding. This manuscript contains:

its variant readings in the critical apparatus. The text is an inferior recension, often a free paraphrase, with frequent addition, contraction, and omission. Even where it corresponds more or less closely to the basic text, it contains many readings obviously corrupt.

* Described by N. Mathews, *Early Printed Books and Manuscripts in the City Reference Library, Bristol* (Bristol, 1899), pp. 66–67.

† f. 119: 'In domo Sancti Marci euangeliste iuxta Bristoliam xxxi die Mensis Octobris. Anno domini, 1502.'

‡ One of the English versions of the treatise of William Flete.

§ Described in *Manuscripts in the Hunterian Library of the University of Glasgow* (Glasgow, 1908), pp. 209–10.

∥ A. I. Doyle hopes to show that U.4.17 is part of the same volume, and that both parts are in the same hand as T.3.15 (dated 1475), probably that of Stephen Dodesham of Sheen.

¶ There is a handwritten *Catalogue of the Old Library of Westminster School* (1889). See also Allen, op. cit., pp. 358–9. A note on f. 230ᵃ of this manuscript reads: 'R. Cloos the wiche is ownere of this boucke 1472.' R. Cloos, or Cloce, appears in the parochial accounts of St. Mary-at-Hill, London, *c.* 1483–1502, where he was churchwarden 1491–3. See *Mediaeval Records of a London City Church*, ed. H. Littlehales, E.E.T.S., 1905, *passim*.

f. 1ª *þe Pater Noster of Richard Ermyte.*
f. 68ª 'Heyl be þow marie . . . .'
f. 73ª A treatise on the Decalogue.*
ff. 88ᵇ–103ᵇ The translation of *Benjamin Minor* (no title).
f. 103ᵇ An exposition of Psalm xxvi: 'How men schulden be pacient in tribulacioun.'
f. 105ª *How men þat beþ in heele schulde visite seke men.*
f. 112ª *þe chartir of heuene* from the *Poor Caitiff.*
f. 115ª A translation of chapter iii of the pseudo-Bonaventuran *Meditationes Vitae Christi.*
f. 117ᵇ *How lordis and housbondemen schulden teche goddis comaunde-mentis.*
f. 121ᵇ *A tretis of weddid men & wymmen & of her children also.*
f. 132ᵇ *A schort reule of lyf for eche man in general & for preestis in special.*
f. 137ª *A noble tretys of maydenhode.*†
f. 162ª Another treatise on the Commandments.
f. 181ª *þe myrour of seynt edmound.*
f. 205ª Rolle's *Form of Living.*

H. E. Huntington Library, California, MS. 127‡ (C)

Vellum; 63 leaves, 7½ × 10½ in.; early fifteenth-century hand; double columns of text, average of 24 lines to a column.

This manuscript includes:

f. 2ª A treatise on the dread and love of God.§
f. 35ª Rolle's *Form of Living.*
f. 52ª 'Crist made to man a faire present . . .', a poem.
f. 54ª The translation of *Benjamin Minor* with the title *De Prae-paratione.*
f. 63ᵇ Poem in English on the seven works of mercy, followed by the Latin *Septem dona Spiritus Sancti.*

W. K. Richardson's Library, Boston, Mass. MS. 22‖ (R)

Vellum; 90 leaves, 6¾ × 10 in.; early fifteenth-century hand; single columns of text, an average of 30 lines to a page; stamped Tudor binding. This manuscript includes:

f. 1ª A translation of the Meditations of St. Augustine.
ff. 52ᵇ–68ᵇ The translation of *Benjamin Minor* with the incipit: 'Here bygynnyþ a tretise þat men calliþ Richarde of seynt victor.'

---

* The common orthodox treatise.
† The treatise in MS. Arundel 286, see above, p. xii.
‡ Described in S. de Ricci, *Census of Medieval and Renaissance MSS. in U.S. and Canada* (New York, 1935), p. 53.
§ Edited by Horstman, op. cit., vol. ii, pp. 72–105.
‖ Described by de Ricci, op. cit., p. 961.

f. 71ᵇ *Carta Redemptoris*, English and in verse.
f. 78ᵃ An English prose commentary on *Ave Maria*.
f. 82ᵇ Christ's address to sinners.

B. The Relationship of the Manuscripts and the Choice of the Basic Text

When there are many manuscripts from which to choose the version which seems best to represent the author's original text, two chief investigations must be made: the relationship of the extant manuscripts must be sought by sifting the evidence of all their variant readings; the texts which seem closest to the original in their line of descent must further be compared, with a weighing of their individual merits and defects. For the present edition these investigations are a difficult and rather unsatisfactory task, for no conclusion can be drawn with absolute certainty. The difficulties lie chiefly, though not entirely, in the number of manuscripts and their nature. The problem is also complicated by the facts that all five treatises do not occur in the same manuscript collections,* and that whereas two are possibly original work, three are translations.†

A further difficulty arises largely through the kind of Middle English manuscripts involved, which were compiled as manuals of devotional reading. Spelling, dialectal and grammatical forms, punctuation, all tend to vary with the scribe, and differences are generally insignificant. Likewise no importance can be attached to variant readings of such words as *and—or, and—but, ben—are,*

* The total number of manuscripts fully collated was sixteen. *Hid Diuinite* occurs in Har¹ Kk; *Þe Stodye of Wysdome* in Har¹ Kk Har² Ar Har⁵ F C R Pw G W Ii; *Pistle of Preier* in Har¹ Kk Har² Pw Bo CP; *Discrecioun of Stirings* in Har¹ Kk Har² Pw CP; *Discrescyon of Spirites* in Har¹ Kk Har² Har⁴ Bo Pw CP Br. All five treatises are therefore present together only in Har¹ Kk, four of them occur in Har² Pw; three in CP; two in Bo. As three of these manuscripts, Har¹ Kk Har², contain also *The Cloud of Unknowing*, closely related in subject-matter and style to these five treatises, it seems justifiable to use the evidence of the relationship of the manuscripts of *The Cloud* in corroboration of the suggested relationship of the manuscripts of the five minor treatises.

† See pp. xxxix–xlvii. Where it is available, the reading of the Latin original must obviously be considered when deciding upon superiority of reading. Yet the Latin evidence is not to be regarded as conclusive. Often the Middle English is not a close word-for-word translation, but rather an adaptation. Moreover, the Latin text used by the Middle English translator might have differed considerably from the text available today.

ne—or, on—in, to—vnto, a—pe, er—or, &c. The substitution of synonyms is often equally unhelpful, for in the manuscripts of Middle English devotional treatises such as these, variants like *bitwix—bitwene, soule—goost, rere—reise, euer—ay, lere—lerne, forpi—perfore, pyne—peyne, hede—kepe,* &c., are common. The evidence such variants may yield might well be corroborative, but it can never by itself be conclusive.

As a final difficulty, the sixteen extant manuscripts probably represent only a small proportion of the manuscripts transcribed, and if the whole number could be collated, the relationship between the surviving texts might prove to be very distant. As it is, it can easily be shown that no one is the author's original, and none is a copy of any other, but that each of the sixteen must be several times removed from the original text. Moreover, the line of descent has not always been single. There is evidence of conflation in several of the existing texts, and the grouping of the variant readings suggests that the parent manuscripts of some of the extant versions must have been subject to similar contamination.

As in the case of *The Cloud,* almost every possible grouping of variant readings is to be found, and with this welter of conflicting evidence it is impossible to establish exactly or conclusively the relationship between the different manuscripts. Yet since all groups of variant readings are not equally important, and since some groups occur more frequently and with more noteworthy variants than others, it seems justifiable to conclude that some manuscripts are more closely connected with each other than they are with any of the rest. It was shown in the introduction to *The Cloud* that Har[1] Kk Har[2] are all good manuscripts, with a dependable text probably closer to the author's original than that in any other manuscript. Har[1] Kk proved better than Har[2], and ultimately Har[1] was chosen as the basic text because it was more complete than Kk, with fewer unique readings and a greater consistency in its language.

The evidence of the manuscripts of the minor treatises is not as clear as with *The Cloud,* but it is not contradictory to conclusions already made. Har[1] has again been chosen as the basic text. This choice has two great advantages: uniformity with the text of *The Cloud* already published and uniformity within the present edition, since Har[1] contains all five treatises. The rest of this section showing relative positions of the different manuscripts will indicate to what extent the readings of Har¹ can be unquestionably accepted, and when the authority of Har¹ ought to be set against that of the other manuscripts.

1. *Deonise Hid Diuinite*

The problem of the relationship of the manuscripts does not occur here. Since there are only two versions, each variant reading must be considered independently on its own merits and on its closeness to the Latin.*

2. *A Tretyse of þe Stodye of Wysdome þat Men Clepen Beniamyn*

As far as can be deduced from the results of the collation of twelve versions, Har¹ is among the best manuscripts, but its readings are not always the most authoritative.†

Two main groupings are postulated:

> Group A (Har¹ Kk Har²)
> Group B (Ar Har⁵ F C R Pw G W Ii).

From their agreement against the rest in certain additions, omissions, and different readings, a common ancestor is assumed for Har¹ Kk Har², which is probably not the author's original text, since in several readings which can be compared with the Latin group A appears to be inferior to group B:‡ e.g.

Readings of Group A longer than those of Group B: 12/6, 7, 8, 21/5.
Readings of Group A shorter than those of Group B: 20/11, 21/10, 25/12, 31/7, 35/9, 36/4.
Readings of Group A different from those of Group B: 12/9, 14/4, 19/3, 21/14, 24/2, 36/12, 39/4, 40/1, 44/1, 46/7.

Though the parent of group B would appear to be closer to the original than the parent manuscript of group A, yet group B can be further subdivided, and it seems impossible to prove that any one of the extant manuscripts of group B is itself closer to

---

* The Middle English versions have been closely compared with the Latin text given in Appendix A.

† The Middle English versions have been compared with the Latin text of *Benjamin Minor* in Migne, *P.L.*, t. cxcvi.

‡ See Note to 20/10–11; cf. also the Latin readings for 12/7 *affectio, diligamus*; 12/9 *sancta*; 19/9 *prioribus*; 19/16 *quis praesumat*; 24/9 *toties*; 28/18 *prius*; 37/2 *intelligamus*; 39/15 *usu*; 40/15 *frequenter*; 44/11 *visionis*.

the original in the majority of its readings than any manuscript from group A.

From the weight of their agreement and the negligible amount of contradictory evidence in significant variants, three clear groups can be discerned within group B, each with its common ancestor, which is not the author's original text: viz. F C R, C R, W Ii.*

Other groupings of significant variants occur, but the evidence is too conflicting to permit any assertion of close relationship. Thus there is occasional striking agreement in Har⁵ F C R, Pw G, Pw F, Ar Har⁵ W G, Har⁵ Pw W G, Ar Pw W G, Ar Pw G W Ii, Ar W, W G, which can only be explained by coincidence or conflation. Repeated contamination by correction from some other manuscript, either in the extant text or in one in its line of descent, is probably the most likely explanation.† The manuscripts of group A contain far fewer signs of conflation than those of group B, and their relationship is accordingly more clearly definable. It would obviously be exceedingly difficult to select the best text from group B since the relationship of its manuscripts is thus obscure.‡

The task is simpler with the three manuscripts of group A. As in the readings of the manuscripts of *The Cloud*, Kk Har² are closer to each other than either is to Har¹: e.g. 22/16, 23/10, 24/1, 25/17, 31/6, 34/11, 35/6, 8, 40/11, 42/8, 43/15, 44/11, 45/2, 5, 11, 12, 14.

Every unique reading in any of the three manuscripts of group A must be regarded with suspicion. Moreover, agreement of either Kk or Har² alone with the manuscripts of group B can only be explained by coincidence or conflation. Har¹ has the fewest unique readings of the manuscripts of group A. These are, in fact,

* F C R: Additions—e.g. 26/16, 42/9, 43/17; Omissions—e.g. chapter-headings 17, 18, 26, 36, 39, also 16/3, 20/3, 25/13, 27/16, 33/ 10–12, 34/5–6, 14, 46/3–4; Different readings—20/7, 21/15, 29/15–16, 33/7–8, 14, 35/5, 37/4, 40/12, 41/8, 43/14, 44/4, &c.

C R: Omissions—14/7, 18/10, 24/1; Different readings—17/6, 18/6, 21/5, 23/4, 10, 26/17, 29/13, 31/8, 36/7, 14, 38/6, 40/2, 43/15, 44/8, 45/13.

W Ii: Additions—20/2, 23/4, 24/9, 33/9, 37/16; Omissions—20/11, 29/5–6, 35/3; Different readings—18/12, 26/15, 27/1, 29/13, 14, 34/12.

† The process of the combining of two readings can occasionally be seen, e.g. Pw 21/7; G 13/13, 22/13, 40/3; Pw F 18/2.

‡ Moreover, each extant manuscript must be many times removed from the author's original text, and each copying would add to the number of inferior readings.

xxii *Introduction*

about forty in number, all very insignificant in kind, being without exception of the sort described on pp. xviii–xix.

Apart from the obvious advantage of uniformity, therefore, the choice of Har[1] as the basic text of *Þe Stodye of Wysdome* can also be defended on textual grounds.

A Pistle of Preier, A Pistle of Discrecioun of Stirings, A Tretis of Discrescyon of Spirites

A full collation of the eight manuscripts of *Discrescyon of Spirites* (Har[1] Kk Har[2] Bo Pw Har[4] CP Br) again confirmed the authority of Har[1], whilst discovering more groupings of manuscripts, which were further established by the agreement of the variant readings in the six manuscripts of the *Pistle of Preier* and the five manuscripts of *Discrecioun of Stirings*, as the footnotes indicate.

The two major groupings most frequently suggested by the significant variants in *Discrescyon of Spirites* are Har[1] Har[4] CP Br and Kk Har[2] Bo Pw.* In the latter, Kk Har[2] can again be shown to be more nearly related to each other than to any other extant manuscript;† and the close relationship of Bo Pw is likewise unquestionable, proved by very frequent and consistent agreement in significant readings.‡ In the former, two readings probably inferior (85/1, 15) and a number of noteworthy variants suggest a common ancestor for Har[4] CP Br.§

---

* Kk Har[2] Bo Pw: Additions—81/16, 82/1, 83/16, 86/3, 88/10, 89/14, 91/8, 92/5; Omissions—82/1, 11, 84/6, 86/10, 20, 87/17, 89/5; Different readings—82/9, 85/2, 88/4; cf. *Preier*, Additions—52/9, 12, 53/15, 54/1, 55/6, 56/20; Omissions—50/13, 52/19, 53/4, 7, 15, 20, 54/14; Different readings—52/2, 21, 53/1, 54/9, 55/3–4, 25, 56/19, 23, 57/7, 58/7.

† Kk Har[2]: Additions—*Preier*, 48/8, 53/6, 56/22, 58/14; *Stirings*, 62/17, 70/15, 73/23, 75/24; *Spirites*, 89/15; Omissions—*Preier*, 56/13; *Stirings*, 63/6, 75/2, 77/4; *Spirites*, 81/16, 92/9; Different readings—*Preier*, 48/18, 49/12, 50/14, 24, 51/13, 52/2, 4, 53/6, 15, 54/23, 55/12, 16, 17, 23, 57/6, 14, 15, 16, 58/7, 11, 19, 59/7, 10, 14, 15; *Stirings*, 63/6, 68/24, 69/5, 10, 17, 70/18, 71/5, 22, 74/4, 11, 13; *Spirites*, 86/17, 87/15, 88/15, 90/9. As Kk Har[2] are descended from a good text, many of these variants are slight.

‡ Bo Pw: Additions—*Preier*, title, 48/12, 16, 49/4, 17, 53/20, 54/20, 58/9, 17, 59/17; *Spirites*, 81/15, 84/6, 88/15, 90/11; Omissions—*Preier*, 48/5, 6, 49/6, 50/18, 22, 51/13–20, 26–27, 54/9, 56/6; *Spirites*, 82/9–10, 83/12, 84/15, 85/2, 4, 86/16, 87/5, 91/1; Different readings—*Preier*, 48/5, 17, 19–20, 49/4, 11, 50/2, 6, 8, 11, 21, 53/8–9, 54/8, 13, 18, 23–24; *Spirites*, 80/1, 12, 82/13, 83/5, 8, 84/1, 85/9, 86/22, 87/16, 88/2, 89/10, 14.

§ Har[4] CP Br: Additions—87/13, 91/19; Omissions—83/18, 85/8, 15,

Judgement of the validity of the readings of Har[1] is more difficult in these three treatises than in the case either of *The Cloud* or *þe Stodye of Wysdome*. Evidence from the readings of all three treatises, including certain corrections in Har[1], suggests that Har[1] is closer to CP than to Kk Har[2] Bo Pw.* Har[4] Br sometimes agree with each other against the rest,† indicating that they are closer to each other than to either Har[1] or CP.‡ Unique readings in any manuscript must be regarded with suspicion. As relatively few of these occur in Har[1] and CP, the choice of the basic text would appear to lie between the two. Har[1] was again selected, for the sake of uniformity, but it must be remembered that where they agree in differing from Har[1], the variant readings of Har[4] CP Br probably have the greater authority.

C. LANGUAGE

The comparative study of the language of all the manuscripts of *The Cloud*§ established the fact that Har[1] was the most uniform in its usage, and that though the other manuscripts differed considerably from Har[1] and from each other in spelling and sometimes had different grammatical forms and vocabulary, basically their language resembled that of Har[1]. It was deduced that the language of Har[1] most closely represented that of the original text, and that this was probably written in a northern part of the central east Midlands late in the fourteenth century. These statements are true also of the language of the minor treatises, where they occur in the same manuscripts as *The Cloud* (viz. Har[1] Kk Har[2] Bo Ii). A close comparison of the linguistic forms in those manuscripts of the minor treatises which do not contain *The Cloud*‖ has led to similar conclusions. The following list of the main differences of these manuscripts from Har[1], complementary to the evidence

89/15, 19, 90/14; Different readings—81/10, 82/17, 83/2, 5, 19, 84/6, 15, 86/19, 91/3, 92/23.

* e.g. 53/1, 56/8, 57/1, 6, 20, 62/8, 18, 64/7, 66/5, 70/17, 80/8, 90/18.

† e.g. 81/3, 3, 82/12, 84/2, 85/1, 88/1, 6, 18.

‡ The frequent agreement of Br both with Bo Pw and with Bo alone, as well as with Har[1] Har[4] CP and Har[4] CP, can only be the result of contamination.

§ *Cloud*, pp. xxvii–li.

‖ i.e. Ar Har[5] F C R Pw G W: *þe Stodye of Wysdome*; CP Pw: *Pistle of Preier, Discrecioun of Stirings, Discrescyon of Spirites*; Har[4] Br: *Discrescyon of Spirites*.

already given in the sections on Phonology and Grammar in *The Cloud*, will show that Har¹ is throughout the most uniform, and that, apart from those in Har⁵ which are generally northern, the variations are slight and insignificant, and, moreover, not always consistently maintained.*

a. PHONOLOGY

(i) *The Development of OE. and EME. Vowels*

1. OE. *æ* (Merc., Kt. *e*)

    Kk *eftyr* occasionally; C R *lest(e)* 34/1.

2. OE. *a* (also ON *a*), EME. *a*

    (1)　Har⁵ *kestes*; Har⁴ CP *waischen*.

    (2)　Har⁵ regularly *-ald*.

    (3) i. Har⁵ *mone*, 'many'.

    　　ii. (*b*) Har⁵ *strang, lange*, 40/7 *lenge*.

3. OE. *e* (also ON. *e*), EME. *e*

    (1)　Br *malencoly, massyngers*.

    (2) i. C R Pw G W CP *togider*; Har⁵ *geyt*, 'get'; *ʒit*, 'yet', usual in all MSS. except F Pw *yet*.

    　　ii. Kk C *brynn-*; Kk Har² *-rynn-*.

    　　iii. CP *stid-*.

    　　iv. Har⁵ *wille*; CP Har⁴ *silf*.†

    　　Other examples: Kk *blyssed*; CP *lifte*.

    (3) Har⁵ CP Pw have *ai, ay* frequently; Kk Har² occasionally *sape*; Ii *weiʒe*.

    (4) Usually *er* in all manuscripts, but Har⁵ G W Pw *marked* 44/7; Pw *harte, darke, clarke*; Br *warke*.

    (5) Har⁵ *dronkune* 14/7, *ordure* 16/3, *vndur-* 38/2; CP often *vndur-*.

4. OE. and ME. *i*

    (1) In certain words with an open syllable Har¹ has both *i* (*y*) and *e*: e.g. *lyue* 26/17, *leuyng* 48/10; *sikyr-* 44/14, *sekir-* 36/5; *witen* 29/4, *wetyn* 28/13; *liv-* forms occur more

---

* The arrangement with its numbering follows that in *Cloud*, pp. xxvii–xlviii. The forms in Har¹ and the variations in Kk Har² Ii are not repeated here when they are the same in the minor treatises as in *The Cloud*; only divergencies from them in the minor treatises are added, and occasionally further examples of interesting points. Line reference is given when the variation occurs only once, or when some contrast is made.

† Possibly from OE. *sylf*.

often than *lev-* in Kk Har⁵ R Pw G Har⁴ CP; *sik-* is usual in Kk Har² Ar F C Pw G W Har⁴. Har¹ prefers *schreuyn, wretin*, where Kk Har² Har⁵ Pw CP have *schryu-*, Kk Har² Ar F C R Pw W Har⁴ CP have *writ-*.

(2) Ar *ȝefte*; C *brengeþ*; R *skelys*; Pw *cheldren*; W *sengulerly*; Ii *cete, pete, skeles*; CP *senguler*; Br *seth, shreft*.

7. OE. *y*

    (1) (See 4 (1)) Har¹ has *besi-* always, where Kk Har² Har⁵ F CP Br have *besi-* and *bisi-*; Ar C R G W Har⁴ prefer *bisi-*. Har¹ *lepir* 58/2, cf. *liper* 41/4; *steriþ* 34/7, cf. *stir-* 75/24.

    Har² C *berþe*; Har² Har⁵ F C Pw G W Ii Br *euelle*; Har⁵ C *ferst*; R *kende*; R G Br *kendlyng*; Har⁵ *preste*.

    (2)   Pw *busy-, churche*; Ii Br *furst*; G Ii *stur-*; Ar *stude, vche*; Ar C G W Ii *þurst, þrust*.

OE. *hwylc*   Ar *whoche* usually; Har⁵ *wilk* often, *wich, weche*; Ii *weche* often; R *wheche*.

OE. *mycel*   Kk *mykel* usually, but also *muche*; Har² *myche, mykelle*; Ar usually *myche*; Har⁵ *mikel, mekil*; C *mochel* most often, but also *mikil, mekil, mechel*; R *moche(l)*, occasionally *mekyl*, rarely *muchel*; Pw *moche*; G *muche, mekel*; W *myche(l), mykil*, Ii *miche(l), meche, mekel, mikel*; Har⁴ *myche*; CP *myche(l), mochel*; Br *much*.

OE. *swylc*   Kk *syche, suche*; Har² F Pw W Br *suche*; Ar CP *siche*; Har⁵ *sclyk, slik, swilk*; C *swich*; G *seche*; Ii *sich, sech*.

OE. *wyrcan*   Kk *wyrk-*; Har² *wyrk-, wirch-, worch-*; Har⁵ *werk-, wyrk-*; C *werk-, wark-*; R Pw *werk-*; W CP Br *worch-*; Har⁴ *wirch-*.

OE. *wyrsa, wyrsta*   C *werse*; Har² Br *werst*.

8. OE. *ā* (also ON. *á*), EME. *ā*

Har⁵ has usually *saule, knawe, gastle*, &c. *a*-forms are rare elsewhere. Kk Har² Ar *saule*; Har² *awne*; Ar G W *sarre* 13/19.

9. OE. *ǣ¹, ē*

    i. Har⁵ *þare, þor*, 'there', *wor(e)*, 'were'.

    ii. G *radde* 16/4.

iii. There is considerable variation in the forms of the words
'either', 'neither'. Har¹ has *eiþer—ouþer, neiþer—nouþer,*
nowþer. Ar Pw have also *noþer;* Har⁵ *aythere, awther,*
auther, nather, nawther; C *auþer;* R *ayþer;* W *noiþer,*
noþer; Ii *noþer, neþer,* CP *neþer.*

10. OE. $\bar{æ}$²

Where conditions exist for shortening, Har¹
has *ledde, lefte, les(se);* Ar F G W Ii *lad(de);*
F R *laffte;* Ar Har⁵ Har⁴ CP *lasse.*

OE. *ǣnig* F G Har⁴ *eny;* Pw Ii Br *ony.*

Before [ʃ] W Har⁴ CP *fleisch.*

11. OE. $\bar{e}$ and EME. $\bar{e}$

i. Har⁵ *beyde, deyde, feile, fleyse, meyde;* Br *meyn.*

iii. G *bith;* Har⁴ *sijknesse;* Br *byn, syme, syknesse.*

12. LOE. $\bar{e}ȝ, \bar{e}h$

Har⁵ *hegh, egh.*

13. OE. $\bar{\imath}$, EME *i*

Br *theyn.*

14. OE. $\bar{o}$

Kk *lukeþ* 23/6; Har² *woudnes* 89/21; Har⁵ *dus* 41/2, *gude.*
Har² *doyne* 18/9, Har⁵ *foyte* 32/11.

16. OE. $\bar{y}$

Kk *kyende* 34/3; Ar *fure* 43/14; Ii *feer* 22/3.

17. OE. *ea*

(1) F *herde* 23/1.

(2) Har¹ *waxeþ* 18/6; C R W Ii *wexiþ.*

18. OE. $\bar{e}a$

Ar *gratnesse** 17/8.

19. OE. *eo*

(2) Kk *reyȝt* 12/8; Har⁵ *reght.*

(3) Har⁵ *warlde;* C *werlde.*

20. OE. $\bar{e}o$

Kk W *four-,* Ii *fouȝr-* 21/2.

See 11 iii above.

21. ME. *ai*

Har⁵ *madens, fare, ma.*

22. ME. *ei*

Where Har¹ has *ei*: Kk *faþ-* 21/9, *rase* 24/6, but *resed* 42/13,

* Possibly a shortened form.

þenes 17/11, *refrened* 28/16; Har⁵ *consawed* 44/12, *desawes* 29/17, *fath-* 21/9, *resawe* 38/14, *santes* 37/16.

Har¹ *sley, slei3, slei3t:* F Pw *slyghe;* C *sliegh, slegh;* R *sly3e;* W *sle3e;* Har⁵ *scleght;* R *slythe.*

Har¹ *di3eþ* 45/6: Kk *deighe,* Har⁵ *deyse,* C *deieþ.*

23. ME. *oi*

Har¹ *distroy-* 25/1: Har⁵ *distro-,* R *destruy-,* Ii *destri-.*

24. ME. *ou*

Har¹ has regularly *þof;* other manuscripts *þou3;* CP also *þei3* (< OE. *þēah*).

(ii) *The Main Consonant Developments*

1. OE. *c*

[ŋk] Ar *drongen, drynge, forþinge* (cf. inverted spellings in *keten* 32/9, *þinkes* 35/12); Ii *drynge, dringke, drongke.*

3. OE. *ċ*

Har⁵ *kirk* 45/14.

Kk Har² Har⁵ F C R Pw G W Har⁴ *lyke.*

See also (i) 7 above.

6. OE. *sc*

Har⁵ *scryue* 21/3, *cho* 16/4, often *sal, sulde.*

Ii *flechli* 23/2; Pw Br have *sh* in initial, *ssh* in medial position.

8. OE. *ŋg*

Har⁵ *strenthand* 35/16.

Ar *þinkes* 35/12, R *kynke* 37/15.

9. OFr. *g*

Ii *charche* 32/1, *ymache* 42/4.

10. OE. *h*

Initially: Har⁵ *is* 'his'; Ii *vnger* 32/2, *is* 43/5.*

11. OE. *hw*

Har⁵ Ii many *w*-forms; C *qweteþ* 45/3; Br *hoo.*

See 20 below.

12. OE., ME. *d*

t in final position: Kk Har² Har⁵ *vyset* 20/10; Ar *cleput, ordeynet;* Br *shewyht, steryt.*

---

* Contrariwise, an inorganic *h* occurs Kk *hou3t* 34/12, Har² *herth* 84/11, Har⁵ *huss* 'use' 42/11, Ii *ham* 25/14, *vnhesi* 27/1.

Loss of *d*: F *kynlyng* 20/9, 12.

13. OE., ME. *t*

Ar *comford, spiride*; Har² *thouched* 91/9; R *slythe* 44/18.

14. OE. *ð*

Pw *broder*; Br *odyr*.

18. OE. *f* in medial and final position

Often *f*, *ff*, in Ar Har⁵ F.

Har⁵ *behose*; Har⁵ F Pw G W Ii *vnlefulle*. But CP *heved*, 65/24.

19. ME. *v, u*

Har⁵ *wayn, woches, hewen, ewere*, &c.; Ii *fouȝchesaf*, 44/4.

20. OE., ME. *w*

Kk W CP *duell-*; Har⁵ *grofe*, 20/8.

wh-forms: Har² *whorthy* 82/6; Ii *whas, whe, whisere*, &c.; C *where*, 'were'.

21. OE. *ȝ*

After back vowel: Har⁵ *oghon, agh, draw*; W *awȝe* 21/7.

OE. *lȝ, rȝ*

Har⁵ *foloing, soroing*, &c.

b. GRAMMAR

Nouns

Genitive singular. Har¹ *Rachelle* 28/13, *Jacob* 41/15, *Dauid* 44/6, where Ar R Pw G W Ii have inflected forms; Ar Pw G W Ii *heuene* 31/2, &c.; Har⁵ *man* 21/4.

Plural. Har¹ *childre* and *chyldren*; Har² Har⁵ *chylder*; F Pw G Ii *children*.

Har¹ *breþren*, Kk Har² Har⁵ *breþire*, Pw *bretherne*.

Pronouns

Personal: third person singular feminine. Har⁵ *scho* (o).

        ,,   ,, plural. Har⁵ *þ*-forms, also *am* (acc. and d.)

Demonstrative pronouns and adjectives. Har¹ *þees, þese, þo*; Kk Har² *þire* often; C Pw CP *þise*.

Relative. See above (i) 7 for forms of 'which'.

Verbs

Present Indicative

(1) Second person singular: Har⁵ often ends -*es*.

(2) Third   ,,   ,,   Har⁵ usually, Ar C sometimes ends -*e*, -*es*.

(3) Third person plural
    i. -*eþ*, -*iþ*   Ar F C Pw G W often.
    ii. -*es*   Har² *fyndes* 30/8; Har⁵ very often.

Past Indicative

(1) OE. Strong verbs
    i. Singular. Har¹ *spak* 25/13, *schone* 44/6, but *come* 25/12, *sawe* 26/7; Kk Har² Ar F C Pw G W *spake*; Ar *sauȝ*; Har⁵ *sagh*; W *siȝe*; Ii *saiȝe*.

(2) Weak verbs
    ii. Plural. W Har⁴ CP *hadden, scholden, wolden*.

Preterite-Present Verbs

'can', 'may', 'shall'. Har¹ keeps the distinction between the singular and plural forms, where the other manuscripts most often use the singular form for both singular and plural. Ar C G W Ii have also *schul(len)*.

Present Participle
    i. -*and*. Har⁵ C W Ii often; C W Ii also -*end*.

Past Participle

In Har¹ the root vowel usually shows the normal development from the OE. form, except in *brokyn, ȝouen, troden* (CP *treden* 82/15); F Pw G *gote(n)*.

OE. prefix *ge*-. Lost, except G *yyouen* 19/13, *yspoused* 12/11.

OE. suffix -*en*. Har¹ usually retains, but *knowe* 21/14; often lost F G Ii; occasionally lost Kk Ar Har⁵ Pw CP Har⁴.

The Verb 'to be'

Present indicative plural. Har¹ *be(n)* usually, but *aren* 56/19; Ar Pw G W Ii CP often *are(n)*; Ar also *er* 14/4, *beþ* 17/11.

Preterite plural. Har² often *ware*, Har⁵ *wor(e)*.

c. VOCABULARY

The conclusions drawn from a study of the vocabulary of the five minor treatises in Har¹ are the same as for *The Cloud*.* There is the same proportion of French and Scandinavian words, and the same kind of borrowing.† The important early and reliable manuscripts agree in the main‡ with Har¹, and generalizations about the vocabulary in Har¹ can be assumed to be true of the author's original text.

The variants of many manuscripts contain later forms than those in Har¹; more noteworthy, however, are those which replace a usage in Har¹ which would appear to be new, or novel, at the end of the fourteenth century.§ The great number of words in all these treatises for which the earliest reference given in the *Oxford English Dictionary* belongs to the last thirty years of the fourteenth century indicates that these treatises, too, are part of the great intellectual and literary activity which produced the poetry of Chaucer, Langland, and Gower, the theological work of Wyclif, and the Wycliffite translations of the Bible. Like them, these treatises introduce late Latin or late French forms (e.g. *formaciouns, passibilite*), and enrich the language with borrowings of abstract terms of philosophy and theology, e.g.:

affeccioun, deuinite (= godhead), *disposicioun, fantasie, fantastik, ymagynatyue, inmaterial, object, sensible, sensibilite, substance.*

The earliest quotations of many of these words are from the Chaucerian translation of Boethius's *De Consolatione Philosophiae*, Trevisa's translation of Bartholomaeus's *De Proprietatibus Rerum*, and Thomas Usk's philosophical *Testament of Love*.

The number of words or phrases in the works associated with the author of *The Cloud* for which the quotation is from Wyclif's

---

* See *Cloud*, pp. xlviii–xlix.

† Most of the Scandinavian words are the same common words which were introduced in *The Cloud*. Further examples are *list*, 'appetite', *ransakiþ, sere, þral*.

‡ As in the manuscripts of *The Cloud*, occasionally common Scandinavian words are substituted for words of native or French origin. Further examples are *ay* for *euer*, *ʒa* for *ʒe*, *ille* for *yuel*, *witterly* for *verrely*, *awe* for *drede*, *rayse* for *rere*, *gare* for *make* 31/6, *sammyn* for *togeders* 45/13, 51/4, *merknes* for *derknes*.

§ e.g. 28/16, 29/13.

work, or the 1382 Wycliffite version of the Bible, is arresting.*
Sometimes the word is a favourite one in Wycliffite writings, e.g.
abound-, auoid-, occasyon; sometimes a particular Wycliffite sense
is given to it, e.g. *ordinaunce* (= practice enjoined), *passeþ*
(= surpasses), *vnderstondynges* (= faculties of understanding),
vnderstandable (= capable of understanding); or the use is figurative, and coloured by the same associations as in the Wycliffite
translation, e.g. *borion-, darte, drounyd, pricke*. Occasionally the
Wycliffite context is very appropriate to the text of these treatises,
e.g.:

> 49/17. Cf. 2 Cor. vi. 2: *In tyme accept, or wel plesynge.*
> 5/17–18. Cf. 1 Cor. iv. 5: *þe hid thingis of derknessis.*
> 28/16. Cf. Ps. xc. 6: *fro þe inrennyng & the midday deuel* (The only
> reference in *O.E.D.* before the nineteenth century for this
> translation of Latin *incursus*).
> 30/11. Cf. Phil. iv. 7: *þe pees of God that passeth al wit.*

Other words for which the earliest reference is Wycliffite are:

*assendiþ, determinid, dissolucioun, enournementes, ensaumplid, Fader-
heed, Firstheed, Ierarchies, propirte, refreyne, refresching, relesyng,
stirer, taasting* (= faculty of taste), *vnknowe, first-felt.*

It seems certain that the author of these treatises was using
a language fresh and up to date. Like his great contemporaries,
however, he made good use of the terms which the heritage of
vernacular devotional literature richly provided. Many of his
words are traceable back to Old English homilies; many more occur
in the west Midland writings of the early thirteenth century. But
the most important source was probably the devotional writings of
the first half of the fourteenth century, for the works of Robert
Mannyng of Brunne, the *Cursor Mundi*, the *Ayenbite of Inwyt*,
The Pricke of Conscience, and especially the writings of Richard
Rolle of Hampole, had already provided a vocabulary well fitted
to describe the experiences and temptations of the spiritual life.
To these the author might well have been indebted for:

*acordaunce, acordeþ, vnder colour of, combrance, comounyng, compassion,
concupiscence, conpunccioun, contryte, corious, corumpid, corupcioun,
dampnable, defoulid, discencioun, discrete, discrecioun, diuersite, erre,
euenheed, exposicioun, fautours, febylnes, felly, ferde, fyling, freel,*

---

* See *Cloud*, p. lxxxv, where attention is drawn to the resemblance
between a passage in *Priue Counseling* and the later Wycliffite version.
Priue Counseling was probably a late work, see *Cloud*, p. lxxviii and footnote.

*freelte, frenesiees, glose, homlynes, illumynyd, ymaginacioun, jangelyng,
langwisching, lyʒtenyng, liking, medeful, onlines, perfeccioun, profiteþ,
queintly, sensualite,* and many other words.

A detailed study of the vocabulary of the five treatises here
edited reveals still more points of interest. At least once a use of a
word—*ruyde,* 'inexperienced'—is the earliest recorded in *O.E.D.,*
which quotes from the translation of *Benjamin Minor.* Several
words described as rare are also to be found herein: *atempereely,
be tymes,* 'now and then', *deuelnes, ensclaundre.* Frequently words
used in these treatises are either not recorded until much later, or
have a particular meaning here which is described as belonging to
a subsequent period. The earliest reference for the following words
or phrases is given in brackets:

acceptacioun (1426), *affirmatyue* (adj., 1509), *formaciouns* (1450),
happynes (1530), *herdesay* (1553), *holdeþ oute* (1583), *inclusid* (1432),
inordynacioun (1612), *knowable* (1449), *lynyng* (1598), *listi* (c. 1440),
listely (c. 1440), *lokest after* (1650), *losable* (1611), *loued* (n., 1435),
passing (quasi-prep., 1449), *spekingly* (1633), *suspeciously* (1549),
sauable (1450), *sonheed* (1602), *visibilite* (1581), *not*+adj., as in *not-
vnderstondable, not-beyng* (sixteenth century), *late*+pp. adj., as in
late-borne, late-getyn (seventeenth century).

Similarly, though the form of the word may have appeared
earlier, the date given in brackets indicates the earliest record of
the meanings obvious in the treatises:

ascension, 'act of ascending' (1596); *assenciouns,* 'ways of ascending'
(1447); *assendiþ* used figuratively (1549); *attemprid* (1474); *being* (adj.)
(1458); *beholding,* 'mental contemplation' (1520), ' things beheld'
(1440); *body,* 'trunk of tree' (1523); *clog* used figuratively (1526);
custume, 'habitual practising' (1526); *deniinges* (1450); *deniingly*
(1824); *doles,* 'deceits' (1563); *godly* (adv., 1530); *negatyue* (sixteenth century); *synguleer,* 'unique' (mid-sixteenth century); *singuleertees* (1663); *scaterst,* 'distract' (1450); *profre* (1523); *crakke*
(nuts 1483); *ungropable* (only reference 1558); *put to* (i.e. for breeding,
1523).

As with *The Cloud* and *Priue Counseling,* some words here are
not recorded at all in the *O.E.D.:* e.g.

not-aʒenstonding (prep.), *apely, aworde, beable, companous, forcostoumid,
goostheed, knittyngly, steedlynes, unmiʒtfulnes, vnpassyngliche,* adv.
(earliest reference to adjective, 1592), *vnresonabiltee, vn-understond-
abely,* adv. (earliest reference to adjective, 1631).

In the case of other words, their signification in the treatises is not paralleled: e.g.

counsel, 'father confessor'; *godly*, 'divinely'; *knowable*, 'that may know';· *losable*, 'in danger of damnation'; *by menes*, 'through intermediate stages'; *ouerlappid*, 'wrapped up in'; *unwise*, 'uninitiated'.

The author of these treatises may justifiably be described as a pioneer in his use of words, an 'inventor', who enriched the language by his attempts to express philosophical and theological conceptions. His ways of working can clearly be seen in the three translations, *Hid Diuinite*, *þe Stodye of Wysdome*, and *Discrescyon of Spirites*. Though closely dependent upon Latin sources for much of his subject-matter, he introduced comparatively few Latinate terms,* but rather followed in the tradition of English translators set by Ælfred and Ælfric of using common native words where available, and customary methods of word-formation where.not. Usually familiar English or French words translate the Latin, which, in a later period, provided the word·in common use today: e.g.

gostely = spiritualis; *syȝt* = visio(n-); *besyly* = diligenter; *jangeling* = garrulitas; *doyng to* = additio(n-); *homlynes* = familiaritas; *seable* = visibilis; *unseable* = invisibilis; &c.

In word-formation much use is made of the prefix **un-**. The suffix *-able* is frequently added to the root to form adjectives from verbs: e.g. *beable, knowable, losable, ungropable, un-understondable,* &c. The suffix *-heed* is favoured for abstract nouns: e.g. *fairheed, Faderheed, firstheed, goostheed, onheed, Sonheed*. Occasionally compounds are introduced such as: *inliche beholder* (= Latin *inspectrix*), *ouerpassyng* (= Latin *excessus*), *late-borne, late-getyn, sonnereborne, not-beyng, not-vnderstondable, ouerlappid*.

At times, in an attempt to communicate the rich associations of the thought, words are strained to bear a load of meaning in a way recognizably individual.† Thus: *Firstheed* = First Cause; *sette* = affirm what can positively be said about God; *list* =

___

* e.g. *ascension(s), affirmatyue, conplexion, formacioun, inclusid, inordinacioun, negative, singuler, singuleerte, visibilite.*

† Cf. the use of 'naked' and 'blind' in *The Cloud*. See *Cloud*, p. 185, note to 17/2, p. 187, note to 22/18.

eager longing of love for God;* *unknowing* = ceasing to know by a deliberate stilling of all the faculties of knowing; *souerein* = Latin *super*, denoting what is infinitely transcendent and ineffable about the being of God.

One may not, of course, with any assurance assess the originality of the vocabulary of these treatises while relatively so little is yet known about the current usage of words at the end of the fourteenth century. The valuable though necessarily inconclusive evidence of the *Oxford English Dictionary*, however, clearly suggests the importance of the works attributable to the author of *The Cloud* in the study of the development of the English vocabulary. It is certain from manuscript evidence and from the early printed edition of 1521 that some of these treatises, at least, were in wide circulation through the fifteenth and sixteenth centuries.

PART II. SUBJECT-MATTER AND STYLE

The authorship† of *The Cloud of Unknowing* is still a vexed question. The attribution of it to Hilton continues to win new supporters;‡ the doubts of those who see in it the work of a different kind of genius remain yet unallayed. External evidence is being sought, but it might well be that it will never be found. Meanwhile the internal evidence must be tested as thoroughly as possible, and a good starting process will be to see how far one can establish the common authorship of *The Cloud*, *þe Book of Priue Counseling*, and the five treatises here edited. Relationship has been generally accepted, but how close it is, not only in theme but in expression and technical details of style, has not hitherto been fully examined.§ The close comparison of the five treatises here attempted, with each other and with the two longer works, will serve both to describe the writings and to collect what stylistic evidence there is for assuming single authorship. Its certain value will lie in the demonstration of the technique behind some masterly

* Cf. *Cloud*, 8/18: listines.

† No separate section on Authorship has been included in the present edition since the editor has little to add to her brief discussion of the problem in *The Cloud*, pp. lxxxii–lxxxvi.

‡ See Helen L. Gardner's review of *The Cloud* in *Medium Ævum*, vol. xvi (1947), pp. 41–42.

§ For a brief treatment see *The Cloud*, pp. lxxvii–lxxxii.

medieval prose; its ultimate achievement may be to provide some material towards a confident answer to the question whether Walter Hilton wrote *The Cloud* as well as *The Scale of Perfection*.

A. The Relationship of the Five Treatises in Subject-Matter

The relationship of the themes of the seven treatises can be easily established by a brief survey of the purpose of the five minor works, set here in order of their closeness to *The Cloud of Unknowing*. *Hid Diuinite* is placed first, with its translator's avowed intent of elucidating certain difficulties in *The Cloud*. It has already been shown that the foundation of the thought of the author of *The Cloud* rests upon the Dionysian tradition.* Thrice† this chief source for the teaching is named, and it seems highly probable that the author of *The Cloud* was himself the translator of the work to which he owed most. From Dionysius, in particular, were drawn the metaphysics explaining the possibility of union between God and His creatures (see *Priue Counseling*, 136/9–24), and the striking paradox that characterizes *The Cloud* that in the search for the Absolute the best way to knowing lies through not knowing, to Divine illumination through the resulting darkness when every conception obtained through the human faculties is set aside. The whole idea of the 'cloud of unknowing' with its distinctive related imagery was ultimately derived from the works of Dionysius.

þe *Stodye of Wysdome*, a short Middle English version of *Benjamin Minor*, is set next, for the author of *The Cloud* was probably indebted to Richard of St. Victor for the systematization of the way to contemplative prayer, some of his allegorical interpretations of Scripture, and possibly for the prevailing antithetical nature of his prose. Richard of St. Victor's longer treatise, *Benjamin Major*, is referred to in *Priue Counseling*, 154/16, and passages in chapters 71–73 of *The Cloud* are translated from it. The Middle English writer nowhere claims to have translated *Benjamin Minor*, but chapters 63–66 of *The Cloud* are largely derived from it,‡ shorter passages are reminiscent of it, and direct

---

* *Cloud*, pp. lvii–lxix.

† *Cloud*, 125/13–15, *Priue Counseling*, 154/17–18, *Hid Diuinite*, 2/5–8.

‡ See *Cloud*, p. lxxv.

reference is made to its allegory in *Priue Counseling*.* The *Pistle of Preier*, which here follows the translation of *Benjamin Minor*, is listed among the author's acknowledged works in *Priue Counseling*, 154/13–15. *Preier* is very close to *Þe Stodye of Wysdome* in the development of its thought, though the resemblance is concealed by the use of different imagery.† Whereas *Hid Diuinite* explains the nature of contemplation, *Þe Stodye of Wysdome* and the *Pistle of Preier* give a psychological explanation of the efforts of the contemplative, and practical advice as to the way of preparation.

The last two treatises in this edition have a more limited theme than those preceding, but in a way they both supplement *Þe Stodye of Wysdome*. In his allegorical interpretation of the story of Jacob, his two wives, their handmaidens, and the twelve sons, Richard of St. Victor shows how in the preparation of the soul for contemplation Joseph must be born long before Benjamyn. Benjamyn signifies the spiritual ecstasy in which the soul attains to a vision of God; Joseph, who must precede, signifies the grace of purity which follows upon a true knowledge of self. Joseph is the virtue of discretion, the guardian virtue of all the others, which recognizes the good and chooses it, and has the power to separate the good from the evil. Joseph, in short, is the 'wisdom, discrecioun, and perfeccioun of vertewe' (65/21), the central theme of the fourth treatise here, *A Pistle of Discrecioun of Stirings*, which amplifies and expounds chapter 42 of *The Cloud*.

A Tretis of Discrescyon of Spirites completes this group of five treatises. Though it is partly a paraphrase of two of St. Bernard's sermons,‡ and closer to the common stock of homiletic material than the preceding four works, yet it too describes an aspect of 'Joseph'. It purposes to teach the contemplative how to recognize the voice of temptation in his spiritual progress, and to know what must be avoided or overcome:

'And þerfore whoso wol haue God contynouly wonyng in him, and liue in loue and in siȝt of þe hiȝe pees of þe Godheed, þe whiche is þe hiȝest & þe best partye of contemplacion þat may be had in þis liif, be he besi niȝt & day to put doun, whan þei come, þe spirite of þe flessche and þe spirite of þe woreld, bot most besily

---

* *Cloud*, 150/10–23.
† See *Cloud*, pp. lxxxv–lxxxvi.
‡ *Sermones xxiii* and *xxiv*, Migne, *P.L.*, t. clxxxiii, cols. 600–5.

þe spirite of malice, of wraþþe, and of wickidnes, for he is þe foulist & þe worst filþe of alle' (85/9–15).

It is possible to compare the pattern of three of these treatises. The *Tretis of Discrescyon of Spirites* may fairly be considered together with the *Pistle of Preier* and the *Pistle of Discrecioun of Stirings*, for, despite its adherence to two of St. Bernard's sermons, it shows independence of arrangement, and the translator passes from one sermon to the next, and back again, with interpolations of his own.* The other two treatises, *Hid Diuinite* and *þe Stodye of Wysdome*, are shaped by the argument of their sources, and discussion of them must be postponed to the next section which deals with the methods of translation.

A Pistle of Preier and *Discrecioun of Stirings*, like *The Cloud* and *Priue Counseling*, are written in the form of letters to a young contemplative who has sought some practical guidance on a specific problem. This might, of course, be only a convention, though at times the tone is noticeably personal, and even intimate.† *A Tretis of Discrescyon of Spirites* is written chiefly in general terms, and in the first person plural, though at 87/19 sqq., where the translator leaves his sources, he changes to the direct and personal address of the second person singular.

The *Pistle of Preier* and *Discrecioun of Stirings* are very closely alike in structure. They both begin with a practical question, plunge straight into the subject, keep to a single theme, treating two main aspects of it, never far from and ever returning to the problem with which they begin. Thus *Preier* propounds the question: 'how þou schalt reule þin hert in tyme of þi preier', 48/2–3; *Stirings*: how far should inclinations towards certain special ascetic practices be followed? The behaviour involved in these questions is next examined, and reasons given for the proffered advice. The theme of *Preier* is the preparation for contemplation which is the goal of prayer; of *Stirings*, the way to self-knowledge which alone leads to true judgement of impulses and inclinations. Direct teaching in each treatise is then followed by imagery which symbolizes the previous thought—in *Preier*, it is

---

* See p. xlvi.

† e.g. *Preier*, 59/6 sqq., and in the final blessing, 59/15; *Stirings*, 63/19–22, 67/8–10, 68/8–16, 70/13–71/2, and final blessing, 77/15. The blessing is given also at the end of *The Cloud*, 133/4–7. This has been taken as evidence that the author was a priest.

the figure of a tree; in *Stirings*, of a ship, followed by that of a crown. The second half of each treatise is more elevated in tone than the first, being devoted chiefly to 'þe pointe & þe prik of perfeccioun, to þe whiche I porpose to drawe þee in my menyng' (*Preier*, 54/16–17), 'þe trewe eendes of oure desire' (*Stirings*, 69/24, cf. 72/3–8, 73/1–2). Here the teaching in the two epistles is the same as in *The Cloud*. Contemplation is essentially an act of love, and not of the mind, of which the workings are in fact an hindrance in this state. The contemplative must transcend the kind of meditations advocated in the first part of the *Pistle of Preier*, must set aside all thoughts of spiritual exercises examined in the first part of the *Pistle of Discrecioun of Stirings*. 'Reuerent affeccioun' must be offered 'sodenly, listely, & likingly, wiþouten mene', *Preier*, 57/5, 14–15. All 'maner of siȝt of any þing bineþe' God must be 'vtterly' voided 'fro þi goostly beholding', *Stirings* 75/4–5.*

There is this same double aspect of subject-matter in *A Tretis of Discrescyon of Spirites*, a practical question of behaviour, a more elevated passage treating of contemplation; but the proportions are different in this discourse, for the practical theme occupies the greater part of it. It is introduced, as in the other two treatises, without preamble, and is similarly based on two main ideas. First the activities of the spirits of the World, the Flesh, and the Devil are described, lest the mistake should be made of not recognizing them and of attributing every thought to a 'mans owne spirite', 80/7. Then the remedy is prescribed when the human spirit is so overcome by any of these three evil spirits that 'it doþ . . . þe office of iche one of hem only itself in itself', 87/5, and 'it may not liȝtly be knowen when it is oure owne spirite þat spekiþ, or when it hereþ any of þe oþer þre spirites spekyng in it', 87/13–15. All this is personal. There is a brief passage, more elevated in tone and comparable in spirit to the second part of *Preier* and of *Stirings*, where the author states the reason for his instruction:

For whoso lackiþ pees and restfulnes of herte, him lackiþ þe liuely presence of þe louely siȝt of þe heiȝe pees of heuen, good gracious God, him owne dere self (84/19–85/2; cf. 85/9–15).

* Cf. *Preier*, 54/9–12, 20–21, 55/11–13, 16–18, 22–23, 56/1, 57/14–18; *Stirings*, 71/22–26, 72/3–12, 21–23, 73/1–3, 75/4–5, 76/6–8.

B. The Translations and their Sources

1. *Deonise Hid Diuinite*

The Middle English prologue to *Deonise Hid Diuinite* (2/2–12) is a good introduction, since it not only names the source of the treatise but also explains the reasons for the method of translation. *Hid Diuinite* is a version from a Latin translation of the *Mystica Theologia* of Dionysius the Areopagite.* But the fourteenth-century writer was a teacher and guide as well as translator, and to expound the Dionysian doctrine he tells us that he used besides the Latin text the interpretation of the 'Abbot of Seinte Victore'. It seems certain that this 'noble' and 'worþi expositour' was Thomas Gallus, Abbot of St. Andrew's, Vercelli, from its foundation in 1219 until his death in 1246, a Canon Regular of the Congregation of St. Victor.† He is known generally as 'Vercellensis', and was one of the most prolific commentators on the works of Dionysius in the Middle Ages, and possibly also the most influential.‡

It has already been clearly shown that the first three chapters of *Hid Diuinite* are a close translation of the Latin version of Johannes Sarracenus,§ and that the last two are based chiefly on the work of Vercellensis.§ Three different works of Vercellensis appear to have contributed towards the Middle English text: the *Paraphrase* or *Extractio*,‖ the *Commentary*,¶ the *Gloss*** on *Mystica Theologia*.

---

* For an account of the pseudo-Dionysius and his works, see notes to Title, pp. 118–19. Also P. Hodgson, 'Dionysius the Areopagite and the Christian Mystical Tradition', in *Contemporary Review*, Nov. 1949.

† See *Cloud of Unknowing*, ed. Dom J. McCann (London, 1924), pp. xii–xiii. This edition will be referred to henceforth as McCann.

‡ A good bibliography for his life and works can be found in the notes to D. A. Callus, 'An Unknown Commentary of Thomas Gallus on the pseudo-Dionysian Letters', *Dominican Studies*, Jan. 1948.

§ See McCann, pp. xii–xiv, 251–83. Both Latin versions are to be found in Denis à Rickel, *D. Dionysii Cartusiani Opera Omnia* (Tournai, 1902), t. xvi. The relevant chapters are given here in Appendix A.

‖ Probably composed 1238–9. See Callus, loc. cit., pp. 65–66.

¶ The Commentary, or Explanatio, was probably written *c.* 1241. See Callus, p. 66. It is extant in England in at least three manuscripts, Brit. Mus. MS. Royal 8. G. iv, Worcester Cathedral Library MS. F 57, Merton College, Oxford, MS. 69. The present editor has consulted the Royal and the Merton manuscripts, and, unless otherwise stated, has quoted in this edition

For note ** see page xl.

Unlike *Þe Stodye of Wysdome* and *Discrescyon of Spirites*, *Hid
Diuinite* follows its Latin sources closely, with only very minor
additions, omissions, and modifications.* It has the same division
into five chapters, preceded by a prayer which, while invoking
divine aid, is an epitome of what follows.

As for contents, the subject of this book is God, and the
teaching describes the profoundest experience of Him attainable
in this life. The Middle English title, like the Latin, has an under-
tone of meaning, though the two are not the same. *Theologia*,
which usually signifies the science which treats of God, is also used
occasionally of Holy Scriptures, and has indeed this sense in the
Latin version of the *Celestial Hierarchy*, 9, § 3, and in a commentary
of Hugh of St. Victor upon Dionysius. In English, *Divinity* can
refer to Godhead as well as to the study of the nature and attributes of God. *Hid* is used to translate not only Latin *mystica*, but
also *clausa* and *occulta*.

Dionysius purposed to teach a truer way of knowing God than
any reached by pagan philosophers striving to rise to knowledge of
invisible things through their knowledge of the visible; a pro-
founder way even than that taught by many of the holy fathers, or
by himself in all his other works; in short, the only way which
could lead to union with God in contemplative prayer. He bases
his teaching throughout on a mystical interpretation of the Scriptures, and prays in the beginning to understand the deepest wisdom
of Christian men lying hidden in the Scriptures and to be drawn up
to the 'souereyn-schinyng hei3t of þi derke inspirid spekynges'
(2/18–19). But the God he would contemplate in His Essence is
transcendent, ineffable, and incomprehensible, hidden from human
powers of knowing in an inscrutable darkness, which can be reached
only in an excess of mind, when all that is lower than God has been

---

from the Royal MS. An attempt has been made in the notes and Appendix A
to show, to some extent, what the translator has drawn from these three
works.

** Thomas Gallus is known to have commented briefly on the *Mystica
Theologia*. See Callus, loc. cit., p. 58, note 3. It seems probable from their
subject-matter and style that his notes were printed by Migne, *P.L.*, t. cxxii,
cols. 267–84, with the title: *Expositiones seu Glossae in Mysticam Theologiam Sancti Dionysii*, and attributed to John Scotus Erigena. These notes
are quoted in the present edition under the title of Gloss.

---

* See Appendix A.

rejected and thrust down. Since the finite created mind can only know finite created things, and since the infinite uncreated God infinitely transcends all finite creation, union is a state when all knowing powers are silenced, and experience of God in His Essence is hidden from normal consciousness, and is therefore inexpressible in words produced by the discursive human reasoning or which describe the perceptions of the senses. All these ideas underlie the initial prayer for the 'ful fayre cleertees' which illumine those who are in a 'darkness of unknowing', not knowing because 'not hauyng iȝen of mynde'.

The first chapter begins by directing the young disciple as to what to reject in contemplative prayer, and by giving warning that this teaching is not for those pursuing worldly wisdom who are not spiritually prepared. It compares the affirmative and the negative paths of contemplation, for by one way of reasoning it is possible to attribute all things to God, by another to deny Him all attributes. This second way is the higher, for it leads on when man's understanding falls short. Moses's ascent of Sinai is typical of the contemplative's progress. When he had climbed to the limits possible to human effort helped by grace he 'entrid by hymself þe derknes of vnknowyng', and in the cloud he experienced the presence of God.

The second chapter explains the direct teaching of the first by means of an elaborate analogy with carving. The last paragraph of chapter 2 and the three remaining chapters compare the two possible ways of approach, and the two possible kinds of statements about God—the positive and the negative. Chapter 3 considers the positive statements made anagogically in Dionysius's earlier works, *Celestial Hierarchy*, *Ecclesiastical Hierarchy*, *Divine Names*, *Symbolic Theology*, wherein the more purely intellectual his conceptions, the fewer congruous words could be found. It is not surprising, therefore, that when the contemplative reaches the level of the 'darkness of unknowing' beyond his understanding, 'it schal al be withouten voice' (8/20–21). The affirmative way rests upon God's immanence in all things, the negative way on God's transcendence of all things. Since what is most universal is nearest to God, and what is most particular farthest away, the way towards knowledge of God by positive statement begins with the highest and works down to the lowest, and contrariwise, the way by negative statement begins at the lowest and works up. Chapter 4 gives illustration of the negative way. Chapter 5 describes both movements, from the highest to the lowest, and back again to the highest, and concludes that neither will bring full knowledge, for the Cause of all incomprehensibly transcends all that can be thought, and is 'vn-vnderstondabely abouen alle affermyng and deniinge' (10/22–23). The affirmative way ends in a negation, for nothing affirmed is God; the negative way paradoxically ends in an affirmative, that God infinitely transcends all knowable things.

With few exceptions the Middle English translator follows phrase by phrase this sequence of thought. But he tells us that he 'moche folowed þe sentence' of Vercellensis as well as 'þe nakid lettre' of the Latin text. It will be seen from the Notes that the Middle English writer was most indebted to Vercellensis in those passages which characterize the exercise of contemplative prayer or show what its operation will be in the mind of the contemplative. Thus, *Hid Diuinite* is following Vercellensis rather than Sarracenus in stressing that this exercise will require great effort (3/1), but that it depends upon grace (2/17, 31–32), that it is an act of love (2/25–26, 4/25, 5/15), that it will lead to illumination through union in a higher cognitive faculty than in the normal working powers of consciousness (2/26, 3/11–12, 16–17). In several passages the Middle English translator follows Vercellensis in expanding or expounding, yet here he does not always agree closely, but sometimes clarifies in a different way (3/13–16, 20–35, 6/32 sqq.). At times he is more personal (3/9–10), at times less vague (2/14), or he has simplified a technical term (3/2–4, 4/33) or a philosophical explanation (3/6–9). Occasionally he borrows from Vercellensis an incidental image (2/17, 5/17) or an illustration (3/25, 33). He incorporated the fourth chapter in its entirety from Vercellensis because it described more directly than the version of Sarracenus the mental process of the contemplative in which he was primarily interested (cf. 3/13–16).

There are comparatively few passages where the Middle English translation has added to the Latin versions of Sarracenus or Vercellensis, or differs significantly from them. Apart from the one long addition in chapter 2, it follows them carefully, and though it may expand to simplify, it omits no link in the thought. The different words or phrases are almost without exception more intelligible because more simple, or they are more suggestive and vigorous. Three times the translator has modified the subject-matter, and by so doing has deepened the meaning of the passage (2/15–16, 4/13, 8/14). Twice he has given a reference (8/8, 3/25); twice has further defined his thought (8/19, 34–35); once he has clarified it by means of a simile (5/8). Often he simplifies Latin abstract terms, trying to express in Middle English the full content of what is very condensed in the Latin (2/19–20, 3/21–22); in 8/7 he translated the abstruse title *Theologicis Hypotyposibus** by 'two bookes of þe Ierarchies'. Like the speculative passages in *The Cloud* and *Priue Counseling*, many of his modifications can be interpreted on two levels—by the learned they can be understood according to the tenets of medieval philosophy and psychology; to the simple and unlettered they still have a meaning according to 'þe comounist wit of kynde',† e.g. 3/3–4, 34–35, 6/25.

More vivid imagery occurs in the Middle English than appears in the Latin sources, and often this is reminiscent of the lively language of *The Cloud* (e.g. 2/32, 3/1, 6/22, 7/4).

2. *A Tretyse of þe Stodye of Wysdome þat Men Clepen Beniamyn*

The Middle English version is little more than a skeleton summary of Richard of St. Victor's *Benjamin Minor*,‡ which, as printed by Migne, occupies over sixty columns of text. It is difficult to generalize about the method of translation, for some chapters from the Latin are followed closely and fully; some are represented by a close translation of a few selected sentences, others by a free paraphrase either of the whole or part; many chapters are not represented at all.§ It must be conceded, however, that though the Middle English treatise gives little more than an outline of the thought of the Latin, and though the Latin is unequally followed, yet in the English translation proportions are well kept, and the work has the homogeneity and finish of an original treatise.

The Middle English translator greatly simplifies, yet follows

* Possibly Dionysius here referred to an entirely different (and now unknown) work.
† *Priue Counseling*, 137/5. ‡ See Notes, pp. 129–130.
§ An attempt has been made in the Notes to indicate the different kinds of translations and borrowings.

Benjamin Minor faithfully in describing the stages of spiritual progress towards perfection through the allegory of Jacob, his wives, and children. The state of perfection comprises knowledge and love of God.* Lya (affection) and Rachel (reason) are both wives to Jacob, that is God. Lya conceived first, for first the heart must be disciplined, and moral purification serves to prepare the way for spiritual progress. Her first four children were Ruben (humility arising through a consciousness of sin and dread of the power of the Divine Judge), Symeon (contrition), Levy (hope of forgiveness), Judas (love of God and heavenly things, arising from a perception of God's goodness). The mind, too, must be disciplined, and there is need to examine what is loved. But the mind at this early stage can proceed only by means of images, rising by and through visible things to the knowledge of invisible things. Therefore Rachel's handmaiden, Bala (imagination), next bears children to Jacob—Dan and Neptalym, who typify the knowledge of what the soul has to dread, and of what to hope for. Next, Zelfa (sensuality), Lya's handmaiden, conceives, for discipline of the body must follow and accompany discipline of the heart. Her children are Gad and Asser (abstinence and patience). To have lasting enjoyment of the interior happiness and the sweetness of soul won by the virtues already acquired, the baser satisfactions of the flesh must be denied, and there must be perseverance and continual effort. Soon the rewards of spiritual progress begin to be felt, and Lya again bears a child, Isachar, who typifies a transitional state when the soul, still bound in by human limitations, and repeatedly dragged down by sin, yet begins to taste inward sweetness and true joy in God. Zabulon must follow, the tenth son of Lya, personifying that true hatred of sin which is only obtainable through an experience of blessedness wherein the soul feels impeded from full participation by sin. Dyna follows, true shame for sinful lapses. Sin is inescapable in the world, and the contemplative must learn a wise attitude towards it, and feel ordained shame, else he may soon fall into despair and bitterness. All these offspring of Lya are virtues, but taken to excess they are soon turned into vices. Discretion is needed to govern them, and discretion can be learnt only by long trial in the bitter school of temptation. And so Joseph, the first child of Rachel, was born late. Joseph signifies

* Cf. *Cloud*, 17/4–5.

discretion,. the guardian virtue of all the others.* Joseph is the
grace which follows from a true knowledge of self, and a true
knowledge of self is the way to knowledge of God, in whose image
man was made. In the last instance, however, the vision of God is a
gift from God. When Benjamyn was born, his mother Rachel died,
for 'in what tyme þat a soule is rauischid abouen hymself by
habundaunce of desires & a greet multytude of loue, so þat it is
enflawmyd with þe liȝt of þe Godheed, sekirly þan dyȝeþ al mans
reson' (45/6–9).† The highest level is touched only in an ecstasy
of mind when all consciousness of self is lost; flooded with divine
light, the soul gazes directly on God without any veils of created
things: 'Ibi Beniamyn adolescentulus in mentis excessu' (46/
12–13).‡

The main outline of Richard of St. Victor's allegory is thus
kept, but in almost every chapter its details have been greatly
reduced. And so, for example, the Middle English writer does not
expound why Rachel is more attractive than Lya (caps. i and ii),
nor does he digress upon the adult adventures of Ruben (caps.
xxviii–xxx) or Dyna (caps. xlix–liii), or the signification of Joseph's
coat of many colours or his dreams (cap. lxviii). Related allegories
are entirely omitted (e.g. the long digression on the Transfigura-
tion in caps. lxxvii–lxxxii), and also the majority of the many
scriptural quotations with their accompanying interpretations.
The treatment of Dan and Gad (caps. xxxi–xxxii) has been reduced
to two lines in Middle English, an example of the drastic simplifica-
tion which is characteristic of much of þe Stodye of Wysdome.

The freedom with which the Middle English translator dealt
with his subject is shown by his introduction of Richard of St.
Victor's quotations from Scripture and interpretation of proper
names in contexts different from those in the source (e.g. 22/7–8,
25/5), and by his reversal of the order of thought (e.g. 18/6 sqq.).

In the translation, the interpretation is always given more
importance than the allegory, and often the explanation is given
directly instead of the details of the story (e.g. 33/7).

Moreover, the Middle English writer was interested only in the
single theme of contemplative prayer and in his purpose of guidance, and whereas he will expand upon the practical application

---

* See above, p. xxxvi.   † Cf. *Priue Counseling*, 150/13–15.
‡ Cf. *Priue Counseling*, 150/19–20.

of his teaching and its effect upon the disciple's mind or feeling (e.g. 14/1 sqq., 26/12–16, 30/13–16), he has no place for the theoretical distinctions dear to scholastic writers. He omits, for example, Richard of St. Victor's development of the two kinds of *rationalis imaginatio*, caps. xvi–xviii, and his account of the different ways in which imagination serves her mistress, reason.

At times he is more explicit and didactic than his source. He is more explanatory in his use of the mirror image (43/5 sqq.), and adds to it the supporting analogy of the candle which is not in the Latin. He further defines and categorizes where the Latin is silent, e.g. 12/12–13, 14/6–7, 15/1–2; in two passages he adduces a further authority, St. Paul in 32/14, St. Augustine in 36/8.

Even though the basic teaching is the same, and the main outline of the allegory kept, often there is a different emphasis, which is best revealed in those passages in the Middle English which do not occur in the Latin.

3. *A Tretis of Discrescyon of Spirites*

In the third derived work there is a treatment of source quite different from the close phrase-by-phrase translation of *Hid Diuinite* and also from the brief outline offered by *þe Stodye of Wysdome*. It is shown in the Notes* that only about a third of it is, in fact, translation, viz. the four sections: (1) 80/2–83/12, (2) 86/22–88/2, (3) 92/4–8, all from no. xxiii of St. Bernard's *Sermones de Diversis*,† (4) 85/16–86/9 from no. xxiv.

Even in the borrowed paragraphs the translator does not draw consecutively from his sources, but inserts part of *Sermo xxiv* among passages taken from *Sermo xxiii*. Nor is his treatment the same, for (1) is a close translation, (2) is greatly expanded and free, (4) is slightly expanded. The borrowed passages are, moreover, neatly fitted into what has already been shown to be a characteristic structure,‡ and the effect of the whole is not so much that of a translation as of an original work comparable with the two Epistles in style. It will be demonstrated in the next section that, despite their derived subject-matter, it is possible to compare the style of these translations with that of *The Cloud* and its related treatises, for apart from certain passages in *Hid Diuinite*, where the language is strained to the utmost to express

---

* Pp. 140 sqq.   † *P.L.*, t. clxxxiii, cols. 600–3.   ‡ Pp. xxxvii–xxxviii.

the difficult meaning, and apart from rare misunderstandings, the fourteenth-century English writer was so little hampered by the Latin that, through his own craft and artistry, he could turn it into highly polished and idiomatic vernacular prose.

C. The Relationship of the Five Treatises in Style

Homogeneity of style in the prose works attributable to the author of *The Cloud* may be felt, but it is not easily demonstrable from treatises on different themes, some of which are translations or adaptations. Certain features, however, are shared by all of them, and in the three pieces certainly not original the evidence for common authorship is all the more convincing since those parts of the translation not paralleled in their source are the most reminiscent of the other treatises of this group. Their resemblance to each other lies partly in their reflection of a like quality of mind, partly in a similar dependence on a tradition inherited from Latin rhetorical writings and earlier English alliterative and rhythmical prose.

Unlike many medieval devotional works, these treatises are composed in what is essentially logical prose, strictly controlled, and appealing to intellect rather than emotion. Their matter appears deceptively plain to a casual reader because of their lucidity and directness; their style seems apparently simple through mastery of syntax and the unobtrusive use and organic function of figures of rhetoric. But here, in fact, is a highly complex prose, with an unusual variety of interwoven and interdependent clauses and phrases in numerous patterns, which leave an impression of sinewy strength and subtle movement. The sentences are skilfully varied in length. It is suggested that their compactness is often the effect of the use of a parenthetic clause or phrase,* frequently within a subordinate clause, or of the substitution of a participial† or prepositional phrase‡ for a subordinate clause.

---

* e.g. *Cloud*, 17/14, 17–18, 19, 18/5–6, 8, 9; *Priue Counseling*, 136/27, 28–29; *Hid Diuinite*, 6/14–18, 19–20, 25–26; *Stodye of Wysdome*, 45/4, 4–5, 8–9, 11–12, 12, 46/1–2; *Preier*, 48/13, 14–15, 17–18, 49/4–5, 7–8; *Stirings*, 62/6, 20–21, 22–63/2; *Spirites*, 81/2, 19–20. These treatises will henceforth be cited as *Cl.*, *P.C.*, *H.D.*, *B.*, *P.*, *D.*, *S.*, in the footnotes.

† e.g. *P.C.* 136/15; *H.D.* 6/23–24, 25, 27–28; *B.* 46/8–9, 9–10; *D.* 62/15–16, 63/3–4.

‡ e.g. *Cl.* 17/17, 19, 18/9; *P.C.* 136/9, 24; *H.D.* 6/28–29; *B.* 44/18, 45/1–2,

These limbs of the sentence, often considerable in number, are commonly held together by the framework of the whole, which, by anticipating the end in the beginning, firmly subordinates one half of the sentence to the other. It is remarkable how many of the sentences from all these treatises can be so divided into two main parts,* as in *The Cloud*, 17/12–18/12:

But forþi . . ., I schal . . .; þis werk askeþ . . . for . . .; It is . . . þe whiche . . .; it is so litil þat . . .; skilful þing it is . . . for . . .; so many . . . as . . .; ȝif . . . þan , . . .

This recurrent major division gives proportion and perspective; more important still: in it lies part of the secret of the movement of the prose.

This is a measured prose based throughout on balance, whether it be one of comparison or distinction. Broadly speaking, the foundation of thought and expression is antithetical, but the balance of comparison is often superimposed. Repeated and dominant patterns may be listed,† but full analysis of this intricate prose is impracticable, for pattern lies within pattern; into a major antithesis is often fitted one or more comparisons, and a major comparison is often partly made up of antithetical members. Antithesis gives edge and precision to the thought; balance satisfies both the mind and the ear by its effect of completion. Yet though contrasts and correspondences are everywhere, it must be noted that the five minor treatises, like *The Cloud*, seem to avoid an exact use of isocola and parison, preferring slight variations in their rhythms to an identity in the number of syllables and in stress.

Within these basic designs of balanced sentences, or clauses, or phrases, paired words or groups of words constantly quicken the rhythm. Certain schemes recur in each treatise:

4–5, 5, 7–8, 46/7, 11–12; P. 48/14–15, 19–20, 49/12; D. 62/10, 63/11–12.

* e.g. H.D. 2/5–12, 6/4–10, 14–25; B. 44/17–46/4.

† An analysis of the antithetical foundation of thought and expression in all the treatises revealed five main ways of expressing contrast, common to all of them: (1) contrast in thought implied in one or more adjacent sentences without an actual antithetical construction; (2) sentences constructed on a dominant antithetical pattern, with medial *bot, ȝit, & not,* &c.; (3) antithetical clauses; (4) antithetical phrases within the sentence; (5) words of opposite meaning placed in close proximity.

The effect of balance is achieved similarly in all the treatises by the construction of consecutive sentences, adjacent clauses, neighbouring phrases, on the same pattern, and by the pairing of words or groups of words.

(*a*) With equal parts

Noun—Noun

Preposition+Noun—do.

Article or *Demonstrative* or *Possessive Adjective+Noun*—do.

Adjective(s)+Noun—do.

Adjective—do.

Adverb—do.

Adverb+Adjective—do.

Verb—do.

Verb+Adverb—do.

Adverb+Verb—do.

(*b*) With unequal parts

Adjective+Noun—Noun

Noun—Adjective+Noun

Noun—Noun+Preposition+Noun

Verb+Adverb—Verb

Verb—Verb+Adverb

Synonyms are sometimes introduced, more frequently perhaps in the translations than in the other treatises, but in the great majority of examples the second word adds to the meaning of the first.

The great diversity of constructions, and the fact that the use of balance within the sentence is not mere ornament but generally consonant with the thought of the passage, prevent monotony. As in *The Cloud*,* one characteristic means of variation in the minor treatises lies in triple movement—sometimes three words,† sometimes three parallel phrases‡ or clauses.§

* See *Cloud*, p. lxxxi.

† e.g. Nouns: *H.D.* 7/18–19; *B.* 21/10, 32/2, 40/16–17; *D.* 64/15, 65/21; *S.* 83/1–3, 18, 84/16, 85/14, 87/3, 88/1, 92/18–19.

Qualified Nouns: *H.D.* 2/15–16, 8/1–2; *P.* 53/13–14; *D.* 62/7–8, 12–13, 15, 63/3–4, 7–8, 64/8, 9, 65/4–5, 68/13–14, 17–18, 72/17–18, 74/25–26, 76/19–20; *S.* 84/12.

Adjectives: *H.D.* 3/1, 14, 6/14; *B.* 13/18, 28/5; *P.* 53/15; *D.* 67/21–22, 72/20; *S.* 87/7–8, 89/2, 92/13.

Adverbs: *B.* 21/11; *P.* 57/14–15; *D.* 64/21–22.

Verbs: *H.D.* 4/1–2, 6/21; *P.* 58/14; *D.* 71/24–25, 72/22–23; *S.* 84/11.

‡ e.g. *H.D.* 4/6, 7/21–23; *P.* 55/7–8; *D.* 62/7–8, 9–10, 65/16–20, 69/22–23, 70/2–4, 73/4–5, 19–20, 74/16–18, 20–21, 75/21–22.

§ e.g. *B.* 26/12–16, 33/3–5; *D.* 63/4–6, 8–10, 65/23–25, 25–66/1, 71/19–21, 75/25–26; *S.* 81/13–16.

Alliteration is abundant, but unobtrusive, for it is neither perfunctory nor merely decorative. It sharpens the outline of the thought and reinforces the rhythm of the sentence. Often it serves to point an antithesis or to weight a balance, and it gives to many a phrase the pithiness of epigram. Here are a few selected from numerous examples in all the treatises:

Cloud
   15/10–11 Look now *f*orwardes, & *l*at be bacwardes. & see what þee *f*aileþ, & not what þou haste:
Priue Counseling
   146/3–5 as is þe *d*erknes of þe *m*oneschine in a *m*ist at *m*idwinters niȝt fro þe *b*riȝtnesse of þe sonne-*b*eme in þe clerest tyme of *m*issomer *d*ay.
Hid Diuinite
   3/34–35 *w*ickyd & *m*anyfolde *f*ormaciouns *m*aad of hemself in here *f*antastik ymagynatyue *w*ittes.
   4/20 not *c*oueryd; bot . . . *c*leerly
   9/19 al *p*assibilitee, & al *t*emporeel flowyng bi *p*roces of *t*ymes.
Stodye of Wysdome
   27/12 *a*bstynence in þe *s*ensualite is *s*elynes in þe *a*ffeccioun.
   41/3–4 betir is a *s*ley man þan a *s*trong man, ȝe, and betyr is *l*ist þen *l*iþer strengþe.
Pistle of Preier
   48/18–20 *f*later & *f*age þi *f*als, *f*leschly, *b*linde *h*erte wiþ *l*esinges and *f*als, *f*eined *b*ehetynges of *l*enger *l*euyng.
   50/18 acceptacioun of þis *l*itil, schort *s*eruise for *s*o *l*onge rechelesnes,
   57/22–24 it is no reson þat þou ete þe swete *k*irnel bot ȝif þou *c*rakke first þe harde schelle & *b*ite of þe *b*itter *b*ark.
Discrecioun of Stirings
   64/17–18 þe *s*ely soule, at þe *l*icnes of a schip, atteineþ at þe *l*ast to þe *l*onde of stabelnes and þe *h*auen of *h*elpe,
   69/19–21 wiþ a trist in *G*od þat his *g*race schal be *l*erner & *l*eder, whan *k*unnyng of *k*inde and of *c*lergie defaileþ.
   76/18–20 *l*ouely and *l*istely to wi*l*ne haue *G*od is *g*rete & *p*assing ese, trewe *g*oostly *p*ees, and erles of þe eendles rest.
Discrescyon of Spirites
   81/8–11 And whiche of þees þre *s*pirites þat *s*pekiþ to oure *s*pirite, we schul not *b*eleue hem, for whi, þei *s*peke neuer bot þat þei *l*ede to þe *l*osse *b*oþe of *b*ody and of soule.
   84/19–85/2 For whoso *l*ackiþ *p*ees and restfulnes of *h*erte, him *l*ackiþ þe *l*iuely *p*resence of þe *l*ouely siȝt of þe *h*eiȝe *p*ees of *h*euen, good gracious *G*od, him owne dere self.

Many of these quotations contain several alliterative units, arranged in larger designs based on two, three, or even more alliterating sounds, often connecting several clauses or phrases. But there are also many examples where the one sound persists, sometimes with onomatopoeic effect, always giving emphasis:

Cloud, 2/20 *ti*þing *t*ellers, rouners & *t*utilers of *t*ales,

Priue Counseling, 138/13–14 alle þe *f*ilþis þat *f*olowen & *f*allen to a wreche. *F*y on hem!; 168/1 *b*areyn in þe *b*ote, *bl*owyn with *bl*undryng,

Hid Diuinite, 3/19–20 Be*w*are þat none of þees vn*w*ise men зit *w*onyng in here *w*ittys

Stodye of Wysdome, 30/10–11 þe cyte is þesid, þan þroueþ a man what þe hiзe þees of God is, þat þasseþ alle mans wit.

Pistle of Preier, 55/5–6 it þlesiþ God in þartie, neuerþeles зit it þlesiþ him not þarfitely;

Discrecioun of Stirings

74/18–19 a *f*oly and a *f*oule presumcioun to soche a *f*reel wrecche; 75/26 þrik on þin hert & þine þee ful sore, and late þee haue no þees; 72/21–22 þan *l*ist *l*oue *l*iue and *l*erne for to plei;

Discrescyon of Spirites

86/7–8 not for he is *d*elited in any *d*ede of *d*euocioun . . . bot for he louiþ *d*iscencioun.

The same kinds of short alliterative units frequently occur separately in all the treatises.*

The evidence already given has shown that each of these treatises was carefully written by a craftsman as attentive to sound as to the shaping of thought. It is to be expected that

---

* There are nineteen favourite combinations common to all the treatises. The following examples from *The Cloud* will illustrate the recurrent types:

Adjective + Noun	besi beholding
Noun + Preposition + Noun	lyame of longing
Noun + Preposition . . . Noun	cause of his creacioun
. . . Noun . . . Noun	in keping & in costume
Noun . . . Noun	clergie & letterly conning
Adjective . . . Noun	Gostly freende in God
	þe heiз & þe next wey to heuen
Participle . . . Noun	fedde in þi bodely felynges
Adverb . . . Noun	stifly in þe state
Noun . . . Adjective	prise of his precious blode
Adjective . . . Adjective	lettred & lewed
Verb + Verb (less common)	lerne to liue
Verb . . . Verb	loke on hym & late
Verb . . . Noun	set þee in þe stede
Verb . . . Adjective	purposid him to be a parfite folower
Noun . . . Verb	schort preier perceþ
Adverb + Verb	speedly springing
Verb . . . Adverb	stonde stifly; leue þee þus liзtly
Adjective . . . Verb	blynd werk behoueþ
Adjective . . . Participle	priue loue put

such a writer would draw upon the traditions of composition known to all cultivated men of the later Middle Ages, and introduce the rhetorical patterns and figures of speech taught in most of the textbooks of medieval rhetoric,* and employed to a greater or lesser extent by prose-writers in the vernacular from the time of King Ælfred. *The Cloud* and all these treatises related to it are as individual in their use of figures frequently introduced as in their omission of other figures common in medieval prose.† Contrasting, for example, with much fourteenth-century devotional prose, these works have essentially a prose rhythm, with but slight use of recognizable cadenced endings, and of Homoeoteleuton, Homoeoptoton,‡ and various devices of assonance. The use of rhyme is so rare that it might well be accidental.§

Much of the forcefulness of this prose depends on different patterns of verbal repetition. Repetition of the same word or group of words either at the beginning‖ or at the end¶ of successive sentences or clauses serves to emphasize the shape of the sentences,

* The teaching of such major works as Cicero's *De Inventione*, the anonymous *Ad Herennium*, Quintilian's *De Institutione Oratoria*, was repeated in innumerable minor treatises. Unfortunately the technical terms for the same figures vary in the different works. In this section the terms are taken, where possible, from *Ad Herennium*, *M. Tulli Ciceronis Scripta Quae Manserunt Omnia*, Teubner ed., Lipsiae, 1925. They are supplemented chiefly from Quintilian.

† See Olmes, A., *Sprache und Stil der englischen Mystik des Mittelalters*, Halle (Saale), 1933.

‡ Examples of similarity in sound in neighbouring final unstressed syllables are rare, and are possibly accidental, e.g. *Preier*, 48/19–20, 49/22–23, 54/4–5, 55/3, 56/7–9, 59/4; *Stirings*, 62/16, 63/1–2.

§ e.g. *Priue Counseling*, 167/3; *Stodye of Wysdome*, 29/16, ? 17/6–7 (if the *u* in OE. *sunu* were lengthened to a long close *o* in open syllables); *Stirings*, 76/19; *Spirites*, 85/18.

‖ Cf. *Repetitio (Anaphora)*, e.g. *Cl.* 15/15, 17, 18, 16/1; 16/10, 12, 13; 21/11, 11, 12; 26/13, 16, 18, 19, 19; 28/17, 18, 19; &c. *P.C.* 154/13, 15, 15, 16, 17, 18, 19; 157/2, 3, 13, 15, 16; 166/15, 16, 16, 17, 18, 19; 167/1, 1, 2, 2, 2, 3; &c. *H.D.* 7/16, 17, 19, 21, 24; 7/33, 33, 34, 34, 35, 8/1, 1, 2, 3; 9/4, 7, 8, 10; &c. *B.* 12/7, 7; 12/12, 12, 13, 13/2, 4; 16/9, 10; 22/8–9, 9–10; 38/4, 5; 38/7, 8, 9, 10; 38/11, 12, 14; 43/6, 8, 8, 10, 11; &c. *P.* 49/21, 50/1; 50/5, 7; 51/21, 24, 25, 27; 52/8, 9; 52/21, 22; 57/13, 14, 16; 57/22, 24, &c. *D.* 66/23, 67/3, 6; 71/13–18; 73/17, 17, 18, 18, 18; 73/20, 22, 74/1; 76/24, 24; &c. *S.* 81/16, 82/3, 12; 82/20, 83/3, 5, 8; 83/16, 19; 91/22, 92/2; &c. Since the analytical structure of Middle English is so fundamentally different from the synthetical structure of Latin, the Middle English examples quoted above and below are, of course, only approximations to the classical rhetorical patterns.

¶ Cf. *Conversio (Epistrophe)*, e.g. *Cl.* 19/11, 12; 21/11, 12, 14, 18, 19; 59/8, 10, 16, 60/8; 69/12, 14, 14; 75/7, 9, 10. *P.C.* 136/10, 11, 11, 17, 17, 18;

and often stresses the relationship of balance or contrast. Less frequently there is repetition both at the beginning and the end of the sentence.* A characteristic means of connexion is to repeat the closing part of a sentence or clause at or near the beginning of the next.† Then there are repetitions within the sentence, indepen-dent of position, which point the thought, or enliven it by giving a subtle twist to the subject. Very often the same word, much reiterated,‡ gives insistency, and at times the use of the same root in different word-formations§ sets the theme in greater relief. Sometimes the repetition includes a play on words;‖ sometimes the effect is one of irony,¶ or of paradox.**

136/15, 20, 21, 21, 22, 23. *B.* 20/4, 6; 21/13, 15; 23/3, 4, 5, 6; 24/5, 7, 10, 15; 26/2, 2, 4; 27/9, 12, 17, 28/2; 32/9, 10; 32/12, 14; 33/9, 10, 12; 34/13, 13, 35/1; 35/9, 10; 36/4, 5, 7, 9. *P.* 48/3, 5, 7, 9, 12; 50/18, 19; 56/9, 10; 57/2, 3; 58/12, 13. *D.* 66/14, 15, 16; 71/20, 20, 20, 21, 21, 21; 76/21, 21, 22, 22, 22, 23; 76/24, 24, 77/1. *S.* 80/2, 4, 7, 7; 87/14, 16, 18; 87/17, 19; 90/2, 6, 7.

* Cf. *Complexio* (*Exoche, Ploche*), e.g. *H.D.* 3/7–9. *B.* 14/8–11, 11–16; 32/8–10; 38/7–11. *P.* 51/26–27; 55/13. *S.* 87/16–19.

† Cf. *Anadiplosis.* (Sometimes this is combined with *chiasmus*, with inversion in the second part of the order followed in the first.) e.g. *Cl.* 17/16–17; 18/17; 19/19; 21/8; &c. *P.C.* 140/17–18; 144/24; 145/20–21. *H.D.* 4/1; 6/23, 25; 7/1–2; 7/5–6. *B.* 29/6; 34/10; 44/5. *P.* 48/13; 48/16; 51/5; 55/6. *D.* 66/13. *S.* 88/3–4; 90/4; 90/21–22.

‡ Cf. *Traductio,* e.g. *Cl.* bodely 113/23–114/10 (8); *P.C.* being 141/4–25 (11); *H.D.* souereyn 2/15–23 (7); wittes 3/2–35 (8); beyng 4/2–10 (6); &c. *B.* ordeynde 16/5–13 (5); mesurid 16/8–14 (4); done to 19/12–20/1 (4); coumfort 20/2–6 (3); schame 36/16–37/14 (10). *P.* preier 48/3–12 (7); tre 53/1–6 (5); God 53/7–54/21 (19); onheed 56/20–24 (3); mene 58/6–21 (4); substaunce 58/17–22 (4). *D.* coroun of liif 65/2–66/10 (7); loue 72/10–25 (8); kun 74/16–22 (7); here, þere 66/11–22 (12). *S.*—not common.

§ Cf. *Polyptoton,* e.g. *Cl.* bodely, *see above,* body 113/21, 114/8, bodelines 114/2; fauorable 100/6, fauored 100/7, fauour 100/9. *P.C.* stinking 138/12, stynche 138/15; foule 138/12, filþis 138/13. *H.D.* Wysdome 2/14, wisdome 2/16, wisest 2/21; derke 2/19, derknes 2/20, derkyst 2/22; pryue 2/19, priuely 2/22; clerest 2/21, cleertees 2/24; vnknowyng 5/17, knowable 5/18, knowing 5/18, 22, 24, vnknowen 5/22, knoweþ 5/23; see- ...know- 5/28, 28, 29, 29; proueþ 6/32, proef 6/33; deuinitee 7/13, 14, deuine 7/17; goodnes 7/19, good 7/20; substancyal 7/24, substaunce 7/24; vnderstond- 10/13, 18, 21, 22. *B.* þristy 13/16, þirst 13/17, þristeþ 13/19; siȝt 17/10, 13, see- 17/11, 18/1, 3, 3; herd 18/10, 12, her- 18/11, 12; schriue 21/3, 6, schrift 21/4, 13; dampne 25/3, dome 25/4, dem- 25/5, 7; happely 27/10, happynes 27/11; harm- 33/13, 13, 14. *P.* worþi- 53/15, 16; good- 53/10, 11, 20; loueli- 53/18, 20, lou- 53/19, 54/1. *D.* holi- 70/22, 23, 24; clep- 73/12, 13 13, 14. *S.* queint- 82/15, 16; foulist, filþe 85/15; -know- 85/16, 17; -sclaundre- 86/9, 13, 13; wise- 86/13, 14, 15, 16; consent- 88/15, 16, 89/9, 10.

‖ Cf. *Adnominatio* (*Paronomasia*), e.g. *Stirings,* 62/3, 77/1.

¶ e.g. *Spirites,* 86/15–16.

** e.g. *Preier,* 49/11–12, 53/22–24; *Stirings,* 72/1–2.

Frequent repetition with slight variation is one of the most individual features of the prose of *The Cloud*, as richly exemplifiable from the use of *Traductio* as from the ways of avoiding monotony in sentence-structure or in the use of alliteration. One short series of permutations and combinations of associated words in *The Cloud* will illustrate the kind of variation which occurs elsewhere* in these works: e.g.

13/18 comoun degree of Cristen mens leuyng, 14/2–3 forme & degree of leuyng, 14/4–5 state & forme of leuyng, 14/7–8 comoun degree of leuyng, 14/12 degre & maner of leuing, 14/13 forme & maner of leuyng, 14/14 state & degre of leuyng.

There are examples of it in *þe Stodye of Wysdome, Discrecioun of Stirings, Discrescyon of Spirites,* works not specifically acknowledged by the author of *The Cloud*.

Characteristic figures of thought no less than common sentence-formations, sound-patterns, devices of repetition, confirm the affinity of all these treatises. Paradoxical statement is distinctive of *The Cloud,* and its Dionysian source is most probably revealed in the all-pervasive paradox of *Hid Diuinite.* Paradox in the *Pistle of Preier* and *Discrecioun of Stirings* is noted above. The theme of *Discrescyon of Spirites* does not lend itself so easily to paradox, but even there one can find traces of it.†

Various modes of statement are common to these treatises. Questions are asked,‡ often rhetorical, sometimes to be answered forthwith; fictitious comments and dialogues are given as direct speech;§ exclamations‖ occasionally interrupt the train of thought;

---

* e.g. *P.C.* nakid—blynde—felyng—beyng 135/20, 136/1–3, 139/12, 24, 141/24–25, 143/10–11, 144/1–2, 146/26–27, 147/9, 17, 152/10–11, 155/28, 156/6, 157/8–9, 158/6, 171/16–17. *B.* inward—trewe—goostly—swetnes—joie—felyng 30/15–16, 31/1, 8–9, 15, 32/6, 12–13, 33/2, 10, 12, 16, 34/1, 35/4–5, 8, 17. *P.* depart—frute—ripe—tre—offre 55/14, 16, 25, 56/4–5, 7–8, 10. *D.* singulere—sodein—steringes 67/5–6, 9–10, 20; *see also* 62/4–5, 7–8, 9–10, 12–13, 15, 18–20; 63/3–4, 6–8, 8–10, 68/13–14, 17–18, 69/1–2, 22–23. *S.* foule—spirite—feend—prince—malice—wraþþe—wickidnes 81/6–7, 7, 16, 82/13, 16, 83/11, 18, 84/16; *see also* 85/1, 4, 10.

† e.g. 87/19–21; 90/16–17.

‡ Cf. *Interrogatio,* e.g. *Cl.* 14/8, 10, 10–12, 16–17, 18–19, 16/1–2, 22/13, 29/5, 35/2–4, 5–8, 39/4–6, &c. *P.C.* 149/29–150/1, 150/10–12, 17, 17–19, 151/6–9, 155/23–26, 160/26–161/1. *H.D.* 3/27–30. *B.* 19/6–8, 36/4–5, 39/13–40/1, 44/12–14. *P.* 50/5–7, 7–10. *S.* 87/16–17, 17–19.

§ Cf. *Sermocinatio,* e.g. *Cl.* 20/16, 17–21/7, 25/13–14, 26/14–15, 16, 19, 29/8–18. *P.C.* 152/23–26, 153/24–27, 154/26–28, 164/15–23, 172/ 4–10. *H.D.* 8/22–24. *D.* 71/12–13.   For note ‖ see page lv.

immediate correction is made, or more frequently a modification, wherein the author, in an apparent afterthought, takes back what has previously been said, or qualifies it further*; aphorisms and maxims abound.† Many interpretations, often introduced by 'þat is to sey', or some equivalent, are added in the *Pistle of Preier*, but are given more sparingly in the other minor treatises.‡ This is explicable, since the *Pistle of Preier* more than the other minor treatises makes persistent use of a single exemplum in the working out of its principal theme.§ Less extensive and less central exempla appear also in *Hid Diuinite*, 5/34–6/10; *Þe Stodye of Wysdome*, 45/13–46/4; *Discrecioun of Stirings*, 64/7–20, 64/20–66/11; *Discrescyon of Spirites*, 90/22–91/6, all developed and expounded in the typical way of medieval allegory. Short incidental similes are comparatively rare.‖ These similitudes are all of the kind common in homiletic writings, but it is perhaps worthy of note that the figures of a tree, a ship, and battle, which are developed at length in the minor treatises, are introduced also in *The Cloud* and *Priue Counseling*.

Like most Middle English devotional and homiletic works, these treatises are all rich in metaphorical statement. Much of their imagery, however, is drawn from common stock, and derived ultimately from the Bible and patristic sources. Though a certain amount of repetition within the group may well be significant, yet the following images are often to be found elsewhere:

Pistle of Preier
  hiʒe mount of perfeccioun 50/13–14; þe pointe & þe prik of perfeccioun 54/16, 19 (cf. *Stirings*, 72/5–6, 10, 73/1; *Priue Counseling*,

‖ Cf. *Exclamatio*, e.g. *Cl.* 21/21, 35/13, 39/4. *P.C.* 149/29, 153/17–19, 19–20, 157/14–15. *P.* 48/17–18, 53/21–24. *D.* 67/14–15; 70/19.

---

* Cf. *Correctio*, e.g. *Cl.* 18/16, 20–21, 25/7, 18–19, 28/7, 34/7–8, 39/20–21. *P.C.* 162/6–7, 25. *H.D.* 4/11. *P.* 48/8–9, 53/12, 55/9–10, 17–18. *D.* 62/20–21. *S.* 90/9–10, 14.
  † Cf. *Sententia*, e.g. *Cl.* 26/4–5, 104/17–18, 112/12–13, 13–14, 132/19–20. *P.C.* 171/27–172/2, 172/2–3. *B.* 17/10–12, 18/7–9, 13–14, 14–15, 19/2–3, 38/11–12, 12–13, 14–15, 15, 15–16, 16–17, 40/11–14, 41/2–3, 3–4, 4–5. *P.* 58/2. *D.* 72/21–22. *S.* 84/10–14, 19–85/2, 85/3–4, 5–7, 7–8.
  ‡ e.g. *P.* 50/14, 54/20–21, 55/14–16, 22–23, 24–25, 57/5, 13–14, 58/1. Cf. *P.C.* 140/16 sqq., 144/17–19, 20–24, 24–26, 145/14 sqq., 154/24 sqq.
  § 52/16–59/5.
  ‖ Cf. *Similitudo*, e.g. *Cl.* 17/16, 18/6–7, 22/8, 24/20–21, 119/8. *P.C.* 168/8–9. *P.* 49/4–5, 54/26–55/1. *S.* 81/6, 82/17–18.

135/11, 141/11–12); kinges mete . . . knaues mete 53/3–4; mariage 56/21; glewe of grace 57/1–2; refresching of . . . goostly miʒtes 55/10; knitteþ 56/13; þe hete & þe feruour 56/22 (cf. *Spirites*, herte . . . brenne 81/19); &c.

Discrecioun of Stirings

fallynges & risinges 64/7; lernid . . . scole of God 64/6; ebbing & flowing liif 64/12; windowes of þi bodily wittes 69/4 (cf. *Cloud* 15/19); holyliche þraldom 70/23 (cf. *Spirites* 87/3); iʒe of þi reson 72/12 (cf. *Hid Diuinite* iʒen of mynde 2/24); ransakiþ 73/3; &c.

Discrescyon of Spirites

troden doune vnder fote 82/15, cf. *Cloud* 22/20; bondage of sinne 90/2; clene paper leef 90/22; write on þe soule 91/2; &c.

But there is a more individual kind of metaphor in *The Cloud* and *Priue Counseling* suggestive of an immediate experience. This particular kind conveys the sense of obstruction between man and God, and describes the exercise of contemplation as one of stripping and blinding. 'Naked' and 'blind' are two operative words,* and these two epithets occur also several times in the minor treatises, sometimes with the same significance,† though not always.‡ *Hid Diuinite* contains a striking image of obstruction not in the Latin, but reminiscent of *The Cloud*.§ *Discrecioun of Stirings* combines the ideas of stripping and blindness in 75/4–5: 'vtterly voiding fro þi goostly beholding', and in 72/12–13 contains a description identical with that in *The Cloud*‖ of the attempt to pierce the obstruction by 'a blinde schote with þe scharp darte of longing loue'.

A study of the choice of words will show the same marked resemblance among these treatises. There is a similar proportion of French and Scandinavian loan-words, the same kinds of borrowing, and the same kinds of word-formation. In all of them verbs of action are often used metaphorically to describe mental and spiritual states, which emphasizes that the contemplative life is not one of passivity but rather of strenuous activity. This sense of

---

* See *Cloud*, notes to 17/2, 22/18.

† e.g. *H.D.* blynde beholdynges, 2/32; *D.* blinde schote, 72/12, blinde stering of loue, 76/6. Cf. *Cloud*, 94/19.

‡ *nakid* is used in a different context in *P.* 51/18, *S.* 91/12, *blinde* in *P.* 48/19, 49/3.

§ Cf. 6/23: 'conielid in a kumbros clog', also 6/25, with *Cloud*, 63/21–22: 'þis combros cloude of vnknowyng bitwix him & God'.

‖ 26/11–12.

continuous energizing is strongly reinforced in all the treatises by the abundant use of the verbal noun in *-ing*.

In short, there is no evidence from a comparison of the five treatises with *The Cloud* and *Priue Counseling* to invalidate the hypothesis of single authorship, but on the contrary much to commend it.

THE TEXT

THE text is from MS. Harleian 674 (Har¹), with occasional emendations indicated by square brackets [ ], based on a full collation of the other manuscripts, and suggested only when the basic text is obviously inferior. Contractions have been expanded; modern punctuation and capitalization have been added.

The footnotes contain all the variant readings of the other manuscripts except those of spelling, inflexional endings, dialectal differences in pronoun forms. Where these are significant they are given in the footnotes; where they are important they are described in the Introd., pp. xxiii–xxix. Insertions and corrections in Har¹ are fully noted, but for the other manuscripts mention is made of them only where they seem significant. To prevent ambiguity when it is not the first occurrence of the word in the line, a superscript number (e.g. þe²) or the adjacent word given in brackets indicates the position of the variant. The manuscripts are quoted in order of their importance and according to their grouping. The following sigla are used:

British Museum	Har¹	MS. Harleian 674
	Har²	MS. Harleian 2373
	Har⁴	MS. Harleian 993
	Har⁵	MS. Harleian 1022
	Ar	MS. Arundel 286
	Pw	The manuscript represented by Pepwell's printed edition of 1521
Cambridge University Library	CP	MS. Ff. vi. 31
	F	MS. Ff. vi. 33
	Ii	MS. Ii. vi. 39
	Kk	MS. Kk. vi. 26
Bodleian Library	Bo	MS. Bodleian 576
City Reference Library, Bristol	Br	MS. 6
Hunterian Library, Glasgow University	G	MS. 258 (U. 4. 16)
Westminster School	W	
Huntington Library, California	C	MS. 127
W. K. Richardson's Library, Boston, Mass.	R	MS. 22

DEONISE HID DIUINITE

Deonise Hid Diuinite

Þe Prolog upon þe Translacioun of *Deonise Hid Diuinite*

Þis writyng þat next foloweþ is þe Inglische of a book þat Seynte
Denys wrote vnto Thimothe, þe whiche is clepid in Latyn tonge
5 *Mistica Theologia*. Of þe whiche book, for-þi þat it is mad minde
in þe 70 chapter of a book wretin before (þe whiche is clepid
Þe Cloude of Vnknowing) how þat Denis sentence wol cleerli
afferme al þat is wretyn in þat same book: þerfore, in translacioun
of it, I haue not onliche folowed þe nakid lettre of þe text, bot for
10 to declare þe hardnes of it, I haue moche folowed þe sentence of þe
Abbot of Seinte Victore, a noble & a worþi expositour of þis same
book.|

             Þis is Seinte Deonise Preier

Þou vnbigonne & euerlastyng Wysdome, þe whiche in þiself arte
15 þe souereyn-substancyal Firstheed, þe souereyn Goddesse, & þe
souereyn Good, þe inliche beholder of þe godliche maad wisdome
of Cristen men: I beseche þee for to drawe us up in an acordyng
abilnes to þe souereyn-vnknowen and þe souereyn-schinyng heiȝt of
þi derke inspirid spekynges, where alle þe pryue þinges of deuiny-
20 tee ben kouerid and hid vnder þe souereyn-schinyng derknes of
wisest silence, makyng þe souereyn-clerest souereynly for to
schine priuely in þe derkyst; and þe whiche is—in a maner þat
is alweys inuisible & vngropable—souereynli fulfillyng wiþ ful fayre
cleertees alle þoo soules þat ben not hauyng iȝen of mynde.
25 And for alle þees þinges ben abouen mynde, þerfore wiþ affeccyon abouen mynde as I may, I desire to purchase hem vnto me
wiþ þis preier.

I Capitulum

How a man schal rise in þis hid deuinite bi doing awey of
30   alle þinges on þis side God

Þou freend Tymothe, what tyme þat þou purposist þee by þe
steryng of grace to þe actueel excersise of þi blynde beholdynges,

---

No title in Har¹ Kk   4 whiche] boke *add.* Kk   16 Good] god Kk

loke þou forsake with a stronge & a sleiȝ & a listi contricyon boþe
þi bodely wittes (as heryng, seyng, smelling, taastyng, & touching),
and also þi goostly wittes, þe whiche ben clepid þin vnderstondable
worchinges; and alle þoo þinges, þe whiche mowe be knowen wiþ
any of þi fyue bodely wittes without-forþe; and alle þoo þinges, 5
þe whiche mow be knowen by þi goostly wittes wiþinne-forþ; and
alle þoo þinges þat ben now, or ȝit haue ben, þof þei be not now;
and alle þoo þinges þat ben not now, or ȝit mow be in tyme for to
come, þof þei be not now. And, as it is possible to me for te speke
& to þee to vnderstonde, loke þat þou rise wiþ me in þis grace,| 10
in a maner þat is þou woste neuer how, to be onid with hym þat f. 122a
is abouen alle substaunces and al maner knowyng. For whi, þorou
þe ouerpassyng of þiself and alle oþer þinges, and þus makyng
þiself clene fro al wordly, fleschly, & kyndely likyng in þin affeccioun, and fro al þing þat may be knowen by þe propre fourme 15
in þi knowyng, þou schalt be drawen up abouen mynde in affeccioun to þe souereyn-substancyal beme of þe godliche derknes,
alle þinges þus done awey.

Beware þat none of þees vnwise men ȝit wonyng in here
wittys here þees þinges. Þees men I clepe alle þoo þat ben fastnyd in 20
knowing & in louyng of þees þinges þat ben knowable and han
bigynnyng, þe whiche han opinion þat noþing is souereyn-sub-
stancyaly abouen þees forseide beyng þinges. Bot þei wenen for to
knowen hym þat haþ 'maad derknes his hidyng place' bi þat
knowyng whiche is after hemself. And siþen, bi witnes of [þe] pro- 25
phete, þe godliche techynges of þees priuetees ben abouen þees
men, what schul we sey þan of þoo þat ben more vnwise, wonyng
ȝit not only in here goostly wittes of natureel philosophy, bot lowe
downe byneþe in here bodely wittes, þe whiche þei hauen bot
in comoun with only beestes? For þees men kun not come to þe 30
knowing of þe first cause, þe whiche is souereynliche set abouen
alle þinges, bot bi making of figures of þe last and þe leest worþi
þinges of þees beyng visible þinges, as stockes or stones, and seyen
þat it haþ noþing abouen þoo wickyd & manyfolde formaciouns
maad of hemself in here fantastik ymagynatyue wittes. 35

4 þinges] *ins. in right margin* Har¹ 9 to] for Kk 11 woste] *om.*
Kk 12 substaunces] substance Kk 19 here] þer Kk 21 in]
om. Kk of] *ins.* Har¹ 24 maad . . . place] *The reference is given*
in rubrics in the left margin of Har¹ his] *ins. in left margin* Har¹
hidyng] bydyng Kk 25 þe] þis Har¹ 26 techynges] techyng Kk

B 2840 B 2

It is noþing þus: bot þus most it be. It behouiþ us for to sette,
for to see, & for to afferme alle þe settynges & þe beynges of alle
f. 122b þees beyng þinges in him þat | is abouen al knowyng & mynde, as
hym being þe cause of alle þees þynges; and more propirly & more
5 miȝtely for to denye alle þees being þinges, as hym souereinly
beyng abouen hem alle, ful heiȝ in hymself, departid fro hem alle;
and not for to haue it in opinyon þat þees deniinges of þees being
þinges ben contrary to þe first affermynges of hem, bot fastliche
for to holde in siȝt of byleue him for to be abouen alle doyng awey
10 of þees beyng or beable þinges, þe whiche in himself is abouen alle,
ȝe! boþe doyng awey and affermyng of hem alle.

And for þis skyle it is þat þe godliche Bertelmewe, þe Apostle of
Criste, seiþ in his writyng þat Cristes deuinitee, it is boþe moche
and it is leest; and þe Gospel is brode and moche, & eftsones he
15 seiþ it is streite & litil. As it semiþ to me, in þis he was rauischid
to beholde abouen kynde, where he seiþ þat þe good cause of alle
is boþe of many wordes & of schorte seiinges, as neiþer hauyng
resoun ne vnderstondyng wiþ þe whiche he miȝt be comen to, þat is
souereyn-substancialy set abouen alle þees beyng þinges. And ȝit
20 naþeles not coueryd; bot verely and cleerly he apperiþ open, not to
alle bot to hem only, þe whiche passen abouen boþe alle vnclene &
clene beyng þinges, and þe whiche comyn abouen alle assenciouns
of alle holy eendes or teermes set vnto man or to aungel, and þe
whiche forsaken alle deuine liȝtes & alle heuenly sounes & wordes,
25 and entren wiþ affeccioun into derknes, where verely he is, as þe
Scripture scheweþ, þe whiche is abouen al.

Ensaumple of þis se by þe story how þe godlich Moyses, mildest
of men, first he is bodyn to be clensid boþe in hymself & also in hys
puple, and after þat to be departyd fro occasyon of fyling. And þan
f. 123a 30 after alle clensyng of hym & his puple, he herd trumpes | of many
voices, & saw many liȝtes wiþ schinyng, sendyng oute fro hem ful
brode and ful clene bemes. Afterwardes he was departyd fro þe
multitude of þis puple, & wiþ preestes þat were chosen he atteynid

11 boþe] but *can.*, boþ *ins. above* Kk   13 it] *om.* Kk   19
souereyn] souereynly Kk   20 to] vnto Kk   24 sounes &] smell
(*can.*) *add.* Har¹   26 Scripture] *The reference is given in rubrics in the
right margin of* Har¹   27 *The reference is given in rubrics in the right
margin of* Har¹   30 of hym] *om.* Kk   &] of *add.* Kk   32 Afterwardes . . .] *The reference is given in rubrics in the left margin of* Har¹
-wardes] -ward Kk

to þe hiȝenes of þe godliche assenciouns, þe whiche is þe teermes &
þe boundes of mans vnderstondyng, be it neuer so holpen wiþ
grace. And ȝit in al þis he was not wiþ God, so as it acordeþ to þe
perfeccioun of þis deuinitee; bot he had in contemplacioun an
obiect not hymself, for he may not be seen by þat iȝe. Bot þe place 5
where he was, þat was his obiecte. And þat place betokeniþ þe
hiȝest godliche beholdynges, passyng abouen & hauyng in subieccioun alle mans resons, as þe lady haþ hir maydens. By þe whiche
godliche beholdynges þe presence of him þat is abouen alle þinkyng
is souereynly schewid to mans vnderstondynges, and setteþ hym 10
abouen þe natureel teermes of hymself. And þan he is assoilid
boþe fro þe vnderstondable worching miȝtes of his soule, & fro
þe obiectes of hem, þat is for to sey, alle þoo þinges in þe whiche
þei worchen.

In þis tyme it was þat Moyses in syngulertee of affeccioun was 15
departid from þees beforeseyde chosen preestes, & entrid by
hymself þe derknes of vnknowyng, þe whiche derknes is vereliche
hid; in þe whiche he schittiþ al knowable knowing; and algates
he is maad in a maner þat is inuisible & vngropable for to fele
in experience þe presence of hym þat is abouen alle þinges, not 20
hauyng felyng ne þinkyng of no beyng þing, ne ȝit of hymself.
Bot in auoidyng of al knowyng þat is algates vnknowen he is
knittyd vnto hym on þe best maner; and in þat þat he knoweþ no-
þing, he is maad to be knowyng abouen mynde. |

II Capitulum

How we schul be onid to þe cause of al, beyng abouen al

In þis souereyn-schining derknes we prey to be done up, &, bi
nouȝt seeyng & vnknowyng, for to see & for to knowe hym þat is
abouen al seing & al knowyng in þis same not se & not knowe; and
souereyn-substancialy for to preise, bi doing awey of alle þees be- 30
yng þinges, hym þat is souereyn-substancial in himself. Þe maner
of whiche doyng awey may be seen bi þis ensaumple þat foloweþ.

Here is a man hauyng a sounde stok of þe grettest quantitee
wiþoutyn hym, liing before hym, and hauyng wiþinne hym entent

---

16 from] fro Kk   17 vnknowyng] vnknowen Kk   is] god (*ins. in
different hand in right margin*) *add.* Kk   18 schittiþ] schyneþ Kk
29 not se &] *written later in left margin* Har[1]

& craft to make an ymage of þe leest quantitee, of þat place of þe
wode, þe whiche is, bi mesuryng of riȝt lynyng, in þe sentre & þe
middes of þat same stok. First þou wost wel by natureel wit þat er
he may com to for to see þat ymage bi cleer bodely siȝt of his out-
5 ward iȝe, or for to schewe it to be seen vnto oþer, þe whiche he
haþ in hymself by cleer crafte of ymaginacioun, þe stok ȝit beyng
hole on euery side, he most algates by craft & by instrumentes
voide awey alle þe outward partyes of þat wode, being aboute &
lettyng þe siȝt of þat same ymage. Riȝt so we must haue us in þis
10 hiȝe deuyne werk, as it is possible to be comyn to in vnderstondyng
by soche a boistous ensaumple of so contrary a kynde.

For we moten be in þis werk as it were men makyng an ymage of
his nakyd, vnmaad, & vnbigonne kynde; þe whiche, þof it be in
itself & to itself euermore free—wiþinne alle creatures, not inclusid;
15 wiþouten alle creatures, not schit oute; abouen alle creatures,
not borne up; bineþe alle creatures, not put doun; behynde alle
creatures, not put bak; before alle creatures, not dreuen forþe—
f. 124a neuerþeles ȝit, to mans vnderstondyng, þe whiles it is | knittyd to
þis corumpid bodi, he is neuermore cleerly schewid, bot as it were
20 a þing þat were couerhid & ouerlappid & ouerleide wiþ vnnoumerable sensible bodies & vnderstondable substaunces, wiþ many a
merueilous fantastik ymage, conielid as it were in a kumbros clog
abouten hym, as þe ymage of þe ensaumple wretyn before is hid in
þe þik, greet, sounde stok. Þe whiche koumbrous clogge, þus con-
25 ielyd of þees vnnoummerable diuersitees, we moten algates craftely
pare awey by sleiȝt of grace in þis deuine werk, as stronge letters
contrariing vnto þis clene hid siȝt. And þus bi þis sleiȝ gracious doyng
awey of hem alle we moten cleerliche preisyn, & abouen mynde,
þe self fairheed in þe self nakid, vnmaad, & vnbigonne kynde; in a
30 maner þat is vnknowen how vnto alle, bot only to þoo þat it proueþ;
and ȝit euermore to þoo same, bot onliche in tyme of þe proef.

It behouiþ us alle þat ben practisers of þis deuinite for to make
oure deniinges on þe contrary maner to oure afferminges; for whi
we settyng oure affermynges begynnen at þe moost worþi þinges

1 & craft] *trs. but order corrected* Har[1]　　　7 euery] euerych a Kk
9 þat] þe Kk　　　11 contrary] contraryouse Kk　　　14 & to
itself] *om.* Kk　　　creatures] a *ins.* Har[1]　　　20 couerhid] couered
Kk　　　24 clogge] *ins. in left margin* Har[1]　　　25 craftely] *om.* Kk
26 awey] craftely *add.* Kk　　　29 nakid] and *add.* Kk　　　31 þe] *om.*
Kk

of þees beyng þinges, & so forþe by þe menes we descende to þe
leest, bot in oure deniinges we begynnyn at þe leest, & stien up to
þe moste, and eftsones by þe menes, from þe hiest to þe last, & fro
þe last to þe hiest aȝein, we foulden alle togeders & done hem
awey, þat we mowen cleerliche knowe þat vnknowyng, þe whiche 5
is wallid aboute from al knowable miȝtes in alle þees being þinges;
and þat we mowen see þat souereyn-substancyal derknes, priueliche hid fro al liȝt in þees being þinges.

[III Capitulum]
Whiche bookes ben of aferming & whiche of deniing diuinitee 10

 And for þis skyle in oure oþer bookes of deuinitee, | & moste in f. 124b
þe bookes þat ben affermyng deuinitee, þe-whiche been þees: þe
first of þe *Ierarchies of Heuen*, & þe secound of þe *Ierarchies of þis
Fiȝtyng Chirche*—in boþe þees we hauen set wiþ preisyng how þat
hiȝe, deuine, synguleer kynde, þe whiche is God, is one; how it is 15
þre, þe whiche after itself is clepid Faderheed & Sonheed & þe
Holi Goostheed; how þe liȝtes of goodnes wonyng in þe herte
borionid oute of þat inmaterial, & þat only good in hymself & of
hymself; & how þat in þis woning in hymself by onheed of substaunce, & in hemself by trinite of persones, & in hem togeders wiþ 20
an euen euerlastyng borionyng, þei dwellyn stille vnpassyngliche;
how þat þe souereyn-substancyal Jhesu is maad substaunce in þe
trewþes of mankynde; and alle oþer soche þinges þat ben expressid
in þe Scripture, ben affermyngliche preisid in þoo two bookes.

 And in þe [booke] of *Goddes Names* it is affermyngliche set & 25
preisid how þat he is namyd Good, how Beyng, how Liif, how
Wisdome, & how Vertewe, & what oþer þat þei be of þe vnderstondable namynges of God. Bot in þe book of þe *Gadering of
Deuine Sentence*, þere I haue affermyngliche set wiþ preising alle
þe names þat ben applied vnto God from þees sensible þinges—as 30
whiche ben þe godliche fourmes, whiche ben þe godliche figures,
whiche ben his partiees & his instrumentes, whiche ben his places
& his enournementes, whiche ben his frenesiees & his heuinesses,

2 &] at Kk   3 from] fro Kk   7 substancyal] substance alle Kk
9 III Capitulum] *om.* Har¹   10 aferming] diuinite *add.* Kk   16 þe]
om. Kk   17 herte] & (*can.*) *add.* Har¹   18 oute] *om.* Kk   23 alle]
om. Kk   25 booke] bookes, s *can.* Har¹, bokes Kk   28 (of) þe] *om.*
Kk   31 godliche] goodliche Kk   godliche] godeliclyche Kk   33
heuinesses] heueynes Kk

whiche ben his woodnesses & his dronkenesses, whiche ben his
gloteniees & his oþes & his cursynges, whiche ben his slepinges
& whiche ben his wakynges—& what oþer sensible formes þat on
f. 125a any maner | in Holy Scripture ben applied vnto God.

5   Alle þees I deme þou hast seen; & how þees last þinges ben of
mo wordes þan þe first þinges. For whi it behouiþ algates be þat
þe first two bookes of þe *Ierarchies* & þe openyng of þe *Godliche
Names* in þe þrid book were of fewer wordes þan þis *Gaderid Book
of Deuine Sentence* touchid here laste. For in-as-moche as we be-
10 holden to þinges þat ben moost hiȝe, in-so-moche þe wordes þat
ben spokyn of hem to oure beholdynges maken streite oure vnderstondyng. As it is now here in þis book, whan we entren into þe
derknes þat is abouen mynde, we schul not onliche fynde þe
schortyng of wordes, bot as it were a madnes & a parfite vnresonabil-
15 tee of alle þat we seyn. And in alle þe oþer bookes oure enditing
descendid fro þe heiȝest þinges to þe lowest; and after þe quantitee
of descendyng, it spred oute to a greet multitude. Bot now it assendiþ in þis book fro þe lowest þinges to þe hiȝest; and after þe
mesure of þe ascencioun—þe whiche is somtyme sodeyner þen oþer—
20 it is maad streite. And after alle soche assencioun, it schal al be
withouten voice, & al it schal be knittid to a þing þat is vnspekable.

    Bot happiliche þou askist: What is þe skyle whi þat in affirma-
tyue deuinitee we begynne at þe moost worþi þinges, & in þe negatyue deuinitee at þe leest worþi þinges? Þis is þe skyle. For whan
25 we wolen merk God bi settyng of alle vnderstondable þinges, þe
whiche in hymself is abouen alle settyng & alle vnderstondyng,
it is moost acordyng þat we set first þoo þinges þat ben moost
worþi & moost niȝe vnto hym. And ȝif we wolen merk hym by
f. 125b doing awey | of alle vnderstondable þinges, it acordeþ moost þat
30 we first do awey þoo þinges, þe whiche be seen to be moost fer
from hym. As þus: more niȝ & more acordyng vnto hym is liif or
goodnes þen is ayer or a stone; and wiþ more acordyng euydence
we schuld do awey from hym glotenye & woodnes, þan spekyng
or vnderstondyng. And ȝit he in hymself is abouen boþe alle
35 spekyng and alle vnderstondyng.

---

1 woodnesses] wodnes Kk   dronkenesses] dronkennes Kk   8 in]
þe (*can.*) *add.* Har¹   24 whan] *ins. in right margin* Har¹   25 God]
by god *add.* Kk   31 from] fro Kk   33 from] fro Kk   34 boþe
alle] *trs., order corrected* Har¹

[IV Capitulum]

Þat he is none of sensible þinges, þe whiche is cause of hem
alle

We put awey first from God þing þat is withoutyn substaunce, and
al þing þat is not, begynnyng fro þe moost fer; for þat þing is more 5
ferþer þen þoo þinges þat bot only ben, & leuen not. [And þen we
put awey þoo þinges þat bot only ben and leuen not,] for þat is ferþer þen þat þat is and leuiþ. And after þat we put awey þoo
þinges þat ben & leuyn & lackyn felyng; for þoo ben ferþer þen
þoo þat hauen felyng. And after þat we put awey þoo þat hauen 10
felyng & lacken reson & vnderstondyng; for þoo ben ferþer þen
þoo þat hauen reson & vnderstonding. And wiþ alle þees þinges we
remowe fro hym al bodely þing, & alle þoo þinges þat fallyn to
body, or to bodely þinges—as is schap, fourme, qualitee, quantitee,
wiȝt, steedlynes, visibilitee, sensibilitee, & al doyng, & suffryng; al 15
inordynacioun of fleschly concupiscence, al troublid conplexion
of material passyon, al vnmiȝtfulnes soget vnto sensible chaunses,
al needfulnes of liȝt; & al generacyon, & al corupcioun, al deuision,
& al passibilitee, & al temporeel flowyng bi proces of tymes. For he
ne is any of þees þinges, ne haþ any of þees, or any or alle þees oþer 20
sensyble þinges.

[V Capitulum]

Þat he is none of vnderstondable þinges, þe whiche is cause
of hem alle |

Also we, ascendyng & begynnyng oure deniinges & oure doinges 25 f. 126a
awey at þe hiȝest of vnderstondable þinges, seyen þat he is
neiþer soule, ne aungel, ne he haþ fantasie, ne opinion, ne resoun,
ne vnderstondyng; ne he is reson, ne vnderstonding; ne he is seyde,
ne vnderstonden. And—þat we renne fro þees hiȝe þinges by
menes to þe last þinges—he is no noumbre, ne ordre, ne greetnes, 30
ne litylnes, ne euenheed, ne licnes, ne vnlicnes; ne he stondeþ, ne he

---

4 from] fro Kk   6–7 And . . . leuen not] *om.* Har¹ Kk. *See note*
9–10 þinges . . . awey þoo] *om.* Kk   11 lacken] lackyng Kk   13 þing]
þinges Kk   14 qualitee] *or add.* Kk   18 corupcioun] and *add.* Kk
19 of] & Kk   25 deniinges] denynynges Kk   27 he] *om.* Kk
28 ne he . . . vnderstonding] *om.* Kk

moueþ, ne he holdeþ no sylence, ne he spekiþ. And—þat we torne
aȝein to þe hiȝest þinges bi som menes, & eend oure denyinges at
þinges moost hiȝe—we sey þat he haþ no vertewe, ne he is vertewe,
ne liȝt, ne he leuiþ, ne he is liif, ne he is substaunce, ne eelde, ne
5 tyme, ne þer is any vnderstondable touching of hym, ne he is
kunnyng, ne trewþe, ne kyngdom, ne wisdom, ne on, ne vnitee, ne
Godheed, or goodnes; ne he is spirit after þat we vnderstonde
spirit; ne sonheed, ne faderheed, ne any oþer þing knowen of us,
or of any þat ben; ne he is anyþing of not-beyng þinges, ne any-
10 þing of beyng þinges; ne any of þoo þinges þat ben knowen,
knowen hym after þat he is; ne he knowiþ þoo þinges þat ben after·
þei ben in hemself, bot after þat þei ben in hym; ne þer is any
wey of reson or vnderstondyng to com vnto hym, ne name, ne
knowyng of hym; ne he is derknes, ne he is liȝt, ne he is errour, ne
15 he is trewþe; ne (knittyngly to sey) þer is of hym no settyng,
ne doyng awey; bot whan we affermingly set or deniingly do awey
alle or any of þoo þinges þat ben not he, hym we mowe neiþer set
ne do awey, ne on any vnderstondable maner afferme him, ne
f. 126b denie him. | For þe parfite & þe singuleer cause of al most nede-
20 lynges be wiþoutyn comparison of þe moost hiȝe heiȝt abouen
alle, boþe settyng & doyng awey. And his not-vnderstondable
ouerpassyng is vn-vnderstondabely abouen alle affermyng and
deniinge.

EXPLICIT

2 denyinges] denynynges Kk   4 ne liȝt] *ins. above* Har¹   he (is)]
ins. in rubrics Har¹   9–10 ne any . . . þinges] *om.* Kk   13 vnder-
stondyng] for *add.* Kk   16 deniingly] denynyngly Kk   22 vn-]
ins. Har¹   23 deniinge] denynynges Kk

A TRETYSE OF ÞE STODYE OF WYSDOME ÞAT MEN CLEPEN BENIAMYN

A Tretyse of þe Stodye of Wysdome þat Men Clepen Beniamyn

f. 111a A greet clerk þat men clepyn Richard of Seinte Victore, in a book
þat he makiþ of þe studie of wisdom, witnessiþ & seiþ þat two
5 miȝtes ben in a mans soule, ȝouen of þe Fader of heuen, of whome
alle good comiþ, þe tone is reson, þe toþer is affeccioun or wille.
Þorow reson we knowe, & þorow affeccioun we fele or loue. Of
reson springeþ riȝt counselles & goostly wittes, and of affeccioun
springeþ goostly desires and ordeynd felynges. And riȝt as Rachel
10 & Lya weren boþe wyues to Jacob, riȝt so mans soule, þorow liȝt [of]
knowyng in þe reson & swetnes of loue in þe affeccioun, is spousid
vnto God. By Jacob is vnderstonden God; by Rachel is vnderstonden reson; by Lya is vnderstonden affeccioun.

Iche of þese wyues, Rachel & Lya, toke to hem a mayden.

No title in Har¹ Ar Har⁵ C G W; Here begynneþ a tretyse of þe stodye of
wysdome þat men clepen Beniamyn Kk Har²; Here begynneth the boke
of the xii patriarkys F; Here bygynnyþ a tretise þat men calliþ Richarde of
Seynt Victor R; Here foloweth a veray deuoute treatyse (named Benyamyn)
of the myghtes and vertues of mannes soule, & of the way to true contem-
placyon/compyled by a noble & famous doctoure. a man of grete holynes &
deuocyon/named Rycharde of Saynt Vyctor Pw; Here beginneþ a book þt
Ricard of Seynt Victore maad vp þe historie of Joseph & of his xii sones and
is callid Beniamyn Ii
3 greet] and a worshipful *add*. G   þat] whom G   men] man Har⁵
clep-] cal(l) Har⁵ F C R Pw G W Ii   Seinte] Sancte Har²   Victore] Victory
G   4 makiþ] þe *add*. Pw   þe] *om*. F Pw   witnessiþ &] *om*. Har⁵
5 miȝtes] or powers *add*. F   ben] are Har⁵ C R Pw G W Ii, *and elsewhere*
6 þe tone] þat one Ar F C R G   tone] one Pw   reson] & *add*. Ar Pw G W Ii
þe toþer] þat oþer Ar C R G   toþer] other Pw   is] *om*. Ar W Ii   or wille]
om. Group B   7 fele or] *om*. Group B   8 springeþ] wise and *add*. G   riȝt]
ryghtwise Har⁵   counselles] counsayle R Pw Ii   wittes] wytte Pw   and]
om. Group B   9 goostly] holy Group B   ordeynd] ordand Kk;
ordenant Har²; ardaunt Ar Pw G; ordred F; ordaund W; ordinat Ii; or
brennyng *add*. G   10 to] vnto Har² C R Pw G W Ii   þorow] for Group B
of] or Group A   11 in] & Ii   12 vnto] to Ar W Ii; into R   By
Jacob . . . God] *om*. F   vnderstonden God] *trs*. Har⁵; be lia is vnderstonden
þe affeccion *add*. Ii   12–13 is vnderstonden] *om*. F C R   13 reson] & *add*.
F C R   by . . . affeccioun] *om*. Ii   is vnderstonden] *om*. Har⁵   14 Iche]
Eyþer Ar Har⁵ F C R G W Ii   þese] two *add*. F   wyues] that is *add*. G
Rachel & Lya] *om*. Har⁵ Pw   to] *om*. Ar Har⁵ C R Pw W Ii; vnto G
hem] hym R; hir G   mayden] mayde Pw G

Rachel toke Bala, and Lya toke Zelfa. Bala was a greet jangler,
and Zelfa was euer dronken & þristy. By Bala is vnderstonden
ymaginacyon, þe whiche is seruaunt vnto reson as Bala was to
Rachel. By Zelfa is vnderstonden sensualite, þe whiche is seruaunt
vnto affeccioun as Zelfa was to Lya. And in so moche ben þees 5
maydens needful to þeire ladies þat wiþouten hem alle þis woreld
my3t serue hem of nou3t. For whi of alle þees outward bodeli
þinges, wiþoutyn ymaginacioun reson may not knowe, and wiþoutyn sensualite affeccioun may not fele.

And 3it ymaginacioun crieþ so vnkunnyngly in þe eres of oure 10
hertes, þat for ou3t þat reson hir lady may do, 3it sche may not
stille hir. And þerfore it is þat oft-tymes whan we schuld praye,
so many diuerse fantasies of yuel þou3tes crien in oure hertes þat
on nowise we mowen by oure owne my3tes driue hem awey. And
þus it is wel prouid þat Bala is a foule jangeler. & also sensualite 15
is euermore so þristy þat al þat affeccioun hir | lady may fele may f. 111b
not 3it sleckyn hir þirst. Þe drinke þat sche desireþ is þe luste of
fleschly, kyndly, & wordly delices, of þe whiche, þe more þat sche
drinkeþ, þe sorer sche þristeþ. For whi for to fylle þe appetite

1 Zelfa] Elfa Ar W, *and elsewhere*   2 euer] ay Har⁵ C G W
dronken] drongen Ar   þristy] þristlew Ii   3 þe] *om.* F   seruaunt]
serwande Har⁵   vnto] to Ar Har⁵ F C R Pw Ii   was] *om.* Har⁵ C R Pw G
W Ii; ys F   to] vnto Kk G   4 -stonden] þe *add.* Ii   þe] *om.* F   seruaunt]
seruande Har⁵   5 vnto] to Ar Har⁵ C Pw Ii   And] an Ii   in] *om.* Pw
6 to] vnto G   þeire] þes Ar C R   woreld] ne *add.* Pw   7 my3t] my
Ar; not *add.* Har⁵   serue] serryf Kk   hem] then F   of nou3t] to pay Har⁵
of] at Ii   nou3t] ought Pw   whi] *om.* F   7–8 of . . . þinges] *om.* Group B
8 not] no3t Kk Har² Har⁵ C Ii *and elsewhere*   and] Nor Pw   wiþoutyn]
þe *add.* Ii   9 sen.] þe *add.* Ii   10 vnkunnyngly] vnconandle Har⁵ C; inportunably F; vncouenabeli R G; enconuenyently Pw; vnkunnendly W
11 hertes] hert Kk Har² Group B   þat] *om.* Pw G   3it] that Pw   12
stille] tille C   it is] *trs.* F C R   it . . . þat] *om.* Ar Har⁵   oft-] often-
Har² Pw G Ii   schuld] *om.* Group B   13 many] sore C; sere or *add.* G
diuerse] sere Ar Har⁵ R Pw   of] oft Ar; ydle and *add.* Pw   yuel] ille
Har² Har⁵ G; or wicked *add.* G   þou3tes] 3oughtes Har²   crien] risin Ii
hertes] eris R   14 on] o Har⁵; in F Pw G W Ii   by] wt F   oure owne] alle
our F   owne] *om.* Har² C R Pw   15 it is] *trs.* Har⁵ C G W   prouid] eproued
Ar   þat] þa W   foule] grete Kk Har² F G   &] *om.* F   also] þe *add.*
Pw Ii   16 so] *om.* Har² Har⁵ F Pw   þat] for F   þat] at Har⁵   fele]
can., forthe *ins. in left margin* Har⁵   17 3it] *om.* Har⁵ Ii   sleckyn] slokyn
Kk Har² Ar Har⁵ C; slake F R; sleke Pw; or quenche *add.* G   luste] luf Har⁵
18 kyndly] kyndelynesse Pw; *om.* Ii   delices] delytes Kk Har² Ar F C R
Pw G   whiche] ay *add.* Ar Har⁵ W; euere *add.* F C G Ii (*ins.* Ii); euermore
add. R   þat] *om.* Group B   19 sorer] sarre Ar Har⁵; sarrer W; more
R Pw G; or the sarrer *add.* G   For whi] *om.* F   fylle] fulfille R G W Ii

of þe sensualite, al þis woreld may not suffise. And þerfore it is
þat oft-tymes whan we praye or þinkyn on God and goostly
þinges, we wolde feyn fele swetnes of loue in oure affeccioun, &
ȝit we mowen not, for we ben so besy to fede þe concupiscence of
5 oure sensualite. For euirmore it is gredyly askyng, & we haue a
fleschly compassion þerof. And þus it is wel prouid þat Zelfa is
euermore dronken & þristy.

And riȝt as Lya conceiuyd of Jacob & brouȝt forþe seuen childre,
and Zelfa conceiuyd of Jacob and brouȝt forþe two childre, and
10 Bala conceyuid of Jacob & brouȝt forþe two childre, and Rachel
conceiuyd of Jacob & brouȝt forþ two chyldren: riȝt so affeccioun
conceiuiþ þorow grace of God and bryngeþ forþe seuen vertewes;
and þe sensualite conceyuiþ þorow grace of God & bringeþ forþ two
vertewes; also ymaginacioun conceiuiþ þorou grace of God, and
15 bryngeþ forþ two vertewes or two beholdynges; and also þe reson
conceyuyþ þorow grace of God, & bryngeþ forþe two vertewes.

1 of] al *add.* W   suffise] it *add.* Ar Pw W; to it *add.* Ii   it is] *trs.* Har⁵
C G W   1–2 it is þat] *om.* F   2 oft-] often Har² Pw   tymes] tyme
F C R; þat *add.* R   or] & Ar   on] of Kk Har² F C; o Har⁵   and] or Har⁵
3 þinges] gudes Har⁵   fele] þe *add.* Har⁵; sum *add.* Ii   loue] liif G W   affec-
cioun] sawle (*ins.*) Har⁵   4 we mowen] *trs.* Ar Har⁵ C R Pw G W Ii
for] *om.* Kk Har² Ar Har⁵ C R Pw G W; & Ii   we ben so] so er (are Har⁵
C R Pw G Ii) we Ar Har⁵ C R Pw G W Ii   so] *om.* F   besy] vs *add.* Ar W
5 askyng] asked F   6 it is] *trs.* Har⁵ C   it] *ins.* Ii   is] *om.* Kk R
prouid] preuiþ R   þat] *om.* R   7 euermore] ay Ar Har⁵ W; euere
F G Ii; *om.* C R; alway Pw   dronken] drongke Ii   &] aye *add.* Pw G
8 riȝt] *om.* Har⁵   forþe] *om.* C   seuen] two C   9 Zelfa] Rachel
Ar Har⁵ C Pw G   and (B.)] *om.* Har⁵   10 Bala] Rachelle Kk Har² F R W Ii;
Zelfa Har⁵   of Jacob] *om.* Har⁵   & brouȝt forþe] *om.* C   10–11 and
Rachel...chyldren] *om.* Ar C   and] *om.* R   Rachel] Bala Kk Har² Har⁵ F R
W Ii; Zelfa Pw G   11 so] þe *add.* Ar C R Pw G W Ii   affeccioun]
gostly (*ins.*) *add.* Har²   12 conceiuiþ] conceiued G   þorow] þe *add.*
F C R Pw G   and] *om.* G   forþe] *can.* Kk   13 and] as Ar; Also
Har⁵; also *add.* F C R Pw G W Ii   þe] *om.* Kk Har² Pw W   sen.]
reson Har⁵   conceyuiþ] *om.* Har⁵; conceiued G   þorow] þe *add.* Kk
Har² Har⁵ F C R Pw   God] consaues *add.* Har⁵   &] *om.* G   14 ver-
tewes] and *add.* Kk Har² Ar Har⁵ R Pw G W   also] & as Ar Har⁵; & Ii;
þe *add.* Ar C R W Ii   ymag.] Reson Har² Ar F C R Pw G W Ii   con-
ceiuiþ] conceiued G   þorou] þe *add.* Kk Har² Har⁵ F C R Pw   and]
om. G   15–16 or two ... vertewes] *om.* Kk   15 or two behold.] *om.*
Har² Ar F C R Pw G W Ii   and also ... vertewes] *om.* Har⁵   and] *om.*
F G   also] *om.* Har²; as Ar   þe] *om.* Har² Ar F G   reson]
ymaginacion Har² Ar F C R Pw G W Ii   16 conceyuyþ] conceiued G   þorow] þe *add.* Har² F C R Pw   vertewes] or els
(els *om.* Ar F C R Pw G W Ii) two beholdynges *add.* Har² Ar F C R
Pw G W Ii

And þe names of þees children & of þeire vertewes scholen be
knowen by þis figure þat foloweþ. |

Husbond
Jacob—God

Wyfe	*Wyfe*
Lya—affeccyon	Rachel—reson

Mayden	*Mayden*
Zelfa—sensualite	Bala—ymagynacioun

þe sons of Jacob of Zelfa	þe sons of Jacob of Lya	þe sons of Jacob of Rachel	þe sons of Jacob of Bala
Gad—abstynence	Ruben—drede of God	Joseph—discresion	Dan—siȝt of peynes to come
Asser—pacyence	Symeon—sorow of synne	Beniamyn—contem-placyon	Neptalym—siȝt of joyes to come
	Leuy—hope of forȝeuenes		
	Judas—loue of good God		
	Isachar—joie of inward swetnes		
	Zabulon—parfite hate of synne		
	Dyna—ordeynde schame of synne		

Figure. See frontispiece

A full comparison of the figures in the different MSS. would be impracticable here. Certain observations however, have value in their further corroboration of deductions made in the chapter on the relationship of the manuscripts (Introd., pp. xx–xxii). Har[1] Kk Har[2] contain the clearest diagram. Kk Har[2] differ from Har[1] only in spelling; Kk also adds numbers to the children according to the order of their birth. The readings of most of the other MSS. indicate a figure in their original, subsequently copied, translated, or summarized, with varying degrees of closeness. Ar F G resemble Har[1] in their arrangement of Jacob, his wives, and their servants, but below in F G there is no attempt at a figure. In the MSS. of Group B the order of the groups of children is unfixed. Ar Har[5] Pw G list in the following order: the children of Lya, Zelfa, Rachel, Bala; F: of Lya, Rachel, Bala, Zelfa; R: of Zelfa, Lya, Bala, Rachel. Ar F Pw G are neat and systematic in their descriptions of the contents of the figure. Har[5] is not so clear. R is wholly confused, its arrangement explicable, perhaps, as a careless transcription of a figure similar to the one in Group A, and in reversed order, with the result that nowhere is clearly expressed the relationship between Jacob and his womenfolk, or the relationship of the different groups of children to their respective mothers. Agreement in the variants of interpretation further adds to the distinctions between Group A and Group B. Thus:

Ruben—drede of God] drede of peyne Ar Har[5] F C R Pw G
Symeon—sorow of synne] sorowȝ of synnes Ar F C R Pw G
Judas—loue of good God] luf of riȝtwysnesse Ar Har[5] F C R Pw G
Isachar—joie of inward swetnes] joye in inwarde swetnesse Pw G
Zabulon—parfite hate of synne] hatreden of synes Ar; hatreden of syne Har[5] C; hatred of synne F R Pw; hate of synne G
Dyna—ordeyne schame of synne] ardaunt (ordaynde Har[5] R; ordred F; ordynate Pw G) schame Ar Har[5]F C R Pw G
Dan—siȝt of peynes to come] siȝt of peyne to (at Har[5]) come Ar Har[5] R Pw G
Neptalym—siȝt of joyes to come] siȝt of ioye to (at Har[5] come Ar Har[5]) F C R Pw G

1–2 And . . . foloweþ] *om.* Ii   þees] þere Kk Har[2] Pw G; þe W
&] are, and *written above* Har[5]   of] *om.* Kk Ar Har[5] F C R Pw G   þeire]
þes Ar Har[5] F C R   2 þis] þe W   figure] scripture G   foloweþ]
here after. In schewynge *add.* R; *no figure follows in* W Ii

f. 112b   In þis figure is schewyd a party of Jacob & of his wyues and
þeire maydens & alle þeire children. Here it is to schewe on what
maner þei were getyn, & in what ordire. First it is to seyn of þe
children of Lya, for whi it is red þat sche first conceyued. Þe sons of
5 Jacob of Lya ben nouȝt elles to bemene bot ordeynde affecciouns
or felynges in a mans soule ; for ȝif þei weren vnordeynd, þan weren
þei not his sones. Also þe seuen children of Lya ben seuen vertewes, for vertewe is not elles bot an ordeynd and a mesurid felyng
of a mans soule. Þan is mans feling in soule ordeynd when it is of
10 þat þing þat it schuld be. Þan is it mesurid when it is as moche as
it schuld be. Þees felynges in a mans soule mowen be now ordeind
& mesurid, & now vnordeind & vnmesurid. Bot when þei ben
ordeynd & mesurid, þan ben þei acomptyd amonges þe sones of
Jacob.

1 In . . . figure] Here Har⁵   1–3 In . . . ordire] *om.* Ii   figure] litel
boke G; it *add.* Har² Ar Har⁵ F C R Pw G Ii   is] apertly *add.* G; it *add.*
W   a party] in parte Har²; *om.* Har⁵ G; apertely F R Pw   (&) of] *om.*
Har⁵ F C Pw G W   and] *om.* Ar Har⁵ F C R•Pw G   2 alle] *om.* Har⁵;
also F   Here] And nowe Ar   to schewe] shewed Pw G W   3 getyn]
goten Pw G; begoten F   & . . . ordire] *om.* F C R   it] *om.* Ii   it . . . seyn]
om. Har⁵   seyn] speke Ar   of] *om.* R; *ins.* Ii   4 whi] *om.* Har⁵ F   it is]
we Har⁵   first conceyued] *trs.* Har⁵ C; first *ins.* Har⁵   sons] sone C; chyldren
Pw   4–5 of Jacob] *om.* Pw G; & *add.* Ii   5 to bemene] *om.* Har⁵; to
vnderstand F Pw   be-] *om.* Kk Har² Ar G   ordeynde] ardaunt Ar; ordred
F; ordynate Pw G W Ii   6 a] *om.* Har² Ar   for] why *add.* Ar Har⁵
C R Pw G W Ii   vnordeynd] vnardaunt Ar; vnordred F; inordynate Pw;
vnordinat G Ii   7 þei not] *trs.* F   his] hyr Ar; þe Pw G   sones] of
Jacob *add.* Pw; of lya *add.* G   Also] *om.* Har⁵   ben] are Har⁵ R W Ii
8 an] & Ii   ordeynd] ardaunt Ar; ordred F; ordynate Pw G Ii   and] or
Pw G W Ii   9 of] in Pw G Ii   a] *om.* Ar   soule] for *add.* Pw G; & *add.* Ii
is] a *add.* R Ii   in] his *add.* F   soule] well *add.* Pw G   ordeynd] ardaunte
Ar; ordred F Pw; ordinat Ii   10 is it] *trs.* Ar R Pw G W Ii   as] so
Ar Har⁵ F C R Pw G W Ii   11 schuld] schul Ii   be] *om.* Har⁵; But (*om.*
Pw G) I supose *add.* Ar Pw G   þees] þire Kk Har²; *om.* Ar; þat Pw G; þose
W; but Ii   felynges] felyng Ar Pw G W Ii   a] *ins.* Har²; *om.* Ar C R W Ii
11–12 ordeind . . . vnmesurid] ardaunt (ordaynde Har⁵ C R W; ordred F; ordynate Pw G Ii) & nowe vnardaunt (vnordaynde Har⁵ C R W; vnordred F;
inordynate Pw; vnordinat G Ii) now mesured & now vnmesured Group B
12 Bot] *om.* F   13 ordeynd] mesured Group B   mesurid] ardaunt Ar;
ordaynde Har⁵ C R W; ordred F; ordynate Pw G W Ii   ben] may Ar
F C R Pw G W Ii; are Har⁵   þei] be *add.* Ar F C R Pw G W Ii
acomptyd] acounted Kk Har² Ar F C R; calde Har⁵; counted Pw; con-
teined G; reckened W Ii   amonges] *om.* Har⁵   Pw *entitles this section* The
Prologue, *and adds*: Here foloweth the chapytres of this present treatyse
Howe þe vertue of drede ryseth in affeccyon. ca. i
Howe sorowe ryseth in the affeccyon. ca. ii
Howe hoope ryseth in the affeccyon. ca. iii   [*note cont. opposite*

HOW ÞE VERTEWE OF DREDE RISEÞ IN ÞE AFFECCYOUN

Þe first childe þat Lya conceyuid of Jacob was Ruben, þat is drede. And for-þi it is wretyn in þe psalme: 'Þe bygynnyng of wysdom, dreed of oure Lorde God.' Þis is þe first felt vertewe in a mans affeccioun, wiþoutyn whiche none oþer may be had. And 5 þerfore, whoso desireþ to haue soche a sone, hym behoueþ besily & oft also beholde þe iuels þat he haþ done. He schal on o partye þink þe greetnes of his trespas, and on anoþer partye þe power of þe domesman. Of soche a consideracioun springeþ drede, þat is to sey he, þat Ruben, þat þorow riȝt is clepid *þe sone of siȝt*. For 10 verrely is he blent þat seeþ not þe peynes þat ben to come & dredeþ not to synne. And wele is þis Ruben clepid *þe sone of siȝt*, for whan he was borne his moder cried & seyde: 'God haþ

1 *No chapter heading in* F C R   How] Here it is to say (seen G) how Kk Har² Ar Har⁵ G W Ii   þe vertewe of] *om.* Har⁵   riseþ] sprynges Har⁵ þe] *om.* Ar; a mans Har⁵   2 Lya] had & *add.* Har²   was] is Kk Har² Group B   3 drede] of þe lord *add.* W·Ii   And] *om.* W Ii forþi] therfore Pw   -þi] *om.* Ar R W Ii; þt F   is] *om.* Har²   þe] *om.* Kk psalme] Inicium sapiencie timor domini *add.* F; of *add.* R; that *add.* G Þe] *om.* Har⁵   4 wysdom] þe *add.* C R; ys þe *add.* F Pw G; is *add.* Ii   oure] þe W Ii   oure Lorde] *om.* Ar   God] *om.* Kk Har² Ar Har⁵ F C R Pw W Ii 5 a] *om.* Ar Har⁵ F C W Ii   wiþoutyn] þe *add.* Ar Har⁵ Pw G W Ii And] *om.* W Ii   6 so] *om.* R; þat Ii ⸝ desireþ] for *add.* C R   haue] loue C   soche] sclyk Har⁵   7 oft] often Pw   also] *om.* Har⁵ G; to F R Pw Ii   iuels] yuele Kk Pw; illes Har²; wickydnes R; wikkednesses C   done] And *add.* Pw G   on o partye] also apertly R   o] oon F W; a C; another Pw G   8 þink] on *add.* F Pw   trespas] gylt Kk Har² Har⁵ F C R Pw G W Ii; ȝifte Ar   on] in W Ii   an-] þe Ar F; þe (*ins.*) R   oþer] toþere F   þe] grete *add.* F   9 domesman] ryȝtwose juge F; and hyghe Juge for *add.* Pw; for *add.* G   soche] sclyk Har⁵; whiche R   a] *om.* R G   10 to] at Har⁵   he þat] *om.* Ar Pw G; is callid *add.* F; is *add.* R clepid] cald Har⁵ F C R Pw G W Ii   siȝt] lihte R   11 verrely] vtterly can. Kk, wytterly Kk Har² Ar Har⁵ C R W Ii; vtterly F Pw G   is he] *trs.* Kk Har² Ar F Pw   blent] blynde Kk Har² Group B   ben] is Kk; beþ Ar; are Har⁵ C R Pw G W   12 þis] *om.* Har⁵ Ii   clepid] clepe Ar; calde Har⁵ F C R Pw G W Ii   þe] *om.* Har⁵ C R G W   13 siȝt] lyht R   whan] *om.* Har²   cried &] *om.* Har⁵   seyde] Vidit dominus humilitatem meam *add.* F   God] Our Lord F

f. 113a seen my meeknes.' And mans soule in soche a consideracioun | of his olde synne & þe power of þe domesman beginniþ þan trewly to se God by feling of drede, and also to be seen of God by rewardyng of pite.

5 HOW SOROW RISEþ IN þE AFFECCIOUN

Whiles Ruben waxeþ, Symeon is borne, for aftir drede it nediþ greetly þat sorow come sone; for euer þe more þat man dredeþ þe pyne þat he haþ deserued, þe bittirlier he soroweþ þe synne þat he haþ done. Lya in þe birþe of Symeon cried and seyde: 'Oure 10 Lorde haþ herd me be had in dispite.' And for-þi is Symeon clepid *heryng*; for when a man bitterly soroweþ & dispiseþ his olde synnes, þan begynneþ he to be herde of God & also to here þis blessid sentence of Goddes owne mouþ: 'Blessed be þey þat sorowen for þei scholen be coumforted.' For in what oure þat a synner 15 soroweþ & turneþ fro his synne, he schal be saaf. þus witnessiþ Holy Scripture. And also by Ruben he is mekyd, and by Symeon

1 seen my] sent me R   a] *om.* Har⁵   2 synne] synnes Ar Har⁵ F C R Pw G W Ii   &] to see *add.* R; of *add.* Pw G W   power . . . domesman] domesmannes (domesman C; or hyghe Juges *add.* Pw) power Ar C R Pw G W Ii; hyghe juges power F   þe] his Har⁵   3 se God] be good F   be seen] see R   by] the *add.* F   5 *No chapter heading* F C R   How] Here it is to say howe Har⁵   riseþ] spryngese Har⁵; ariseþ Ii   in þe affeccioun] *om.* Har⁵   þe] *om.* G   6 Whiles] þe whyles Ar; In þat whiles (while R) C R; whyle Pw G; þt *add.* F R   Symeon] Simon C   7 greetly] *om.* Har⁵ sone] after *add.* G   euer] ay Kk Har² Ar Har⁵ G   þat] *om.* Ar Har⁵ C R W; a F Pw G; a *add.* Har² Ii   8 pyne] payne Kk Har² Ar Pw G W Ii; paynes Har⁵ F C; pynes R   8–9 he haþ . . . he] *om.* C   þe] *om.* Har⁵   bittirlier] more bitterly F   soroweþ] for *add.* R   þe] þat Har⁵ synne] synnes F R Pw G   9 he] *om.* Har²   Symeon] Symon, e *ins.* Har¹ cried and] *om.* Ar Har⁵ F C R W Ii   seyde] thus. Audiuit me dominus haberi contemptui *add.* F   10 herd me be] *om.* C R   me] to *add.* C   F had] me *add.* C R   for-þi] þerfor F Pw   Symeon] is *add.* F   clepid] cald Har² F C R Pw G W Ii; *om.* Har⁵   11 when] *om.* Ar Har⁵ C Pw W Ii   man] whan he *add* Ar Har⁵ C Pw W Ii   &] he W Ii   synnes] syne Har⁵   12 þan] *om.* Ar Har⁵ C; he R; & W Ii   begynneþ he] *trs.* Har⁵ F   he] *om.* Ar C R W Ii also] for *add.* Ar F C R Pw G W Ii   þis] the Pw   blessid] blyssed Kk Har² Har⁵; blisful Ii   13 of] of *add.* Kk   mouþ] Beati qui lugent quoniam ipsi consolabuntur *add.* F   Blessed] Blyssed Kk Har² Har⁵   13–14 Blessed . . .] *The reference is given in rubrics in the left margin of* Har¹   14 coumforted] comforde Har⁵   14–15 For . . .] *The reference is given in rubrics in the left margin of* Har¹   þat] *om.* Har⁵ F Pw G   a] the Pw G synner] synful Ar   15 fro] from Pw   his] *om.* R   þus] as Ar; þis Har⁵ F G   16 Scripture] writte Ar Har⁵ F C R G W Ii; seyng. In quacumque hora homo ingemuerit saluus erit *add.* F   And] *om.* Ar F R he is] *trs.* Har⁵ F C R G W Ii   mekyd] mekened Ar

he is contrite, & haþ conpunccioun of teres. Bot as witnessiþ
Dauid in þe psalme: 'Hert contrite & mekyd, God schal not dispise.' And wiþouten doute soche sorow bringeþ in trewe coumforte.

HOW HOPE RISEþ IN þE AFFECCYON   5

Bot I prey þee what coumforte may be to hem þat dreden
trewly & bitterly sorowen here olde synnes, ouȝt bot a trewe hope
of forȝeuenes, þe whiche is þe þrid sone of Jacob? þat is Leuy,
þe whiche is clepid in þe story *doyng to*. For when þe oþer two
children, drede & sorow, ben ȝouen of God to a mans soule, 10
wiþouten doute he, þis þrid þat is hope, schal not be delaied. Bot
he schal be done to, as þe story witnesseþ of Leuy þat when his
two breþren, Ruben & Symeon, weren to here moder Lya,
he, þis Leuy, was done to.

Take hede of þis worde þat he was done to & not ȝouen. And þer- 15
fore it is seyde þat men schul not presume of hope | of forȝeuenes f. 113*b*
before þe tyme þat his herte be mekyd in drede & contryte in
sorow. Wiþoutyn þees two, hope is presumpcioun; and where

1 he is] *trs.* Har⁵ F C G W Ii   contrite] conuertede Har⁵   1–2 Bot . . . Dauid]
And dauid þe prophete seiþ Ar   Bot] *om.* F ; And G   1–2 witnessiþ Dauid] *trs.*
Har⁵ G   2 þe] *om.* Kk ; a Pw G   psalme] seyng. Cor contritum & humiliatum deus non despicias. The *add.* F ; The *add.* G ; A *add.* Ii ; *The reference
is given in rubrics in the right margin* of Har¹   Hert] þat ys *add.* F   schal]
schal *add.* Ii   3 wiþouten doute] *om.* Ar   bringeþ in] is Group B   trewe]
om. R   coumforte] to the (the *om.* C W) modyr *add.* F C R W Ii ; of (the *add.*
G) herte *add.* Pw G   5 How . . . affeccyon] Here is to say of hop *follows at
end of chapter in* Har⁵ ; *om.* F C R   riseþ] arisith G   þe] *om.* G   6 þee]
om. W   to] vnto Ar W Ii   hem] þo (*ins.*) Har⁵ ; hym R   6–7 dreden trewly]
trs. Group B   7 sorowen] for *add.* Pw   olde] *om.* Pw G   ouȝt] elles *add.* G
a] *om.* Pw   8 þe] *om.* F   is] *om.* C R   9 þe] *om.* Ii F ; þat C R
whiche] *om.* C R   clepid] calde Har⁵ F C R Pw G W Ii   þe] *om.* Ii
story] a *add.* Group B   oþer] toþer Kk Har² ; first Group B   two] twey
G   10 ben] are Har⁵ C R Pw G W Ii   to] into G   a] *om.* R Pw W Ii   mans]
menes C   11 wiþouten doute] *om.* R   he] *om.* Har⁵ F ; is *add.* Kk   þis] þe
Kk   he . . . hope] The thyrde is that hope Pw   þis] þe Har⁵ ; þe *add.*
Har²   þrid] leuy R ; son *add.* F   12 he] *om.* Ii   of] of *add.* W   his]
these Pw G   13 breþren] breþire Kk Har² Har⁵   here] þe C R   14 he]
om. Pw   done] or added *add.* Pw   15 hede] kepe Ar Har⁵ C R G W Ii
of] o Har⁵ ; to Pw   worde] *om.* Har⁵ Ii   not] *om.* R   þerfore] herfore
Ar C R G W Ii ; forþi Har⁵   16 it is] *trs.* Ar Har⁵   men] a man Group B
17 þe] *om.* Har⁵ ; þat W   þat] *om.* W Ii   contryte] conuertede Har⁵
18 sorow] for *add.* Pw   þees] þer Kk Har²   where] þt *add.* F ; so *add.* C R

þees two ben, hope is done to. And þus after sorow comeþ sone
coumforte, as Dauid telleþ in þe psalme þat 'after þe mochilnes of
my sorowes in myn herte', he seiþ to oure Lorde þat his coum-
fortes han gladid his soule. And also þerfore it is þat þe Holy
5 Goost is clepid Paraclitus, þat is coumfortour, for ofte he voucheþ-
saaf to coumforte a sorowful soule.

HOW LUF RISIþ IN AFFECCIOUN

Fro now forþ begynneþ a maner of homlynes for to growe
bitwix God & mans soule, and also on a maner a kyndelyng of
10 loue; in-so-mochil þat oft-tymes he feliþ hym not only be visityd
of God, bot greetly coumfortyd in his comyng. þis homlynes & þis
kyndelyng of loue first felt Lya when, after þat Leuy was borne,
sche cried wiþ a greet joie & seyde: 'Now schal myn housbonde be
couplid to me.' þe trewe spouse of oure soule is God. And þan ben
15 we trewly couplid vnto hym when we drawe nere hym by hope &

1 þees] þer Kk Har² Har⁵; þe R   ben] are Har⁵ C R Pw W Ii
comeþ sone] *trs.* Har⁵   2 as] and Har⁵   telleþ] sayes Har²
þe] his R; a Pw   psalme] sauter Ar; & *add.* Ar; Secundum multitudinem
dolorum meorum consolaciones tue letificauerunt animam meam *add.* F;
þus *add.* W Ii; *The reference is given in rubrics in the left margin of*
Har¹   þat] *om.* F Ii; Lord R   mochilnes] mykylnes Kk Har² F; mekelnes
Har⁵ G Ii; mekenes Ar W; mochelnessis R; gretenesse Pw   3 sorowes]
sorowe Ar Har⁵ Pw G W Ii   3–4 he . . . gladid his] þe comford of oure lord
haþ gladed my Ar   3 he . . . Lorde] *om.* F C R   þat his] thy F C R Pw
coumfortes] comforte R Pw G W Ii   4 han] haþe Kk Har² C R Pw G W Ii
his] my F C R Pw   And] *om.* F   also] *om.* Har⁵ F Pw   þerfore . . .
þat] *om.* Ar   it is] *trs.* Har⁵ G   5 clepid] cald Har⁵ F C Pw G W Ii   is] a
add. Har² G; to sey a *add.* F; the *add.* Pw   coumfortour] comforte Pw   ofte]
om. Har⁵; often tymes Pw; often Ii   voucheþ] woched Kk   6 saaf] for *add.*
C R G   sorow-] sore- Har⁵   soule] gooste Kk Har⁵ C R G W Ii; for nowe
forþe *add. in rubrics* Ar   7 How . . . affeccioun] Here it ys to sey of lufe
(lyf C R) in the affeccion F C R; Here is to say of luffe *at end of chapter
in* Har⁵   risiþ] arisiþ Ii   in] þe *add.* Kk Har² Ar Pw W Ii   8 Fro]
For Ar G; From Pw   now forþ] hensfurth F; -warde *add.* G   for] *om.* F
growe] grofe Har⁵; grewe F   9 bitwix] betwyn F Pw G W Ii   &] a *add.*
C R Pw   and] *om.* F Pw   on] *om.* Har⁵ F C R   a] nother *add.* Har² Pw
G   a] of Har⁵ F C R; *om.* W   10 only] to *add.* F   be] *om.* Pw   visityd]
vyset Kk Har² Har⁵   11 bot] & Ar Har⁵ F C R Pw G   bot . . . coum.] *om.*
W Ii   greetly] *om.* Ar Har⁵ F C R Pw G   coum.] comford, d *ins.* Har⁵
comyng] conynge Ar G; but (also *add.* F) ofte (often Pw) tymes (tyme F)
also (*om.* F) he feliþ hym fyld wiþ an (*om.* Ii) vnspekeable ioye *add.* Group B
homlynes] holynes Ar   þis] *om.* Har⁵ R   13 cried] & saide *add.* Har⁵
joie] voyce Ar Pw G W Ii; *ins.* Har⁵   & seyde] *om.* Har⁵; Nunc quoque
copulabitur mihi maritus meus *add.* F   14 to] vnto Ar C R   is] *om.* W Ii
15 vnto] to Har⁵ Pw G W Ii   hym] gode Har⁵   nere] to *add.* G Ii   hope
&] *om.* Ar Har⁵ F C R W Ii

soþfast loue. And as after hope comeþ loue, so after Leuy was
Judas borne, þe feerþe sone of Lia.

Lya in his birþe cried and seyde: 'Now schal I schriue to oure
Lorde.' And þerfore in þe story is Judas clepid *schrift*. Also mans
soule in þis degre of loue offreþ it cleerly to God, and seiþ þus: 5
'Now schal I schryue to oure Lorde.' For before þis felyng of loue
in a mans soule, alle þat he doþ is done more for drede þen for
loue. Bot in þis state a mans soule feliþ God so swete, so mercyful,
so good, so curteis, so trewe, & so kynde, so feiþful, & so louely, &
so homly, þat þer leuiþ noþing in hym—miʒt, kunnyng, ne wylle— 10
þat he ne offreþ it cleerly, frely, & homly vnto hym. Þis schrift is
not only of synne, bot of þe goodnes of God. | Greet tokyn of loue f. 114*a*
it is whan a man telliþ to God þat he is good. Of þis schrift spekiþ
Dauid ful oft-tymes in þe psalme whan he seiþ: 'Makiþ it knowe to
God for he is good.' 15

Lo, now haue we seyde of foure sones of Lya. And after þis tyl
eftsones sche left beryng of children. And so mans soule weniþ þat

1 soþfast] trew Ar; stedfast F   And] riʒt *add.* Ar Har⁵ F C R Pw G W
Ii   was] comes Har⁵   2 borne] *om.* Har⁵   feerþe] fourte Kk Har²
of Lia] *om.* Ar Har⁵ F C R W Ii   3 seyde] Modo confitebor domino *add.*
F   schal] *om.* G   schriue] me *add.* F R Pw G   4 is] *om.* F Ii   Judas]
was *add.* F; is *add.* Ii   clepid] calde Har⁵ F C R Pw G W Ii   schrift] And
add. Har²; or confessioun *add.* F   Also] for F   mans] man Har⁵   5 soule]
is *add.* C R   offreþ] offrid C R   it] self *add.* F; *om.* R   þus] *om.*
Group B   6 schryue] me *add.* F Pw G   before] afor F   7 a] *om.* Ar F R W
Ii   more] rather Pw; fore *add.* Ii   for] awe or *add.* Pw   drede] awe Ar
Har⁵ F C R G W Ii   8 state] astate Ar   a] *om.* F   9 so (trewe)] *om.*
Har⁵   &] *om.* Ar C R W Ii   so] *om.* Ar Har⁵ F W   so] *om.* W   feiþful]
triste Ar   &] *om.* Kk Har² Group B   louely] louy Ar   10 þer] he F Pw
hym] but *add.* Ar G W Ii; selfe be it *add.* Pw   miʒt] witte *add.* Ar Har⁵
F C Pw G W Ii; ne *add.* F C; wiþ none *add.* R; or *add.* G   kunnyng]
knowynge Pw G   ne] or Ar Har⁵ F C R Pw W Ii; & G   11 þat] þaten Kk
Har² Har⁵; þat ne Ar; but þat F   ne] *om.* Kk Har² Ar Har⁵ F   homly]
homelyly Kk   vnto] to Group B   schrift] & (or Pw) confession *add.*
F Pw   12 not] al *add.* Ar Pw G W Ii (*ins.*)   bot] also *add.* Har² Ar F   þe
goodnes of] *om.* Ar   tokyn] tokunyng Har⁵   13 it] *om.* Har⁵   schrift]
shryf Kk; confession F   14 ful oft-tymes] *om.* Kk Har² Group B   psalme]
sauter Group B; ful (*om.* Har²) oft (often Har² Pw Ii) tymes *add.* Kk Har² Ar
F C R Pw G W Ii   whan he] & Har⁵   seiþ] Confitemini domino quam bonus.
þat is (þat is *om.* F) *add.* Har² F; þus *add.* G; *The reference is given in rubrics
in the left margin of* Har¹   Makiþ] Make ye F Pw G W Ii   15 for] þat
F C R   16 Lo] *om.* Har⁵   haue we] *trs.* Pw   of] þe *add.* Har⁵
F C R   after] -ward *add.* Ar   þis] þes Group B (this Pw)   tyl] to
Kk Har² C G; twoo Ar F R W; *om.* Har⁵ Pw Ii   17 eftsones] *om.* Har⁵ Pw
Ii; eftere born sonnys F   of] *om.* C   children] childringe Ar; tille anothere
tyme *add.* Har⁵   so] a *add.* Har⁵

it suffiseþ to it when it feliþ þat it loueþ þe trewe goodes. And it is
inow to saluacion, bot not to perfeccioun; for it falliþ to a parfite
soule boþe to be enflaumyd wiþ þe fiir of loue in þe affeccioun, and
also to be illumynyd with liȝt of knowyng in þe reson.

5 HOW ÞE DOUBLE SIȜT OF PEYNE & IOY RISEÞ IN ÞE YMAGINA-
CIOUN

Þus when Judas [was borne], þat is to sey when loue & desire of
vnseen trewe goodes is rysing & waxing in a mans affeccioun,
þan coueiteþ Rachel for to bere some children. Þat is to sey, þan
10 coueiteþ reson to knowe þees þinges þat affeccyon felyþ. For as
it falleþ to Lya, þe affeccioun, for to loue, so it falleþ to Rachel, þe
reson, for to knowe. Of Lya, affeccioun, springeþ mesurid and
ordeynd felynges; and of Rachel, reson, springeþ riȝt knowynges
& cleer vnderstondyng. And euer þe more þat Judas waxeþ, þat
15 is to sey loue, so mochel more desireþ Rachel beryng of children.
Þat is to sey, reson studieþ after knowyng.

1 to it] hym F   it] he F   it] he F   þe] *om.* Kk. Har² þe
trewe goodes] to clens it clene to gode Har⁵; of God *add.* Pw G And]
so *add.* Group B   2 inow] *om.* Har⁵; now R; as *add.* W   (not) to] vnto
G   a] *om.* R   3 boþe] for Har⁵   þe] *om.* W Ii   4 il-] en- R   with]
þe *add.* Har² Pw F   þe] *om.* Kk   5 How . . . ymag.] Here it is to
say of doubulle syght in ymaginacion *at end of chapter* Har⁵; Here it ys to
sey of (of *om.* C R) þe dowbyl syȝte that rysyth of ymaginacion F C R þe]
om. Ar Pw G W Ii   double] *om.* Pw   þe] *om.* Ar   7 Þus] Than Pw
was borne] waxeþ Har¹. *See Note*   was] is Ar C R   is] so Har⁵   to] at Kk
when] *om.* Group B   8 vnseen] inuisible F; one sene Pw; seen Ii; and
invysyble *add.* Pw   goodes] gudenes Har²   is] *om.* Pw Ii   a] *om.* Ar R
mans] soule *add.* Har² Har⁵ (*can.* Har⁵); þt is in hys *add.* Har²   9 for] *om.*
Har⁵   some children] *trs. but corrected* Har¹   some] *om.* Pw   to] at Kk
Har²   10 þees] þo Har⁵ C R; those F   þat] at Har⁵; þe *add.* Har⁵   as]
om. Har⁵   11 it] *om.* Har²   to] *ins.* Ar; to *add.* Har¹   Lya] *can.*
Har¹   þe] *om.* Ar Har⁵ F C R W Ii   for] *om.* Ar Ii   Rachel] *can.* Har¹
þe] *om.* Kk Har² Ar Har⁵ F C R W Ii   12 for] *om.* Har⁵   Lya] *can.*
Har¹; the whiche is *add.* Pw   springeþ] by *add.* G   mesurid] ordeyned
Ar Har⁵ C R W; ordred F; ordynat Pw G; ordeinet Ii   13 ordeynd]
mesured Group B   felynges] felynge vs Ar   and] also *add.* C   Rachel]
can. Har¹; whiche is *add.* Pw   reson] *ins. in left margin* Ar   springeþ] by
add. G   knowynges] conynge Ar Har⁵ F C Pw; counssayles R; knowing
G W Ii; or kunnyng *add.* G   14 cleer] clene Ar Har⁵ C R W Ii   vnder.]
vnderstandyndynges Pw   euer] ay Ar G W; *om.* Har⁵   þe] *om.* R   þat]
om. Ar F C W; as (*ins.*) R   15 to] at Har²   mochel] the *add.* Pw
G W Ii   16 to] at Kk Har²

Bot who is þat þat wote not how hard it is & niȝhond inpossible to a flesc[h]ly soule, þe whiche is ȝit ruyde in goostly studies, for to rise in knowyng of vnseable þinges, & for to set þe iȝe of contemplacioun in goostly þinges? For whi a soule þat is ȝit ruyde & fleschly knowiþ nouȝt bot bodely þinges, and noþing comeþ ȝit 5 to þe mynde bot only seable þinges. And neuerþeles ȝit it lokyþ inward as it may, and þat it may not se ȝit cleerly by goostly knowyng, it þinkiþ by ymagynacioun.

And þis is | þe cause whi Rachel had first chyldren of hir may- f. 114b den þan of hirself. And so it is þat þof al a mans soule may not ȝit 10 gete þe lyȝt of goostly knowyng in þe reson, ȝit it þinkeþ it sweet to holde þe mynde on God & goostly þinges in ymagynacioun. As by Rachel, reson, so by hir mayden Bala we vnderstonde ymagynacioun. And þerfore reson schewiþ þat it is more profitable for to þink on goostly þinges in what maner so it be—ȝe, ȝif it be in 15 kyndelyng of oure desire wiþ som fayre ymagynacioun—þan it is for to þink vanitees & diseyuable þinges of þis woreld. And for-þi of Bala weren borne þees two, Dan & Neptalym. Dan is to sey siȝt of peynes to come, and Neptalym siȝt of joies to come.

1 þat] he Har⁵ F ; om. C ; it G   is] ȝa add. Har²   niȝ-] ner- Kk Har²
Group B   in-] vn- Har⁵   2 to] til C   þe] om. Ar F G W Ii ; and Pw
whiche] that G   ȝit] om. R   in] to add. Ar   goostly] goost C   3 of]
os, of written above Har⁵   vnseable] inuisible F   &] om. Har²   þe] his
Pw G   iȝe] eyes Pw   4 in] god and add. Har²   whi] om. F   ȝit] om. Ar
Ii ; riȝt C R   ruyde] in bodily þingis add. W Ii   5 nouȝt] not ȝitt Har⁵
bodely] body C   comeþ ȝit] trs. W Ii   6 þe] þi C; om. Ii   only] om.
Har⁵ Pw   seable] visible F; stable C; feble Pw; or vysyble add. Pw
And] bot Har²   neuer-] no- Ar; na G; nere W   7 þat] þat add. Har²
Ar F R Pw; at add. Har⁵ C   se ȝit] trs. Har⁵ F C R   se] so Har⁵   ȝit] om.
Ar W Ii   cleerly] om. Pw   8 it] hi C   þinkiþ] seeth F C R   9 And]
also add. Pw   þe] om. F C R   whi] that add. Pw G   had] iacob (ins. in
rubrics)add. Har⁵   first] or rather add. Pw G   chyldren] om. Har²   mayden]
mayde R; Bala add. F   10 þof] of Kk Har²; om. Har⁵ C R   al] om.
Ar F Pw G W Ii; ȝif C R; if add. Har⁵   a] om. F   11 of] the add. Pw
it] om. F R G W   sweet] and gude add. Har²; for add. Ar F C R Pw G W Ii
12 holde] beholde F   on] of Kk Har² Har⁵ F C R W Ii   &] on add. Pw G
in] the add. F Pw G W Ii   13 Rachel] is vnderstand add. Har⁵ R   so] to
Ar   mayden] mayde Pw   mayden] is Har⁵ F C R   14 it] om. Har²   15 on]
om. G W Ii   in] on Ar F C R Pw G W Ii   in . . . be] watso þa be Har⁵
so] þt R ; om. Pw   ȝe] ȝa Kk Har² C ; so R   ȝe . . . be] om. Pw G W Ii
ȝif] þowȝe F; þouȝt Ar   16 is] be R   17 for] om. Ar   þink] on add. Kk
Har² Ar C R Pw G W Ii; of add. Har⁵ F   þis] þe Group B   And] om.
W Ii   for-þi] þerfore Ar Pw   -þi] that F; whi Ii   18 þees] þire Kk Har²   to]
at Kk Har²   19 peynes] pynes R; þat is add. Ii   19–24/1 peynes . . . speed-
ful] nedfulle þinges F   19 Nept.] is to sey add. R   siȝt] liȝt Ii   joies] ioy Har⁵

Þees two children ben ful needful, & also speedful vnto a worching soule, þe tone for to put doun alle sogestyons of synnes, & þe
toþer to rere up oure wille in worching of good, & in kyndeling of
oure desire. For as it falliþ to Dan to put doune yuel sogestyons of
5 synne by si3t of peynes to come, so it falliþ to þe toþer broþer,
Neptalym, to reyse up oure willes in worching of good, & in
kyndelyng of holy desires by þe si3t of ioies to come. And þerfore
holy men whan þei ben sterid to any vnleueful þing, be it in rising
of any foule þou3t, als sone þei set before here mynde þe peynes
10 þat ben to come, & so þei sleckyn here temptacioun in þe begynnyng, er it rise in any foule delite in þeire soule. And as ofte as þeire
deuocioun and þeire likyng in God & goostly þinges cesen & waxen
colde (as oft-tymes it befalliþ in þis liif for corupcioun of flesche
& many oþer skyles) : soo oft þei set before þeire mynde þe ioie þat
15 is to come. And so þei kyndelen here wille wiþ holy desires, &

1 þees] There Kk, Þir Har²   ful] right G   & . . .speedful] *om.* C R
also] *om.* Har⁵ ; full Pw W Ii ; right G   vnto] to Ar Har⁵ Pw W Ii   a]
om. C   worching] werk and C   2 þe] *om.* F ; þat C R G W   tone]
oon F C R Pw G W   for] *om.* Ar Har⁵ R Pw G W Ii   to put] putteth Pw
alle] yuel Ar C R Pw G W Ii ; ille Har⁵ F   synnes] synne Ar F C R Pw G
W Ii   2–5 & . . . synne] *om.* Har⁵   2 &] *om.* F   2–3 þe toþer] þat oþer C
R Pw G W   3 to] *om.* Pw   rere] rayse Har² F C R G W Ii ; reysoune
Ar ; rayseth Pw   wille] welthe Pw   in] to *add.* Ar   good] dedys *add.*
F ; thynges *add.* Pw ; werkes *add.* Ii   in] *om.* Ii   4 yuel] ille Har² F
5 peynes] payne Har⁵ ; þat is *add.* Har⁵   þe toþer broþer] *om.* Ar   þe
toþer] þat oþer C R Pw G W Ii   6 Neptalym] for *add.* Group B   willes]
welthes Pw   of] *om.* Pw   good] dedys *add.* F   (&) in] *om.* R ; to G
7 of] *om.* R   holy] oure Har² Ar R ; *ins.* Har⁵   desires] desire R
þe] *om.* Ar Har⁵ Pw G W Ii   ioies] ioye Ar Har⁵ ; þat is *add.* Har⁵
8 whan] þat *add.* Ar   to] tyl Kk   any] *om.* Har⁵   vnleueful] vnlefulle
Kk Har⁵ F C G W Ii ; vnlawfull Pw   þing] þinges Har² Ar Har⁵ Pw G
W Ii   be it] by Ar Har⁵ F R   it] *om.* C Ii   in] *ins.* Har² ; *om.* F C W
Ii   rising] reisyng G ; entryng F   9 foule] fulle Kk ; foole C ; vnleful
Ii   sone] ofte (often Ii) Group B ; as *add.* Pw   þei set] *trs.* R   here]
i3en *add.* W Ii   mynde] of *add.* W Ii   þe] *om.* W Ii   10 ben] for *add.* W
þei] *om.* F C   sleckyn] slokyn Kk Har² C, slake(n) Ar F W Ii ; scloknen
Har⁵ ; quenchen G ; schal aslake R ; sleke Pw   temptacioun] temptacions
R   11 er] or Kk Har² Har⁵ F R Pw G W Ii   rise] come Har⁵   in] to Ar
Har⁵ F C R Pw W Ii ; vnto G   foule] defoule *add.* Har²   þeire] þe Ii
soule] soules G   ofte] often Ii   12 likyng] lykynges Pw G   God]
good Ii   &] in *add.* Har⁵   13 as] for R   oft-] often C R Pw   -tymes]
in þis lyfe *add.* Group B   be-] *om.* Group B ; so (*ins.*) *add.* R   in . . . liif]
om. Group B   for] the *add.* F   of] þe *add.* Har² Ar Har⁵ F Pw Ii   14
skyles] & *add.* R   soo] als Kk Har² Ar Har⁵ F C Pw W Ii   oft] often
Pw Ii   ioie] peynes Ar   15 is] ben Ar   kyndelen] kyndeld Har⁵   wille]
wylles Ar   desires] desire Har⁵

distroyen | þeire temptacioun in þe biginnyng, er it come to any f. 115a
werynes or heuynes of slewþe.

And for-þi þat wiþ Dan we dampne alle vnleueful þouȝtes, þerfore he is wel clepid in þe story *dome*. And also his fader, Jacob,
seide of hym þus: 'Dan schal deme his folk.' And also it is 5
seyde in þe story þat when Bala brouȝt forþ Dan, Rachel seide
þus: 'Oure Lorde haþ demed me.' Þat is to sey: 'Oure Lorde haþ
euenyd me vnto my sister, Lya.' And þus seiþ reson when þe
ymagynacioun haþ geten þe siȝt of peyne to come, þat oure Lorde
haþ euenyd hir wiþ hir sistre, affeccioun. And sche seide þus, for 10
sche had þe siȝt of peynes to come in hir ymagynacioun, of þe
whiche sche had drede & sorow in hir felyng. And þan come Neptalym, þat is to sey: þe siȝt of ioies to come. And in his birþe spak
Rachel and seyde: 'I am maad liche to myn sistre, Lya.' And for-
þi is Neptalym clepid in þe story *lyknes*. And þus seiþ reson þat sche 15
is liche to hir sistre, affeccioun, for þere sche had hope & loue of
ioye to come in hir felyng, scho haþ getyn siȝt of ioie to come in
hir ymagynacioun. Jacob seide of Neptalym þat he was an hert,

---

1 tempt.] temptacions Ar R Pw G   er] or Kk Har² Har⁵ F R Pw G W Ii
to any] *om*. C   2 werynes] hirkyng Har⁵ F C R Pw G W Ii   3 forþi] *om*.
Ar ; for F ; for þys, s *ins*. R ; therfore Pw   þat] *om*. Har⁵   wiþ Dan] *om*.
F   dampne] wt Dan *add*. F   alle] *om*. Kk Har² Group B ; mone Har⁵   4
he is] *trs*. Har⁵ F C R G   he] it Pw   clepid] calde Har⁵ F C R Pw G W Ii
dome] or Jugement *add*. Pw   And] *om*. F   5 seide] þan *add*. Ar   of]
to Ii   þus] Dan iudicabit populum suum *add*. F   folk] peple F   And]
om. F   6 þat] *om*. Har⁵ F C R   Rachel] than *add*. Pw   seide] þan
add. Ar F C R G W Ii   7 þus] *om*. Har⁵ ; Judicauit mihi dominus *add*. F
to] at Kk Har² Ar   8 euenyd] even C   me] and made me equall *add*.
Pw   vnto] to Ar F R Pw G W Ii ; with Har⁵   sister] sustyr F C R G   reson]
om. Har²   þe] *om*. Ar   9 þe] *om*. F C R W Ii   peyne] pyne Kk Har² ;
peynes Ar F C R Pw G W Ii ; þat is *add*. Har⁵   10 wiþ] to F   sistre]
suster Kk F C R G   And] þus *add*. Har⁵   þus] *om*. Har⁵   11 þe]
om. Ar Har⁵   siȝt] syhtys R   of] þe *add*. Ar G W Ii   peynes] payne (*ins*.)
Har⁵   to come] *om*. Kk Har² Group B   ymagynacioun] ymagynaciouns
R   12 þan] *om*. Kk ; after *add*. Group B   13 to] at Kk Har²   to sey] *om*.
F C R   þe] *om*. Group B   ioies] pese Har⁵ ; þat is *add*. Har⁵   come]
comes Har⁵   14 maad] meked Kk ; maked Har² ; *om*. Ii   to] vnto Pw
sistre] suster Kk F C R G   for-þi] þerfore Ar C R Pw ; for þt F   15 clepid]
om. Ar Pw G W Ii ; cald Har⁵ F C R   story] cleput *add*. Ar ; called *add*.
Pw G W Ii   16 is] made *add*. Har⁵   to] *om*. G   sistre] suster Kk
F C R G   þere] were Har⁵ ; þat W Ii ; as *add*. Pw   had] bothe *add*. Har²,̣ ;
getyn *add*. Har⁵   of] & W Ii   17 in] to R   felyng] And *add*. Kk Har²
scho] sho, c *ins*. Har¹   haþ] hade Har⁵ ; nowe *add*. Pw   18 Nept.] thus.
Neptalim ceruus emissus dans eloquia pulcritudinis *add*. F   þat he was]
Neptalim ys F   an] a Har⁵ W

sent oute, ȝeuyng speches of fairheed. So it is when we ymagyn
of þe joies of heuen. We seyen þat it is feyre in heuen. For wonderfuly kyndelyþ Neptalym oure soules wiþ holy desires, as oft as we
ymagyn of þe worþines & þe faireheed of þe joyes of heuen.

5 HOW þE VERTEWES OF ABSTYNENCE & PACYENCE RISEN IN þE SENSUALITE

When Lya sawe þat Rachel, hir sistre, maad greet joie of þees
two bastardes borne of Bala, hir mayden, sche ·clepid forþ hir
mayden, Zelfa, to put to hir housbonde, þat sche miȝt make joie
10 wiþ hir sistre, hauyng oþer two bastardes getyn of hir mayden,
Zelfa. And þus it is semely in a mans soule for to be, þat fro þe
f. 115b tyme | þat reson haue refreinid þe greet jangelyng of þe ymagyna-
cioun, & haþ put hir to be vnderloute to God, & makiþ hir to
bere sum frute in helpyng of hir knowyng, þat riȝt so þe affeccioun
15 refreyne þe lust & þe þrist of sensualyte, and make hir to be vnderloute to God, & so to bere sum frute in helpyng of hir felyng.

Bot what frute may sche bere, ouȝt bot lerne to lyue atem-

---

1 oute] *om.* Har²; of *add.* W Ii   speches] speche Ar Pw G W Ii   -heed] -hode
Har²; -nes F   is] þat *add.* Ar Har⁵ C R Pw G W Ii   2 it] þare Kk Har² Har⁵
F C R Pw G W   is] be F   feyre] thynges *add.* F   For] ful Har⁵   3 soules]
soule Kk Har² Group B   holy] *om.* R; hol C   desires] desyre Ar Har⁵ C R
Pw G W Ii; and *add.* C   4 & þe fairheed] *om.* C   þe] *om.* F   fairheed]
beautye Pw   -heed] -hode Kk Har²; -nes F G   5–6 *No chapter heading* F C R;
Here it is to say of doubulle syght in ymaginacion Har⁵ (*see* 22/5)   5 þe]
doble *add.* Kk Har² Ar G W Ii   þe … of] *om.* Pw   vertewes] wertew Kk·
Har² Ar G W Ii   risen] ryseþ Kk Har² Pw G W Ii   7 When] Han Pw   sawe]
siȝe W, saiȝe Ii   sistre] suster Kk F C R G   8 mayden] maide Ii   clepid] cald
Har⁵ F C R Pw G W Ii   9 mayden] mayde F   put] hir *add.* F C R Ii   to]
vnto G   housbonde] Jacob *add.* Group B   10 sistre] suster Kk F C R
G   getyn] goten F Pw G   mayden] mayde F   11 a] *om.* Ar F C R Pw
W Ii   fro] from Pw   12 refreinid] restreyned Ii   (of) þe] *om.* Group B
13 &] also *add.* Har²; so *add.* Ar   haþ] *om.* Ii   put] puttude Har⁵, puttide
W   be] *om.* R   vnderloute] subdwed F   &] also *add.* Har²; so *add.* Group B
makiþ] to make Ar Pw G W Ii; make F; (to R) do C R   makiþ hir] *om.*
Har⁵   to] *om.* Ar F C R Pw G W, *ins.* Ii   14 frute] profyte Ar W Ii
þat] *om.* F Har⁵   so] þt *add.* Har⁵   15 refreyne] refreneþ Kk Ar F G; res-
seyueþ W Ii   &] in F C   þe] *om.* F   þrist] þrust C; furst Ii   of] þe
add. Group B   16 -loute] -lowed F   so] for *add.* F C R   17 may] schal Ii
bot] to *add.* Kk Har²; þat (*om.* R) scho *add.* Ar Har⁵ F C R Pw G W Ii
lerne] *ins. in left margin* Har¹; lere Kk Har² G W Ii; *om.* Har⁵ F C R   to]
om. Har⁵ F C R   atempereely] temperaly Ar; atempere, ly *ins.* Har⁵;
temperatly F Pw G W Ii; a tempre C R

pereely in esy þinges, and pacyently in vnesy þinges? Þees ben
þei, þe children of Zelfa, Gad & Asser. Gad is abstynence, & Asser
is pacyence. Gad is þe sonner borne childe, and Asser þe latter; for
first it nediþ þat we be attemperid in oure self wiþ discrete abstynence, and after þat to bere outward disese in streng of pacyence. 5
Þees ben þe children þat Zelfa brouȝt forþe in sorow, for in abstynence & pacyence þe sensualite is greetly ponyschid in þe flesche.

Bot þat þat is sorow to þe sensualyte turneþ to moche joie
and blis to þe affeccioun. Þerfore it is þat when Gad was borne
Lya cried and seyde: 'Happely.' And for-þi Gad is clepid in þe 10
story *happynes* or *selynes*, wheþer þou wilt. And so it is wel seyde
þat abstynence in þe sensualite is selynes in þe affeccioun. For whi
euer þe les þat þe sensualite is delityd in hir lust, þe more swetnes
feliþ affeccioun in hir loue. Also after whan Asser was borne,
Lya seide: 'Þis schal be for my blis.' And for-þi was Asser 15
clepid in þe story *blissidheed*. And so it is wel seyde þat pacyence in þe sensualite is blis in þe affeccioun. For whi euer þe more

1 esy] nesche Ar; prosperite & welthfulle F; erþely W Ii　　vnesy]
vnnesche Ar; aduersite & in vnwelthfulle F　　ben] ay *add*. Kk
2 þei] *om*. Ar Har⁵ F R G W Ii　　(abst.) &] *om*. Kk Har² Group B
3 þe] *om*. Har⁵　　sonner] raþer Ar F C R; titter Har⁵　　childe]
om. Har⁵ F C R　　Asser] is *add*. Ar Pw G W Ii　　þe] *om*. Har⁵ Ii　　latter]
latere Kk Ar Ii　　4 nediþ] is nedefulle F　　attemperid] attemptyd F
C; temperid Ii　　wiþ] by F C R　　5 and] þt Har⁵　　after] -ward *add*. W Ii
þat] *om*. Har⁵　　to] we Kk Har² Ar Har⁵ F C Pw G W Ii　　bere] were Har²
disese] dysesis F C　　in] be R　　streng] strenþe (þ *erased* Har²)
Har² Group B; strenght Har⁵　　6 þees] Thyre Kk Har²　　þat]
of Har² Pw　　Zelfa] þat scho *add*. Har²　　7 is] *om*. Ii　　greetly] *om*.
Ar F C R Pw G W Ii　　7–8 greetly . . . sensualyte] *om*. Har⁵　　ponyschid]
pyned Har²; punecheþ Ii　　8 þat] thilke G　　þat] at C　　to] of Pw
turneþ] torned Har⁵　　joie] comforth Kk Har² Group B (comforthed
Har⁵)　　9 þe] *om*. R　　affeccioun] and *add*. Ar Har⁵ F C R Pw G
W Ii　　is] was Ar F C R Pw G W Ii　　þat] *om*. Ii　　10–11 Happely . . .
story] *om*. Ar　　10 Happely] Feliciter. happy or blessidly F　　for-þi] for þat
F; þerfore C R Pw; in þe story *add*. F　　Gad is] *trs*. Har⁵ F C R W Ii
clepid] cald Har⁵ F C R Pw G W Ii　　10–11 in þe story] *om*. Har⁵ F　　11
happynes] hapnes W　　or *selynes* . . . wilt] *om*. F C R Pw　　wheþer . . . wilt]
om. Har⁵　　is] *om*. Har²　　12 þe] *om*. Har²　　selynes] happynes F C R Pw
whi] *om*. F ,　　13 euer] ay Kk Har² Har⁵ G W　　þat] *om*. Kk　　14
feliþ affeccioun] *trs*. Ar　　feliþ] þe *add*. Kk Har² Har⁵ F C R Pw G W Ii
loue] lust Ar Pw G W Ii; lyf C R　　after whan] *trs. but corrected* Har¹　　whan]
om. C　　15 seide] thus. Hoc quoque pro beatitudine mea *add*. F　　for-þi]
þerfore Ar C R Pw; for þat F　　was] *om*. Ar　　Asser] is *add*. Ar; was *add*. F
16 clepid] calde Har⁵ F C R Pw G W Ii　　*blissid*-] blessid F C Pw G W Ii
-heed] -hode Kk Har²; *om*. Group B　　so] *om*. Pw　　is] *om*. Har²; whas Ii
wel] *om*. F C R　　17 þe] *om*. Har²　　whi] *om*. F　　euer] ay Kk Har² Har⁵ G W

disese þat sensualyte suffreþ, þe more blessid is þe soule in þe affeccioun.

And by abstynence & pacyence we schul not onliche vnder-stonde attemperaunce in mete and drynke, & suffring in outward
5 tribulacioun, bot also al maner of fleschly, & kyndely, & wordly delices, & al maner of disese, bodely & goostly, wiþinne or wiþ-

f. 116*a* outen, resonable | or vnresonable, þat by any maner of oure fyue wittys turmenten or delyten þe sensualyte. On þis wise bereþ þe sensualite frute in helpe of affeccioun, hir lady. Moche pees &
10 rest is in þe soule þat nowþer is drounyd in þe lust of sensualyte, ne gruchid in þe pyne þerof. Þe first of þees is getyn by Gad, and þe latter by Asser.

Here it is to wetyn þat first was Rachelle mayden put to þe housbond or þe mayden of Lya. And þis is þe skyle whi. For
15 trewly bot ʒif þe jangelyng of þe ymagynacioun, þat is to sey þe inrennyng of veyne þouʒtes, be first refreynyd, wiþoute doute þe lust of þe sensualyte may not be attemperid. And þerfore whoso wil absteyne hym from fleschly and wordly lustes, hym behouiþ seeldom or neuir þink any veyne þouʒtes. And þerfore neuer in

1 þat] þe *add.* Har² Harˢ F C R Pw G W Ii   blessid] blyssed Kk Har²
Harˢ R   3 And] þus *add.* Group B   abstynence] abstyinence Har¹
4 attemp.] temperans F   in] *om.* C   in] of Kk Har² Group B   5
trib.] tribulacions F C R   also] of *add.* Harˢ   of] *om.* Harˢ R   &] *om.*
Group B   6 delices] delytes Kk Har² Ar F C Pw G; delite Harˢ   of]
om. Harˢ F C R   disese] deseases Kk Har² F C R   &] or Ar Harˢ F C R Pw
G W   7 resonable] resonably Ar Pw G W Ii   or vnres.] *om.* R   vn-
resonable] vnresonably Ar Pw G W Ii   maner] *om.* Ar Harˢ F C R Pw
G W Ii   fyue] *om.* Harˢ   8 delyten] in *add.* Pw   þe] in *add.* G
bereþ] berieþ C   9 þe] *om.* Pw   in] wt F; and C   of] þe *add.* Ar F   affec-
cioun] on *add.* C   9–10 pees—rest] *trs.* F   10 þe] þat Ar Harˢ F C R Pw
G W   nowþer] neyther F R G   drounyd] drounkned Kk Har²; drounk-
e(n) Group B   þe] *om.* Ar Pw G W Ii   lust] luf Harˢ   of] þe (*ins.* Har²)
add. Har² F C R Pw G W Ii   11 ne] nor Pw   gruchid] grutcheþ Ar F R Pw
W Ii; crutched Harˢ   pyne] peyne Ar Harˢ F Pw G W; peynes Ii   pees] þer
Kk; þises C   getyn] gotyn F Pw G   12 latter] later Ar Harˢ Ii   13 Rachelle]
h *ins.* Har¹   mayden] mayde F R   13–14 put ... housbond] *om.* F   þe] *om.*
C R   14 or] er Ar F C W; than Pw   mayden] mayde F R   þis ... whi] for
þis skille Harˢ   skyle] reson F   15 ʒif] *om.* Harˢ Ii   (of) þe] *om.* Kk Har²
Ar Harˢ C R Pw G W Ii   to] at Kk Har²   þe in-] in the Pw   16 inrennyng]
murmuryng Har² Ii; chyrmyng F   17 be] *om.* Ii   attemperid] tem-
peryd F Ii   -so] þat R   18 from] fro Kk Har² Ar Harˢ F C G W Ii
fleschly ... wordly] *trs.* F C R   and wordly] *om.* Ii   lustes] lust Kk Har²
Ar Harˢ F C Pw G W Ii; & wordly lust *add.* Ii   behouiþ] fyrst *add.* Ar
Harˢ Pw G W Ii   19 þouʒtes] thoght Harˢ; at þe leest wyllyngly *add.*
Pw   And] *om.* F   þerfore] also Kk Har² Group B

þis liif may a man parfytely dispise þe ese of þe flesche & not drede
þe disese, bot he haue before besyli beholden þe medes & þe tour-
mentes þat ben to come.

Bot here it is to witen how þat wiþ þees foure sones of þees
two maydens, þe cite of oure concyence is kepte wonderfuly from 5
alle temptaciouns. For alle temptacyon ouþer it riseþ wiþinne by
þou3t, or elles wiþouten by somme of oure fyue wittys. Bot
wiþinne schal Dan deme and dampne yuel þou3tes by si3t of
pyne, & wiþouten schal Gad put a3eyn fals delices by vse of
abstynence. Dan wakiþ wiþinne, and Gad withouten. And also 10
þees oþer two breþren helpen hem ful mochel. Neptalym makiþ
pees withinne wiþ Dan, and Asser biddeþ Gad haue no drede of his
enmyes. Dan feriþ þe hert with horribilite of helle, and Neptalym
cherischiþ it wiþ hetyng of heuenly blis. Also Asser helpiþ his
broþer wiþouten, so þat þorow hem boþe þe cytee walles ben not 15
brokyn. Gad holdeþ oute ese, and Asser pursueþ | diseese. Asser f. 116b
sone deceyuiþ his enemye when he bringiþ to mynde þe pacyence

---

1 þis] hys Ar 2 bot] 3if *add.* Ar Har⁵ F C R Pw G haue
before] *trs.* Ar F C R Pw G W Ii before] *om.* Har⁵ (&) þe] *om.* Har⁵
tourmentes] paynes Har⁵; turnementes C 3 ben] for *add.* W Ii 4
þat] *om.* Kk Har² Har⁵ F C R wiþ] by (*ins.* Ar) Ar G W Ii; *om.* Pw þees]
þere Kk, þir Har² sones] sone R þees] þere Kk, þir Har² 5 mayd-
ens] kepeth wonderfully *add.* Pw is . . . wonderfuly] *om.* Pw kepte
wonderfuly] *trs.* F C R wonder-] wordyr- Kk from] fro Kk Har² Ar Har⁵
R C 5–6 from . . . temptaciouns] *om.* W Ii 6 tempt.] temptacioun Kk
Har² Har⁵ F alle] ilk Har⁵ temptacyon] temptacions C R Pw G W Ii
ouþer] eyther Pw G W it] þei C R Pw G W Ii 7 or] oþer R
8 dampne] dempne C yuel] ille Har² Har⁵; alle ylle F by] þe
add. F si3t] drede Har⁵ of] þe *add.* Har² 9 pyne] peyne Kk Har² Ar
Har⁵ Pw G W Ii; peynes F C R; to come *add.* Har² a3eyn] awey
F C R W Ii; downe Pw; ayenst G delices] delyttes Har² Ar Har⁵ F C R Pw
G vse] vsynge Ar 10 Gad] wakeþ *add.* Ar F C Pw G W Ii And]
om. C 11 þees] þeire Kk Har² Har⁵ Pw, hir Ar G W Ii; the F C R oþer]
om. Ar breþren] breþire Kk Har² Har⁵ mochel] mekely R; wel G
12 wiþ] *om.* Pw 12–13 Asser . . . Dan] *om.* F biddeþ] bedeþ C 13 fer-
iþ] flays Har⁵; frayeth F; driueþ C R; stireþ W Ii with] the *add.* F Ii
horribilite] oglynes Ar F Pw; vgsomnes Har⁵; horibilnesse C R; hidousnesse
G W Ii helle] paynes *add.* Pw 14 cherischiþ] chereþ Kk Har²; com-
fordeþ Ar; cheris, ses *written above* Har⁵; cleryth F C R Pw G W Ii wiþ]
the *add.* F Ii hetyng] hetynges Har⁵; promysse F Pw; or behyghtynge
add. Pw heuenly] heuen W Ii Also] & Ii 15 cytee] *om.* Pw
walles] walle Kk Har² Ar Har⁵ C R Pw G W Ii; of þe cyte *add.* Pw
ben] is Kk Har² Ar Har⁵ C R Pw G W Ii 15–16 not brokyn] kepte
vnbroke F C R 16 Asser] Asseres Ar pursueþ] pursuit C 17
deceyuiþ] dysesyth F

of his [parte], & þe behetyng of Neptalým. And þus oft-tymes euer
þe moo enmyes he haþ, þe more mater he haþ of ouercomyng. And
þerfore it is þat when he haþ ouercomen his enemyes, þat is to sey
þe aduersitees of þis woreld, sone he turneþ hym to his broþer Gad
5 to helpe to distroye his enemyes. And wiþoutyn faile, fro þat he be
comen, sone þei torne þe bak & fleen. Þe enemyes of Gad ben fleschly
delites. Bot trewly fro þe tyme þat a man haue pacyence in þe pyne
of his abstynence, fals delites fynden no wonyng stede in hym.

HOW IOY OF INWARD SUETNES RISIþ IN þE AFFECCIOUN

10   Þus, when þe enemyes fleen & þe cyte is pesid, þan proueþ a
man what þe hiȝe pees of God is, þat passeþ alle mans wit. And
for-þi it is þat Lya left beryng of children tyl þe tyme þat Gad
& Asser weren borne of Zelfa, hir mayden. For trewly, bot ȝif it be
so þat man haue refreinyd þe lust & þe pyne of his fyue wittys in
15 his sensualite by abstynence & pacyence, he schal neuir fele inward swetnes & trewe joie in God & goostly þinges in þe affeccioun.
Þis is þat Isachar, þe [fifþe] sone of Lya, þe whiche in þe story is
clepid *mede*.

1 parte] fader Har¹ Kk Har² Group B; *can.*, broder *written above* Kk.
See Note   þe] he Kk   be-] *om.* Ar Har⁵ C R G W Ii   -het-]-hyȝt- Pw
oft-] often G Ii   tymes] *om.* Pw   euer] ay Har⁵ G W   2 þe] *om.*
R   moo] more C R Ii   enmyes] þat *add.* Har⁵   more] *ins. in left
margin* Har¹, *ins.* Har⁵   he] *om.* W   of ouercomyng] to euercome his
enemyes Pw   2–3 And . . . enemyes] *om.* Pw   3 his] here R
to] at Kk Har²   4 þis] þe Ar Har⁵ F C R   5 to helpe] & helpiþ
hym Ar; hym *add.* F C R   distroye] stroy Har⁵   fro] after Ar;
whan R   þat] *om.* Kk Har² Har⁵ F C R G W Ii   be] is (*ins.*) R   6 þe]
om. Har⁵; her F   bak] backes F   þe] þere Har⁵; Thei G   ben] þe *add.*
Kk Har²   7 delites] delices C W   haue] haþe Kk F   pyne] peyne
Ar Har⁵ F Pw Ii; tyme C R G   8 delites] delyte Ar Har⁵ Pw G W Ii
wonyng] dwellyng F Pw Ii   stede] stude Ar; place Har⁵ F C R Pw G Ii
9 How] Here it is to sey howe F C R; the *add.* F W Ii (*ins.* Ii)   ioy] *om.*
C   þe] a mans Har⁵ F C R; *om.* G   affeccioun] saul Har⁵   10 cyte]
of conscience *add.* Har⁵   pesid] made pesebule Har⁵ F C R   proueþ]
bygynneþ Group B   11 man] to proue *add.* Group B; here *add.* G
what] that *add.* Pw   þe] þat Ar F C R G   hiȝe pees] philipens ₄ *added
in rubrics in left margin* Har¹   hiȝe] *om.* Pw G   pees] is *add.* Ii   is] *om.*
Ii   alle] *om.* Pw   12 for-þi] þerfore Ar C R Pw; for þat F   tyl] to
Kk Har²; vnto Group B   þe] þis Ar Har⁵ C R Pw G   13 mayden] mayde F
14 þat] a *add.* Har² Har⁵ F C R   refreinyd] restreyned Ii   & þe pyne]
om. Har⁵   &] of Ar G W Ii   pyne] peyne Ar F Pw G W Ii   15 his] the Pw
fele inward] *trs.* Ar G W   16 trewe] turne G   17 is] it (*can.*) *add.* Har¹;
he *add.* C   þat] he þilke Ar; *om.* Har⁵ F R Ii; he that hyght Pw F; he G
fifþe] first Har¹ Kk Har² (r *partly erased* Har²) F C Ii; fifte Har⁵ Pw G; fyueþ
W   þe] *om.* F W Ii   þe] *om.* Har⁵   18 clepid] cald Har⁵ F C R Pw G W Ii

And wele is þis ioie of inward swetnes clepid mede; for þis joie is þe taast of heuenly blis, þe whiche is þe eendeles mede of a deuoute soule begynnyng here. Lya in þe birþe of þis childe seyde: 'God haþ ȝouen me mede, for þat I haue ȝouen my mayden to myn housbonde in beryng of children.' And so it is good for-þi þat we 5 make oure sensualite bere frute in abstynence of it fro alle maner fleschly and wordly [ese, and in fruteful suffryng of alle fleschly and wordly] disese, for-þi oure Lorde of his greet mercy ȝeueþ us joie vnspekable & inward swetnes in oure affeccioun, in erles of þe souereyn ioie and mede of þe hiȝe kyngdome | of heuen.   10 f. 117*a*

Jacob seide of Isachar þat he was a stronge asse, dwellyng bitwix þe teermes. And so it is þat a man dwellyng in þis state, & þat feliþ þe erles of þat lastyng joie in his affeccioun, is as an asse, stronge & dwellyng bytwix þe teermes, for-þi þat be he neuer so fylled in soule of goostly gladnes and joie in God, ȝit for corupcioun 15

1 And . . . mede] *ins. at top of column* Har¹; *om.* Ar Har⁵; *ins. in right margin* Ii   swetnes] þat *add.* R   clepid] cald Har⁵ F C R Pw G W Ii   þis] *om.* Har⁵   joie] þat (*ins.*) *add.* Har⁵   2 is] in (*ins.*) *add.* Har⁵   of] þe (*ins.* Har⁵) *add.* Har⁵ F C R   heuenly] heuely Har²; heuene Ar Pw G W Ii   heuenly blis] blise of hewen Har⁵ F C R; *of add.* G   þe . . . mede] þis inward swetenes for þis is þe inwarde mede Ar   þe²] *om.* F   þe³] *om.* Har⁵ W Ii   3 seyde] Dedit deus mercedem mihi *add.* F   4 me] *om.* C Ii   for] þi *add.* Har⁵ C G W Ii; bycause Pw; þis *add.* R   mayden] mayde F   5 children] childrynge Ar   good] *om.* Group B   for-þi] for Ar; *om.* Har⁵ F; þerfore C R; bycause Pw   6 make] gare Kk Har², gere Har⁵   oure] *om.* F   sensualite] sensualitees W   bere] berynge Ar   in] of Kk Har²   abstynence] abstenynge Group B   of it fro] and pacyence in Kk Har²   of] *om.* Ar Har⁵ F Pw G W Ii   fro] from F Pw G Ii   maner] of *add.* Kk Group B   7 fleschly] of *add.* Ar; (& *add.* R) kyndely *add.* Group B   ese and] *om.* Har¹   ese] delyte Ar Har⁵ C R Pw G W Ii; delytes F   7–8 in fruteful . . . wordly] *om.* Har¹ Kk Har². *See Note*   of] & R   8 disese] disesys F   for-þi] so þat Kk Har²; For F; þerfore C R; wherfore Pw   greet] *om.* Ar   joie] of *add.* Har⁵   9 erles] ernes Ar F G W; tokenynge C R; ernest Pw Ii   10 and] þe *add.* Har⁵   of] *can.*, in *ins.* Kk   hiȝe] *om.* Group B   heuen] whiche is to come *add.* Pw   11 of] Isakar thus *add.* F   Isachar] asinus fortis accubans inter terminos. Isaker *add.* F   þat he] *om.* F   he] *ins.* R   was] is F   a] asse C   a] alle] *om.* bitwix] betwyn F Pw G W Ii   dwellyng] *om.* Ar Har⁵ F C R Pw G W Ii   state] astate Ar   &] *om.* F C R W Ii   13 þat] *om.* R   erles] ernes Ar F G W; gladnes C R; ernest Pw Ii   þat] euer Ar F C R Pw G W Ii; euer *add.* Har²; ay *add.* Har⁵   is] *om.* C R   asse] & *add.* Ar G   13–14 asse stronge] *trs.* F   14 &] *om.* F W Ii   bytwix] betweyn Har⁵ F Pw G W Ii   for-þi . . . neuer] for he þat byholdiþ Ar   for-þi . . . so] þerfor ȝif he be euer R   for-þi] For thouȝe F; þerfore C; thoughe Pw   þat] *om.* F; ȝif C   be he] *trs.* F C Pw Ii   so] *om.* F C; so *add.* Har²; ful- *add.* Ii   15 in] his *add.* F   soule of] *om.* Har⁵   of] þe *add.* Har² Pw; wiþ F R   for] þe *add.* F

of flesche in þis deedly liif hym behoueþ bere þe charge of þe
deedly body, as hungre, þrist, & colde, and oþer many diseses.
For þe whiche he is licnyd to an asse as in body. Bot as in soule
he is stronge for to distroie alle passyons & lustes of þe flesche by
5 pacyence and abstynence in hys sensualyte, and by aboundaunce
of goostly joie & swetnes in þe affeccyon. And also a soule in þis
state is dwellyng bitwix þe teermes of deedly liif and vndeedly
liif. He þat dwelliþ bitwix þe teermes haþ niʒhonde forsaken deedlynes, bot not fully; & haþ niʒhond getyn vndeedlynes, bot not
10 fully. For whiles þat him nedeþ þe goodes of þis woreld, as mete &
drynk, cloþing, as it falliþ to iche a man þat leuiþ, ʒit his oo fote is
in þis deedly liif; and for greet habundaunce of goostly joie &
swetnes þat he feliþ in God—not seeldom, bot ofte—he haþ his
oþer foot in þe vndeedly liif. Þus I trowe þat Seinte Poule felt
15 whan he seyde þis worde of greet desyre: 'Who schal delyuer
me fro þis deedly body?'; and when he seide þus: 'I coueyte to be

1 of] þe *add.* Har² Har⁵ F Pw   hym] he Ar   behoueþ] mote Ar ; to *add.*
F Pw G Ii   þe²] þis Ar F C R Pw G W Ii   2 þrist] tryst Kk ; sclep
add. Har⁵   oþer many] *trs.* Ar Pw   oþer] diseses (*ins.*) *add.* R   diseses]
desesease Kk ; *om.* Ar Har⁵ F C R Pw W Ii ; moo G   3 whiche]
skyl *add.* Ar F C R Pw G W Ii   to] tylle Kk   as] *om.* Har⁵   4 for]
om. R   to] *om.* Ii   distroie] stroy Har⁵   alle] þe *add.* Group B   &] þe
add. Har⁵ ; alle þe *add.* Ii   &] of C R   lustes] lust Ar Pw G W Ii   5
and] in W   hys] þe Group B   6 And] *om.* F   a] the Pw G   7 state]
astate Ar   dwellyng] dwelled C ; dwellid (*can.*) *add.* R   bitwix] betwyn F
Pw G W Ii   vndeedly] euerlastyng Ar   8 liif] *om.* Har⁵ G ; And *add.* R
bitwix] betwyn F Pw G W Ii   þe] *om.* Kk Har² Ar Har⁵ Pw G ; þese R
niʒ-] nere Kk Har² Har⁵ F C R Pw W Ii   deedlynes] delynes Ar   9–
10 & . . . fully] *om.* R   9 niʒ-] nere Kk Har² Har⁵ F C Pw W Ii   getyn]
keten Ar   10 For] euere *add.* F; alwey *add.* C R   whiles] whil C R Pw
G W Ii   þat] *om.* Har⁵ ; he is here (*ins. in left margin*) *add.* Ii   him] he F
þe] *om.* Ar Ii   þis] þe Ii   woreld] lyfe Har²   &] or C ; *om.* G W
11 drynk] & *add.* Group B   cloþing] cleþing Kk Har⁵   it] *om.* Group B
iche] ilk Har⁵ ; euery F C R G   a] *om.* Ar F C R Pw G W Ii   his] *om.* Ar
C Pw G W Ii ; is Har⁵   oo] a Ar Har⁵ W Ii ; oon F C R Pw   is] *om.*
Har⁵   12 þis] the F   for] the *add.* F   of] in F C R   goostly] goodis &
gostly *add.* Ar   13 swetnes] in god (gode Har⁵, good Pw) *add.* Group
B   in God] *om.* Group B   ofte] tyme *add.* G   he] *om.* W Ii   14
felt] ferde *ins.* Har⁵   15 seyde] þus *add.* Har²   þis . . . desyre]
om. Har⁵   þis] thes F   worde] wordys F ; werlde C ; bywerke R   desyre]
Quis liberabit me de corpore mortis huius *add.* F   15–16 Who . . .] *The
reference is given in rubrics in the right margin of* Har¹   16 fro] from Ar
Pw ; of Har⁵   and] also *add.* Har² Pw   þus] Cupio dissolui & esse cum
Christo *add.* F   16–33/1 I coueyte . . .] *The reference is given in rubrics
in the right margin of* Har¹   I] he Ar W   coueyte] desyre F ; coueyted
Ar R W

lesid, & to be wiþ Criste.' And þus doþ þe soule þat feliþ Isachar in his affeccioun ; þat is to sey, þe joye of inward swetnes, þe whiche is vnderstonden by Isachar. It enforceþ it to forsake þis wrechid liif, bot it may not. It coueitiþ to entre þe blessid liif, bot it may not. It doþ þat it may, & ȝit it dwelliþ bitwix þe teermes. 5

HOW PARFITE HATE OF SYNNE RISEþ IN þE AFFECCYOUN |

And þerfore it is þat after Ysachar Zabulon is borne ; þat is to f. 117b sey, hateredyn of synne. And here it is to wetyn whi þat hatere- dyn of synne is neuir parfitely felt in mans affeccioun er þe tyme þat goostly joie of inward swetnes be felt in þe affeccioun. And þis 10 is þe skyle. For er þis tyme was neuer þe trewe cause of hatereden felt in þe affeccioun. For þe felyng of goostly ioie techiþ a man what synne harmiþ þe soule ; and after þe harme in a soule is felt, moche or lytyl, þerafter is þe hatereden mesurid vnto þe harmyng. Bot when a soule by þe grace of God & longe trauayle is comyn to 15 þe felyng of goostly joie in God, þan it feliþ þat synne haþ be þe cause of þe delaying þerof. And also whan he feliþ þat he may not

1 lesid] losed Ar Har⁵ F Pw G W Ii; or vnbounde *add.* Pw   to] *om.* F W Ii   þe] þe *add.* F   1–3 in . . . Isachar] *om.* W   2 affec- cioun] affeccions R   to] at Kk Har²   to sey] *om.* Ii   of] the *add.* F þe] *om.* F   3 It] þat R   it (to)] *om.* G   4 It . . . not] *om.* Ar F C R   blessid] blyssed Kk Har² Har⁵ Ii   5 þat] what Ar   ȝit] *om.* W Ii   it] *om.* R   bitwix] betwyn F Pw G W   6 How] Here it is to sey how F C R   parfite] *om.* Har⁵ C R; ordred F   hate] hattre- den Kk Har² Ar Har⁵ W; hatred F C R Pw G Ii   þe] a (*om.* Har⁵) mans Har⁵ F C R; *om.* G   affeccyoun] Zabuloun *add.* R   7 And] *om.* F C R   þer-] her- Ar Har⁵ F C W Ii   it is] *trs.* Ar Har⁵ G   after] þis *add.* Ar F C R W   Zab.] *om.* C R   borne] Zabuloun *add.* C   þat] þe whyche Kk Har² Ar Har⁵ C R G W Ii; whiche F   7–8 to sey] seyde F C R 8 hateredyn] hatred F R Pw G   synne] synnes F C R   here] herto W Ii it] *om.* W   to] say & *add.* Har⁵   whi] *om.* Pw   hat.] hatred F R Pw G W Ii   9 synne] sinnes C   is] and (also *add.* Ii) here it is to write þat hatereden (hatrade Ii) of synne is *add.* W Ii   neuir] nermore Har⁵   par- fitely] *om.* Group B   in] a *add.* Kk Har⁵ F C R Pw G W Ii   er] or Kk Har² Har⁵ F C R Pw G W Ii   þe] þat R   10 þat] of Ar G W Ii   joie of] and Pw   10–12 And . . . affeccioun] *om.* F C R   11 er] or Kk Har² Har⁵ G Pw Ii   hatereden] hatred Pw G Ii; of synn *add.* Har²   12 (For) þe] *om.* W Ii   13 harmiþ] and hurteth *add.* Pw   and] al *add.* Group B   after] as F; þat *add.* Ar Har⁵ C R Pw G W   harme] ys felte *add.* F C R Pw   a] þe Group B   is felt] *om.* F C R Pw   14 hatereden] hatred F Pw G Ii mesurid] more or less *add.* Har⁵   vnto] to Ar F C R   harmyng] harm F C R; harmand W Ii   15 þe] *om.* Ar Har⁵ Pw G W Ii   16 þe] *om.* Har⁵ G Ii   þan] þat Har⁵   synne] þat (*can.*) *add.* Har¹   þe] *om.* Ar F C R W Ii   17 þe] *om.* F Ii   And] *om.* F   also] als Har⁵   not] alwey *add.* Ar C R Pw G W Ii, always *add.* F

last in felyng of þat goostly joye for þe corupcioun of flesche,
of þe whiche corupcioun synne is þe cause, þan he riseþ wiþ
a stronge felynge of hateredyn aȝens alle synne & alle kynde
of synne. Þis felyng tauȝt Dauid us for to haue where he seiþ
5 in þe psalme: 'Wrappes, & willeþ not synne.' Or þus: 'Beeþ
wroþe, & synniþ not.' Þat is þus to mene: beeþ wroþe with þe
synne, bot not wiþ þe kynde; for kynde steriþ to dede, bot not
to synne.

And here it is to wyten þat þis wrappe & þis hatereden is not
10 co[n]trary to charite. Bot charite techiþ how it schal be had boþe
in a man self, & in his euen-Cristen. For a man schuld hate synne
in his kynde; and as anemste oure euyn-Cristen, us auȝt to hate
synne in hem, & to loue hem. And of þis hatereden spekiþ Dauid
in þe psalme where he seiþ þus: 'Wiþ parfite hateredyn I hatid

---

1 last] allway *add.* Har⁵   in] þe *add.* Group B   þat] *om.* Har⁵   þe]
om. Har⁵   of] þe *add.* Har² Group B   2 þe] *om.* F C R   þe] *om.* Ar
F C R   he riseþ] is he reysyd R   3 a] *om.* R   hateredyn] hatred F Pw
G Ii; hateredynge R   aȝens] aȝeyn Kk Har² Ar Har⁵ C W Ii, ayenst F R
Pw G   alle] *om.* Ar   &] in Pw G W Ii; in *add.* Ar   alle] þe Har⁵;
þe *add.* Ar   4 for] *om.* Group B   seiþ] seyde Ar Pw G W Ii   5 in þe
psalme] *om.* Har⁵   þe] þis Ii   psalme] *The reference is given in rubrics in
the right margin of* Har¹; Irascimini et nolite peccare *add.* Har² F; þat is *add.*
Har²   Wrappes] wraþe ȝe Ar G; bes wroth Har⁵; Waxe ye wrath F;
Wrethes ȝow C R; Be ye wrothe Pw; Wrappiþ W; Wrathid Ii   &] in R
willeþ] wylle Kk Har² F C R; wyl ȝe Ar Har⁵ Pw G W Ii   not] ye *add.* F
5–7 Or þus . . . bot not] *om.* Har⁵   5–6 Or þus . . . not] *om.* F C R
Pw   6 synniþ] synn Har²   þat] it *add.* Ii   þus] *om.* Ar F; for *add.* G   þus
to mene] *om.* C R   mene] sey F; bymene W Ii   beeþ] be ye F Pw; be C
þe] *om.* Ar; *ins. in right margin* Ii   7 bot] & Ar F C R   to] þe *add.* Kk
Har² Group B   dede] & noȝt *add.* Ar   8 to] þe *add.* Kk Har² F C R
Pw G W Ii   synne] not toye Har⁵   9 here] fore *add.* W Ii   þis] is C
wrappe] wreth C R   & . . . hatereden] *om.* Ar Har⁵   &] in G W Ii   þis]
his Ii   hatereden] hatred F Pw G F Ii   11 a] *om.* Kk Har²   man]
mans Har⁵; hym *add.* Kk Har² Ar F C R Pw G W Ii   schuld] schal R; noȝt
add. Ar Har⁵ F C Pw G W Ii   12 in his] so þat he dystroye (destroyd C
Pw G W; nat *add.* C R) his (his *om.* Ar) Group B   kynde] hynde Pw; but so
þat he dystroye (destroied G) þe synne & þe appetyte of (þe *add.* W) synne in
his kynde *add.* Ar C R Pw G W Ii   and] *om.* Kk   as] *om.* R; also G
anemste] anence Kk Har², anentes Ar Har⁵ W; to F; aȝens C, aȝenst R Pw;
anemptes Ii   us] we F C R Pw G   us auȝt] as how W Ii   auȝt] owȝeþ Ar;
ogh Har⁵, owe F C R   hate] þe *add.* F C R G   13 hem] hym Ar Har⁵
Pw G W Ii   &] for *add.* Ar   hem] hym Ar Har⁵ Pw G W Ii   hatereden]
hatred F C R Pw G Ii   14 þe] *om.* Kk   where he seiþ (þus *om.* Har⁵ F)]
om. F C R; & says Har⁵; Perfecto odio oderam illos *add.* Har² F; *The refer-
rence is given in rubrics in the right margin of* Har¹   hateredyn] hatred
F C R Pw G Ii

hem.' And in anoþer psalme he seiþ þat he had in hateredyn alle
wickyd wey.

Þus is wel prouid þat er Zabulon were borne, Judas & Ysachar
weren boþe borne. For bot ȝif a man haue had charite and goostly
joie in his felyng first, he may on nowise fele þis | parfite hateredyn 5 f. 118a
of synne in his affeccioun. For Judas, þat is to sey charite, techiþ
us how we schul hate synne in oureself, & in oure breþren. And
Isachar, þat is to sey goostly felyng of joie in God, techeþ whi we
schul hate synne. Judas biddeþ hate synne, & loue þe kynde; and
Isachar biddeþ us distroie þe synne, & saue þe kynde. And þus 10
it falleþ for to be þat þe kynde be maad stronge in God and in
goostly þinges by parfite hateredyn & distroying of synne.

And herfore is Zabulon clepid *a dwellyng stede of strengþe*
in þe story. And Lya seide in his birþe: 'My housbonde schal
dwelle wiþ me.' And so it is þat God, þat is þe trewe housbonde 15
of oure soule, is dwellyng in þat soule, strengþing it in þe
affeccioun with goostly joie & swetnes in his loue, þat trauayliþ besily to distroye synne in hymself and in oþer by parfite

1 psalme] *The reference is given in rubrics in the right margin of* Har¹
he seiþ] *om.* Ar; Omnem viam iniquam (iniquitatis F) odio habui; *add.*
Har² F; þat is *add.* Har²   þat] *om.* Har² F G   he] I Har² F; haue *add.* F
hateredyn] hatred F C Pw G Ii   2 wey] ways Har⁵   3 Þus] it *add.*
Ar F C R Pw G W Ii   is] it *add.* Har⁵   wel] wile Har⁵; *om.* W Ii   þat]
om. G   þat er] *trs.* Har⁵   er] or Kk Har² Har⁵ F C R Pw G; that *add.* G
were] was Kk Har² Group B   5 his] *om.* F   felyng first] *trs.*
Pw   first] elles F C R   may] not (*can.*) *add.* Har¹; nouȝt *add.* Kk Har²
on] oo Kk; in F R Pw G   hateredyn] hatred F C R Pw G Ii   6 of synne]
om. Kk Har² Group B   to] at Kk Har²   to sey] *om.* Har⁵   7 schul]
shuld F   &] also *add.* Har²   breþren] breþire Kk Har² Har⁵ C;
broþer Ar Pw G W Ii   8 to] at Kk Har²   to sey] *om.* Har⁵   techeþ]
vs *add.* Kk Har² Ar Har⁵ F C R Pw G W Ii   9 schul] shuld F   synne] in oure
selfe & in (in *om.* Ii) oure broþer (brethere Har⁵, brethren G) *add.* Ar Har⁵
F C Pw G W Ii   Judas . . . synne] *om.* R   Judas] charite (*ins.*) *add.*
Har⁵   biddeþ] vs *add.* Kk Har² Ar Har⁵ F C Pw G W Ii   hate] þe *add.*
C W Ii   10 Isachar] gastle felyng (*ins.*) *add.* Har⁵   biddeþ us] *om.* Har⁵
distroie] stroy Har⁵   þe] *om.* Har⁵   11 kynde] may *add.* Har⁵   (and) in]
om. Har⁵ R Ii   12 hateredyn] hatred F C R Pw G Ii   di-] *om.* Har⁵   synne]
synnes Ar   13 her-] þer- F Pw   -fore] in þe stori *add.* Har⁵   clepid]
calde Har⁵ F C R Pw G W Ii; in þe story *add.* Har² Ar F C R Pw G W Ii   a] the
F; *om.* C R   stede] stude Ar; place Pw   strengþe] strenghe Kk, strenght
Har⁵   14 in þe story] *om.* Har² Group B   seide] *om.* Har⁵   his] *om.*
Ar   birþe] seyd *add.* Har⁵; thus. Mecum erit maritus meus *add.* F   schal] now
(*ins.*) *add.* Har⁵   15 þat is] *om.* Har⁵   þe] *om.* F R; *ins.* Ii   16 in]
om. Har²   þat] þe Ii   strengþing] strengþenynge Ii   it] þat C R   17 his]
om. Ar   18 hym-] hem- Ar C R W; þame Har⁵   oþer] others Pw

hateredyn of þe synne, & alle þe kynde of synne. & þus it is seide
how Zabulon is borne.

HOW ORDEINDE SCHAME RISEþ & GROWEþ IN þE AFFECCYOUN
    Bot þof al þat a soule fele in it parfite hateredyn of synne,
5 wheþer it may ȝit lyue wiþoutyn synne? Nay, sekirly. And for-þi
no man presume on hymself, when þe Apostle seiþ þus: 'ȝif we
seye we haue no synne, we disceyue oureself, & soþfastnes is not
in us.' And also Seinte Austyne seiþ þat he dar sey þat þer is no
man leuyng wiþoutyn synne. And I preye þee who is he þat
10 synnyþ not in ignoraunce? ȝe, and oft-tyme it falliþ þat God
suffriþ þees men falle ful greuously, by þe whiche he haþ ordeynde oþer mens errour to be riȝtyd, þat þei mowen lere by
þeire owne fallyng how mercyful þei scholen be in amendement of
oþer. And for-þi þat men oft-tymes fallen greuously in þoo same
15 synnes þat þei moste hate, þerfore after hateredyn of synne
springiþ ordeynde schame in a mans soule.

1 hateredyn] hatred F C R Pw G Ii   þe] *om.* Ar C   &] *om.* C   it is]
trs. Har⁵ F G W   seide] at say Har⁵   2 how] þat *add.* Har² Ii   3 *No
chapter heading in* F C R   ordeinde] ardaunt Ar; ordynate Pw G Ii;
ordaund W   & groweþ] *om.* Har² Har⁵   þe affeccyoun] a mans sawle Har⁵
4 þof] of Kk; ȝif C   þof al] *trs.* Har⁵ R Pw   al] *om.* F W Ii   þat] *om.*
R W Ii   a] þe Ar   soule] þurȝe grace *add.* Group B; of god *add.* F   in
it] þat it hath F   in] *om.* C   it] selfe *add.* Ar Pw   hateredyn] hatred
F C R Pw G Ii   5 wheþer] whyder Pw; wher W Ii; ȝit *add.* Kk Har²
it] ȝit *add.* Har⁵   ȝit] *om.* Kk Har² Har⁵   lyue] leue C   for-þi] þerfore
Ar F C R Pw; let *add.* Pw   6 on] of Group B   when] syne Har⁵;
sith G   seiþ] Si dixerimus quod peccatum non habemus. nos ipsos seduci-
mus & veritas in nobis non est *add.* F   þus] *The reference is given in rubrics
in the right margin of* Har¹; That *add.* Kk Har² Ar Har⁵ Pw G W Ii; *om.* F
7 seye] þat *add.* Ar F C Pw G W   soþfastnes] trewþe Ar F   not] noon
C R   8 And] *om.* F   dar] well *add.* Pw G   þat] *om.* Har⁵ G W Ii
8–9 no man] none Ar Har⁵ Pw G W Ii   9 he] þat Ar Har⁵ W Ii; *om.* C R
10 synnyþ] liueth G   ȝe] ȝa Kk Har²   oft-] often Ii   -tyme] tymes Kk
Har² Ar F C R Pw G Ii; syth Har⁵   11 þees] þoo Ar Har⁵ C R W Ii; somme
F; those Pw; thilke G   men] to *add.* Har⁵ (*ins.*) F G   ful] *om.* Har⁵
þe] *om.* W Ii; þe *add.* Ar   þe whiche] whom G   12 errour] errours Har⁵
F C R   riȝtyd] regthede Har⁵   lere] lerne Group B   13 fallyng]
fallynges Ar   mercyful] þat *add.* Ar F C R   scholen] shuld F   in] to
the F   amendement] amendynge Ar Pw   14 oþer] others Pw   And...
oft-tymes] ffor ofte tymes men F   for-þi þat] þerfore C R   -þi] *om.* Ar;
þt Pw; it is *add.* Kk Har²   men] *om.* Har⁵ C R Pw G W Ii   oft-] often G
Ii   -tymes] *om.* Ar; (þt *add.* Ii) men *add.* Har⁵ C R Pw G W Ii   greuously]
om. Ar   þoo] þe Group B   same] *om.* Ar   15 synnes] synne Pw G W Ii
moste] must R G   þer-] wher- Pw   after] of (*ins.*) Har⁵   hateredyn]
hatred F Pw G Ii   synne] synnes F C R   16 ordeynde] ordenand Har²;
ardaunt Ar; ordred F; ordynat Pw G Ii; ordaund W   a] *om.* Ar; a *add.* F

And so it is þat after | Zabulon was Dyna borne. As by Zabulon f. 118*b*
hateredyn of synne, so by Dina is vnderstonden ordeynde schame
of synne. Bot wite þou wel he þat felt neuer Zabulon, felt neuer
ȝit Dyna. An yuel man haþ a maner of schame, bot it is not þis
ordeynd schame. For whi and þei had parfite schame of synne, 5
þei schuld not so costomably do it wiþ wyl & auisement. Bot
þei schame more wiþ a foule cloþe on here body þan wiþ a foule
þouȝt in here soule. Bot whatso þou be þat wenyst þat þou haste
getyn Dyna, þink wheþer þee wolde schame as moche & a foule
þouȝt were in þin herte, as þee wold and þou were mad stonde 10
nakid bifore þe kyng &,alle þe rewme. And sekirly ellys wite þou
riȝt wel þat þou hast not getyn ȝit ordeinde schame in þi felyng,
ȝif it so be þat þou haue lesse schame wiþ þi foule herte þan wiþ þi
foule body ; and ȝif þou more schame wiþ þi foule body in þe siȝt of
men þan wiþ þi foule herte in þe siȝte of þe kyng of heuen & of alle 15
his aungelles & holy seyntes in heuen.

1 þat] *om.* Kk   borne] ffor *add.* F   As] Als C   Zabulon] þe *add.*
Har⁵   2 hateredyn] hatred F Pw G Ii   so by] *om.* R   is] we Group
B   ordeynde] ordenand Har² ; ardaunt Ar ; orden Har⁵ ; ordred F ; ordynat
Pw G Ii ; ordaund W   3 of] for Har⁵   wite] witeþ Ar   þou] *om.* Ar
Har⁵ C R W Ii ; ye F   wel] wille Har⁵ ; þat *add.* Ar F C Pw   he] *om.* R
felt neuer] *trs.* F   felt] feleþ C   neuer] nere Har⁵ ; ȝit *add.* Kk Har²
neuer ȝit] *trs.* W   4 An] *om.* Ar Har⁵ Pw G W Ii   An yuel] Euery F R ;
Iche a C   yuel] ille Har² Har⁵   man] men Ar Har⁵ Pw G W Ii   haþ]
han Ar G W Ii ; haue Har⁵ Pw   a maner of] *om.* Ar   þis] *om.* Kk Pw
5 ordeynd] ordenande Har² ; ardaunt Ar ; ordred F ; ordynat Pw G Ii ;
ordaund W   schame] of synne *add.* Pw   whi] *om.* F   and] yf F ;
yf *add.* Pw   6 schuld] wold F   not] neuir C   costomably] cous-
tomable Kk Ar Har⁵   wiþ] *om.* R   auisement] vysement W   7
schame] muche *add.* G   on] o Har⁵ ; or G   body] boþi Kk ; bake
Har²   þan] þai do *add.* Har²   8 so] euere *add.* F G   þou be] *trs.* Har²
þat (þou)] *om.* Har⁵   þou] *om.* R   haste] haue Kk, haþe Har², has
Har⁵   9 þink] wel *add.* G   wheþer] wher W ; or Ii   þee] þoue F R Pw W Ii
wolde] wolt W Ii   &] in Ar ; yf F Pw W Ii ; of G   10 were] *om.* Ar G
herte] sowle F C R   þee] þu Har² Ar F C R Pw G W Ii   and] if F
Pw G W Ii   mad] *om.* Har⁵ ; to *add.* Ar Pw W Ii   11 &] in G W   þe] is
Har⁵ ; his Pw Ii   rewme] reyme Har² ; royalme Pw   sekirly] surely
Pw   ellys] *om.* Har⁵   þou] it Pw   12 riȝt] *om.* Har⁵ C Pw   þat] *om.* Ii
getyn ȝit] *trs.* Kk Har² Group B ; ne *add.* R   ordeinde] ordenand Har² ;
ardaunt Ar ; ordred F ; ordynat Pw G Ii ; ordaund W   þi] þe C   13 it] *om.*
Kk Har² Har⁵ Pw   so be] *trs.* F C R   haue] hast G   14 þou] *ins.*
Har⁵ ; þink *add.* Har⁵ ; haue *add.* F C R Ii   more schame] *trs.* Pw G
þe] *om.* Har⁵   15 men] man Ar Pw W Ii   þan] *om.* R   herte] þouȝt
W Ii   þe] *om.* Har⁵   (&) of] *om.* Ar F   16 &] þe *add.* Har⁵   in
heuen] *om.* Ar   in] of Har⁵ Ii   heuen] þou hast not ordaund (ordynat Ii)
schame *add.* W Ii ; than hast thou not gete Dyna *add.* G

Loo, it is now seyde of þe seuen children of Lya, by þe whiche
ben vnderstonden seuen maners of affecciouns in a mans soule, þe
whiche mowen be now ordeynde & now vnordeynde, now mesurid
and now vnmesurid. Bot whan þei ben ordeinde & mesurid, þan
5 ben þei vertewes. And whan þei ben vnordeynde & vnmesured,
þan ben þei vices. Þus behoueþ a man haue warnes þat þei be not
only ordeynde bot also mesurid. Þan ben þei ordeynde, when þei ben
of þat þing þat þei schuld be. And þen be þei vnordeynde, when þei
ben of þat þing þat þei schuld not be. And þan ben þei mesured,
10 whan þei ben as mochel as þei schuld be. And þan ben þei
vnmesured, when þei ben more þen þei schuld be. For whi ouer
moche drede bryngiþ in dispeyre. And ouer moche sorow castiþ
f. 119a a man into bitternes | & heuines of kynde, for þe whiche he is
vnable to receyue gostly coumforte. And ouer moche hope is pre-
15 sumpcioun. And outrageous loue is flateryng & glosyng. And
outrageous gladnes is dissolucioun and wantonnes. And vntemprid hateredyn of synne is woodnes. And on þis maner þei ben

1 Loo] nowe *add.* Group B   it is] *trs.* Har⁵ F C R   now] *om.* Ar Har⁵ F
C R Pw G W Ii   þe] *om.* Ar G W Ii   by] *om.* Ar G W Ii   þe] þo Ar
2 maners] manere F C R Pw G W   affecciouns] affeccion G W Ii   þe]
om. F   3 be now] *trs.* F C R Ii   ordeynde] ardaunt Ar; ordred F;
ordynat Pw G Ii; ordaund W   vnord.] vnardaunte Ar; vnordred F;
inordynate Pw; vnordinat G Ii; vnordaund W   4 Bot] *om.* F   Bot
whan] bot when *add.* Kk   ordeinde] mesured Har²; ardaunt Ar; ordred F;
ordynate Pw G Ii; ordand W   4–5 & mesurid . . . vnordeynde] *om.* Kk,
but ins. at foot of page in a different later hand   mesurid] ordeynd Har²   þan]
þai Har²   5 vertewes] vertuous Pw   ben] ben (*can.*) *add.* Har¹   vnor-
deynde] vnmesured Har²; vnardaunt Ar; vnordred F; inordynat Pw; vnordinat G Ii; vnordand W   vnmesured] vnordeynd Har²   6 þan] þai Har²
þus] it *add.* G   man] to *add.* F Pw G Ii   warnes] children Ar Pw G W Ii; warn-
inge C R   7 ordeynde] ardaunt Ar; ordred F; ordynate Pw G Ii; ordand W
ordeynde] ardaunt Ar; ordred F; ordynat Pw G Ii; ordand W   ben] of
add. Har²   8 be] of *add.* Har²   þen] *om.* Kk; *ins.* R   vnordeynde]
vnardaunt Ar; vnordred F; inordynate Pw; vnordinat G Ii; vnordand W
8–9 when þei ben] *om.* Pw   þei] *om.* Ar   9 ben] not *add.* F   þei] *om.* R
not] *om.* F   þan] *om.* Kk   10 as] so Ar Har⁵ Pw G W Ii   as mochel as] no
more than F C R   And] *om.* Har⁵ C R   10–11 And . . . schuld be] *om.*
Pw   11 more] or lesse *add.* Ar   þei] þa Har⁵   whi] *om.* F   12 in] *om.* Kk
Har² Ar Har⁵ F C G W Ii; *ins.* R; to Pw   13 -to] *om.* Ar Har⁵ F C R W
14 vnable] for *add.* Pw G W   15 outrageous] outerage Har²   is] bot *add.*
Kk Har² Group B   glosyng] fagyng Kk Har² Ar Har⁵ C Pw G W Ii;
fadyng F; faynynge R   16 gladnes] *om.* Ar   vntemprid] an vntempre
Ar, vnatempere Har⁵; vntemperatte F Ii; vnatempred C R; outragyous
Pw; vnattemperat G   17 hateredyn] hatred F C R Pw G W Ii   maner]
whan *add.* Ar; if *add.* Har⁵ F Pw G; and *add.* C W Ii

vnordeynd & vnmesured, & þus ben þei tornyd vnto vices. &
þan lese þei þe name of vertewes, & mowen not be acomptyd
amonges þe sones of Jacob, þat is to sey God. For by Jacob is
vnderstonden God, as it is schewid in þe figure before.

HOW DISCRECIOUN & CONTEMPLACIOUN RISEN IN ÞE RESOUN 5

Þus it semiþ þat þe vertewe of discrecioun nediþ to be had,
wiþ þe whiche alle oþer mowen be gouernyd. For wiþouten it, alle
vertewes ben tornid to vices. Þis is he, þat Joseph, þat is þe late-
borne childe. Bot ȝit his fader loueþ hym more þen hem alle, for
whi trewly wiþouten discrecioun may nouþer goodnes be getyn ne 10
kepte. And for-þi no wonder þof þat vertewe be syngulerly loued,
wiþoutyn whiche no vertewe may be had, ne gouerned.

Bot what wonder þof þis vertewe be late getyn, when we mowe
not wynne to þe perfeccioun of discrecioun wiþouten moche
custume and many trauayles of þees oþer affecciouns comyng be- 15

1 vn-] *ins.* Har² Ii   vnordeynd] vnardaunt Ar; vnordred F; inordynate
Pw; vnordinat G Ii; vnordand W   &] or W Ii   & þus] *om.* Ar Pw
G W Ii; þen Har⁵ F C; þat R   ben þei] *trs.* Ar C R Pw G Ii   þei]
om. Har⁵   vnto] into Har² Ar Har⁵ F C R Pw G W Ii   2 þan] *om.*
W Ii   lese] lose Har² Ar Har⁵ Pw G   þei] *om.* W Ii   acomptyd]
acounted Kk Har² Group B   3 amonges] wiþ Kk Har² Group B   sones]
sone R   to] at Kk Har²   4 vn-] *om.* Pw   as] and so Group B
as . . . before] *om.* Ii   is] *om.* G W   before] sayde *add.* Har²
5 *Chapter
heading*] Here it is to say of þe two sons of Rachel. Joseph & Beniamyn Har⁵; *om.* F C R   þe] *om.* G   resoun] affeccion Kk Har² Pw G
6 þat] þe Kk   nediþ] is ful (ful *om.* R) nedefulle Har⁵ F C R   7 wiþ] bi
W Ii   þe] *om.* W Ii   oþer] vertues F C R; others Pw; vertus *add.* Har⁵   be]
kepude & *add.* Har⁵ F C R   For] why (*can.*) *add.* Kk; qwy *add.* Har²
alle] othere *add.* Har⁵ F C R   8 to] into Har² Ar F C R Pw G W Ii   is he,
þat] þilke Ar; hyght *add.* Pw F   he þat] *om.* Har⁵   þat] *om.* G   þat is]
om. W   is þe] *om.* R Ii   þe] *om.* Har⁵   late-] last Ar W Ii   9 Bot] bo
Har⁵   loueþ] loued Har² F   þen] *om.* Har²   10 whi] *om.* F   trewly]
om. Pw   nouþer] ne neuere Ar; neuere F; neyþer C R; no Pw G; noiþer
W; þere no Ii   goodnes] goodes Ii; nother *add.* F; neiþer *add.* G   getyn]
kept Ar C R   ne] noþere F; nor Pw; be *add.*   11 kepte] geten Ar
C; begetyn R   for-þi] þerfore Ar C R Pw G; for that F   þof] yf Kk Har²
C R; of Har⁵   be syng.] *trs.* W Ii; be- *add.* Pw F   12 wiþoutyn . . .
gouerned] *om.* Har⁵   -outyn] *om.* Har²; þe *add.* Har² F C R   whiche]
may *add.* W Ii   no] not Ii   may] *om.* W Ii   ne] nor F Pw; be *add.*
Ar F C R Pw   13 þof] if *can.*, þouȝe Har²; is of Har⁵; ȝif C R   we] he Pw
14 to] *om.* Pw   þe] *om.* Ar R G W Ii; no Har⁵   15 custume] vse Group
B   of] and Ar Pw G W Ii   þees] þis Ar C R; those Pw   oþer] others Pw
aff.] affeccyon Pw

fore ? For first behouiþ us be custumed in iche a vertewe by hymself, and gete þe profite of hem alle seerly, er we mowen haue ful
knowing of hem alle, or elles kun deme sufficyently of hem alle.
And when we vsen us besily in þees felynges & beholdynges before-
5 seyde, oft-tymes we fallen, oft-tymes we risen. Þan, be oure ofte
fallyng, mowe we lere how moche warnes us behoueþ haue in þe
getyng & keping of þees vertewes. And þus sumtyme, by longe vse,
a soule is led to ful discrecioun. & þan it may ioie in þe birþe of
Joseph.

f. 119b 10   And before þis vertewe be conceyuid in a mans | soule, alle þat.
þees oþer vertewes done is withouten discrecioun. And for-þi, in-as-
moche as a man presumiþ and enforceþ hym in any of þees felynges
before-seide ouer his miȝte & oute of mesure, in-so-moche þe
fouler he falleþ, and failiþ of his purpos. And þerfore it is þat after
15 hem alle, & last, is Dyna borne, for after a foule fal and a faylyng
comeþ sone schame. And þus after many fallynges and faylynges,
& schame folowyng, a man lerneþ by þe proef þat þer is noþing

1 first] it *add.* F   us] to *add.* Pw F   custumed] vsed Group B   iche]
vche Ar ; ilk Har⁵ W ; euery F G   a] *om.* F C R Pw G   hym-] þam
Har⁵, hem C R W Ii   2 and] to *add.* F   þe] in Pw   profite] profe
Har⁵ F C R Pw G W Ii   alle] or elles R   seerly] sunderlye Ar ; sothly
C R ; swrely F Pw G W Ii   er] or Kk Har² Har⁵ F C Pw G ; *om.* R
mowen] not *add.* R   haue] *om.* W Ii   ful] *om.* F C ; þe R   3 knowing]
kunnynge Ar Har⁵ F C Pw W Ii ; cnwyg R ; or konnynge *add.* G ; haue *add.*
W Ii   alle] *om.* Har² ; or *add.* Har⁵   or] nor R   elles] *om.* R ; we
add. F   kun] not *add.* F ; we not *add.* G   alle] nowþer R   4 us] *om.* Har²
&] in þe (*ins.*) *add.* R   5 oft-] often Pw G Ii   fallen] & *add.* Group B   oft-]
often Pw G Ii   6 mowe we] *trs.* F   lere] lerne Ar F C R Pw G W Ii
us] we F   behoueþ] to *add.* Ar F Pw Ii   haue] *om.* G   7 &] in þe
add. Ar F   þees] þis Ar Pw G W Ii   vertewes] vertue Ar Pw G W Ii
sum-] vm- Kk Har² ; hom Har⁵ ; oþer Ar R ; ouer- C   -tyme] whyle Kk
Har² Ar Har⁵ C R   8 to] into Ar Har⁵ R ; vnto F C Pw   may] see þe
add. Ar Pw G W Ii   in] of Ar F C R Pw G W Ii   10 a] *om.* Ar Ii   11
þees] þere Kk, þeir Har² ; þis Ar   vertewes] vertu Ii   done] doþ Kk
Har² ; it *add.* Group B   for-þi] þerfore Ar C R Pw G ; for that F   12 en-
forceþ] enstresses Har⁵ ; comfortith F C R   þees] þis Ar   13 in-] *om.* Pw
14 falleþ and] *om.* R   his] of is *add.* Har⁵   15 & last] *om.* F   for]
ofte (often Pw Ii) *add.* Group B   foule] sodeyn Har⁵ ; soule C R   fal] is
dyne (dyne *can.*) *add.* Ar   and a faylyng] *om.* Har⁵   15–17 and a
faylyng . . . faylynges &] *om.* Ar   a] *om.* F C R Ii   faylyng] fayle
Kk Har² F C R   16 comeþ . . . schame] schame comeþ soune after-
ward R   sone schame] *trs.* Pw ; after *add.* Pw   many] *om.* W Ii   fallynges]
fallyng W Ii   and faylynges] *om.* F C W Ii   and] vs G   faylynges]
failynge G   17 schame] shames Pw   lerneþ] lers Har⁵ ; ofte *add.* Ar
by] *om.* Ii   þe] *om.* Ar W ; this G   þat] *om.* Har⁵

betyr þan to be rewlyd after counsel, þe whiche is þe rediest getyng
of discrecioun. For whi he þat doþ alle þing by counsel, he schal
neuir forþink it. For betir is a sley man þan a strong man, 3e,
and betyr is list þen liþer strengþe. And a sley man spekiþ of
victories. 5

And here is þe open skyle whi þat neiþer Lya, ne Zelfa, ne Bala
mi3t bere soche a childe, bot only Rachel. For, as it is seide before,
þat of reson spryngeþ ri3t counselles, þe whiche is verrey discrecioun, vnderstonden by Joseph, þe first sone of Rachel. And
þan at þe first bryng we forþe Joseph in oure reson, when al þat 10
we ben sterid to do, we do it wiþ counseyl. Þis Joseph schal not
only knowe what synne we ben moste sterid to, bot also he
schal knowe þe weyknes of oure kynde. And after þat eiþer
askeþ, so schal we do remedye and seek counsel at wyser þen
we, and do after hem. Elles be we not Joseph, Jacob sone, borne 15
of Rachel.

And also by þis ilke Joseph he is not only lernyd to eschewe þe

1 after] be Har⁵   þe] om. F Pw G   getyng] goten G   2 whi]
om. F   2–5 The references are given in rubrics in the left margin
of Har¹   þing] om. Har² R; þinges Ar Pw G W Ii   by] wiþ Ar
Har⁵ F C R Pw G W   he] hym Har⁵   3–4 is . . . is] om. Har⁵
3 (strong) man] om. F C R   3e] 3a Kk Har² C   3–4 3e, and] also R
3–4 3e . . . strengþe] om. Ar   4 is] om. Har⁵   strengþe] strenghe Kk
Har² C   4–5 And . . . victories] om. Har⁵   And] for Ar   a] om. Ii
5 victories] victorie W Ii   6 is] om. Har²   þe] om. F   neiþer]
nouþere Kk Har⁵ C, nawther Har⁵, nother Pw W, neþer Ii   ne] nor Pw;
neþer Ii   ne] nor Pw G; noþer Ii   ne Zelfa] om. W Ii   Bala] ne Zelfa
(ins.) add. Ii   7 childe] schilde Har⁵   is] om. Pw   8 þat] om.
F C R   reson] Rachel F C R   spryngeþ] comen (ins.) Har⁵   counselles]
conseyle Ar Pw G W Ii   þe] om. F   8–9 discrecioun] þat is add. R   9 vnderstonden . . . Rachel] so of rachel springeþ forþe Joseph Ar   vnder-
stonden] vndirstondenge C R   And] for Ar; om. R   10 bryng we] trs.
Ar; bringer G   forþe Joseph] trs. C R   10–11 al . . . counseyl] we doo
by conseyle al þat we ben styred to doo Ar   al] þing (ins.) add. R   11 do]
om. W Ii   we] om. W   we do] be done Pw; om. G; to don Ii   it] om. F Pw
wiþ] be Har⁵ F C R Pw G W Ii   12 synne] synnes Group B   we ben] he was R
to] vnto Pw; doo add. Ar F C R   13 weyknes] waykes Har²; feblenesse Ar;
wickydnes R   13–14 after . . . askeþ] om. Ar   after] om. Pw   eiþer]
other Pw   14 schal we] he schal Ar   we] he Har⁵ F C R Pw G W Ii
at] þat Har²; of W Ii   15 we] he Group B; is add. R   do] þer add. R
hem] om. R; or add. Pw   be we] he is Ar Pw G W; is he Har⁵ C R; he nys
Ii; ys not he F   not] ins. Har⁵; om. F   Jacob] Jacobes Ar R Pw G Ii
17 And] om. Ar C R   by] om. Har⁵   þis ilke] om. Ar   ilke] foresayd Pw;
same F   he . . . only] is no3t a man onely Ar; is a (a om. Ii) man noght
onle Har⁵ F C R W G Ii   he] a man Pw   lernyd] ledde R   þe] om.
Ar Har⁵ F C R Pw G W Ii

deceyte of his enemyes, bot also oft a man is led by hym to þe
parfite knowyng of hymself. And al after þat a man knoweþ hymself, þerafter he profiteþ in þe knowyng of God, of whom he is þe
ymage & þe liknes. And þerfore it is þat after Joseph is Beniamyn

f. 120a 5 borne; for as by Joseph discrecyon, | so by Beniamyn we vnder-
stonde contemplacioun. And boþe ben þei borne of oo moder, &
getyn of oo fader. For þorow þe grace of God lyȝtenyng oure reson,
come we to þe parfite knowyng of oure self and of God, þat is to
sey, after þat it may be in þis liif.

10   Bot longe aftyr Joseph is Beniamyn borne; for whi trewly bot
ȝif it so be þat we vse us besyly & longe in goostly trauayles, wiþ
þe whiche we ben lernid to knowe oure-self, we mowen not be
reisyd to þe knowyng & contemplacioun of God. He doþ for nouȝt
þat liftyþ up his iȝe to þe siȝt of God, þat is not ȝit able to see

15 hymself. For first I wolde a man lered hym to knowe þe vnseable
þinges of his owne spirit, er he presume to knowe þe vnseable
þinges of þe spirit of God. And he þat knoweþ not ȝit hymself, and
weniþ þat he haue getyn somdele knowing of þe vnseable þinges of

1 deceyte] deceytes Group B   his] oure Ar Harˢ F C R Pw G W Ii
also oft] als oft os (os *ins.*) Harˢ   also] as R   oft] *om.* Ar Pw; often Ii; as
add. R; is *add.* G W Ii   is] *om.* G W Ii; ofte *add.* Ar Pw   hym] hem Ii
to] vnto F; into R Pw   þe] *om.* Kk Harˢ R Ii   2 al] *om.* Ar G
al after þat] also þat after R   knoweþ] haþ knowynge of Ar   3
þe] *om.* Ar Harˢ Ii   4 þe] *om.* Ar Harˢ   it is] *trs.* F C R   is] *om.*
Ar Pw; was G W Ii   Ben.] was *add.* Ar Pw   5–6 borne . . . cont.]
om. F   5 borne] *ins.* R   for . . . Ben.] be whom (*ins.*) R   by] holy
Ar   Joseph] is *add.* Ar   we] is Ar   6 ben þei] *trs.* Ar F Pw G
ben] were Harˢ; are C R Pw W Ii   oo] a Kk Har² Harˢ; oon F C R
(*ins.*) Pw Ii   7 oo] a Kk Har² Harˢ; one F C R Pw Ii   lyȝten-
yng] lyghtand Harˢ; liȝtned C; lyhtnyþ R; lighting G   reson] & þan
add. R   8 come we] *trs.* F   þe] *om.* Kk   8–9 þat . . . sey] *om.* Ar   to] at
Kk Har²   9 be] hadde *add.* F C R   10 is Ben.] *trs.* Ar   whi] *om.* F
trewly] *om.* Ar   11 it . . . þat] *om.* Ar   it] *om.* Harˢ   so be] *trs.* F C R
Pw G W Ii   trauayles] traueil Ii   12 þe] *om.* Harˢ   whiche] wyþ Kk;
þe whyche *add.* Kk   lernid] lered Ar   13 to] into Group B   þe] *om.*
G W Ii   &] of R   14 ȝit] *om.* Har²   15 I wolde] *om.* Harˢ; þat *add.*
Ar F C R Pw G W Ii   man] suld *add.* Harˢ   lered] lerned (lerne Harˢ)
Group B; for *add.* F   hym] *om.* F; *can.* Ii; ffor *add.* C R; selfe *add.* Pw
to] *om.* C   þe] *om.* Harˢ   vnseable] inuisible F; vnseasable Pw   16 er]
or Kk Har² Harˢ R Pw G Ii; ar C; þat *add.* F   presume] presumed Kk Har²
Ar Harˢ C R W Ii; for *add.* Ar Harˢ F C R   knowe] kunne Ar F C R G W Ii;
see *add.* F C R   vnseable] inuisible F; vnseasable Pw   17 þe] *om.* Harˢ R
þat] yet *add.* Pw   ȝit] *om.* Pw Ii   and] he Ar   18 weniþ] weneneþ Har²
haue] haþe Kk Har² Group B   getyn somdele] *trs.* Ar Pw G W Ii   getyn]
a *add.* C   vnseable] inuisible F; vnseasable Pw

God, I doute it not þat he ne is disceyuid. And for-þi I rede þat
a man seke first besily for to knowe hymself, þe whiche is maad to
þe ymage and þe licnes of God, as in soule.

And wite it wel þat he þat desireþ to se God, hym behoueþ to
clense his soule, þe whiche is as a mirour in þe whiche alle þing is 5
cleerly seen when it is clene. And when þe mirour is foule, þen
maist þou see noþing cleerly þerin. And riȝt so it is of þi soule.
When it is foule, neiþer þou knowest þiself, ne God. As when þe
kandil brenniþ, þou maist see þe self kandel by þe liȝt þerof, &
oþer þinges also: riȝt so when þi soule brenniþ in þe loue of God, 10
þat is when þou felist contynowely þin herte desire after þe loue
of God, þan by þe liȝt of his grace þat he seendeþ in þi reson, þou
maist boþe see þin vnworþines, & his greet goodnes. And for-þi
clense þi myrour, and profre þi candyl to þe fiir. And þanne,
when it is clensid & brennyng, and it so be þat þou wittirly | be- 15 f. 120b
holde þerto: þan byginniþ þer a maner of cleerte of þe liȝt of God
for to schyne in þi soule, and a maner of sonnebeme þat is gostly

1 not] but *add.* F   þat he ne] þaten (þat ne C) he Kk Har² Har⁵ C
þat] but Pw   ne] *om.* Kk F R Pw   for-þi] þerfore Ar F Pw   -þi] þat R
rede] counsayle R   þat] *om.* Pw G   2 first] *om.* Har⁵   þe] *om.* F
3 ymage and þe] *om.* Pw   and þe licnes] *om.* Har⁵   þe] *om.* Ar
G W Ii   as] *om.* F   4 wite] knowe Ar   it] þo Har⁵; þu F C R G Ii;
om. Ar Pw W   þat] *om.* Kk Har² W Ii   desireþ] for *add.* Ar Har⁵ F C R W
hym] hem Har²   to] *om.* Har⁵ C R W   5 þe] *om.* F Pw   as] *ins.* Har¹;
om. C R Pw G Ii   þing] þinges Group B   is] ben Ar F; are Har⁵
C R Pw G W Ii   7 maist] myȝt Ar   it is] *om.* Har⁵   þi] þe Har⁵ Ii
8 neiþer] nouþire Kk Har² Ar, nather Har⁵, nother Pw, noiþer W; neþere Ii
ne] nor Pw   As] And Kk Har² Har⁵ F C R Pw G W Ii   9 brenniþ]
brynneþ Kk Har² C; þan *add.* Kk Har² Group B   þou maist] *trs.* Ar Har⁵
F C R Pw G (þo *ins.* Har⁵)   þe] þi Har⁵ F C R   self] same Ar; & þe *add.*
Har⁵ F   kandel] *om.* R   10 also] *om.* Har⁵   þi] þe Kk Ar C G W Ii
brenniþ] byrneþ Kk; brynneþ Har² C   11 contynowely] *om.* F C R
þin] þe Ii   herte] continuelly *add.* R   desire] contynually *add.* F C   after]
om. Har⁵   12 in] into Ii   þi] þe C   13 maist] myȝt Ar   boþe
see] *trs.* Har⁵ R Pw Ii   þin] owne *add.* Kk Har² Ar Har⁵ Pw G W Ii   &] also
add. Har²   his] godes Har⁵   for-þi] þerfore Ar C R Pw; for that F
14 profre] beede Ar Har⁵ G W Ii; put F C R; lyght Pw   to] at Pw   15 it]
þi myroure Har⁵   &] þi candel *add.* Group B   brennyng] brynnyng Kk
Har² C; lyghted Har⁵   and] if *add.* G   it] *om.* Kk Har²   þat] than
add. Pw   wittirly] trewly Ar; vtterly F; stedfastly C R; wyttely Pw;
and dylygently *add.* Pw   16 þer] *om.* Har⁵ F   of] the *add.* F
cleerte . . . liȝt] cler liȝt Ii   cleerte] clerenes F   þe] *om.* Ar C Pw G W
17 for] *om.* W Ii   to] *om.* C   of] þe *add.* Ar F C R Pw G; a *add.* Har⁵
15–44/1 gostly . . . þi] *om.* Pw   gostly] vndirstandyng *add.* F C R; for
add. F C R G W Ii

to apere before þi goostly siȝt, þe whiche is þe iȝe of þi soule and
is openid to beholde God & godly þinges, heuen & heuenly þinges,
and alle maner of goostly þinges. Bot þis siȝt is bot be tymes,
whiles God wil vouche-saaf to ȝeue it to a worchyng soule, þe
5 whiles it is in þe batayle of þis deedly liif. Bot after þis liif it schal
be euerlastyng. Þis liȝt schone in Dauid soule when he seyde þus
in þe psalme: 'Lorde, þe liȝt of þi face is merkyd vpon vs. Þou
hast ȝouen gladnes withinne myn herte.' Þe liȝt of Godes face is þe
schinyng of his grace, þat reformeþ in us his ymage þat haþ ben
10 disfygurid wiþ þe derknes of synne. And þerfore a soule þat
brenniþ in desyre of his liȝt, ȝif it hope for to haue þat þat it desireþ, wite it wel þat it haþ conceyuid Beniamyn. And þerfore what
is more heleful þan þe swetnes of þis siȝt, or what softer þing may
be felt? Sikyrly none. And þat wote Rachel ful wel; for whi reson
15 seiþ þat in comparyson of þis swetnes alle oþer swetnes is soure,
& bittyr as galle forby hony.

Neuerþeles ȝit may a man neuer come to soche a grace by his
owne sleiȝt, for whi it is þe ȝift of God withoutyn deseert of man.

---

1 before] to Ar Har⁵ F C R G W Ii   þi] þe R   þe whiche is] þurȝ
þe whoche Ar Har⁵ F C R Pw G W Ii   is] *om.* R   þe] *om.* Har²
and] *possibly can.* Har¹; *om.* Group B   2 beholde] þi *add.* Ar   godly]
goostli *written first, but can.* Har¹; gostely Har² Ar Har⁵ F C R Pw G Ii
þinges] & *add.* Ar   heuen] *om.* R   3 and . . . þinges] *om.* Ar   of] *om.* Har⁵
F C R   4 whiles] whan Ar Har⁵ F C R Pw G W Ii   saaf] for *add.* Ar
Har⁵ C R Pw G (it) to] vnto Har⁵ F C   a] *om.* Ii   worchyng] wakyng Pw
þe] *om.* Har⁵; euere F C R   5 whiles] whyle Ar W Ii; whiche Pw G   it]
yet Pw; *om.* G   þe] *om.* Kk Har² Group B   it schal] *trs.* Har⁵   6
euer-] ay Har⁵ G W   Dauid] daviþes Ar W; Dauid is, is *can.* Ii   Dauid
soule] þe soule of Dauyd Pw   when] whils Har⁵   þus] *om.* Ar   7
psalme] 4 *added in rubrics in left margin* Har¹; Signatum est super nos lumen
vultus tui domine *add.* F   þe] thy F   7–8 Þou . . . herte] *om.* Ar   8
gladnes] fayrnes Kk; faynes Har² Har⁵; veines C, vaynes R   9 his] *om.* Ii
ymage] ymagynacion R   haþ ben] be F   10 disfygurid] defoulede Har⁵
derknes] merknes Har⁵ C G   11 brenniþ] brynneþ Kk Har²   in] the *add.*
F C W Ii   his] þis Ar Har⁵ F R Pw G W Ii; *om.* C   liȝt] siȝt Group B   þat]
thilke G   þat] at Har⁵   12 þat] *om.* Pw   13 þe] *om.* Har⁵ R; *ins.*
Ii   siȝt] liht R W   or] and F C R   þing] þingis W   14 Sikyrly] Surely Pw
whi] *om.* F; þe *add.* Har⁵   15 seiþ] seiȝt Ii   þat] *om.* Ar G W Ii   þis]
his F   oþer] ouþer Har²   is] ben Ar F; are Har⁵ C R Pw G W Ii   soure]
sorwe C Pw   16 forby] byfore Ar F C R Pw G W Ii   17 neuer] *ins.*
Har¹; *om.* Ar   a] *ins.* F; *om.* Ii   grace] neuer *add.* Ar   18 sleiȝt]
myȝte F   for whi] þerfore C R   whi] *om.* F   þe] a (*ins.*) Har⁵   of]
onely *add.* Har²   18–45/1 withoutyn . . . grace] *om.* R   -outyn] þe *add.*
Pw   deseert] deseruyng F   man] but wiþoute doute þouȝ (of Har⁵) it be
noȝt þe (þe *om.* Har⁵) deserte of (a *add.* G) man *add.* Ar Har⁵ Pw G W Ii

And ȝit no man may take soche grace wyþoutyn greet study [and] brennyng desires comyng before. And þat wote Rac[h]el ful wel. And for-þi sche multyplieþ hir study, & whetteþ hir desires, iche desire on desire, so þat at þe laste, in greet habundaunce of brennyng desires and sorow of þe delaiing of hir desire, 5 Beniamyn is borne, and his moder Rachel diȝeþ. For whi in what tyme þat a soule is rauischid abouen hymself by habundaunce of desires & a greet multytude of loue, so þat | it is enflawmyd with f. 121a þe liȝt of þe Godheed, sekirly þan dyȝeþ al mans reson.

And þerfore whatso þou be þat coueytest to come to contempla- 10 cioun of God, þat is to sey, to bryng forþe soche a childe þat men clepyn in þe story Beniamyn, þat is to sey, siȝt of God: þan schalt þou use þee in þis maner. Þou schalt clepe togeders þi þouȝtes & þi desires, and make þee of hem a chirche, & lerne þee þerin for to loue only þis good worde Jhesu, [so þat alle þi desyre and þi þouȝt 15

1 And] om. Group B   no] a F C   may] neuere add. F C   soche] a add. F Ii   wyþoutyn] wiþ R   study] studies Ar Pw G W Ii   2 and] of Har¹   brennyng] brynnyng Kk Har²   desires] desire Har⁵   comyng] comen R   wote] om. W Ii   Rachel] Raclel Har¹   3 wel] wist add. W Ii   for-þi] þerfore Ar C R Pw; for þat F   multyplieþ] multiplied G Ii   study] studyes F C R G   3–4 whetteþ . . . desires] om. Har⁵   whetteþ] quykeþ R; swetyth F; whettid G Ii   4 iche] sechynge Ar Pw G W Ii; hekand Har⁵; encresyng F; ekend C; & knyttiþ R   desire on desire] oon desire W Ii   on] one Kk; vnto Har⁵; vpon F Pw G   5 brennyng] brynnyng Kk Har²   desires] desire Har⁵   and] in add. Ii   þe] om. Ar Ii   6 and] Rachel add. F C R   Rachel] om. F C R   For whi] þerfore C R   whi] om. F   in] om. Har⁵   7 þat] om. G   hym-] it Group B   8 &] in Ii; in add Har⁵   9 al] a add. Ar   10 -so] euere add. F Pw   þou] he Har⁵ F C R   coueytest] coueyteþ Har²; desires Har⁵ F C R   come to] þe add. F C R   11–12 þat is . . . siȝt of God] lete hym lere (lerne F C R) for to gedire samen (& examyn F; togyder R; togedere add. C) þe myghtes of his sawle, & lete hym study for (om. F) to refreyne þe outpassyng of is mynde, & schape (ordeyne F) hym for (om. F) to wone (dwelle F) with hymself os a kyng in is reme to wome þat (om. F C R) non of his sugetes wore contrari (and add. F C R) Har⁵ F C R   to] at Kk Har²   12 clepyn] calleth Pw G W Ii   to] at Kk Har²   God] And add. R   þan] om. F   12–13 schalt þou] trs. F   13 use þee] witt so þat (ins.) þou be wise Har⁵   þee] om. F; thyse Pw G   þou schalt] om. Ar Pw G W Ii; & (ins.) Har⁵   clepe togeders] examyn F   clepe] calle Kk Har² Har⁵ Pw G W Ii; gedere C R   togeders] sammyn Kk Har² Har⁵   14 þee] om. Group B   lerne] lere Kk Har²   þee] om. F W Ii   for] om. Har⁵ Pw   15 loue] one add. Pw   only] loue add. Pw   þis . . . Jhesu] whiche is god Pw   þis] om. R   good] om. Har⁵   worde] Lord F G; god R; Jhesu ins. in left margin Har¹ Ar; om. G   15–46/1 so . . . Jhesu] om. Har¹   15 desyre] desires Ar R Pw G W Ii   and] all add. Pw   þouȝt] þouȝtes Ar R Pw G W Ii

be onely sette for to loue Jhesu,] and þat vnsesyngly, as it may
be here, so þat þou fulfille þat is seyde in þe psalme: 'Lorde,
I schal bles þee in chirches,' þat is in þouȝtes and desires of þe
loue of Jhesu. And þan, in þis chirche of þouȝtes and desires, & in
5 þis oneheed of studies & of willes, loke þat alle þi þouȝtes & þi desires & þi studyes & alle þi willes be only set in þe loue & þe
preisyng of þis Lorde Jhesu, wiþouten forȝetyng, as fer forþ as
þou maist by grace & as þi freelte wil suffre, euer more mekyng
þee to preier & to counsel, pacyently abidyng þe wille of oure
10 Lorde, vnto þe tyme þat þi mynde be rauischid abouen itself to be
fed wiþ þe feire foode of aungelles in þe beholdyng of God & godly
þinges. So þat it be fulfillid in þee þat is wretyn in þe psalme: 'Ibi
Beniamyn adol[es]centulus in mentis excessu.' Þat is: 'Þere is
Beniamyn, þe ȝonge childe, in rauesching of mynde.'

15   AMEN

1 onely sette] *trs.* Har⁵   for] *om.* Har⁵   Jhesu] *om.* C Pw G   vnsesyngly]
vsynglich Ar; vnseshandle Har⁵; incessantly F; vnsessandly C; wiþowten
seesyng R; vncessingly G; vncessauntly W; vncessandly Ii   2 fulfille] þat
add. Ar Pw W; thilke *add.* G   seyde] sette G   psalme] *The reference is given
in rubrics in the left margin of* Har¹; In ecclesijs benedicam te domine *add.*
F   Lorde] *om.* Ii   3 bles] blysse Kk Har² C R   in] alle *add.* Ar   chirches]
kirkes Har⁵; þe chyrche Pw   in] gatherynge of good *add.* Pw   þouȝtes]
thoght Har⁵ F C R   desires] desyre Ar Har⁵ F C R W Ii   þe] *om.* W Ii
3-4 þe loue of] *om.* F C R   4 Jhesu] god Pw G   (&) in] *om.* Kk   5 &
of] þe *add.* Har⁵   of] *om.* F C R   willes] wilk Har⁵; wellis C   alle] *om.*
Pw W   þouȝtes] þoghte Har⁵   &] alle *add.* C R Pw G W Ii   þi] *om.* F
6 &] alle F R; alle *add.* Kk Har² Har⁵ C Pw G W Ii   6 & . . . willes]
om. Ar   þe] *om.* C R   &] in *add.* Ar R Ii   þe] *om.* F G   7
preisyng] loouynge Groupe B   þis Lorde] *om.* Har⁵   þis] good *add.* F
Lorde] worde C R; god *add.* R   Jhesu] *om.* Pw G   forȝetyng] Also *add.* R
fer] *om.* Har⁵ F C R W   forþ] for F   8 maist] may Kk Har² Har⁵ F
W; myȝt Ar   by] throgh F C R   þi] þt Kk; *om.* F C R   suffre] it *add.*
Ar   8-9 mekyng þee] make þe redy Ar   9 counsel] counseiles G
abidyng] bidinge C R; vpon *add.* C R   10 Lorde] Jhesu *add.* Ar W Ii   vnto]
into Ar; to Pw W Ii   11 þe] *om.* Ii   11 feire foode] beautye Pw
feire] fadir W; swete F   aungelles] and *add.* Pw G W Ii   in] *om.* W Ii
þe] *om.* Kk Har² Group B   godly] gostely Har² Har⁵ F C R Ii (godly *written
in right margin* Ii); goodly Ar   12 be] *om.* C   (þee) þat] þat *add.* Ar R;
ilke that *add.* G   psalme] *The reference is given in rubrics in the right margin of*
Har¹   13 -es-]-o- Har¹   is] to sey *add.* F W Ii   þere is] *om.* Ar Har⁵   is] *om.* G
14 þe] ȝe C   ȝonge childe] yonglyng F   mynde] þe grace of Jhesu kepe
þe euermore *add.* Har²; Explicit de xij filiis Jacob *add.* Ar; of Jhesu. Jhesu.
Jhesu. Mercy Jhesu. Graunt Mercy. Jhesu *add.* Har⁵; Here endythe the
tretys of the xii patriarkys *add.* F; *No explicit* C; To the whiche vs brynge our
blessyd Beniamyn Cryst Jhesu. Amen *add.* Pw; Hic explicit libellus Studium
Sapiencie Vocitatus *add.* G; Explicit. Þus endiþ Beniamyn *add.* W Ii

A PISTLE OF
PREIER

A Pistle of Preier

f. 12b Goostly frende in God, as touching þin askyng of me how þou
schalt reule þin hert in tyme of þi preier, I answere vnto þee febely
as I kan, and I sey þat me þink þat it schuld be ful speedful to
5 þee at þe first biginnyng of þi preier, what preier soeuer it be,
longe preier or schort, for to make it ful knowen to þin hert
wiþouten any feinyng þat þou schalt diȝe in þe ende of þi preier,
and, bot þou spede þee þe raþer, er þou come to þe ende of þi
preier. And wite þou þat þis is no feinid þouȝt þat I telle þee, & se
10 whi. For trewly þer is no man leuyng in þis liif þat dar take apon
him to sey þe contrary: þat is to sey, þat þou schalt liue lenger
þen þi preier. And þerfore þou maist þink it saueliche.

And I counsel þee to do it, for, if þou do it, þou schalt see þat,
what for þe general siȝt þat þou hast of þi wrechidnes and þis
15 specyal siȝt of þe schortnes of tyme of amendement, it schal
bring into þin hert a verrey worching of drede. And þis worching
schalt þou fele verrely folden in þin herte, bot ȝif it so be (þe
whiche God forbede!) þat þou flater & fage þi fals, fleschly,
blinde herte wiþ lesinges and fals, feined behetynges of lenger
20 leuyng. For þof it may be soþ in þee in dede þat þou schalt liue

Title: Here biginneþ a pistle of preier Har¹ Kk Har²; Herafter folowith
a devowte treatyse callyd the pystle (Epystle Pw) of prayer Bo Pw; Þis
matere suyng techiþ how þou schalt dispose þee to preie CP   2 God] cryst
Iesu Har²   3 schalt] *om.* Kk   in] the *add.* Kk Har² CP   þi] *om.* Bo Pw
þee] so *add.* Kk Har²; thus *add.* Pw; as *add.* CP   4 þat] *om.* Bo   ful] *om.*
Bo   to] vnto Kk Har² Bo Pw CP   5 first] *om.* Bo Pw   soeuer] that Bo Pw
6 preier] *om.* Bo Pw   to²] vnto Bo Pw   7 schalt] schat Har²   in] at
Bo Pw   ende] of thi *add.* Kk   8–9 and . . . preier] or peradventure before
Bo; *om.* Pw   8 bot] yf *add.* Kk Har²   er] or Kk Har²   9 wite] knowe Bo
þou] wele *add.* Har² Bo Pw; riȝt wel (*ins. in left margin*) *add.* CP   þis] it
Bo Pw   is] *om.* Har²   þee] of *add.* Bo Pw   10 trewly] *om.* Kk Har² Bo
Pw CP   þer] *om.* Kk   man] trewly *add.* Kk Har² CP   11 sey] To say *add.*
Pw   leng-] long- Har² Bo Pw   12 preier] is on (in Pw) doynge *add.* Bo Pw
þerfore] *added later in* Har¹ *in right margin, probably by the same scribe*   13
þee] so *add.* Bo   14 what] *ins. in right margin of* Har¹, *probably by the same
scribe; om.* CP   of] for CP   15 of] for CP   þe] *om.* Bo Pw   16 verrey] trew
add. Bo Pw   worching¹ *and* ²] wrycheyng Har²   17 fele] fynde Bo Pw
þe] *om.* Bo   18 fage] deceyve Bo   fals, fleschly] *trs.* Kk Har²   19 fals]
om. Kk Har² Pw   -het-] -hight- Bo Pw   19–20 of . . . leuyng] that thow
shalt longer lyve Bo Pw   leng-] lang- Har²   20 þee] *can.* CP; þat *add.* Har²;
and *add.* Kk Bo Pw; & in (*can.*) *add.* CP   þat] *om.* Har²   schalt] *om.* Kk

lenger, ȝit it is euer in þee a fals lesing for to þink it before and for
to behote it to þin hert. For whi þe soþfastnes of þis þing is only in
God ; and in þee is bot a blinde abiding of his wille wiþouten cer-
teinte of moment, þe whiche is as litel or lesse as a twinkeling of an
iȝe. And þerfore, | ȝif þou wilt preie wiseliche, as þe prophete bid-
deþ whan he seiþ in þe psalme: 'Psallite sapienter', loke þou gete
þee in þi beginnyng þis verrey worching of drede ; for, as þe same
prophete seiþ in anoþer psalme: 'Inicium sapiencie est timor
Domini' ; þat is: 'Þe biginnyng of wisdom is drede of oure Lorde
God.'

Bot for-þi þat þer is no sekir stonding upon drede onliche for
drede of sinking into ouer moche heuines, þerfore schalt þou knit to
þi first þouȝt þis oþer þouȝt þat foloweþ. Þou schalt þink sted-
fastliche þat ȝif þou maist þorou þe grace of God distincteliche
pronounce þe wordes of þat preier and winne to þe ende, or ȝif
þou diȝe bifore þou come to þe ende, so þat þou do þat in þee is,
þat þan it schal be accept of þee unto God as a ful seeþ of alle þi
rechelesnes fro þe beginning of þi liif into þat moment—I mene
þus, stonding þat þou hast beforetyme, after þi connyng and þi
concience, lawfulich amendid þee after þe comoun ordinaunce of
Holy Chirche in confession. Þis schort preier, so litil as it is, schal
þan be accept of þee vnto God, to þi ful saluacioun ȝif þou þan
diedest, and to þe grete encrese of þi perfeccioun if þou leuedist

5 f. 13a

10

15

20

1 leng-] long-, *and elsewhere* Pw (and) for] *om.* Bo Pw   2 -hote] -hete Kk
Har² Bo Pw   þin] *om.* Har²   soþfastnes] trewthe Bo ; soþfast *written in
right margin* CP ; & certaynte *add.* Bo Pw   þing] *om.* Bo Pw   4 of] one
add. Bo Pw   as] a Pw   as] then Bo Pw   6 seiþ] thus *add.* Bo Pw   in þe
psalme] *om.* Bo Pw. *The reference is given in rubrics in the left margin of* Har¹
Psallite] pallite Bo   loke] that *add.* Bo Pw   7 þi] the Bo Pw   same] *om.*
CP   8 *The reference is given in rubrics in the left margin of* Har¹   Inicium]
Iudicium Pw   est] *The abbreviated form* é *is inserted in* Har¹ ; *om.* Kk Bo
Pw   9 (wis.) is] þe *add.* Kk Har² Bo Pw CP   11 for-þi] for Bo Pw   þat]
om. Bo   þer] this Bo   no] fulle *add.* Kk Har² Pw   sekir] sykernesse Bo Pw
stonding] fully *add.* Bo   12 drede] *can.*, ferde *add.* Kk, ferde Har² ;
feare Bo Pw   schalt þou] *trs.* Har²   14 þat] *om.* Har²   ȝif]
þat *add.* Har²   þe] *om.* Bo   15 winne] comme Bo ; or come *add.* Bo
ende] therof *add.* Bo Pw   or ȝif] er þat CP   16 þou] fortowne to *add.*
Bo   bifore] or Bo Pw   bifore . . . ende] *can.* CP   þat] *om.* Kk Bo Pw
þat] is *add.* Bo   is] *om.* Bo   17 seeþ] asethe Kk Har² Bo Pw ; or
amendes *add.* Bo Pw   18 fro] from Bo Pw   into] vnto Bo Pw   19
stonding] so *add.* Bo ; thus *add.* Pw   20 lawfulich] lowefullyche Har²
21 it is] *trs. but order corrected in* Har¹   22 þan] *om.* Bo Pw   vnto]
to Bo Pw   to] for Bo Pw   23 diedest] dyest Kk ; sholdest dye Bo ;
dydest dye Pw   þe] þi Kk Har² Pw

lenger. Þis is þe goodnes of God, þe whiche, as þe prophete seiþ,
forsakeþ none þat trewly tristen in him wiþ wille of amendement.

And siþ alle amendement stonden in two, in leuyng of iuel and
doing of good, menes to gete þees two ben none redier þan ben
5 þe goostly worching of þees two þouȝtes touchid before. For what
reuiþ fro a liif more rediliche þe affeccioun of sinning þan doþ
a trewe worching of drede of deeþ? And what moueþ a liif more
feruentliche to worching of good þan doþ a certein hope in þe
mercy & þe goodnes of God, þe whiche is brouȝt in bi þis secound
f. 13b 10 þouȝt? For whi þe goostly | feling of þis secound þouȝt, whan it is
þus trewlich ioined to þe first, schal be to þee a sekir staf of hope
to holde þee bi in alle þi good doinges.

And bi þis staf þou maist sekirliche climbe into þe hiȝe mount of
perfeccioun, þat is to sey, þe parfite loue of God, þof al þis begin-
15 nyng be inparfite, as þou schalt here after. For, what for þe general
siȝt þat þou hast of þe mercy and þe goodnes of God, and þis
special experience þat þou felist of his mercy and his goodnes in
þis acceptacioun of þis litil, schort seruise for so longe rechelesnes,
as it were in a ful seeþ of so moche rechelesnes (as it is seide be-
20 fore), it may not be bot þat þou schalt fele a grete stering of loue
vnto him þat is so good and so merciful vnto þee, as þe steppes of
þi staf hope pleinly schewiþ unto þee in þe time of þi preier, if
þou do it deweliche as I haue tolde þee bifore. Þe goostliche
experience of þe profe of þis worching, it stondeþ al in a reuerent
25 affeccioun þat a man haþ to God in þe tyme of his preier, causid

1 þe (wh.)] *om.* CP   2 *The reference is given in rubrics in the
right margin of* Har¹   none] not them Bo Pw   tristen] trusteth Bo
Pw   of amendement] to amende Bo Pw   3 siþ] senne Kk; that
add. Bo Pw   two] that is *add.* Bo Pw   of] þe *add.* Har²   iuel]
ille Har²   and] in *add.* Bo   4 of] þe *add.* Har²   ben] *om.* Bo Pw
5 þe] *om.* CP   worching] worchingis CP   þouȝtes] poyntis CP   For] *om.* Bo
Pw   6 reuiþ] takethe Bo   fro] from Bo Pw   liif] sowle Bo Pw   7 trewe]
om. Har²   liif] sowle Bo Pw   8 of good] in god Bo Pw   9 þe] *om.* Bo Pw
10 For whi . . . þouȝt] *om.* CP   þouȝt] þout, 3 *ins.* Har¹   11 sekir] sure Bo Pw
13 sekirliche] sewerly Bo   into] to Bo   hiȝe] *om.* Kk Har² Bo Pw
14 to] at Kk Har²   sey] to *add.* Bo Pw   þof al] all thowghe Bo   15 here]
om. Har²   after] -warde *add.* Har²   16 and] of *add.* Bo Pw   17 mercy
—goodnes] *trs.* Bo Pw   and] of *add.* Kk   his] *om.* Bo Pw   18 þis] the
Bo Pw   schort] *om.* Bo Pw   19 seeþ] aseþe Kk Har²; satysfaccioun Bo
Pw   21 as] Also Bo Pw   22 þi] *om.* Har²   schewiþ] will shew Bo Pw   in
. . . preier] *om.* Bo Pw   23 þee] *om.* Kk   bifore] or not *add.* Bo Pw   24 of]
or Kk Har²; and Bo   it] *om.* Bo Pw   a] *om.* Kk   25 to God] *ins. in right
margin* Har¹   þe] *om.* Bo Pw · his] þis Kk Har² CP; *om.* Bo Pw

of þis drede in þe grounde of þis werk and of þis stering of loue,
þe whiche is brouȝt in bi þe goostly steppis of þis staf hope touchid
before. For whi reuerence is not elles bot drede and loue medelid
togeders wiþ a staf of certein hope. Me þink þat þe profe of þis
worching is deuocioun; for deuocioun is not ellis, as Seinte Thomas 5
þe doctour seiþ, bot a redines of mans wile to do þoo þinges þat
longen to þe seruise of God. Iche man proue in himself; for he
þat doþ Goddes seruise in þis maner, he feleþ hou redy þat his
wille is þerto. Me þink þat Seinte Bernard acordeþ to þis worching
where he seiþ þat alle þinges schuld be done swiftlich & gladliche. 10
And se whi: swiftliche for drede, and gladliche for hope and loueliche trist in his mercy.

And what more: sekirliche I had leuer haue his mede þat lasteþ
in soche doyng, þof al he neuer did bodiliche penance | in þis liif f. 14a
bot onlich þat þat is enioined to him of Holi Chirche, þan of alle 15
þe penaunce doers þat haue ben in þis liif, fro þe beginning of
þe woreld into þis day, wiþouten þis maner of doing. I sey not
þat þe nakid þinking of þees two þouȝtes is so medeful; bot þat
reuerent affeccioun, to þe whiche bringing in þeese two þouȝtes ben
souerein menes on mans partie, þat is it þat is so meedful as I sey. 20
And þis is onliche it bi itself, wiþouten ani oþer maner of doing, as
is fasting, waking, scharp weryng, & alle þeese oþer, þe which onliche bi itself pleseþ to Almiȝty God and deseruiþ to haue mede of
him. And it were inpossible any soule to haue mede of God
wiþouten þis. And alle after þe quantite of þis schal stonde þe 25
quantite of mede; for whoso haþ moche of þis, moche mede schal
he haue, and whoso haþ lesse of þis, lesse mede schal he haue. And

3 not] nothinge Bo; nought Pw   4 togeders] sammyn Kk; same
Har²; *om*. Bo Pw   5 not] nothinge Bo; nought Pw CP   Seinte]
sancte Har²   6 þe] de Kk   þoo] thos Bo Pw   7 God] let *add*.
Bo   Iche] every Bo   9 Seinte] sancte Har²   10 schuld] shalle
Kk Har² Bo Pw; schulen CP   swiftlich] swiftily CP   11-12 loueliche]
louyngly CP   13-20 And . . . meedful as I sey] *om*. Bo Pw   13 I]
iche Kk Har²   lasteþ] lastyd Kk   14 neuer did] *trs*. CP
17 þe] þis Kk Har² CP   18 þe] *om*. Kk   19 bringing] beyng CP; þus
add. CP   two] menes (*can*.) *add*. Har¹   20 þat is] *can*. CP   it] *om*. CP
21 And] *om*. Bo Pw   is] *om*. Bo Pw   it] *om*. Bo Pw CP   22 weryng]
onelynes *add*. Har²   &] with Bo Pw   þeese] suche Bo Pw   oþer] others
Pw   þe which] *om*. Bo Pw   23 pleseþ] blesyth Har²   to] *om*. Kk
Har² Bo Pw   deseruiþ] for *add*. Kk Har² CP   24 soule] for *add*. CP
25 þe quantite of] *om*. Bo   þe . . . stonde] *om*. CP   26 quantite of] *om*.
Bo Pw   26-27 moche . . . haþ] *om*. Bo Pw   27 he] *om*. Bo

alle þeese oþer þinges, as is fasting, waking, scharp wering, and alle
þeese oþer, þei ben meedful in as moche as þei ben helpliche to
gete þis; so þat withouten þis þei ben nouȝtes, and þis wiþouten
hem is somtyme sufficient at þe fulle by himself, and it is ofte times
5 ful worþelich had & comen to of ful many, wiþouten any of þe
oþer. Alle þis I sey, for I wolde bi þis knowing þat þou chargedest
& comendist iche þing after þat it is, þe more þe more and þe
lesse þe lesse. For oft-tymes vnknowing is cause of moche errour.
And ofte-tymes vnknowing makeþ men charge more & comende
10 more bodeliche excersise, as is fastyng, wakyng, scharp wering, &
alle þeese oþer, þan þei do goostliche excersise in vertewes or in þis
reuerent affeccioun touched before. And þerfore, in more declaracioun of þe mede and þe worþines of þis reuerent affeccioun, I schal
seie a litil more þerof þen I ȝit haue seide, so þat bi soche declaring
f. 14b 15 þou maist be betir lernid bi þis worching þen | þou ȝit arte.

Alle þis maner of worching before-seide of þis reuerent affeccioun, when it is brouȝt in by þeese two þouȝtes of drede and of
hope comyng before, may wel be licned to a tre þat were ful of
frute. Of þe whiche tre drede is þat party þat is wiþinne in þe erþe,
20 þat is þe rote, and hope is þat partye þat is aboue þe erþe, þat is
þe body with þe bowes. In þat þat hope is certein & stable, it is
þe body; in þat it steriþ men to werkes of loue, it is þe bowes. Bot
þis reuerent affeccioun is euermore þe frute. And þan euermore as

---

1 fasting. . . wering] fastynges wakynges scharpe werynges Kk   waking]
and *add.* Bo Pw   2 oþer] others Pw   meedful] nedefulle Kk Har² Bo Pw
as] also Kk Har²   helpliche] helpers Kk; helpynge Bo Pw   3 nouȝtes]
nowght Bo Pw   4 -self] one Kk Har²   ofte-] often Bo Pw   6 oþer] tho-
þer Har²; others Pw   for] that *add.* Bo Pw   7 comendist] commenddid
Kk Har²; commawn(d)ed Bo Pw   iche] every Bo   þat] *om.* Har²   (more)
þe] *om.* Pw   8 þe] *om.* Bo Pw   oft-tymes] *om.* Kk Har² Bo Pw CP   is]
of tyme *add.* Kk; oft tymes *add.* Har²; often tymes *add.* Bo Pw   cause]
ofte tymes *add.* CP   9 ofte] often Har² Bo Pw   men] to *add.* Kk Har²
Bo Pw   11 alle] *om.* Kk Bo Pw CP   þeese] suche Bo Pw   oþer]
others Pw   vertewes] vertuows Bo Pw   12 affeccioun] exercyse Bo
Pw   þerfore] ȝit *add.* Kk Har² Bo Pw   12-13 in . . . declaracioun] for
the more (playne *add.* Bo) declaracioun Bo Pw   13 of . . . worþines]
om. Bo Pw   affeccioun] & of the mede and worthynes therof *add.* Bo
Pw   14 þerof] *om.* Bo Pw   ȝit] thowghte to Bo Pw   15 bi] in Kk
Har² Bo Pw CP   16 before-] afor- CP   17 drede] hope CP   of] *om.*
Kk Har² Bo Pw   18 hope] *can.*, drede *ins. in left margin* CP   to] tylle
Kk Har² CP   19 party] parte Bo Pw   in] *om.* Kk Har² Bo Pw   20
is] to saye Bo   partye] parte Bo Pw   21 with] and Bo; and and Pw
þat] *om.* Kk   certein—stable] *trs.* Kk Har² Bo Pw   22 þat] þat *add.*
Kk Har² CP   to] the *add.* Bo Pw   23 (þan) euermore] *can.* Har¹

longe as þe frute is fastned to þe tre, it haþ in party a grene smel
of þe tre. Bot whan it haþ a certein tyme ben departed fro þe tre
and is ful ripe, þan it haþ lost al þe taste of þe tre and is kinges
mete, þat was bifore bot knaues mete. In þis tyme it is þat þis
reuerent affeccioun is so meedful as I seide. And þerfore schape 5
þee for to departe þis frute fro þe tre and for to offre it up bi itself
to þe hiȝe kyng of heuen. And þan schalt þou be clepid Goddes
owne childe, louing him wiþ a chast loue for himself and not for
his goodes.

I mene þus: þof al þat þe vnnoummerable good dedes, þe whiche 10
Almiȝti God of his gracious goodnes haþ schewid to iche soule in
þis liif, ben sufficient causes at þe fulle and more to iche soule to
loue him fore with alle his mynde, wiþ alle his witte, and wiþ alle
his wile, ȝit if it miȝt be, þat may nowise be, þat a soule were as
miȝti, as worþi, and as witty as alle þe seintes and aungelles þat ben 15
in heuen gadered on one & had neuer taken þis worþines of God, or
to whom þat God had neuer schewid kindenes in þis liif, ȝit þis
soule, seing þe louelines of God in himself and þe habundaunce
þerof, schuld be raueschid ouer his miȝt for to loue God til þe hert
brast, so louely and so liking, so good & so glorious he is in him- 20
self. | O [what] wondirful a þing, & hou hiȝe a þing is þe loue of f. 15a
God for to speke of, of þe whiche no man may speke parfitely to
þe vnderstonding of þe lest partie þerof, bot bi inpossible ensaum-
ples & passing þe vnderstonding of man! And þus it is þat I mene

---

1 fastned] festende Kk   to] by Kk Har² Bo Pw   tre] it is but
churles mete for *add.* Bo Pw   haþ] euermore (*can.* Har¹) *add.* Har¹ CP
2 haþ] ben *add.* Bo Pw   ben] *om.* Bo Pw   fro] from Bo Pw   3 ful]
fully Bo   þe] *om.* Kk   and] it *add.* Har²   4 þat . . . mete] *om.* Bo Pw
6 for] *om.* Kk Har² Bo Pw   fro] from Bo Pw   for] *om.* Bo Pw   -self]
one Kk Har²; rype *add.* Kk Har²   7 hiȝe] *om.* Kk Har² Bo Pw
clepid] called Bo; or called *add.* Pw   8–9 not . . . goodes] for nothinge els
Bo Pw   10 þof] þe (*can.*) *add.* Har¹   þat] *om.* Kk Bo   þe] *om.* Kk
Har² Pw   vn-] in- Bo Pw   11 iche] a *add.* Har²   13 (mynde) wiþ]
and Bo Pw   wiþ] *om.* Bo Pw   14 ȝit] *om.* Kk Har² Bo Pw CP   may]
in *add.* Bo   15 (miȝti) as] also Kk   (and) as] also Kk Har²   as]
ben *add.* Kk Har² Bo Pw   þe] *om.* Bo   seintes] sanctes Har²   and] the
add. Bo   þat ben] *om.* Kk Har² Bo Pw   16 gadered] gardderd Har²
on] in (on *ins. above* Kk) Kk Bo Pw   17 þat] *om.* Bo   19 for] *om.*
Bo Pw   til] to Kk Har² CP   20 and] *om.* Kk Har² Bo Pw   good]
so swete *add.* Bo Pw   21 what] hou Har¹   a] *om.*
Kk Har² Bo Pw   22 (speke) of] *om.* Har²   22–23 to . . . of] *om.* Bo
23 partie] parte Bo Pw   ens-] ex- Bo   24 &] *ins.* Har¹   24–54/1
I mene whan] *ins. in left margin of* Har¹

whan I sey 'louyng him wiþ chast loue for himself and not for his
goodes'. Not as ȝif I seide, þof al I wel seide, mochel for his goodes,
bot wiþoute comparison more for himself; for ȝif I schal more
heilich spekin in declaring of my mening of þe perfeccioun & of
5 þe mede of þis reuerent affeccioun, I say þat a soule, touched in
affeccioun bi þe sensible presence of God as he is in hymself & in a
parfite soule, & illumind in þe reson by þe clere beme of euerlastyng
liȝt, þe whiche is God, for to se and for to fele þe louelines of God
in himself, haþ for þat tyme and for þat moment lost alle þe mynde
10 of any good deed or of any kindnes þat euer God did to him in
þis liif; so þat cause for to loue God fore feleþ he or seeþ he none in
þat tyme oþer þan his God.

So þat þof al it may be seide, in speking of þe comoun perfeccioun, þat þe grete goodnes & þe grete kindnes þat God haþ
15 schewed to us in þis liif ben hie and worþi causes for to loue God
fore; ȝit, hauyng beholding to þe pointe & þe prik of perfeccioun, to
þe whiche I porpose to drawe þee in my menyng and in þe maner
of þis writyng, a parfite louer of God, for drede of lettyng of his perfeccioun, sekiþ now, þat is to sey in þe pointe of perfeccioun, none
20 oþer cause to loue God fore bot God himself. So þat by þis menyng
I sei þat chast loue is to loue God for himself and not for his goodes.

And þerfore, folowing þe reule of myn ensaumple, schape þee to
departe þe frute fro þe tre and for to offre it up bi itself vnto þe
king of heuen, þat þi loue be chaste. For euermore as longe as þou
f. 15*b* 25 offrest him þis frute grene and hanging on þe tre, þou | mayst wel
be licned to a womman þat is not chast, for sche loueþ a man more

1 wiþ] a *add.* Kk Har² Bo Pw   2 goodes] good Bo Pw   ȝif] *om.*
Kk Bo Pw   I] hafe *add.* Kk   al] *om.* Bo Pw   goodes] good Bo
Pw   3 more] *om.* Bo Pw   6 he] *om.* Bo   7 (soule) &] *om.* Bo
Pw CP   þe] *om.* Bo   8 þe whiche] that Bo Pw   God] hym selfe
add. Har²   (and) for to] *om.* Bo Pw   louelines] blessednes
Bo Pw   9 þat] the Bo   and] or Kk Har² Bo Pw   for þat] *om.* Bo
Pw   alle] *om.* Bo Pw   10 (or) of] *ins.* Har¹   of any] *om.* Bo Pw
11 God] *om.* Har²   feleþ he] none *add.* Har²   12 his] is Har² Bo Pw
God] hymselfe *add.* Bo Pw   13 þof al] ther of all Bo Pw   14 þe]
om. Bo Pw   þe grete] *om.* Kk Har² Bo Pw   15 for] *om.*
Kk Har² Bo Pw CP   16 pointe—prik] *trs.* Kk Har² Bo Pw CP   17
maner] meaner Bo   18 drede] feare Bo Pw   of] his (*can.*) *add.* Har¹
20 cause] for *add.* Bo Pw   þis] hys Kk   21 is] for *add.* CP   22 ens-]
ex- Bo   23 fro] from Bo Pw   up] alone *add.* Bo Pw   -self] one Kk Har²
23–24 þe king of heuen] god Bo Pw   25 offrest] to *add.* CP   hang-
ing] hyngyng Kk Har²   25–26 wel be] *trs.* Bo Pw   26 sche] qwo so Har²

for his goodes þan for himself. And se whi þat I licne þee þus: for
it semeþ þat drede of þi deeþ and schortnes of tyme, wiþ hope of
forȝeuenes of al þi rechelesnes, makeþ þee to be in Goddes seruise
so reuerent as þou arte. And ȝif it so be, þen haþ þi frute a grene
smel of þe tre. And þof al it plesiþ God in partie, neuerþeles ȝit 5
it plesiþ him not parfitely; and þat is for þi loue is not chaste.
Chaste loue is þat when þou askest of God neiþer relesing of
peyne, ne encresing of mede, ne ȝit swetnes in his loue in þis liif,
bot ȝif it be any certeine tyme þat þou coueitest swetnes as for a
refresching of þi goostly miȝtes þat þei faile not in þe wey; bot 10
þou askest of God noȝt bot himself. And neiþer þou rechest ne
lokest after wheþer þou schalt be in pine or blis, elles þat þou haue
him þat þou louest. Þis is chaste loue. Þis is parfite loue. And
þerfore schap þee to departe þe frute fro þe tre, þat is to sey þi
reuerent affeccioun fro þe þouȝtes of drede & of hope coming be- 15
fore, so þat þou maist offre it ripe & chast to God bi itself, not
causid of any þing bineþe him, medelid wiþ him, ȝe, þof al it be þe
cheef, bot onliche of him bi himself.

& þan it is so meedful as I sey þat it is. For it is pleinly knowen
wiþouten any doute vnto alle þoo þat ben experte in þe sience of 20
deuenite and of Goddes loue, þat as often as a mans affeccioun is
sterid vnto God wiþouten mene, þat is wiþouten messenger of any
þouȝt in special causing þat stering, as ofte it deserueþ euerlastyng
liif. And for-þi þat a soule þat is þus disposid, þat is to sey, þat
offreþ þe frute ripe and departeþ it fro þe tre, may vnnoumerable 25

3 al] *om.* Bo Pw   be] so reuerent *add.* Kk Har² Bo Pw   4 so reuerent]
om. Kk Har² Bo Pw   be] *add.* sotly Kk, sothlyche Har² Bo Pw
5 þof al] therof Bo Pw   6 him not] *trs.* Pw   not] ȝit (*ins.* Kk)
add. Kk Har² Bo Pw   7 neiþer] nouþer Kk Har², nother Pw   of] *om.*
Kk   8 ne¹ ᵃⁿᵈ ²] nor Kk Har² Bo Pw   11 noȝt] nothinge Bo   neiþer]
noythere Har², nother Bo Pw   rechest ne] *om.* Bo Pw   ne] nor Kk Har²
12 after] *om.* Bo Pw   pine] blys Kk Har²; payne Bo Pw   or] in
add. Kk Har² Bo Pw CP   blis] pyne Kk Har²   elles] so Bo Pw CP
13 þou . . . loue. Þis] *om.* CP   14 þee] for *add.* Kk Har² Bo Pw CP
fro] from Bo Pw   þi] The Kk Har²; this Bo Pw   ᶦ 15 fro] from Bo Pw   16
to] vnto Kk Har² Bo Pw   -self] one Kk Har²   17 bineþe him]
ins. in right margin Har¹   him] or *add.* Bo Pw   ȝe] ȝa Kk Har²   þof al
it] if he therof all Bo; ther of all he Pw   it] he Kk Har²   18
cheef] cawse *add.* Bo   him] self *add.* Bo Pw   20 vnto] to Bo Pw
þoo] them Bo Pw   21 often] oft Kk Har² CP   a] *om.* Har²   23 þat]
the Bo   ofte] often Bo   euer-] ay Kk Har²   24 -þi] that Bo Pw   25
departeþ it] departyd Kk Har² Bo Pw   fro] from Bo Pw   vn-] in- Bo Pw

tymes in one oure be reisid into God sodenly wiþouten mene;
þerfore, more þen I kan sey, it deserueþ þorow þe grace of
God, þe whiche is þe cheef worcher, for to be reisid into ioye.
f. 16a And þerfore | schape þee to offre þe frute ripe and departid fro
5 þe tre.

Neuerþeles þe frute apon þe tre continuely offrid as mans freelte
wil [s]uffre, deserueþ saluacioun. Bot þe frute ripe and departid
fro þe tre, sodenly offrid vnto God wiþowten ani mene, þat is perfeccioun. And here maist þou se þat þe tre is good, þof al I bid
10 þee departe þe frute þerfro for more perfeccioun. And þerfore I
sette it in þi gardine, for I wolde þat þou gaderist þe frute þerof and
keptest it to þi Lorde, and for-þi þat I wolde þat þou knewest what
maner of worching þat it is þat knitteþ mans soule to God and
þat makiþ it one wiþ him in loue and acordaunce of wile.

15   After þe worde of Seint Poule seiing þus: 'Qui adheret Deo, vnus
spiritus est cum illo.' Þat is to sey: 'Whoso draweþ nere to God,' as
it is bi soche a reuerent affeccioun touchid before, 'he is o sperit
with God'; þat is, þof al þat God & he ben two and sere in kynde,
neuerþeles 3it in grace þei aren so knitte togeders þat þei ben [bot]
20 o sperit. And alle þis is for onheed of loue and acordaunce of wile.
And in þis oonheed is þe mariage maad bitwix God and þe soule,
þe whiche schal neuer be broken, þof al þe hete & þe feruour of
þis werk ceese for a tyme, bot by a deedly sinne. In þe goostly
feling of þis onheed may a louyng soule boþe sey and singe, 3if
25 it list, þis holy worde þat is wretyn in þe *Book of Songes* in þe
Bible: 'Dilectus meus mihi et ego illi.' Þat is: 'My loued vnto me

---

3 for] *om.* Bo Pw   into] vnto Bo   4 þee] for *add.* Kk Har² Bo Pw   fro]
from Bo Pw   6 apon þe tre] *om.* Bo Pw   as] a *add.* Bo Pw   7 s-] f- Har¹
8 fro] from Bo Pw   ani] *ins.* Har¹; *om.* Kk Har² Bo Pw   9 þof] that *add.* Bo
Pw   al] *om.* Bo Pw   10 -fro] -of CP   11 þat] *om.* Bo Pw   þou] settest þ (*can.*)
add. Har¹   gaderist] gaddyrd Kk Har²; sholde gather Bo Pw   and] b (*can.*)
add. Har¹   12 keptest] kepe Har² Bo Pw   -þi] *om.* Bo; that Pw   knewest]
knowe Har²   13 worching] worsching Har¹   þat] *om.* Bo Pw CP   it]
om. Kk Har²   15 seiing] sayand Kk Har²   17 it] *om.* Bo Pw   18 God]
hym Har²   al] *om.* Bo Pw   þat] *om.* Bo   and] *om.* Bo Pw   sere] sondry
Bo; sere, diuerse *written in right margin* CP; persons *add.* Bo; or sondry
add. Pw   19 togeders] togidyr Kk Har² Pw CP; together Bo   ben]
ar Kk Har² Bo Pw   bot] *om.* Har¹   20 o] in *add.* Kk Har² Bo Pw
and] in Bo   21 bitwix] betwene Bo Pw   22 al] that Bo Pw; þat
add. Kk Har²   hete—feruour] *trs.* Bo Pw   23 bot] onely *add.* Bo   þe] þis
Kk Har² Bo Pw   24 louyng] louand Kk; lofened Har²   26 *The reference
is given in rubrics in the right margin of* Har¹   et] *om.* Bo   vnto] to Bo Pw

and I to him' vnderstond 'schal be knittyd with þe goostly glewe of grace on his partye, and þe louely consent in gladnes of sperite on þi partye.'

And þerfore climbe up bi þis tre, as I seide in þe biginnyng, and when þou comest at þe frute, þat is to þe reuerent affeccioun, þe 5 whiche alweis wil be in þee and þou þink hertly þe oþer two þouȝtes bifore and glose not þiself with no liȝe, as I seide: þan schalt þou | take good kepe of þat worching þat is maad in þi soule þat tyme, f. 16b and schape þee, in as moche as þou maist þorou grace, for to meek þee vnder þe heiȝt of þi God, so þat þou maist use þee in 10 þat worching oþer tymes bi itself, withouten any climbing þerto by any þouȝt. And sekirli þis is it þe whiche is so meedful as I seide. And euer þe lenger þat it is kept fro þe tre, þat is to sey fro ani þouȝt, and euer þe ofter þat it is done sodenly, listely, & likingly, wiþouten mene: þe swetter it smelleþ, & þe betir it 15 plesiþ þe hiȝe king of heuen; and euer whan þou felist swetnes and coumforte in þi doing, þan he brekiþ þis frute and ȝeueþ þee parte of þin owne present.

And þat þat þou felest it so harde & so streitliche stressing þin herte wiþouten coumforte in þe first biginnyng, þat [bemeneþ] 20 þat þe greenes of þe frute hanging on þe tre, or elles newely pullid, eggen þi teeþ. Neuerþeles ȝit it is speedful to þee; for it is no reson þat þou ete þe swete kirnel bot ȝif þou crakke first þe harde schelle & bite of þe bitter bark. Neuerþeles, ȝif it so be þat þi teeþ

1 I] *om.* Kk   to] vnto Har² Bo Pw   vnderstond] ing (*can.*) *add.* Har¹; vndurstonding CP; God *add.* Kk Har²; that god *add.* Bo Pw   2 þe] þi Har²   on] in CP   5 at] to Bo Pw   þe] þi CP   6 alweis] algate Kk Har²; ever Bo Pw   and] if Bo Pw   hertly] on *add.* Bo Pw oþer] toþer Kk Har²   7 glose] fage Kk Har² Bo Pw; or flatter *add.* Bo Pw 8 kepe] hede Bo Pw   maad] naked Kk; maked Har²   9 schape] steppe Bo Pw   þee] *om.* Bo Pw   þorou] by Har²   10 heiȝt] lyght Bo þee in] *om.* Bo Pw   11 it-] þi CP   -self] one Kk Har²   any] *om.* Kk Har² Bo Pw CP   12–14 And . . . þouȝt] *om.* Har²   12 þouȝt] goynge before *add.* Bo   sekirli] truly Bo   13 euer] ay Kk   þat] *om.* Bo Pw   fro] from Bo Pw   14 fro] from Bo Pw   euer] ay Kk Har² ofter] oftener Bo Pw   listely] lustely Bo Pw   &] *om.* Kk Har² Bo Pw   15 likingly] lykandly Kk Har²   16 euer] ay Kk Har²   19 (þat) þat] at Kk; whiche Bo   it] is Bo Pw   20 bemeneþ] ben menes Har¹ CP, n *in* ben *can.* CP; or betokeneth *add.* Bo Pw   21 þat] *om.* Bo Pw   (of) þe] *om.* CP hanging] hangand Kk   on] of Har²; apon Bo Pw   22 eggen] eggiþ Kk eggen þi teeþ] (whiche Bo) settith thy tethe on edge Bo Pw   22–24 Neuerþeles . . . Neuerþeles] *added later in* Har¹   it] *om.* Har² CP   is] *om.* Kk   23 ȝif] *om.* Har²

be weike, þat is to sey þi goostly miȝtes, þan it is my counsel þat
þou seke sleiȝtes, for 'Betir is list þan leþir strengþe'.

Anoþer skile þer is whi þat I sette þis tre in þi gardyn for to climbe
up þerby. For þof al it be so þat God may do what he wyle, ȝit, to
5 myn vnderstonding, it is inpossible any man to atteyne to þe perfeccioun of þis worching wiþouten þees two menes, or elles oþer
two þat ben acording to hem, comyng before. And ȝit is þe perfeccioun of þis werk sodeyn withouten any menes. And þerfore I
rede þeese be þine; not þine in propirte, for þat is noȝt bot sinne,
10 bot þine ȝeuen gracyously of God and sent bi me as messenger, þof
I be vnworþi. For wite þou riȝt wel þat iche a þouȝt þat stereþ
þee to þe good, wheþer it come fro wiþinne bi þin aungel messenger or fro wiþouten by any man messenger, it is bot an instru-
f. 17a ment of grace, ȝeuen, sent, & chosen of God himself for | to worche
15 wiþinne in þi soule.

And þis is þe skile whi þat I counsel þee to take þees two before
alle oþer. For as a man is a mengid þing of two substaunces, a
bodily and a goostly, so it nediþ for to haue two sere menes to
come by to perfeccioun (siþ it so is þat boþe þees substaunces
20 scholen be onid in vndeedlines at þe uprising in þe last day), so þat
eiþer substaunces be reisid to perfeccioun in þis liif by a mene
acordaunce þerto. And þat is drede to bodily substaunce and
hope to þe goostly. And þus it is ful semely and according to be,
as me þink. For as þer is noþing þat so sone wol rauische þe body

---

2 seke] some *add.* Bo   sleiȝtes] therfore *add.* Bo Pw   list] lust Pw
leþir] lyddyr Har²   3 þat] *om.* Bo Pw CP   sette] þe *add.* Kk   4 þof] *om.*
Har²; þeiȝ CP   al] *om.* Bo Pw   5 atteyne] comme Bo   6 þees] þis Har²
7 ben] ar Kk Har² Bo Pw   acording] acordand Kk Har²; acordaunt CP
comyng] comand Kk Har²   8 any] *ins.* Har¹   menes] meene Kk
Har² Bo Pw   9 rede] or cownsell the that *add.* Bo Pw   propirte]
propriete Bo Pw   10 ȝeuen] gevynge Bo   as] a *add.* Bo Pw   11 iche]
ilke Kk Har²; euery Bo Pw   a] *om.* Bo Pw   12 þe good] god Bo Pw
it] *om.* Bo   fro] from Bo Pw   13 fro] from Bo Pw   by] from Bo Pw   14
worche] wiþ *add.* Kk Har²   15 in] *om.* Bo Pw   16 þis] *om.* Kk   skile]
cawse Bo   two] yowthes Bo Pw   17 oþer] others Pw   as] *om.* Har²   a]
om. Kk Har² Pw CP   mengid] or a myxt *add.* Bo Pw   a] of Bo   18 a]
om. Bo Pw   for] *om.* Bo Pw   sere] dyuerse Bo Pw; sere, diuerse *in right
margin* CP   19 by] *om.* Bo Pw   perfeccioun] by *add.* Bo Pw   siþ] senne
Kk Har²   it] *om.* Kk Har² Bo Pw CP   so] it *add.* Bo   þees] þere Kk
Har² Bo Pw   20 in vndeedliness] *om.* Bo Pw   at] in Kk Har² CP   in]
at Kk Har² Bo Pw CP   day] in vndedlynesse *add.* Bo Pw   21 sub-
staunces] substance Kk Bo Pw   22 acordaunce] accordynge Bo Pw;
acordant CP   23 þe] *om.* Bo Pw   acording] accordand Kk Har²

fro al affeccioun of erþely þing as wile a sensible drede of þe deeþ:
so þer is noþing þat so sone ne so feruentliche wol reise þe affeccioun of a sinner soule vnto þe loue of God as wole a certein hope
of forȝeuenes of alle his rechelesnes. And þerfore I haue ordeined
þi climbing by þees two þouȝtes.   5

Bot ȝif it so be þat þi good aungel teche þee withinne þi goostly
conseite, or any oþer man ouþer, oþer two þat ben more acording
to þi disposicioun þan þee þink þees two ben, þou maist take hem
and leue þees sauelich, withoutyn any blame. Neuerþeles to my conseite, til I wite more, me þink þat þees schuld be ful helply unto 10
þee, and not moche unacording to þin disposicioun, after þat I
fele in þee. And þerfore, ȝif þee þink þei do þee good, þan þank
God hertlich. And for Goddes loue prey for me. Do þan so, for I am
a wreche, and þou wost not how it stondeþ wiþ me. No more at
þis tyme, bot Goddes blessing haue þou & myne. Reed ofte; forȝete 15
it not; sett þee scharply to þe profe; and fle alle letting and occasion of lettyng, in þe name of Iesu. Amen.

1 fro] from Bo Pw   of] all *add.* Bo Pw   erþely] bodely Bo Pw   þing]
þinges Har² Bo Pw   a] the Bo   þe] *om.* Bo   2 ne] nor Kk Har² Bo
Pw   reise] ravyshe Bo Pw   3 sinner] synners Bo Pw   vnto] up to Kk Bo
Pw   4 I haue] *trs.* Kk Har² Bo Pw   5 climbing] vp *add.* Bo   6 it] *om.*
Kk Bo Pw   7 ouþer] or any Bo Pw; oþer CP   oþer] *can.* CP   ben]
are Kk Har² Bo Pw   acording] accordant Kk Har²   8 to] vnto Bo Pw
þink] that *add.* Bo   ben] are Bo   9 any] *om.* Bo Pw   10 til] to
Kk Har²   wite] knowe Bo   helply] helpyngly Bo   unto] to Bo Pw
11 unacording] unaccordant Kk; unacordande Har²; vnaccordyngely Bo
to] vnto Bo Pw   12 ȝif] *om.* Kk   þee] thow Bo Pw   þink] that *add.* Bo
Pw   þan þank] *trs.* Kk Har² Bo CP   þan] *om.* Bo Pw   13 Do þan so]
om. Bo Pw   14 wost] wate Kk Har²   how] þat *add.* Har²   more]
to the *add.* Bo   15 blessing] blyssyng Kk Har²   myne] Amen *add.* Bo
ofte] often Bo Pw; this *add.* Bo; and *add.* Bo Pw   16 not] and *add.* Bo
letting] lettinges Bo Pw   16–17 occasion] occacyons Bo Pw   17 lettyng]
lettynges Bo Pw   in] for Bo   name] love Bo   of] our lorde *add.* Bo Pw
Iesu] christe *add.* Bo Pw

A PISTLE OF
DISCRECIOUN OF
STIRINGS

A Pistle of Discrecioun of Stirings

f. 5b Goostly freend in God, þat same grace & ioie þat I wil to myself I
wil to þee at Goddes wile. Þou askist me counsel of silence and of
speking, of comoun dietyng & of singulere fastyng, of dwelling in
5 companye & of only wonyng by þiself. And þou seist þou arte in
grete were what þou schalt do; for, as þou seist, on þe to partye
þou arte greetly taried wiþ speking, with comoun etyng as oþer
folk done, and wiþ comoun wonyng in companye; and, on þe toþer
party, þou dredist to be streitly stille, singulere in fasting, and only
10 in woning, for demyng of more holines þen þou arte worþi, and
for many oþer periles. For oft-tymes now þees dayes, þei ben demid
for most holy and fallen into many periles, þat most aren in silence,
in singulere fastyng, & in only dwellyng.
f. 6a   And soþ it is þat þei ben most holy ȝif grace | only be þe cause
15 of þat silence, of þat singulere fastyng, & of þat only dwelling, þe
kinde bot suffring and only consentyng. And ȝif it be oþerwise,
·þen þer is bot perile on alle sides. For it is ful perilous to streine
þe kynde to any soche werk of deuocioun, as is silence or spekyng,
comoun dietyng or singuleer fastyng, dwelling in companye or in
20 onlines (I mene, passing þe comoun custom & þe cours of kynde
and degre), bot it be ledde þerto bi grace; and namely to soche
werkis, þe whiche in hemself ben indiferent, þat is to sey, now

Title (In þe name of iesu Har²) Here biginniþ a pistle of discrecioun of
(in·Kk Har²) stirings Har¹ Kk Har²; Here foloweth also a veray necessary
Epystle of dyscrecyon in styrynges of the soule Pw; *om.* CP   2 God]
crist Iesu Har²   grace] þat (*can.*) *add.* Har¹   I wil] *trs.* Kk Har²
Pw CP   4 fastyng] & *add.* Har²   5 (&) of] *om.* Pw   only] *om.* Pw
wonyng] dwellynge Pw; alone *add.* Pw   And] For Har²   seist] þat *add.*
Kk Har² CP   6 were] doubte Pw   to] one Pw   7 arte] summe
tyme *add.* Kk Har² Pw   7–8 as...and] *om.* Pw   8 and] þou seist (*can.*
Har¹) *add.* Har¹ CP   wonyng] dwellynge Pw   toþer] other Pw   9
stille] in kepynge of scylence *add.* Pw   singulere] syngulerly Pw   in] *om.*
Pw   only] *om.* Pw   10 in] onely *add.* Pw   woning] dwellynge Pw   þen...
worþi] in þe than þu hast Pw   11 þees] a Pw   14 only be] *trs.* Kk
Har² Pw   16 kinde] of nature *add.* Pw   17 þer] *om.* Kk Har² Pw CP
is] þare noo þing *add.* Kk Har² Pw CP   perilous] for *add.* Kk Har²   18
spekyng] or (*can.* Har¹) *add.* Har¹ CP   19 fastyng] or (*can.* Har¹) *add.* Har¹
CP   20 comoun custom—cours] *trs.* Kk Har² Pw   21 bot] if *add.*
Kk Har² Pw   22 hem-] hym Pw

good and now iuel, now wiþ þee and now aȝens þee, now helping
& now lettyng. For it miȝt befalle þat ȝif þou foloudist þi singuler
stering streitly streining þee to silence, to singuler fastyng, or to
only dwellyng, þat þou schuldest be oft-tymes stille whan tyme
were to speke, oft-tyme fast whan tyme were to ete, oft-tyme to be 5
only whan tyme were to be in companye: or if þou ȝeue þee to
spekyng alweis whan þee list, to comoun etyng, or to companous
wonyng, þan parauenture þou schuldest somtyme speke when
tyme were to be stylle, somtyme ete whan tyme were to fast,
somtyme be in companye whan tyme were to be only. And þus 10
miȝt þou liȝtly falle into errour, in grete confusion not only of þin
owne soule bot also of oþers. And þerfore, in eschewing of soche
errour, þou askest of me, as I haue parceyued bi þi lettre, two
þinges: þe first is my conseite of þee and þi steringes, and þe toþer
is my counsel in þis caas, and in alle soche oþer whan þei comen.   15

As to þe first, I answere and I sey þat I drede ful moche in þis
mater & in soche oþer to put forþ my rude conseite, soche as it is,
for two skyles. And on is þis: I dar not lene to my conseite,
affermyng it for fast trewe. Þe toþer is: þin | inward disposicioun f. 6b
and þin abelnes þat þou hast vnto alle þees þinges, þat þou spekist 20
of in þi lettre, ben not ȝit so fully knowen vnto me as it were speedful þat þei weren, ȝif I schuld ȝeue fulle counsel in þis caas. For it
is seide of þe apostle: 'Nemo nouit que sunt hominis nisi spiritus
hominis, qui in ipso est'; 'No man knowiþ whiche ben þe priue
disposiciouns of man bot þe spirite of þe same man, þe whiche is 25
in hymself.'

1 iuel] ille Har²   and] *om.* Pw   aȝens] aȝeyn Kk Har² CP; agaynst
Pw   2 þat] *om.* Kk Har² Pw CP   4 schuldest] *om.* Har²   be
ofttymes] *trs.* Kk Har² Pw CP   oft-] often Pw   5 speke] and *add.* Pw
oft-] often Pw   -tyme] tymes Kk Har² Pw   oft-] often Pw   -tyme]
tymes Kk Har² Pw   to] *om.* Kk Har² Pw   6 tyme] bettyr Kk
Har²   to be] *om.* Kk Har²   if þou] *om.* Har²   7 alweis] *om.* Pw
þee] thou Pw   8 wonyng] company Pw   9 tyme] better Pw
tyme] better Pw   10 tyme] better Pw   only] alone Pw   11 errour]
errours Pw   12 oþers] oþere CP   13 lettre] letters Pw   13-14 two
þinges] *om.* Pw   14 steringes] styrryng Kk Har² Pw   toþer] other Pw
15 oþer] others Pw   16 (and) I] *om.* Pw   17 (&) in] *om.* Kk Pw
oþer] others Pw   18 skyles] causes Pw   19 it for] that it is Pw   fast]
and *add.* Pw   toþer] other Pw   20 and . . . abelnes] *om.* Pw   vnto]
to Pw CP   þees] þis Har; those Pw   21 lettre] letters Pw; whiche
add. Pw   as] at Har²   22 caas] cause Pw   23 apostle] Paule *add.*
Har². *The reference is given in rubrics in the left margin of* Har¹   24 ben]
arn Kk Har² Pw   25 þe³] *om.* CP

And parauenture þou knowest not ȝit þin owne inward disposicioun þiself so fully as þou schalt do herafter, when God wole
late þee fele it bi þe profe amonge many fallynges and risinges.
For I knewe neuer ȝit no synner þat myȝt come to þe parfite
5 knowing of himself and of his inward disposicioun, bot if he were
lernid of it before in þe scole of God, by experience of many temptaciouns [and by many fallynges and risinges]. For riȝt as amonge
þe wawes and þe flodes and þe stormes of þe see on þe to partye, þe
pesible winde and þe calmes and þe softe weders of þe ayre on
10 þe toþer partye, þe sely schip at þe last atteineþ to þe londe and þe
hauen: riȝt so amonge þe diuersite of temptaciouns and tribula-
ciouns þat fallen to a soule in þis ebbing and flowing liif (þe which
ben ensaumpled bi þe stormes and þe flodes of þe see on þe to
partye) and amonges þe grace and þe goodnes of þe Holy Goost,
15 þe manyfold visitacioun, swetnes and coumforte of spirite (þe
whiche ben ensaumplid bi þe pesible winde and þe softe weders of
þe eire on þe toþer partye) þe sely soule, at þe licnes of a schip,
atteineþ at þe last to þe londe of stabelnes and þe hauen of helþe,
þe whiche is þe clere and þe soþfast knowing of himself and of alle
20 his inward disposiciouns; þorow þe whiche knowing he sitteþ
quietly in hymself, as a king crouned in his rewme, miȝtly, wisely,
and goodly gouernyng himself and alle his þouȝtes & steringes, |
f. 7a boþe in body & in soule.
    Of soche a man it is þat þe wise man seiþ þus: 'Beatus vir qui
25 suffert temptacionem, quoniam cum probatus fuerit accipiet
coronam vite, quam repromisit Deus diligentibus se'; 'He is a

1–2 disposicioun] of *add.* Pw   3 amonge] amonges Kk Har²   many]
om. Har²   4 neuer ȝit] *trs.* Pw   come] perfytely *add.* Pw   þe]
om. Kk   parfite] *om.* Pw   5 disposicioun] dysposycyons Pw   7 and
. . . risinges] *om.* Har¹ CP   8 and] of Pw   and] of Har²   to] one
Pw   partye] & *add.* Pw   9 calmes] calme Pw   and] of CP   þe] *om.*
Kk Har² Pw CP   of þe ayre] *om.* Pw   10 þe] þat CP   toþer] other
Pw CP   at þe last] *om.* Pw   atteineþ] at þe laste *add.* Pw   10–11 and
þe hauen] *om.* Pw   11 þe] þe *add.* Har²   diuersite] dyuersytes Kk
Har² Pw   12 fallen] in *add.* Har²   a] þe Pw   13 ben] ere Kk Har² Pw
þe] *om.* Pw CP   to] one Pw   14 amonges] omonge Pw CP   15 coum-
forte] comforthes Kk Har² CP   of] þe *add.* Har²   16 ben] ere Kk
Har² Pw CP   (and) þe] *om.* Pw   17 toþer] other Pw   18 (to) þe] *om.*
Pw   and] to *add.* Pw   19 whiche] *om.* Har²   21 in] *om.* Har²
rewme] royalme Pw   23 soule] And *add.* Har²   24 wise man]
apostle saynt James Pw. *The reference is given in rubrics in the left margin
of* Har¹   25 quoniam] qui Pw

blisful man þat suffringly beriþ temptacioun, for, fro he haue ben
prouid, he schal take þe coroun of liif, þe whiche God haþ hiȝt
vnto alle þoo þat louen him.' Þe coroun of liif may be seide on two
maners: on for goostly wisdom, for ful discrecioun, and for perfeccioun of verteue; þees thre knittid togedir may be clepid 5
a coroun of liif, þe whiche bi grace may be comyn to here in þis liif.
On anoþer maner þe coroun of liif may be seide: þat it is þe eendles ioie þat iche trewe soule schal haue after þis liif in þe blis of
heuen. And sekerly neiþer of þees corouns may a man take, bot he
before haue ben wel prouid in suffring of noye and of tempta- 10
cioun, as þis text seiþ: 'Quoniam cum [p]robatus fuerit, accipiet
coronam vite'; þat is, 'Fro þat he haue ben prouid, þan schal he
take þe coroun of liif.' As who seiþ acording to myn vnderstonding
touchid before: bot if a sinner man haue ben prouid before in
diuerse temptacions, now rising, now fallyng, fallyng by freelte, 15
rising by grace, he schal neuer elles take of God in þis liif goostly
wisdome in clere knowyng of hymself and of his inward disposiciouns, ne ful discrecioun in teching and counselyng of oþer, ne ȝit
þe þrid, þe whiche is þe perfeccioun of vertewe in louyng of his
God and his broþer. 20

Alle þees þre—wisdom, discrecioun, and perfeccioun of vertewe—
ben bot one, and þei mowe be clepid þe coroun of liif. In a coroun
ben þre þinges. Gold is þe first, precious stones ben þe secound, and
þe toretes of þe floure-de-lices reisid up abouen þe heed, þoo
ben þe þrid. By golde wisdom, bi precious stones discrecioun, and 25
bi þe toretes of þe floure-de-lices I vnderstonde þe perfeccioun of

1 blisful] blyssed Har²; blessid CP; blessydfull Pw   suffringly
beriþ] suffers wylfully Har²   fro] frome Pw   3 vnto] to Pw   þoo]
those Pw   on] in Pw   4 and for] fulle (can.) add. Har¹   5 clepid]
kallyd Kk Har² Pw CP   6–68/3 a coroun . . . þin owne] om. Har²   6 bi
grace] om. Kk Pw   may] be grace add. Kk Pw   to] men add. CP   8
iche] euery Pw   soule] ins. in left margin of Har¹   9 sekerly] sikyr
Kk; surely Pw   neiþer] none Pw   þees] ii add. Pw   man] ta add.
Har¹   bot] yf add. Kk Pw   10 noye] trouble Pw   of] om. CP
11 þis] þe CP   probatus] brobatus Har¹   12 Fro] frome Pw   13
þe] ins. Har¹   14 man] om. Pw; may CP   haue ben] be Pw   15
fallyng] om. Pw CP   16 neuer elles] trs. Kk   17 in] and Kk Pw
disposiciouns] disposisiciouns Har¹   18 teching — counselyng] trs. Kk
Pw   teching] tekyng Kk   oþer] others Pw   19 his] om. Kk Pw
20 and] of add. Kk Pw   broþer] bretherne Pw   22 mowe] om. CP
clepid] callyd Kk Pw   23 ben] is CP   secound] toþer Kk   24 reisid]
reryd Kk Pw   abouen] in Pw   heed] toppe Pw   þoo] they Pw
26 toretes of þe] om. Pw   þe] om. Kk Pw

verteue. Gold enuirouneþ þe heed ; and bi wisdom we gouerne oure
f. 7b goostly werk in euery side. | Precious stones ȝeuin liȝt in beholding
of men ; and bi discrecioun we teche and counseilen oure breþren.
Þe toretes of þe floure-de-lices ȝeuyn two side braunches spreding,
5 on to þe riȝt side, anoþer to þe left, and on euen [up] aboue þe
heed ; and by perfeccioun of vertewe, þe·whiche is charite, we
ȝeue two side braunches of loue, þe whiche ben spreding oute, to
þe riȝt side to oure freendes, and on þe left side to oure enemyes,
and one euen up unto God, abouen mans vnderstondyng, þe
10 whiche is þe heed of þe soule. Þis is þe coroun of liif, þe whiche by
grace may be getyn here in þis liif.

And þerfore bere þee lowe in þi bataile, & suffre meekly þi temptaciouns tyl þou haue ben proued. For, [fro þou haue ben proued],
þan schalt þou take ouþer þis coroun here or elles þe toþer þere, or
15 boþe þis here and þe toþer þere. For whoso haþ þis here, he may
be ful sekir of þe toþer þere. And ful many þer ben þat ben ful
graciously prouid here and ȝit comen neuer to þis þat may be had
here in þis liif ; þe whiche, ȝif þei meekly contynow and paciently
abyde þe wille of oure Lorde, schal ful aboundingly resceiue þe
20 toþer þere in þe blis of heuen. Þee þink þis coroun feire þat may be
had here. Ȝe, bere þee as meekly as þou maist bi grace, for, in
comparison of þe toþer þere, it is bot as a noble to a woreld ful of
gold. Alle þis I sey to ȝeue þee coumfort and euidence of strengþe

1 enuirouneþ] ennourneþ Kk; or compasseth *add*. Pw   2 in] on Kk
Pw   euery] euere yche Kk   2-3 Precious . . . men] *om*. CP   5
side] and *add*. Kk Pw   up] *om*. Har¹ CP   6 vertewe] vertewes
Kk Pw   is] *om*. Kk   7 þe whiche ben] *om*. Kk Pw   oute] one
Kk Pw   8 on] one to Kk Pw   side] *om*. Kk CP   10 heed]
hygher parte Pw   11 in . . . liif] *om*. CP   12 And þerfore bere]
if þu *ins. in right margin* CP   12-13 temptaciouns] temptacyon Pw
13 tyl . . . proued] *om*. CP   fro . . . proued] *om*. Har¹   fro] from
Pw ; if CP   14 ouþer] eiþer CP   þis] þe to (one Pw) Kk Pw ;
om. CP   here] *om*. Kk Pw CP   elles] *om*. Pw ; þe ton or *add*.
CP   toþer] other Pw   þere] *om*. Kk Pw CP   15 þis] þat
oon CP   and] *om*. CP   þe] þat CP   toþer] other Pw CP   16
sekir] and sure *add*. Pw   toþer] other Pw   þere] *om*. Pw   ben] err
Kk, are Pw   17 ȝit] neuer *add*. Pw   neuer] *om*. Pw   18 in þis]
presente *add*. Pw   þis] *om*. CP   19 ful] worthely and *add*. Pw
aboundingly] haboundauntely Pw   resceiue] *ins. in right margin of*
Har¹   20 toþer] other Pw   þere] thre Pw   þe] hyghe *add*.
Pw   21 ȝe] ȝa Kk   22 þe] that Pw   toþer] other Pw
a] one Pw   woreld ful] worfulle Kk   23 and] in CP

in þi goostly batayle, þe whiche þou hast taken on hande in þe
trist of oure Lorde.

And alle þis I sey to late þee se hou fer þou arte ȝit fro þe
trewe knowyng of þin inward disposicioun, and þerafter to ȝeue
þee warnes not ouersone to ȝeue stede ne to folow þe singulere 5
sterynges of þi ȝong hert for drede of disseite. Alle þis I sey for to
schewe vnto þee my conseite þat I haue of þee & of þi steringes, as
þou hast askid of me. For I conseiue of þee þat þou arte ful able
& | ful gredely disposid to soche sodein steringes of singulere f. 8a
doynges, and ful fast to cleue vnto hem when þei ben resceyued; 10
and þat is ful perilous.

I say not þat þis abilnes and þis gredy disposicioun in þee, or
in any oþer þat is disposid as þou arte, þof al it be perilous, þat it
is þerfore iuel in itself; nay, so say I not. God forbede þat þou take
it so! Bot I say þat it is ful good in itself, and a ful grete abelnes to 15
ful grete perfeccioun, ȝe, and to þe grettest perfeccioun þat may
be in þis liif; I mene, ȝif þat a soule þat is so disposid wil besily,
niȝt and day, meke it to God and to good counsel, & strongly rise
and martir itself, wiþ castyng doun of þe owne witte and þe owne
wile in alle soche sodein & singulere steringes, and sey scharply 20
þat it wil not folow soche steringes, seme þei neuer so liking, so
heiȝ, ne so holy, bot if it haue þerto þe witnes and þe consentes of
som goostly techers (I mene soche as haue ben of longe tyme experte in singuler leuyng). Soche a soule for goostly continouaunce
þus in þis meeknes, may deserue, þorow grace & þe experience of 25
þis goostly bataile þus wiþ itself, for to take þe coroun of liif
touchid before.

And as grete an abilnes to good, as it is þis maner of disposicioun
in a soule þat is þus mekid as I sey, as perilous it is in anoþer soule,
soche one þat wil sodenly, wiþouten auysement of counsel, folow 30
þe steringes of þe gredy hert by þe owne witte & þe owne wyle.
And þerfore for Goddes loue bewar wiþ þis abilnes and wiþ þis

2 trist] truste Pw   3 fro] frome Pw   5 warnes] warnynge Pw
6 ȝong] *om.* Kk Pw   for] *om.* Pw   7 my . . . þee] *om.* CP   9
gredely] gretly Kk Pw   to] reseue *add.* Kk Pw   11 and] *om.* Pw
13 is] so *add.* Kk CP; thus *add.* Pw   al] *om.* Kk Pw   14 þerfore] *om.* Pw
15 (þat) it] *om.* Kk   a] *om.* CP   16 ȝe] ȝa Kk   17 a] *om.* Kk Pw CP
disposid] dyspysed Pw   19 it-] hym- Kk Pw   witte . . . owne]
om. Pw   20 in] to CP   sodein] stiringes *add.* CP   steringes] *om.* CP
22 witnes] wyttes Kk Pw CP   23 of] *om.* Pw   25 þe] *om.* Pw
29 (is) in] *ins.* Har[1]   30 þat] as Pw

maner of disposicioun þat I speke of, ȝif it be in þee as I sey, and
meek þee continowly to preyer and to counsel. Breke down þin
owne witte & þi wil in alle soche sodein & singulere steringes,
and folow hem not ouer liȝtly, til þou wite whens þei comen and
5 wheþer þei be acording for þee or not.

And touching þees steringes, of þe whiche þou askist my conseit
f. 8b & my counsel: | I say to þee þat I conseyue of hem suspeciously;
þat is, þat þei schold be conceyuid on ape maner. Men sein comonly þat ape doþ as he oþer seeþ. Forȝeue me ȝif I erre in my
10 suspecioun, I prey þee. Neuerþeles, þe loue þat I haue to þi soule
stereþ me by euydence þat I haue of a goostly broþer of þine and ·
of myne, þat was now late in ȝoure contrey, touchid wiþ þoo
same steringes of ful [streite] silence, of ful singulere fastynges, and
of ful only dwellyng, on ape maner, as he graunted vnto me after
15 longe comounyng wiþ me and when he had proued hymself and
his steringes. For, as he seyde, he had seen a man in ȝoure cuntre,
þe whiche man, as it is wel knowen, is euermore in grete silence, in
singulere fastyng, and in only dwellyng. And certes, as I suppose
fully, þei ben ful trewe steringes, þoo þat þat man haþ, causid al
20 only of grace þat he feliþ bi experience wiþinne, and not of any
siȝt or herdesay þat he haþ of any oþer mans silence wiþoutyn, þe
whiche cause ȝif it were, schuld be clepid apely, as I sei in my
simple meenyng.

And þerfore beware, and proue wel þi sterynges & whens þei
25 come. For houso þou arte steryd, wheþer fro wiþinne by grace or
fro wiþouten on ape maner, God wote and I not. Neuerþeles, þis
may I sey þee, in eschewing of perile liche vnto þis: loke þat þou be

1 in þee] *om.* Kk Pw   3 & þi wil] *added in right margin of* Har¹
4 til] to Kk Har²   whens] whyne Kk Har²; when CP   5 wheþer] why-
ther Pw   6 And] as *add.* Pw   þe] *om.* Kk   askist] me *add.* Har² Pw
my] *om.* Pw   conseit] counsayle Pw   7 my] *om.* Pw   counsel] con-
ceyte Pw   8 on] þe *add.* Pw; an *add.* CP   ape] apes Pw   9 þat]
the *add.* Pw; an (*ins.*) *add.* CP   oþer] others Pw   oþer seeþ] *trs.* Kk
Har² Pw; do *add.* Har² Pw   10 þe] *om.* Kk Har²   11 a] one Kk
Har² Pw   12 of] *om.* Pw   þat . . . contrey] *om.* Pw   þoo] the Pw
13 streite] grete Har¹   fastynges] fastyng Kk Har² Pw   14 ape] apes Pw
vnto] to CP   16 seyde] he seide (*can.*) *add.* Har¹   seyde, he] *om.* Pw
17 as] *om.* CP   18 certes] certaynly Pw   as] a CP   19 þoo] those Pw
þat] *om.* Pw   al] *om.* Pw   20 of] by Kk Har² Pw   22 were] it *add.* Kk
Har² Pw   clepid] called Kk Har² Pw   as] *om.* Kk   24 whens] whythen Kk
Har²   25 -so] *ins.* Har¹; *om.* Pw   fro] from Pw   26 ape] apes Pw   I not]
trs. Har²   27 þee] *om.* Kk Har² Pw CP   perile] perilles Kk Har² Pw CP

none ape ; þat is to sey, loke þat þi steringes to silence or to spekyng, to fastyng or to etyng, to onlines or to companye, wheþer þei
ben comyn fro wiþinne of habundaunce of loue & of deuocioun in
spirite and not fro wiþouten bi windowes of þi bodily wittes, þin
eren and þin iȝen ; for, as Ieremie seiþ pleinly, 'Bi soche windowes 5
comeþ in deeþ', 'Mors intrat per fenestras.' And þis suffiseþ, as
litel as it is, for answere to þe first, where þou askist of me what
is my conseite of þee and of þees steringes | þat þou spekist of to me f. 9a
in þi lettre.

And touching þe secound þing, where þou askist of me my 10
counseile in þis caas and soche oþer when þei falle: I beseche Almiȝti Iesu, as he is clepid þe 'Aungel of Grete Counseile', þat he
of his mercy be þi counselour and þi coumfortour in alle þi noye
and þi nede, and wisse me wiþ his wisdom to fulfille in party by
my teching, so simple as it is, þe trist of þin herte, þe whiche þou 15
hast to me bifore many oþer, a simple lewid wreche as I am, vnworþi to teche þee or any oþer for litelnes of grace & for lackyng of
kunnyng. Neuerþeles, þof I be neuer so lewid, ȝit schal I sumwhat
seie, answering to þi desire at my simple kunnyng, wiþ a trist in
God þat his grace schal be lerner & leder, whan kunnyng of kinde 20
and of clergie defaileþ.

Þou wost wel þiself þat silence in itself ne spekyng, also singulere fastyng ne comoun dietyng, onlines ne companie, alle þees,
ne ȝit any of hem, þei ben not þe trewe eendes of oure desire. Bot
to som men, and not to alle, þei ben meenes helping to þe eende, 25

1 steringes] styrryng Kk Har² Pw   3 fro] from Pw   in] of
Pw ; þe *add.* Kk Har² Pw   4 and not] or Pw   fro] from Pw   bi]
fro (from Pw) Kk Har² Pw ; þe *add.* Kk Har² Pw   wittes] as *add.* Pw
5 and] *om.* Pw   as] sancte *add.* Har² Pw   Ieremie] Jerome Kk Har² Pw
seiþ] precheþ Kk Har²   windowes] wiþ outen *add.* Har². *The reference is
given in rubrics in the right margin of* Har¹   6 And] *om.* CP   as] so
Kk Har² Pw CP   7 for] ane *add.* Kk Har² Pw CP   8 (and) of] *om.* Kk
10 And] as (*ins.*) *add.* CP   touching] towchand Kk Har²   11 and]
in *add.* Kk Har² Pw   12 clepid] called Kk Har² Pw. *The reference is
given in rubrics in the left margin of* Har¹   13 þi] *om.* CP   noye]
noyaunce Pw   14 wisse] ordre Pw   15 teching] tehing Har²   trist]
trust Pw   16 to] vnto Kk Har² Pw   many] in any, in *can.* CP   oþer]
others Pw   a] as CP   17 lackyng] wantyng Kk Har² ; lacke Pw
18 þof] yf Kk Har² Pw   neuer so] *om.* Pw   19 trist] trust Kk Pw ;
treste Har²   20 & leder] *om.* Pw   21 defaileþ] defalleþ Kk ; fayleth Pw
22 wost] wote Kk Har² ; ryȝt *add.* Kk Har² Pw   wel] in (*can.*) *add.* Har¹
also] *om.* Pw ; and *add.* Har²   23 ne] *om.* Pw   dietyng] etynge Pw
24 þei] *om.* Pw   eendes] ende Pw

ȝif þei ben done lawfuly & wiþ discrecioun; and elles ben þei more
lettyng þan forþering. And þerfore pleinly to speke ne pleinly to
be stylle, pleinly to ete ne pleinly to fast, pleinly to be in companye or pleinly to be only, þink I not to counsel þee at þis tyme;
5 for whi perfeccioun stondeþ not in hem. Bot þis counsel may I
ȝeue þee generaly to holde þee by in þees sterynges and in alle
oþer liche vnto þeese, euermore where þou fyndest two con-
traries as ben þeese, silence & spekyng, fastyng & etyng, onlines &
companye, comoun cloþing of Cristen mens religion & singulere
10 abites of diuerse & deuisid broþerhedes, with alle soche oþer
whatso þei be, þe whiche in hemself ben bot werkes of kynde &
of men.

    For þou hast it bi kynd and bi statute of þin vtter man now for
f. 9b to speke & now for to be stylle, now for | to ete and now for to fast,
15 now for to be in company & now to be only, now to be comoun
in cloþing & now to be in singulere abite, euer when þee list and
whan þou seest þat any of hem schuld be speedful and helply
to þee in noresching of þe heuenly grace worching wiþinne in þi
soule, bot ȝif it be so (þat God forbede!) þat þou or any oþer be so
20 lewid & so bleendid in þe·sorouful temptaciouns of þe midday
deuel, þat ȝe binde ȝow by any crokid auowe to any soche singulertees, as it were vnder colour of holines feined vnder soche an
holyliche þraldom, in ful and fynal distroiing of þe fredom of
Criste, þe whiche is þe goostly abite of þe souereyn holines þat
25 may be in þis liif or in þe toþer, by þe witnes of Poule seiing þus:

1 wiþ] by CP   ben] ere Kk Har²; by Pw   2 forþering] helpynge
Pw   3 ne] *om.* Pw   7 vnto] to Pw   where] when Har²
8 ben] ere Kk Har² Pw   (fastyng) &] *om.* Pw   &] *om.* Pw   9
Cristen mens] crysteyns Kk; crystines Har²; crysten Pw   10 broþer-]
bredyr- Kk Har² CP   alle] *om.* Pw   11 ben] ere Kk Har² Pw
bot] not (*can.*) CP   13 and bi statute] *om.* Pw   for] *om.* Pw   14 &] *om.*
Pw   for to be] *om.* Pw   for to] *om.* Pw   and] *om.* Kk Har² Pw   for
to] *om.* Pw   15 for to be] *om.* Pw   now] for *add.* Kk Har²   to be] *om.*
Pw   only] alone Pw   to be] *om.* Pw   15–16 comoun in] *trs.* Kk Har² Pw
16 now] *om.* Har²   to be] *om.* Pw   þee] thou Pw   17 seest] doost fele Pw
any] *corrected from* many Har¹ CP   helply] helpefull Pw   18 to] vnto Kk
Har²   to þee] *om.* Pw   in] to the Pw   þe] *om.* Kk Har² Pw   in] *om.* Kk Har²
Pw   þi] the Pw   19 be] by Pw   þat] whiche Pw   so] *om.* Pw   20 bleendid]
blyndyd Kk Har² Pw CP   21 deuel] enmy Har²   binde] blynde Pw   22
vnder] ouþer Kk   vnder] -neþe *add.* Kk Har² Pw   23 holyliche] holy
Pw; holich CP   þraldom] I meane excepte the solempne vowes of holy
relygyon *add.* Pw   25 toþer] other Pw   witnes] wytnessyng Kk Pw   of]
sancte *add.* Har² Pw. *The reference is given in rubrics in the left margin of* Har¹

'Vbi spiritus Domini, ibi libertas'; 'Þere where þe spirite of God is, þer is fredom.'

And þerto when þou seest þat alle soche werkes in þeire use mow be boþe good & iuel, I preie þee leue hem boþe, for þat is þe most ese for þee for to doo if þou wilt be meek. And leue þe corious 5 beholdyng & seching in þi wittes to loke wheþer is betir. Bot do þou þus: sette þe tone on þe to honde and þe toþer on þe toþer, and chese þee a þing þe whiche is hid bitwix hem, þe whiche þing when it is had, ȝeueþ þee leue, in fredom of spirite, to beginne and to seese in holding any of þe oþer at þin owne ful list, wiþouten 10 any blame.

Bot now þou askest me what is þat þing. I schal telle þee what I mene þat it is. It is God for whom þou schuldest be stille, ȝif þou schuldest be stylle; and for whom þou schuldest speke, ȝif þou schuldest speke; and for whom þou schuldest fast, ȝif þou schuldest 15 fast; and for whom þou schuldest ete, ȝif þou schuldest ete; and for whom þou schuldest be only, ȝif þou schuldest be only; and for whom þou schuldest be in companie, if þou schuldest be in | com- f. 10a panie; and so forþ of alle þe remenant, whatso þei be. For silence is not God, ne speking is not God; fastyng is not God, ne etyng is 20 not God; onlines is not God ne companye is not God; ne ȝit any of alle þe oþir soche two contraries. He is hid betwix hem, and may not be founden by any werk of þi soule, bot al only bi loue of þin herte. He may not be knowen by reson. He may not be þouȝt, getyn, ne trasid, by vnderstonding. Bot he may be loued and chosen 25 wiþ þe trewe, louely wille of þin herte. Chese þee him; and þou

1 þe spirite] *om.* Har² 4 iuel] ille Har² 5 ese] esye Kk for] to Kk Har² for] *om.* Pw 7 tone] one Pw to] tone Kk Har²; one Pw toþer] other Pw toþer] other Pw 8 þee] *om.* Har² þe whiche] þat Kk Har² Pw CP hid] bydde Pw bitwix] bytwene Pw 10 seese] chese Kk holding] of *add.* Kk Har² Pw oþer] toþer Kk Har² CP; others Pw owne] *om.* CP list] lust Pw 12 askest] at *add.* Pw 13 þat] and what Pw God] good Pw 13–14 ȝif . . . stylle] *om.* Pw 15 and] *om.* Pw fast] etc. *add.* Pw 15–19 ȝif . . . companie] *om.* Pw 16 (ete) and] *om.* Kk Har² CP 19 forþ] forsoþe CP -so] euer *add.* Pw silence] it *add.* CP 20–22 ne speking . . . bitwix] ne fastynge / ne etynge / ne onelynesse / ne company / ne harde werynge of synguler habytes / ne comune werynge are not god / but he is hyd bytwene Pw 20 speking] it *add.* CP fastyng] it *add.* CP etyng] it *add.* CP 21 onlines] it *add.* CP companye] it *add.* CP 22 oþir] toþer Kk Har² 24 He . . . reson] *om.* Kk þouȝt] *om.* Kk Har² Pw 25 getyn] þouȝte *add.* Kk; by þouȝte *add.* Har² Pw ne] *om.* Pw ne trasid] *trs., but corrected* Har¹ trasid] concluded Pw 26 þee] þou Kk Har² Pw

arte silently spekyng & spekingly silent, fastyngly etyng and
etyngly fasting; and so forþ of alle þe remenant.

Soche a louely chesing of God, þus wisely lesing and seking
him oute wiþ þe clene wille of a trewe herte bitwix alle soche to,
5 leuyng hem boþe whan þei come and profren hem to be þe poynt
and þe pricke of oure goostly beholding, is þe worþiest trasing and
sekyng of God þat may be getyn or lerned in þis liif (I meene, for
a soule þat wil be contemplatife); 3e, þof al þat a soule, þat þus
sekiþ, see noþing þat may be conseiued wiþ hir goostly i3e of reson.
10 For 3if God be þi loue and þi menyng, þe cheef and þe pointe of þin
herte, it suffiseþ to þee in þis liif, þof al þou se neuer more of him
wiþ þe i3e of þi reson alle þi liif tyme. Soche a blinde schote with
þe scharp darte of longing loue may neuer faile of þe prik, þe
whiche is God; as himself seiþ in þe *Book of Loue*, where he spekiþ
15 to a langwisching soule and a louyng, seiing þus: 'Vulnerasti cor
meum, soror mea, amica mea, sponsa mea, vulnerasti cor meum in
vno oculorum tuorum'; 'Þou hast wounded myn hert, my sistre,
my lemman, & my spouse, þou hast woundid myn herte in one of
þin i3en.' I3en of þe soule þei ben two, reson & loue. By reson we
f. 10b 20 mowe trace how | mi3ty, how wise, & how good he is in his crea-
tures, bot not in himself. Bot euer whan reson defaileþ, þan list
loue liue and lerne for to plei; for bi loue we may [fynde] him,
[fele] him, and hit him euen in himself. It is a wonderful i3e loue,
for of a louing soule it is seide of oure Lorde: 'Þou hast woundid
25 myn herte in one of þin i3en'; þat is to sey, in loue þat is blinde to
many þinges and seeþ bot þat o þing þat it sekiþ, and þerfore it

1 silently] scylence Pw   1–2 fastyngly . . . fasting] *om.* Har²   2
remenant] toþer Har²   4 clene — trewe] *trs.* Kk Har² Pw   bitwix]
bytwene Pw   5 hem] hym *add.* Har²   7 getyn or lerned]
had Kk Har² Pw   8 3e] 3a Kk Har²   al] *om.* Pw   9 may]
om. Kk   hir] the Pw   10 cheef] chose Kk Har²; choyse Pw   11 to]
om. Pw   al] *om.* Pw   se neuer] *trs.* CP   of him] *om.* Pw   12 i3e]
eyes Pw   13 þe] a Pw   faile] defayle Kk Har²   15 a] þe Pw
a] *om.* Pw   and a louyng] *added in right margin of* Har¹   seiing] sange
Kk. *The reference is given in rubrics in the right margin of* Har¹   16 amica
mea] et *add.* Kk Har² Pw   17 tuorum] þat is *add.* Har²   sistre] suster
Kk   18 &] *om.* Pw   19 þei] *om.* Kk Har² Pw; þere CP   two] that is to
say *add.* Pw   By] the *add.* Pw   20 trace] and fynde *add.* Kk Har² Pw
&] *om.* CP   good] þat *add.* Kk Har² Pw   21 defaileþ] fayleþ Har² Pw
þan] *om.* Har²   22 liue] *om.* Pw   for] *om.* Pw   22–23 fynde — fele] *trs.*
Har¹ CP   23 and] *om.* Pw   in] *om.* Kk Har² Pw CP   i3e] this *add.*
Pw   24 of] *om.* CP   is] onely *add.* Kk Har² Pw   25 in] with Pw
in] *om.* Kk Har² Pw   þat] *ins.* Har¹

findeþ and feliþ, hitteþ and woundeþ þe point and þe pricke þat
it scheteþ at wel sonner þan it schuld, ȝif þe siȝt were sondrid in
beholding of many þinges, as it is whan þe reson ransakiþ & sekiþ
amonges alle soche sere þinges as ben þees—silence and [speking],
singulere fastyng and comoun etyng, onlines or companie, and 5
alle soche oþer—to loke wheþer is beter.

Lat be þis maner of doing, I preie þee, and late as þou wist not
þat þere were any soche menes, I mene for to gete God bi; for
trewly no more þer is, ȝif þou wilt be verrey contemplatyfe & sone
sped of þi purpos. And þerfore I preie þee and oþer liche vnto þee 10
wiþ þe apostle seiing þus: ;Videte vocacionem vestram, et in ea
vocacione qua vocati estis, state'; 'Seeþ ȝoure cleping, and in þat
cleping þat ȝe ben clepid, stondeþ' stifly and abideþ in þe name
of Iesu. Þi cleping is to be verrey contemplatyfe, ensaumplid by
Mary, Martha sister. Do þan as Mary did. Set þe poynte of þin herte 15
upon o þing. 'Porro vnum est nesessarium'; 'For o þing is nesessarie', þe whiche is God. Him woldest þou haue; him sekist þou;
him list þee loue; him list þee fele; him list þee holde þee bi; and
neiþer by sylence ne bi spekyng, by singulere fasting ne by
comoun etyng, by onlines ne by companous wonyng. For sum- 20
tyme silence is good, bot þat same tyme speking were betir; and
aȝensward, somtyme speking is good, bot þat same time silence
were | beter; and so forþ of alle þe remenaunt, as is fastyng, etyng, f. 11a

2 þe] *om.* Pw   sondrid] sonderyng Kk Har²; sondry Pw   3 ransakiþ &] *om.* Pw   4 amonges] among Kk Har² Pw   sere] ∧ *mark*
added, diuerse written in left margin CP   ben] ere Kk Har² Pw   þees]
om. Pw   speking] spekinges Har¹   5 singulere] *om.* Pw   comoun
. . . and] *om.* Pw   6 soche] these Pw   oþer] lyke *add.* Pw   8 mene]
ordenyd *add.* Kk Har² Pw CP; for þe *add.* Har² CP   for] *om.* Har² CP
9 verrey] verrely Kk   10 and] also *add.* Har²   vnto] to Pw CP   11
apostle] Paule *add.* Har². *The reference is given in rubrics in the right*
margin of Har¹   12 cleping] callyng Kk Har² Pw   13 cleping]
callyng Kk Har² Pw   clepid] called Kk Har² Pw   and abideþ] *om.* Pw
14 cleping] callyng Kk Har² Pw   15 Martha sister] Magdaleyne Pw
sister] suster Kk   þan] þou CP   16 *The reference is given in rubrics in*
the right margin of Har¹   Porro] Pario Pw   17 whiche] þing *add.* Har²
sekist] sekeþ Kk Har²   18 þee] to *add.* Pw   þee] to *add.* Pw   fele]
& *add.* CP   fele] hym lyst þe (to *add.* Pw) see and *add.* Kk Har² Pw   þee]
to *add.* Pw   19 neiþer] nother Pw   20 by onlines . . . wonyng] and so
of alle þe toþer Har²   companous] company Pw   wonyng] *om.* Pw; by
harde werynge ne by easye *add.* Pw   21 þat . . . speking] spekyng were
þe (þat Pw) same tyme Kk Har² Pw   22 aȝens-] aȝene Kk Har² Pw CP
23–74/1 and so . . . soche oþer] lykewyse of fastynge & of al þe remenaunt Pw
23 alle] *om.* Har²   remenaunt] toþer Har²   fastyng] and *add.* Kk Har²

onlines, and companie, & alle soche oþer. For somtyme þe tone is
good, bot þe toþer is betir; bot neiþer of hem is any time þe best.
And þerfore lat be good al þat is good, and betir al þat is betir,
for boþe þei wil fayle and haue an ende; and chese þee þe best,
5 wiþ Mary þi mirour, þat neuir wil defaile. 'Maria, inqui[t] opti-
mus, optimam partem elegit, que non auferetur ab ea.' Þe best is
Almiȝty Iesu, and he seide þat Mary, in ensaumple of alle con-
templatiues, had chosen þe best, þe whiche schuld neuer be take
fro hir. And þerfore, I preie þee, wiþ Mary leue þe good and þe
10 betir, and chese þee þe best.

Lat hem be, alle soche þinges as ben þeese—silence & speking,
fasting & etyng, onlines & companie, & alle soche oþer—and take no
kepe to hem. Þou wost not what þei bemenen, and, I preie þee,
coueite not to wite. And ȝif þou schalt any tyme þenk on hem or
15 speke, þink þan and sey þat þei ben so heiȝ & so worþi þinges of
perfeccioun—for to kun speke or for to kun be stille, for to kun
fast & for to kun ete, for to kun be only & for to kun be in companie—þat it were bot a foly and a foule presumcioun to soche a
freel wrecche as þou arte for to medel þee of so grete perfeccioun.
20 For whi for to speke & for to be stille, for to ete & for to fast, & for
to be only and for to be in companie euer whan we wile, mow we
haue bi kinde; bot for to kun do alle þees, we may not bot bi
grace.

And withouten doute soche grace is neuer getin bi any mene of
25 soche streite silence, of soche singulere fastyng, or of soche only
dwellyng þat þou spekist of, þe whiche is causid fro wiþouten by

1 tone] one Pw   2 toþer] other Pw   is] were Har²   neiþer] nowþir
Kk Har², nother Pw   is] at *add*. Pw   3 good] & *add*. Pw   betir]
with *add*. Pw   4 fayle] defale Kk Har²   an] *om*. Kk Har² CP
and] but Pw   þee] *om*. Kk   5 defaile] fayle Pw. *The reference is
given in rubrics in the left margin of* Har¹   inquit] inquid Har¹ Pw CP
optimus] *om*. Kk   9 fro] from Pw   þee] lyue *add*. Pw   leue]
om. Pw   10 þee] *om*. Pw   11 hem] *om*. Pw   ben] ere Kk Har²; is Pw
þeese] *om*. Pw   11–12 & speking . . . oþer] & these other Pw   13 wost]
wote Kk Har²   be-] *om*. Pw   14 schalt] at *add*. Pw   on hem]
om. Kk Har² Pw   15 speke] of þeim *add*. Kk Har² Pw   and] to Pw
ben] ere Kk Har² Pw   16 kun] *om*. Pw   or] and Kk Pw CP   for to
kun] *om*. Pw   kun] *om*. Pw   17 for] *om*. Pw   kun] *om*. Pw   kun]
om. Pw   for] *om*. Pw   kun] *om*. Pw CP   20–21 for to speke . . . com-
panie] *om*. Pw   21 (only) and] or Har²   mow] *om*. Pw   we] may *add*.
Pw   22 haue] them *add*. Pw   for] *om*. Pw   kun] *om*. Pw   þees]
this Pw   we may] *trs*. Kk Har² Pw   25 streite] forȝette CP   of] *om*. Pw
26 þat] as Kk Har² Pw   fro] from Pw

occasion of hering & of seing of any oþer mans soche singulere
doinges. Bot ȝif euer schal þis grace be getin, it behoueþ to be
lerned of God fro wiþinne, vnto whom þou hast listeli lenid many
day before wiþ alle þe loue of þin herte, | vtterly voiding fro þi f. 11b
goostly beholding alle maner of siȝt of any þing bineþe him, þof al 5
þat som of þoo þinges, þat I bid þee þus voide, schuld seme in þe
siȝt of som man a ful worþi mene to gete God bi. Ȝe, say what men
say wile, bot do þou as I say þee, and lat þe proue witnes. For to
him þat wil be sped of his purpos goostly, it suffiseþ to him for
a mene, and him nediþ no mo bot þe actuele minde of good God 10
only, wiþ a reuerent stering of lastyng loue; so þat mene vnto
God gete þee none bot God, ȝif þou kepe hole þi stering of loue,
þat þou maist fele bi grace in þin hert, and scaterst not þi goostly
beholding þerfro.

Þen þat same þat þou felest schal wel kun telle þee when þou 15
schalt speke and when þou schalt be stille. And it schal gouerne
þee discretly in al þi leuyng withouten any errour, and teche þee
mistely how þou schalt beginne and seese in alle soche doinges of
kinde wiþ a grete & souerein discrecioun. For if þou maist by
grace kepe [it] in custom and in contynuel worching, þan ȝif it be 20
needful to þee for to speke, for to comounly ete, or for to bide in
cumpanye, or for to do any soche oþer þing þat longeþ to þe
comoun trewe custom of Cristen men and of kynde, it schal first
stire þee softely to speke or to do þat oþer comoun þing of kynde,
whatso it be; and þan, ȝif þou do it not, it schal smite as sore as 25
a prik on þin hert & pine þee ful sore, and late þee haue no pees
bot ȝif þou do it. And on þe same maner, ȝif þou be in spekyng or

2 euer schal] *om.* Pw   grace] shall euer *add.* Pw·   to] *om.* Kk
Har²   3 fro] from Pw   listeli] lustely Pw   lenid] lyued Har²; lined
CP   many] a *add.* Pw   4 herte] or (*can.*) *add.* Har¹   vtterly] entyerly
Pw   voiding] wodyng Kk   fro] from Pw   5 him] selfe *add.* Har²
al] *om.* Pw   6 þoo] *ins.* Har¹; these Pw   6–7 in þe siȝt of] to Pw
7 man] men Har² Pw   3e] Ȝa Kk Har²   what] *om.* Pw   men] what
they *add.* Pw   8 do] saye Pw   þee] *om.* Pw   9 þat] sone *add.*
Har²   wil] sone *add.* Kk   be] soone *add.* Pw CP   to] *om.* Pw   10
him] he Pw   12 þee] thou Pw   15 kun] *om.* Pw   17 þi] doing
(*can.*) *add.* Har¹   18 mistely] pryuely Pw   soche] thy Pw   doinges]
doyng Kk Har² Pw   19 &] a *add.* Kk Har² CP   20 it] þee Har¹   (and)
in] *om.* Kk Pw   21 needful] s (*can.*) *add.* Har¹; or spedefulle *add.* Kk Har²
Pw   (or) for] *om.* Pw   22 for] *om.* Pw   23 comoun] *om.* CP   24
þee] fulle *add.* Kk Har² Pw   or] for *add.* Kk Har²   25 -so] euer *add.* Pw
smite] stryke Kk Har² Pw   26 pine] payne Pw   pees] rest Pw

in any soche oþer werk þat is comoun to þe cours of kynde, ȝif it
be needful and speedful to þee to be stille and to sette þee to þe
contrary, as is fastyng to etyng, onlines to companie, and alle.
soche oþer, þe whiche ben werkes of singulere holines, it wil stire
5 þee to hem.

So þat þus by experience of soche a blinde stering of loue unto
f. 12a God, a contemplatyfe soule | comeþ sonner to þat grace of dis-
crecioun for to kun speke and for to kun be stille, for to kun ete
and for to kun fast, for to kun be in companye and for to kun be
10 only, and alle soche oþer, þan by any soche singulertees as þou
spekist of, taken by þe steringes of mans owne witte and his wile
wiþinne in himself or ȝit bi þe ensaumple of any oþer mans doing
wiþouten, whatso it be. For whi soche streynid doinges vnder þe
steringes of kynde, wiþouten steringes of grace, is a passing pine
15 wiþouten any profite, bot ȝif it be to hem þat ben religious or þat
han hem bi enioinyng in penance, where profite riseþ only bicause
of obedience & not bi soche streitnes of doyng; wiþouten, þe
whiche is pinful to alle þat it proueþ. Bot louely and listely to
wilne haue God is grete & passing ese, trewe goostly pees, and
20 erles of þe eendles rest.

And þerfore speke whan þee list & leue whan þee list; ete
whan þee list and fast whan þee list; be in companie whan þee list
& be by þiself whan þee list; so þat God and grace be þi leder.
Late fast who fast wil, and be only who wil, and lat holde silence

1 any] *om.* Pw   is] to (*can.*) *add.* Har¹   comoun] come Pw   cours]
curse Kk   2 and] or Kk Har² Pw   to] be (*can.*) *add.* Har¹   and]
for *add.* Kk Har² Pw   3 fastyng . . . companie] onelynesse to company
fastynge to eatynge Pw   4 oþer] others Pw   ben] ere Kk Har² Pw
6 unto] to Pw   7 sonner] more sone Kk Har² Pw   þat] þe Kk   8 kun]
lerne to Pw   kun] lerne to Pw   8–10 for to kun ete . . . be only] *om.*
Har²   9 and] or CP   kun] lerne to Pw   kun] lerne to Pw   kun]
lerne to Pw   10 alle soche oþer] so in alle þe toþer Har²   oþer] others
Pw   11 steringes] styrryng Kk Har² Pw   of] a *add.* Kk Har² Pw CP
12 in] *om.* Kk Har² Pw CP   13 -so] euer *add.* Pw   14 steringes]
tochyng Kk Har² Pw   pine] payne Pw   15 to] in Kk Har² Pw   ben]
erre Kk Har² Pw   16 han] do Pw   in] of Pw   17 not bi] any
add. Kk Har² Pw   18 whiche] it (*can.*) *add.* Har¹   pinful] paynfull
Pw   listely] lustely Pw   to] *om.* Pw   19 wilne] wyllen Kk Har²;
wyllynge Pw; to *add.* Har² Pw   haue] loue Pw   and passing] *om.* Pw
20 erles] ernest Pw; ernes CP   þe] *om.* Har²   22 be] wonne Kk Har²
CP   23 be] *om.* Kk CP   by þiself] alone Pw   so þat] els Kk Har² Pw
24 fast] *om.* Kk Har² Pw; so CP   who fast wil and] *om.* Pw   who] so *add.*
CP   who wil] *om.* Pw   lat] *om.* Pw

who hold wil; bot holde þee bi God, þat no man begileþ. For
silence & speking, fastyng & etyng, onlines & companye, alle may
begile. And ȝif þou here of any man þat spekiþ or of any þat is
stille, of any þat eteþ or of any þat fasteþ, or of any þat is in companye or elles by himself, þink þou & sey, if þou schalt, þat þei 5
kun do as þei schuld do, bot ȝif þe contrary schewe in aperte. Bot
loke þou do not as þei do; I mene, for þei do so, on ape maner.
For neiþer þou kanst, ne parauenture þou arte not disposid as þei
ben. And þerfore leue to worche after oþer mens disposicions; and
worche after þin owne, if þou maist knowe what it is. And vnto 10
þe tyme be þat þou maist wite what it is, worche after þo mens |
counseile, þat knowen here owne disposicioun, bot not after þeire f. 12b
disposicioun. For soche men schuld ȝeue counsel in soche cases,
and elles none. And þis suffiseþ for an answere for alle þi lettre.
Þe grace of God be euermore wiþ þee, in þe name of Iesu. Amen. 15

1 who] so *add.* Kk, Har² (*ins.*), Pw CP   hold] *om.* Kk Har² Pw   no
man] *om.* Pw   begileþ] dothe begylde Pw; þe *add.* Kk; no man *add.* Pw
2 &] *om.* Pw   fastyng] onelynesse Pw   etyng] company Pw   onlines]
fastynge Pw   companye] eatynge Pw   3 begile] begylde Pw; the
add. Pw   of] *om.* Pw   or] *om.* Pw   4 stille] or *add.* CP   4–5
of any . . . himself] moche fastynge or alone or dothe the contraryes of
these Pw   of] *om.* Kk   or] *om.* Kk Har²   5 him-] hem- CP   þou
schalt] the lyste Pw   6 aperte] a parte Pw   Bot] loke (*can.*) *add.*
Har¹   7 loke] that *add.* Pw   for] that *add* Pw   on] an *add.* CP
ape] apes Pw   8 neiþer] nouþer Kk Har², nother Pw   not] ȝit
add. Har²   9 ben] ere Kk Har² Pw   to] *om.* Pw   disposicions]
dysposicion Kk Har²   10 worche] þu *add.* Har²   what it is] it Pw
11 be] *om.* Pw   wite] knawe Kk Har² Pw CP   þo] no Pw   12 counseile]
consels Kk; but syth *add.* Pw   knowen] well *add.* Pw   12–13 bot . . .
disposicioun] *om.* Pw   13 cases] causes Pw   14 elles none] *trs.* Pw
an] *om.* Kk CP   for] to Kk Har² Pw   lettre] as me thynketh *add.* Pw
15 (in) þe] *om.* Kk

A TRETIS OF
DISCRESCYON OF
SPIRITES

A Tretis of Discrescyon of Spirites

For-þi þat þer ben diuerse kindes of spirites, þerfore it is needful to
us discrete knowing of hem, siþ it so is þat we ben lernid of þe
apostle Seinte Iohun not to bileue to alle spirites. For it miȝte seme
5 to somme, þat ben bot litil in kunnyng and namely of goostly
þinges, þat iche þouȝt þat souniþ in mans herte schuld be þe
speche of none oþer spirite, bot only of mans owne spirite. And
þat it is not so, boþe beleue and witnes of Holy Scripture prouen
apeertly. 'For I schal here,' seiþ þe prophete Dauid, 'not what I
10 speke myself, bot what þat my Lorde God spekiþ in me.' And
anoþer prophete seiþ þat an aungel spak in him. And also we ben
leernid in þe psalme þat wickid spirites senden iuel þouȝtis into
men. And ouer þis, þat þer is a spirite of þe flessche not good, þe
apostle Poule schewiþ apeertly, where he seiþ þat som men ben
15 fulle blowyn wiþ þe spirite of here flessche. And also þat þer is þe

1 *Title* Here biginniþ a tretis (pystylle Har²) of discrescyon (in knowynge
add. Kk Har²) of spirites Har¹ Kk Har²; Here followeth a devowte treatyse
of dyscerninge of spyrites very necessarie for gostly lyvers Bo Pw; Here
begynneþ a tretys of iij dyuers þouȝtes þt come ofte to men & ask to know
to wiþstond hem CP; Here begynnyth A profytable ynformacyon techyng
a man to knowe the kynd of spyrytys whych ben good and whych not Br
2 For-þi] For because Bo Pw Br   need-] spede- CP   3 us] to haue *add.*
Br   knowing] knowlege Br   so is] *trs.* Bo Pw Br   lernid] tawghte Bo Pw
of] by Br   4 Seinte] sancte Har²   not . . . spirites] *The reference is given
in rubrics in the left margin of* Har¹   to] yeue *add.* Br   to] *om.* Har²
5 bot] *om.* Br.   in] in *add.* Har¹   kunnyng] connynynge Pw   6 iche]
every Bo Pw Br   souniþ] semys Kk   in] a *add.* Bo   be] bee *add.* Br
6–7 þe speche . . . spirite] *om.* Br   7 only] *om.* Bo Pw Br   of]
a Br; a *add.* Bo Pw   8 it] *om.* Har² Bo Pw CP Br   so] sothe
Har²   boþe] as Br; by *add.* Bo Pw   beleue and] *om.* Br   and witnes]
written after Scripture, *but order altered by scribal correction in* Har¹ *to that
of* Kk Har² Bo Pw Br; CP *retains original order of* Har¹   and] also *add.*
Bo   Scripture] shall *add.* Br   8–9 prouen apeertly] *om.* Bo Pw   9
apeertly] openly Br   I schal here seiþ] as Br   seiþ þe prophete] Har⁴ *here
begins*   seiþ] davyd *add.* Bo   þe] holy *add.* Br   Dauid] *om.* Bo; sayth y
shall heere *add.* Br. *The reference is given in rubrics in the left margin of* Har¹
what] þt thyng that Br   10 bot] y shall heere *add.* Br   þat] *ins.* Har¹;
om. Bo Pw Br   my] our Br   God] *om.* Br   11 *The reference is given in
rubrics in the left margin of* Har¹   12 leernid] tawght Bo Pw. *The reference
is given in the left margin of* Har¹   þat] the *add.* Bo Pw   13 þat] *om.* Har²
CP   of] in Bo Pw   14 apeertly] playnly Bo Br   where he seiþ] sayyng Br   ben] are Bo Pw   15 blowyn] or inflate *add.* Bo Pw   here] the Bo
Br. *The reference is given in rubrics in the left margin of* Har¹   þe] a Har⁴ Bo

spirite of þe woreld he declariþ pleinly, where he makiþ ioye in
God, not only for himself bot also for his disciples, þat þei had
not takin þat spirite of þe woreld bot þat þat is sent of God, þe
whiche is þe Holy Goost.

And þees two spirites of þe flessche and also of þe woreld ben, 5
as it were, seruauntes or seriauntes of þat cursid spirite, þe foule
feend of helle; so þat þe spirite of wickidnes be lorde of þe spirite
of þe flessche and also of þe spirite of þe woreld. And whiche of
þees þre spirites þat spekiþ to oure spirite, we schul not beleue
hem, for whi þei speke neuer bot þat þei lede to þe losse boþe of 10
body and of soule.

And whiche [spirite] it is þat spekiþ to oure spirite, þe speche of
þat same spirite þat spekiþ schal fully declare. For euermore þe
spirite of þe flessche spekiþ softe þinges and esy to þe body, | þe f. 1b
spirite of þe woreld veine þinges and couetyse of worschip, and 15
þe spirite of þe feende felle þinges and bitter. As ofte-tymes as any
þouȝt smiteþ on oure hertes of mete, of drinke, and of slepe, of
softe cloþing, of lecherie, & of alle oþer soche þinges, þe whiche
longin to besines of flessche, and makiþ oure herte for to brenne, as
it were, in a longing desire after alle soche þinges, be we ful sekir 20

1–2 where . . God] sayyng y doo yoy yn our lord Br   2 -self] he
sayd *add.* Br   3 takin] receyuyd Br   þat] þe Har⁴ Br. *The reference
is given in the right margin of* Har¹   þe] thys Br   þat] *om.* Bo Pw;
spyryt *add.* Br   sent] *om.* Har⁴ Br   3–4 þe whiche is] sent by Br   5
two] tweyn CP   also] *om.* Br   6 seruauntes or seriauntes] too massyngers
and seruantys Br   or seriauntes] *om.* Har²   of] vnto Br   þat] þe Kk
Har² Bo Pw Br   spirite] of *add.* Kk Har⁴ CP Br   7 feend] olde enmy Har²
wickidnes] þe feend Br   be] is Bo Pw   lorde] both *add.* Br   of] to Br
8 þe] *om.* Br   9 þre] *om.* Bo Br   spirites] it be *add.* Bo   spekiþ]
speken Har⁴ CP   schul] shuld Kk Har² Bo Pw Br   not] yn no wyse Br
beleue] to *add.* Har⁴   10 hem] hym, y *can.*, e *ins.* Kk; him Har⁴ CP Br
speke neuer] *trs.* Bo   bot] anone by that their spekynge *add.* Bo Pw   þat]
om. Bo Pw   þat þei lede] tho thyngys þt ledeth vs Br   þe] *om.* Kk Har²
Bo Pw Br   losse] lesse Kk   11 of] *om.* Bo   12 spirite] *All MSS.*
except Har¹   13 þat spekiþ] *om.* Br   schal] tell vs and *add.* Br   fully]
fulle Kk   14 esy] ese Har²   15 woreld] spekythe *add.* Br   coue-
tyse] couetyng Br; or ambysion *add.* Bo Pw   16 spirite] of malece *add.* Kk
Har² Bo Pw   of þe feende] *om.* Kk Har²; of hell (*om.* Pw) spekythe *add.*
Bo Pw   felle] full sotell Bo; byttyr Br   bitter] deceytfull Br; Wherfore
add. Bo Pw   As] Also Br   ofte-] often Bo Pw   -tymes] tyme Har⁴; *om.* Bo
Br   17 on] to Bo Pw   (mete) of] or Kk Bo   and] *om.* Har² Har⁴ Bo
CP Br   slepe] and *add.* Br   18 cloþing . . . soche] *om.* Br   19 to] the
add. Bo Pw Br   of] þe *add.* Har² Bo Pw CP Br   herte] hertes Bo
for to] *om.* Br   brenne] brynne Kk   20 longing] to *add.* Br   þinges]
to have them *add.* Bo; than *add.* Br   sekir] suer Bo Br

þat it is þe spirite of þe flesche þat spekiþ. And þerfore put we him
awey in as moche as we goodly may be grace, for he is oure aduer-
sary. As oft-tymes as any þou3t smitiþ on oure herte of veyne ioye
of þis woreld, kindelyng in us a desire to be holden feire & to be
5 fauourid, to be holden of grete kynne & of grete kunnyng, to be
holden wise & worþi, or elles to haue grete degre & hi3e office in
þis liif (soche þou3tes & alle oþer, þe whiche wolde make a man to
seme hei3 & worschipful, not only in þe si3te of oþer bot also in
þe si3te of hymself) no doute bot it is þe spirite of þe woreld þat
10 spekiþ alle þees, a fer more perilous enmye þan is þe spirite of
þe flessche, and wiþ moche more besines he schuld be put of. And
ofte-tymes it befalleþ þat þees two seruauntes & seriauntes of þe
foule feend, þe spirite and prince of wraþþe and of wickidnes, ben
ouþer by grace and goostly slei3t of a soule stifly put doune and
15 troden doune vnder fote, or elles by queintise of here malicious
maister, þe foule feend of helle, þei ben queintly wiþdrawen, for
he þenkiþ himself for to rise wiþ grete malice and wraþþe, as a
lyon rennyng felly, for to asaile þe seeknes of oure sely soules. And
þis befalleþ as ofte as þe þou3t of oure herte steriþ us, not to þe
20 lust of oure flessche, ne 3it to þe veine ioye of þis woreld, bot it

1 þat] *om.* Kk Har² Bo Pw   þat spekiþ] *om.* Br; it *add.* Kk Har² Bo Pw
put we] lett vs put Br   2 goodly] *om.* Br   3 As]And as Bo   oft-tymes]
often Bo Pw Br   on] yn Br   herte] hertes Kk Har² Bo Pw   of] of *add.* Pw
4 in us] *om.* Pw   desire] in vs *add.* Pw   (&) to be] well Bo   5 fauourid]
hadde yn fauoure Br; or *add.* Br   of] vp wt Br   kynne] kunyng
Har²; kynrede Bo   &] or Bo Br   of grete] *om.* Br   kunnyng] kynne
Har²   6 holden] callyd Br   wise] holy *add.* Bo   &] or Bo   hi3e]
hyth Br   7 þis] thy Br   oþer] *om.* Br   þe] *om.* Har⁴   þe whiche] þt Br
wolde] wyll Br   8 oþer] others Bo Pw   9 it] þis Kk Har² Bo Pw   9–10
þat . . . a] *om.* Bo Pw   þat] thus *add.* Br.   10 spekiþ] doth speke Br   alle
. . . fer] And thes ys a Br   perilous] *om.* Bo Pw   enmye] and more
peryllows *add.* Bo Pw   11 flessche] by a gret dele *add.* Br.   and] therfor
add. Br   moche] *om.* Bo Pw Br   he] *om.* Kk Har² Bo Pw; we Br
be put] put hym Br   12 ofte-] often Har² Bo Pw   -tymes] *om.* Br
be-] *om.* Har⁴   & seriauntes] *om.* Har²   13 feend] olde enmy
Har²   þe spirite and] whych ys the Br   and] þe *add.* Har²   wraþþe]
warre Bo Pw   of] þe Kk   14 ouþer] eiþir Har⁴ Bo CP   and] or Br; by
add. Bo Pw   slei3t] and wysdom *add.* Br.   of a soule] *om.* Br   stifly]
ben *add.* Br.   doune] *om.* Bo Pw; by a soule *add.* Br   14–15 and troden
doune] *om.* Har²   15 doune] *om.* Bo Pw Br   by] þe *add.* Br   queintise]
sotelte Br   16 feend] enmy Har²   queintly] craftely Bo   17 himself
. . . rise] to reyse hymself Br   for] *om.* Bo Pw CP   wraþþe] ire Har⁴ CP Br
18 rennyng] rynnyng Kk Har²; *om.* Br   felly] fellyþ Kk; sottelly Bo
for] *om.* Bo Pw   19 þis] þes Kk Har²   ofte] often Bo   þe] a Har⁴
oure] *om.* Har²   20 oure] the Bo Br; *om.* Pw   ne] nor Bo Br   3it] *om.* Br

steriþ us to murmuryng, | to grucching, and to greuance, to bitter- f. 2a
nes of soule, to pine, & to inpacience, to wrapþe, to malencoly, and
to iuel wille, to hate, and to enuye, and to alle soche sorow. It
makiþ us to bere [us] heuily, ȝif ouȝt be done or seyde vnto us not
so louely ne so wisely as we wolde it were. It reiseþ in us alle iuel 5
suspecioun ; ȝif ouȝte be schewid in signe, in contenaunce, in worde
or in werk, þat miȝt bi any maner be turnid to malice or to heuines
of hert, it makiþ us as fast to take it to us.

To þees þouȝtes and alle soche, þat wolde put us oute of pees &
restfulnes of herte, we schulde none oþerwise aȝeinstonde bot as 10
we wolde þe self feend of helle ; and as moche we schuld fle þerfroo
as fro þe losse of oure soule. No doute bot boþe þe oþer þouȝtes of
þe spirite of þe flessche and also of þe spirite of þe woreld, þei
worchen and trauailen in alle þat þei kan to þe losse of oure soule ;
bot moste perilou[sl]y he þis. For whi he þis bi himself, and þei 15
not wiþoutyn him þis. For ȝif a soule be neuer so clene of flesschly
lust and of veine ioye of þis woreld, and ȝif it be defoulid wiþ þis
spirite of malice, of wrapþe, & of wickidnes, not aȝenstonding al
þe oþer clennes bifore, ȝit it is losable. And ȝif a soule be neuer so

1 murmuryng] mournyng Br ; and *add.* Kk Har² Bo Pw   and] *om.*
Bo Pw   greuance] & *add.* Har⁴ Bo Pw   2 to pine] *om.* Br   pine]
peyne Har⁴ Bo Pw   &] in *add.* Har⁴   in-] vn- Har²   wrapþe] ire
Har⁴ CP Br ; and *add.* Br   3 iuel] ille Har²   and] *om.* Kk Har² Bo Pw,
ins. Har⁴   enuye] enmy Har²   sorow] sorwes Har⁴ Bo Pw   4 us]
can. Har¹ ; *om.* Br   heuily] heuy Br   ouȝt] any thinge Bo   done —
seyde] *trs.* Br   vnto] to Bo   5 louely] louelyly Kk Har²   ne] nor Kk
Har² Bo Pw ; not Har⁴ CP Br   wisely] gladly Bo Pw   iuel] ille Har² ;
all Bo ; *om.* Pw   6 in signe] *om.* Br   signe] synne Pw   in] or Bo
7 in] *om.* Bo   bi] yn Br   to] yn to Br   malice] heuynesse Br
to] *om.* Br   7–8 heuines of hert] malyce Br   8 as fast] euer redy Bo Pw
to] vnto Bo Pw   9 and] to *add.* Bo Pw Br   10 none] not Br   aȝein-
stonde] or resyste them *add.* Bo   11 wolde] do *add.* Har⁴ ; wᵗstond *add.* Br
þe] same *add.* Bo Br   self] felff *add.* Br   feend] enmy Har²   we schuld]
shull we Br   12 þe] *om.* Br   soule] and *add.* Har⁴   boþe] *om.*
Bo Pw   þe] tho Br   oþer] toþer CP   oþer] two *add.* Bo Pw ; that
is the *add.* Bo   13 þei] *om.* Bo Pw   14 in] *om.* Bo Pw   þe] *om.* Bo
Pw   losse] lose Bo Pw ; and deceyve *add.* Bo   of] *om.* Bo Pw   15 bot]
yet *add.* Bo ; þe *add.* Br   perilously] periloulsy Har¹ ; perylous Br ; of all
add. Bo   he þis] the spyrite of malyce Bo Pw ; ys þᵗ spyryte of malyce Br
þis] is Bo Pw Br   and] but Bo Pw   þei] be *add.* Bo Br   16 þis] *om.*
Bo Pw Br   a] mans *add.* Kk Har² Bo Pw   of] froo Br   17 of] fro
Br   ȝif] *om.* Har²   it] he Br   þis] the Bo   18 of wrapþe . . .
wickidnes] *om.* Har⁴ CP Br   (&) of] *om.* Bo   aȝen-] wiþ- Har⁴ Br
19 þe] þt Br   oþer] toþyr Kk Har² CP   clennes] clennesses CP
bi-] to- Har⁴ CP Br   ȝit] *om.* Br.   is] yet *add.* Br   losable] dampnable Br

moche defoulid bi luste of flessche & veine ioye of þis woreld and
it may bi grace kepe it in pees & in restfulnes of herte vnto þe
euen-Cristen, þof al it be ful harde for to do lastyng þe costume of
þe oþer two, ȝit it is [lesse] losable, not aȝeinstonding al þe toþer
5 filþe of þe flessche & of þe woreld touchid before. And þerfore,
þof al þat oure lusty þouȝtes of oure foule flessche be iuel, for
þei reuyn fro þe soule þe list of deuocioun ; and þof al þat þe veine
ioye of þe woreld be worse, for it reuiþ us þe trewe ioye þat we
schuld haue in contemplacioun of heuenly þinges, ministred and
10 tauȝt to us bi þe aungeles of heuen (for whoso lustly | desireþ
to be worschepid, fauored, and seruid of men here in eerþe, þei
deserue to forgoo þe worschip, þe fauour, and þe seruise of aungelles in goostly contemplacioun of heuen & of heuenly þinges al
þeire liif-tyme, þe whiche contemplacioun is betir & more worþi in
15 itself þan is þe list and þe likyng of deuocion) ; and for þis betirnes
I clepe þe spirite of malice, of wraþþe, & of wickidnes þe worst
spirite of hem alle. And whi? Ce[r]tes, for it reuiþ us þe best
þing of alle ; þat is charite, þe whiche is God.
    For whoso lackiþ pees and restfulnes of herte, him lackiþ þe

2b (margin, line 10)

1 bi] with the Bo Pw   of] þe add. Har² Bo Pw   &] of add. Br
þis] the Bo Pw   and] if add. Bo Br   2 kepe it] self add. Bo   in]
þe add. Br.   rest-] ryst- Kk ; riȝt- Har⁴ Br   þe] his Har⁴ Br ; þin
CP   3 þof al] althowghe Bo Br   for] ins. Har⁴ ; om. Bo Pw ; soo
Br   4 lesse] lesser Har¹ ; om. Br   losable] sauable Br   aȝein-] wiþ-
Har⁴   al] om. Br   þe] þat Har⁴   toþer] oþir Har⁴ Bo Pw ; om.
Br   5 touchid] touche Br   6 þof al] althowghe Bo ; if al Har⁴
CP Br   oure] þe Har⁴ CP ; om. Br.   lusty] and voluptuows
add. Bo Pw   þouȝtes] thowghes Bo   oure] the Br   foule] om. Kk
Har² Bo Pw   iuel] ylle Har²   for] by cause Br ; becawse add.
Bo Pw   7 reuyn] take Bo Br   fro] from Har⁴ Bo Pw Br   þe]
a Br   soule] man Br   list] luf Kk ; lust Har⁴ CP ; lyfe Bo Pw
Br   þof al] althowghe Bo ; thought Br   þat] om. Br   8
þe] þis Har⁴ CP Br   reuiþ] taketh Bo   us] from add. Bo Pw
8–9 þat . . . in] of Br   9 contemplacioun] þt we shullen haue
add. Br   10 aungeles] aungel Har² Har⁴ CP   -so] ever add. Bo
lustly] lustili Har⁴ CP Br ; and voluptuowsly add. Bo Pw   12 worschip]
and add. Br   þe] om. Bo Pw   aungelles] aungell Bo Pw   13 1
of] yn Br   14 is] more add. Bo Pw   more] om. Bo Pw   15 list]
lust Har⁴ Bo Pw CP Br   þe] om. Har⁴ Br   for . . . betirnes]
om. Bo Pw   þis] hys Br   betirnes] bittirnesse Har⁴ CP Br   16 clepe]
calle Har⁴ Bo CP Br   17 whi] for add. Kk Bo Br   Certes] cetes
Har¹ ; truly Bo   for] om. Bo Br   reuiþ] takethe Bo   us] from add. Bo
18 alle] and add. Bo Pw   þe] om. Br   19 lackiþ] wantiþ CP ; om.
Br   herte] wantythe add. Br   him] he Bo Br   lackiþ] wantith
CP Br

liuely presence of þe louely siȝt of þe heiȝe pees of heuen, good gracious God, him owne dere self. Þus witnessiþ Dauid in þe psalme, where he seiþ þat þe steed of God is maad in pees and his wonyngplace in Syon. Syon is as moche to sei as þe siȝt of pees. Þe siȝt of þe soule is þe þouȝt of þe same soule. And certes in þat soule þat 5 moste is ocupied in þouȝtes of pees haþ God maad his woningplace. And þus seiþ himself bi þe prophete whan he seiþ: 'Upon whom schal my spirite rest, bot upon þe meek & þe restful?'

And þerfore whoso wol haue God contynouly wonyng in him, and liue in loue and in siȝt of þe hiȝe pees of þe Godheed, þe 10 whiche is þe hiȝest & þe best partye of contemplacion þat may be had in þis liif, be he besi niȝt & day to put doun, whan þei come, þe spirite of þe flessche and þe spirite of þe woreld, bot most besily þe spirite of malice, of wraþþe, and of wickidnes, for he is þe foulist & þe worst filþe of alle. 15

And it is ful needful & speedful to knowe his queintyse and not for to vnknowe his doelful deseites. For somtyme he wol, þat wickid cursid wiȝt, chaunge his licnes into an aungel of liȝt, þat he may, vnder colour of vertewe, do more dere. Bot ȝit þanne, and we loke rediliche, it is bot seed of | bittirnes and of discorde þat þat 20 f. 3a

---

1 liuely] loueli Har⁴ CP Br   of] and Har⁴ Br; *partly erased, & in right margin* CP   heiȝe] *om.* Br   pees] of god *add.* Br   heuen] oure *add.* Bo; þe *add.* Br.   good] moste Bo; *om.* Pw; and þe *add.* Br   2 him] hys Br owne dere] *om.* Bo Pw   þus] Thys Kk Har² Bo Pw   witnessiþ] by the prophet *add.* Bo   psalme] *The reference is given in rubrics in the left margin of* Har¹   3 where] whanne Har⁴ CP   where . . . þat] sayng Br; Factus est in pace locus eius et habitacio eius in Syon *add.* Br   he seiþ] *corrected from* seiþ he Har¹   steed] place Bo Pw; or the place *add.* Br wonyng-] dwellynge Bo Pw Br   4 place] *om.* Bo Pw   to] *om.* Bo 5 (of) þe] that Pw   certes] truly Bo; certenly Br   6 moste] *om.* Bo Pw ocupied] moste *add.* Bo Pw   in] wyth Br   woning-] dwellynge Bo Pw Br 7 þus] so Har⁴   seiþ] he *add.* Bo; our lord *add.* Br   whan] where Bo whan he seiþ] *om.* Br   8 (&) þe] *om.* Har⁴ CP Br   9 so] þt Br   contynouly] *om.* Bo   wonyng] dwellynge Bo Pw; restyng Br; contynually *add.* Bo   10 and liue] *om.* Bo   þe] *om.* Bo Br   11 best] *om.* Kk partye] parte Bo Pw   14 besily] of all *add.* Bo   malice] and *add.* Br   (and) of] *om.* Bo Pw Br   15 &] and *add.* Pw   worst] moste Bo Pw   filþe] folȝe Bo Pw; *om.* Har⁴ CP Br   16 And] yet *add.* Br   &] also *add.* Bo   queintyse] couetyse Br   17 vnknowe] know Bo Pw   he] *om.* Br   18 wickid] and *add.* Bo   wiȝt] feende Bo   an] *om.* Har⁴. *The reference is given in the right margin of* Har¹   19 vnder] ouþer Kk   do] þe *add.* Br   dere] harme Bo; hurt Br; or harme *add.* Pw and] if Bo Pw   20 loke] more *add.* Har² Bo Pw   (and) of] *om.* CP Br þat] *om.* Br; thinge *add.* Bo

he schewiþ, seem it neuir so holi ne neuer so feire at þe first
schewing. Ful many he steriþ vnto singuleer holines, passing þe
comoun statute and costume of here degree, as is fastyng, wering,
and many oþer deuoute obseruaunces and outward doinges, in
5 open reprouing of oþer mens defautes, þe whiche þei haue not of
office for to doo. Alle soche, and many oþer, he steriþ hem to do, &
alle vnder colour of deuocioun & of charite; not for he is delited
in any dede of deuocioun & of charite, bot for he louiþ discencioun
and sclaundre, þe whiche is euermore causid of soche vnseemly
10 singulertees. For wheresoeuer þat any one or two ben in any
deuoute congregacioun, þe whiche any one or two vseþ any soche
outward singuleertees, þan in þe siʒt of alle foles al þe remenaunt
ben ensclaundred by hem; bot in siʒt of þe wise man þei ensclaundre hemself. Bot for-þi þat foles ben moo þen wise men, þerfore,
15 for fauour of foles, soche singulere doers wenen þei be wise, when,
& it were wisely determinid, þei and alle here fautours schuld be
seen aperte foles & dartes schotte of þe deuil to slee trewe simple
soules vnder colour of hele & of charite. And þus many disceites
kan þe feende bring in on þis maner. Whoso wil not consente,
20 bot mekiþ him trewly to preier and to counseil, schal graciously
be deliuerid of alle þees doles.

Bot it is sorou for to sey, & more for to fele, þat somtyme oure

---

1 ne] or Bo   neuer] *om.* Bo Pw   2 vnto] to Bo Pw   3 statute].
stature Har⁴ CP   fastyng] sharpe *add.* Kk Har² Bo Pw; and harde
add. Br   4 many oþer] *trs.* CP   deuoute] *om.* Br   6 for] *om.*
CP   doo] *om.* Br   hem] for *add.* Kk Har² Bo Pw   7 &] or Br
of] for Br   8 (&) of] *om.* Har⁴   for] *om.* Har²   10 þat] the Bo;
om. Br   any] *om.* Kk Har² Bo Pw   10–11 ben . . . two] *om.* Br   any
. . . two] *om.* Bo   11 soche] *om.* Har⁴   12 outward] *om.* Br   alle] *om.*
Bo Pw   13 ben] by Kk   en-] dis- Har⁴; *om.* Bo Pw   in] þe *add.* Kk
Har² Bo Pw Br   þe] *om.* Bo   man] men Bo   en-] *om.* Har⁴ Bo Pw   14
for-þi] for (*om.* Br) because Bo Pw Br   þat] *om.* Br   foles . . . moo] ther
ben more fooles Bo   moo] more Pw   15 wenen] þat *add.* Har⁴ Bo Pw Br
wise] men *add.* Bo   when] that *add.* Bo Pw   16 & . . . determinid] *om.*
Bo Pw   &] yf Br   fautours] flaturers Br; if it were wysely deter-
myned *add.* Bo Pw   17 seen] fond Br   aperte] openly Bo   schotte]
om. Br   deuil] enmy Har²; shotyng *add.* Br   slee] sla Kk Har²   18
hele] holynes Bo Pw Br   of] *om.* Bo Pw   þus] full *add.* Bo   19 feende]
enmy Har²   þis] thus Br   maner] wise Har⁴ CP Br   Whoso] But he
þt Br   20 mekiþ] mekely gevythe Bo; meke Br   him] self *add.* Bo
trewly] *om.* Kk Har²Bo Pw   preier — counseil] *trs.* Br   21 doles]
deceytes Bo Pw   22 is] *om.* Kk; more *add.* Bo Pw   for] *om.* Har²
for . . . for] *om.* Bo Pw   fele] (of *add.* Pw) our owne spyrites deceytes
add. Bo Pw   þat] for Bo Pw

owne spirite is so ouercomen, parauenture, wiþ iche of þees þre
spirites of þe flessche, of þe woreld, & of þe fende, & so brou3t in
daunger, boundin in bondage, in þraldom, and in seruage of hem
alle, þat sorow it is to wite, in grete confusion and losse of itself,
it doþ now þe office of iche one of hem [only] itself in itself. And 5
þis befalliþ when, after longe vse & customable consentyng vnto
hem when þei come, at þe last it is | maad so fleschly, so wordly, f. 3b
and so malicious, so wickid, and so froward, þat now pleinly of
itself, wiþoutyn sogestion of any oþer spirite, it gendriþ and
bringiþ forþ in itself not only lusty þo3tes of þe flesche and veine 10
þo3tes of þe worild, bot, þat worst of alle þees ben, bitter þo3tes &
wickid, in bacbiting and deming and iuel suspecioun of oþer.

And when it is þus wiþ oure spirite, þan I trowe it may not
li3tly be knowen when it is oure owne spirite þat spekiþ, or when it
hereþ any of þe oþer þre spirites spekyng in it, as it is touchid be- 15
fore. Bot what þar reche who spekiþ, when it is alle one & o þing
þat is spokyn? What helpeþ it to knowe þe persone of him þat
spekiþ, when it is sekir and certeine þat alle is iuel and perilous
þat is spokyn? 3if it be þin enemye, concent not to him, bot meek
þee to preier & to counsel; and so may þou mi3tly wiþstonde þin 20
enemye. 3if it be þin owne spirite, reproue him bitterly, & si3ingly

---

1 parauenture] *om.* Bo Pw Br   wiþ iche] *om.* Br   iche] euery Bo; one
add. Pw   þre] *om.* Har⁴   2 of] *om.* Br   flessche] and *add.* Bo Pw   of]
om. Br   fende] olde enmy Har²; spyrite of malyce Bo   so] ferr *add.* Bo
in] into Har²   3 (bondage) in] and Br   in] *om.* Br   4 wite] and *add.* Har⁴
in] to *add.* Har⁴   5 it doþ . . . self] *om.* Bo Pw   only] *om.* Har¹, *but the
reading of* Kk Har² Har⁴ CP Br   6 befalliþ] it fallyth Br   longe] tyme
of *add.* Bo Pw   7 when . . . last] *om.* Br   come] and (*can.* Har¹) *add.* Har¹
Kk Har² Har⁴ CP   it] *om.* Har⁴   8 malicious] at þe laste and *add.* Bo
wickid — froward] *trs.* Bo   9 -self] it bringethe forthe *add.* Bo
Pw   9–10 it . . . forþ] *om.* Bo Pw   gendriþ] engendreth Br   10
in itself] *om.* Bo Pw   lusty] lustely Har²; voluptuows Bo Pw   11 þat]
þo Har⁴ CP; *om.* Bo Pw; the Br   worst] worse Bo Pw   of] then
Bo Pw   þees] whiche Har⁴ CP; as *add.* Bo Pw; þt *add.* Br   12
in] as Br   and] fals *add.* Br   and] in *add.* Har²   iuel] ille Har²   oþer]
others Bo Pw; afor rehercyd *add.* Br   13 oure] out hys owne Br   not]
ful *add.* Har⁴ CP Br   14 oure] his Br   or] oþer Br   15 þe] þere Kk
Har²   oþer] toþer CP   þre] *om.* Br   spekyng] spekyn Kk   it] *om.* Br
16 what] who Br   þar] þere Kk Har²   þar reche] dare þee recke Har⁴;
makethe it mater Bo Pw; shall rech Br   who] it is that *add.* Bo; þat *add.*
Pw   &] soo *add.* Bo Pw   oon Har⁴; the same Bo Pw; same *add.* Kk
Har²   17 it] *om.* Kk Har² Bo Pw   18 iuel] ille Har²   and perilous]
om. Bo Pw   19 spokyn] And *add.* Bo; of hyt *add.* Br   concent] thou
add. Br   20 mi3tly] my3tili Har⁴ CP Br   21 enemye] And *add.* Br

sorou þat euer þou fel in so grete wrechidnes, bondage, and þraldom
of þe deuil. Schriue þee of þi costum consentes and of þin olde sinnes ;
and so maist þou come to bi grace to recouer þi fredom aȝein.

And by þe gracious fredam may þou sone come to wisely for to
5 knowe and soþfastly for to fele by þe proue when it is þin owe
spirite þat spekiþ þees iueles, or it ben þees oþer iuel spirites þat
speken hem in þee. And so may þis knowyng be a souerein mene
& help of aȝenstonding; for oft-tymes vnknouing is cause of
moche errour, and, aȝensward, knowing is cause of moche trewþ.
10 And to þis maner knowing maist þou winne þus as I sey þee. Ȝif
þou be in doute or in were of þees iuel þouȝtes whan þei come,
wheþer þat þei be þe speche of þin owne spirite or any of þe toþer
f. 4a of þin enemyes, loke þan besily by | þe witnes of þi counsel and
þi concience, ȝif þou haue be schreuyn and lawfuly amendid,
15 after þe dome of þi confessour, of alle þe consentes þat euer þou
consentid to þat kynde of synne þat þi þouȝt is aworde of. And
ȝif þou haue not be schreuen, schriue þee þan as trewly as þou
maist by grace and by counsel. And þan wite þou riȝt wel þat alle
þe þouȝtes þat comen to þee aftir þi schrift, stering þee eft to þe
20 same sinnes, þei ben þe wordes of oþer spirites þan þin owne,

1 fel] dedyste fele Bo Pw   in] to *add.* Har⁴ Br ; the *add.* Bo Pw   2
deuil] olde enmy Har²   costum] customed Bo Pw ; and *add.* Br   con-
sentes] conseites *written first, but altered to* consentes Har¹ ; conceites
Har⁴ CP Br   3 to] *om.* Bo Pw Br   þi] wold *add.* Br   4 þe] þi Kk Har²
Bo Pw   sone come] *trs.* Har⁴   wisely] wysdom Br   for] *ins.* Har² ; *om.*
Pw   5 for] *om.* Br   þe] trew Br   proue] preff Br   6 þees] þis
Har⁴ Br   iueles] illes Har² ; yuel Har⁴ Br   or] oþer Br ; els that *add.* Bo
ben] is CP Br   þees] of Br   oþer] *om.* Har⁴   iuel] ille Har²   iuel
spirites] *trs., but order corrected in* Har¹   7 þis] þing (*can.*) *add.* Har¹
8 & help] *added in right margin of* Har¹   oft-] often Bo Pw   -tymes]
tyme Har⁴ CP Br   9 aȝens-] aȝeyn- Kk Har² Har⁴ Bo Pw CP Br
-ward] *om.* Bo Pw   10 maner] of *add.* Kk Har² Bo Pw   winne]
comme Bo Br   sey] to *add.* Bo Pw   11 or in were] *om.* Bo Pw Br   þees]
this Bo Pw   iuel] ille Har²   12 þat . . . þe] it by Br   or] of *add.* Kk Har²
Bo Pw   þe] þat Har⁴   12–13 þe toþer of] *om.* Bo   toþer] oþir Har⁴
Br ; others Pw   13 þin] theyn Br   enemyes] enemy Br ; that is to saye
of the other thre spyrites aforesayde *add.* Bo   besily] wysely Har²
þe] þi Har⁴ ; *om.* Br   witnes] wyttes Bo Pw ; councell Br   þi] þe Br
counsel] wytnesse Br ; of thy councell *add.* Br   and] in Har⁴ CP
14 lawfuly] laweful Har⁴   15 dome] and iudgment *add.* Bo Pw   þe] þi
Kk Har²   16 to] vnto Bo ; yn Br ; in *add.* Bo Pw   is] *om.* Bo
aworde] aware Bo Pw Br   18 þan] þt Br   wite] know Bo   riȝt] *om.*
Har⁴ ; *ins.* Br   19 þe] þo Har⁴   eft] often tymes Bo Pw ; ofte Br   20
sinnes] synne Br   þei] þee Kk   of] þe *add.* Har⁴   þan] not Har⁴ ; of
add. Bo Pw Br

I mene som of þe þre touchid before. And þou for none soche
þouȝtes, be þei neuer so þicke, so foule, ne so many, I mene for
here first comyng in, bot ȝif it be for rechelesnes of aȝenstonding,
arte no blameworþi. And not only relesing of purgatory þat þou
hast deseruid for þe same synnes don before, whatso þei be, þou 5
maist deserue ȝif þou stifly aȝenstonde hem, bot also moche grace
in þis liif & moche mede in þe blis of heuen.

Bot al þoo iuel þouȝtes comyng into þee, stering þee to any sinne,
after þat þou hast consentid to þat same synne and bifore þat
þou hast sorow for þat consent and arte in wil to be schreuen: 10
it is no perile to þee to take hem to þiself, and for to schriue þee of
hem as of þouȝtes of þin owne spirite. Bot for to take to þiself alle
oþer þouȝtes, þe which þou hast by verrey profe, as it is schewid
bifore, þat þei ben þe speches of oþer spirites þan þiself, þerin liþ
grete peril. For so miȝst þou liȝtly misreule þi consience, charging 15
a þing for sinne, þe whiche is none. And þis were grete errour and
mene to þe grettest perile. For, & it were so þat iche iuel þouȝt and
stering to sinne were þe werk & þe speche of none oþer spirite bot
only of mans owe spirite, þan it wolde folow bi þat þat mans owne
spirite were a feend, þe whiche is apertly fals | and dampnable 20 f. 4b
woodnes. For þof al it be so þat a soule may, bi freelte and custom

1 þou] *om.* Kk; than Bo Pw   2 þicke — foule] *trs.* Br   for]
om. Bo   2–3 for here first] after shreft Br   4 arte] is Kk Bo
Pw; þou *add.* Har⁴; thou art Br   no] not Br   not only] alsoo it
shall be a gret Br   of] the peynys of *add.* Br   5 before] by Br
whatso þei be] *om.* Kk Har² Bo Pw   -so] euyr *add.* Br   þei] þt Br   5–6
þou . . . deserue] *om.* Br   6 deserue] discerne Har⁴   6 aȝen-] with- Bo
bot] And Br   also] they shall be to þe a meyn of *add.* Br   6–7 grace
. . . mede] *om.* Kk   8 þoo] thos Bo Pw; þe Br; other *add.* Bo   iuel]
ille Har²   9 þat] *om.* Bo   þat] the Br   10 hast] haddest Br
arte] were Br   be schreuen] shryve the therof Bo Pw   11 and] *om.*
Kk   for] *om.* Bo Pw   12 (for) to] *om.* Br   14 þat þei ben] by Bo Pw
þan] of *add.* Kk Har² Bo Pw   liþ] ys Br   15 so] thow *add.* Bo Br
þou] *om.* Bo Br; ryȝt *add.* Kk Har²   liȝtly] *om.* Har⁴ CP Br   charg-
ing] charyng Har²   16 þe] *om.* Bo Pw Br   none] no synne Bo Pw
þis] thus Br   and] þe *add.* Har⁴ Br; a *add.* Bo Pw   17 iche] an Har⁴
iuel] ille Har²   18 to] of Bo   þe werk . . . spirite] none other
spyrites werke & speche Bo Pw   speche] spekyng Br   none oþer] no
noþer Br   19 only] *om.* Br   of] a *add.* Br   mans] *om.* Har²; thyne
Bo Pw   spirite] *om.* Bo Pw   it wolde] *trs.* Br   wolde] wole Har⁴
þat] *om.* Br; a *add.* Kk Har² Har⁴ Bo Pw   owne] *om.* Har⁴ CP Br   20 a]
veray *add.* Bo Pw   is] *om.* Har⁴ CP   apertly] *om.* Br; is *add.* Har⁴ CP
and] a *add.* Bo Pw   21 woodnes] to thynk *add.* Br   þof al] all þoue
Br   al] *om.* Bo Pw

of sinnyng, falle into so moche wrechidnes þat it takiþ on itself bi
bondage of sinne þe office of þe deuil, stering itself to sinne euer
more & more wiþoutyn any sogestion of any oþer spirite, as it is
seide before, ʒit it is not þerfore a deuel in kynde. Bot it is a deuel
5 in office and may be clepid deuely, for it is in þe doing liche to
þe deuel, [þat is to sey a stirer of itself vnto sinne, þe whiche is þe
office of þe deuel.] Neuerþeles ʒit, for al þis þraldome to sinne and
deuelnes in office, it may bi grace of contricioun of schrift and of
amending, recouer þe fredom aʒein and be mad sauable, ʒe, and a
10 ful special Goddes seint in þis liif, þat before was ful dampnable
and ful cursid in þe leuyng.

And þerfore as grete a peril as it is, a soule þat is fallen in sinne
not for to charge his consience þerwiþ ne for to amende hym
þerof, as grete a peril it is, and, ʒif it may be seide, a gretter, a man
15 for to charge his concience wiþ iche þoʒt and stering of sinne þat
wil come in him. For by soche nice charging of concience miʒt he
liʒtly renne into errour of concience, and so be ledde into dispeire
alle his liiftyme. And þe cause of alle þis is lackyng [of] knowing of
discrecioun of spirites, þe whiche knowing may be getyn in verrey
20 experience, whoso rediliche wil loke sone after þat a soule haue
ben trewly clensid by confession, as it is seide before.

For fast after confession a soule is, as it were, a clene paper leef

1 sinnyng] synne Har⁴   so] *ins.* Har¹; *om.* Kk Har² Pw CP Br
wrechidnes] wyckydnesse Br   -self] *om.* Br   5 clepid] called Bo; or
called *add.* Pw   deuely] dcvelysshe Bo Pw; a deuyle Br   in] *om.* Br
þe] *om.* Bo Pw   6–7 þat ... deuel] *All MSS. except* Har¹   7 þe] a Bo Pw
þis] thus Br   þraldome] custume Br   8 deuelnes] devylysshenes Bo Pw
of] sorowe of *add.* Br   of] and Har⁴   of] *om.* Bo Pw Br   (and) of] *om.* Bo Pw Br
9 amending] amendment Bo Pw   þe] bi Har⁴   ʒe] ʒa Kk Har²   10 ful]
om. Kk Har² Pw   seint] sancte Har²   was] a *add.* Bo Pw   ful]
fowle Bo   11 and] a *add.* Bo Pw   cursid] fende *add.* Bo Pw   þe] his
Bo Pw; euyle Br   12 a] *om.* Har⁴ CP Br   is] of *add.* Br   in] into
Bo Br   13 for] *om.* Bo Pw   13–14 þerwiþ ... þerof] *om.* Br   for]
om. Har⁴ Bo Pw   14 a] *om.* Har⁴ CP Br   it is] *trs.* Br; ye *add.* Bo;
for *add.* Br   and ... gretter] *om.* Br   man] soule Br; not fall yn
synne *add.* Br   15 iche] euery Bo Pw   16 in] to Bo Pw   soche]
scrupylosyte of *add.* Bo   nice] vyse Br   charging] gayrgyng Kk   miʒt
he] *trs.* Bo   17 renne] rynne Kk Har²; renewe Br   into] in Har⁴   so]
to Br   into] in Har⁴ Br   18 þis] þes Kk Har²   lackyng] wantynge Har⁴
Pw CP Br   of] and (*can.* Har¹) Har¹ CP; and not Br   knowing] connynge
Bo Pw   19 knowing] connynge Bo Pw; vnknowyng Br   in] by
Bo Pw   20 rediliche] *om.* Bo   loke] redely *add.* Bo   21 ben trewly]
trs. Br   22 fast] anonne Bo Pw; soone Br   as] and *add.* Br   paper]
pauper Kk

for abilnes þat it haþ to receiue what þat men wil write þerupon.
Boþe þei prese for to write on þe soule, whan it is clene in itself
maad bi confession, God and his aungelles on þe to partye, and
þe feend and his aungelles on þe toþer partye. Bot it is in þe free
choise of þe soule to receiue whiche þat it wole. Þe resceyte of þe 5
soule is | þe concent of þe same soule. A newe þouȝt and a stering f. 5a
to any sinne, þe whiche þou hast forsaken bifore in þi schrift, what
is it elles bot one of þe þre spirites, þe whiche ben þin enemyes
touchid before, profring to write on þi soule þe same sinne aȝen.
Þe speche of þiself is it not, for whi þer is none soche þing wretin in 10
þi soule. For al it is wasschin awey bifore in þi schrift, and þi soule
lefte nakyd and bare, noþing þerupon bot a freel and a free consent, more enclining to þe iuel forcostoumid þerin þan it is to þe
good, bot more abil to þe good þan to þe iuel for clennes of þe
soule & vertewe of þe sacrament of schrift. Bot of itself it haþ 15
nouȝt þan whereþorou it may þink or stire itself to good or to
iuel; and þerfore it foloweþ þat, what þouȝt þat comeþ þan in it,
wheþer þat it be good or iuel, it is not of itself. Bot þe consent to
þe good or to þe iuel, wheþer þat it be, þat is euirmore þe werk of
þe same soule. 20

And al after þe worþines & þe wrechidnes of þis consent, þerafter it deseruiþ pine or blisse. Ȝif þis consent be to iuel, þan as

1 for] þe *add.* Br   to receiue] *om.* Bo Pw   what] þing *add.* Har² men]
om. Bo Pw   wil] wold Br   wil write] shal be writen Bo Pw   2 þei] do *add.*
Bo Pw; dothe ther deuour and *add.* Br   prese for to] *ins. in right margin*
of Har¹   prese] profe Br; and desire myche *add.* Bo Pw   for] *om.* Bo
Pw Br   3 aungelles] Angel Kk Har² Bo Pw   þe] þat Har⁴ CP Br   to]
o CP, oon Har⁴ Bo Pw Br   and] *om.* Har⁴; & *add.* Pw   4 aungelles] Angel
Kk Har² Bo Pw   þe] þat Har⁴ CP Br   toþer] oþer Har⁴ Bo Pw CP Br
is] thought els but *add.* Br   8 bot] þe speche of *add.* Kk Har² Bo Pw
þe] tho Br   þe] *om.* Br   þin] *om.* Br   9 touchid before] touchyng and
Br   10 is it] *trs.* Har²   wretin] wryttyng Har²   in] on Br   11 al]
that *add.* Pw   it] *om.* Har²; that Bo   wasschin] wasted Bo Pw   þi] þe
Br   and] yn *add.* Br   12 lefte] is Har⁴   bare] and *add.* Br   noþing] lefte
add. Bo Pw   -upon] on Br   13 enclining] enclynyd Br   iuel] ille Har²
forcostoumid] for coustome Har² Bo Pw; for by cause it ys soo custummed
Br   þe] *om.* Har⁴ CP   14 iuel] ille Har²   15 (sacrament) of]
om. Br   16 nouȝt] nothinge Bo   þink or] *ins. in left margin of* Har¹
stire] store Br   (or) to] *om.* Har⁴   17 iuel] ille Har²   what] þing or
add. Har²   þat] than Br   þan] *om.* Bo Pw Br   in] into Bo Pw;
of Br   18 þat] *om.* Bo Pw Br   or] eiþer CP; els *add.* Br   iuel] ille Har²
19 þe] *om.* Har⁴ CP   or] ellis *add.* Har⁴ CP Br   to] *om.* Bo Pw   þe]
om. Bo CP Br   iuel] ille Har²   be] good or euylle *add.* Kk   21
al] *om.* Br   22 pine] peyne Har⁴ Bo Pw Br   iuel] ylle Har²

fast it haþ bi combrance of sinne þe office of þat same spirite þat
first maad him sogestion of þat same sinne. And ȝif it be to [þe]
good, þan as fast it haþ bi grace þe office of þat same spirite þat
first maad him stering to þat same good. For as ofte as any heelful
5 þouȝt comeþ in oure minde, as of chastite, of sobirnes, of dispising
of þe woreld, of wilful pouert, of pacience, of meeknes, & of
charite, wiþoute doute it is þe spirite of God þat spekiþ, ouþer by
himself or elles by som of his aungelles: þat is to sey, ouþer his
aungelles of þis liif, þe whiche ben trewe techers, or elles his
10 aungelles in blis, þe whic[h]e ben trewe stirers and inspirers of good.

And as it is seide of þe oþer þre iuel spirites þat a soule for longe
f. 5b vse and costomable consentyng vnto hem may be | maad so
fleschly, so wordly, & so malicious þat it takiþ upon it þe office of
hem alle, riȝt so it is aȝensward þat a soule, for longe use and
15 custume in goodnes, may be mad so goostly by clennes of leuing
and deuocioun of spirite aȝens þe spirite of þe flesche, and so
heuenly aȝens þe spirite of þe woreld, and so godly by pees and bi
charite & by restfulnes of herte aȝens þe spirite of malice, of
wraþþe, & of wickidnes, þat it haþ hem now of office alle soche
20 good þouȝtes to þink whan him list wiþoutyn forȝeting, in as greet
perfeccion as þe freelte of þis liif wil suffre.

And þus it may be seen how þat iche þouȝt þat smiteþ on oure
hertes, wheþer þat it be good or iuel, it is not euermore þe speche

1 it haþ] *trs.* Br   bi] *om.* Br   þat] þe Har⁴   2 sinne] synne *add.*
Pw   þe] þee Har¹; *om.* Har⁴ Bo   3 fast] as *add.* Pw   4 stering]
suggestion Bo Pw   þat] þe Pw   heelful] helthefull Bo   5 in] into Bo
CP Br   (sobirnes) of] þe *add.* Kk Har² Bo Pw   6 woreld] and
add. Br   pouert] pouerte Har² Bo Br; pouertye Pw   of pacience] *om.*
Br   &] *om.* Bo Pw   7 of] gude *add.* Har²   ouþer] eiþer Har⁴
Bo   8–9 þat . . . aungelles] *om.* Br   ouþer] eiþer Har⁴ Bo   9 aungelles]
Angelle Kk Har² Bo Pw   þis] hys Br   liif] sylf Br   elles] *om.* Kk
Har²   10 aungelles] Angel Kk Har²   in] of his Bo Pw   þe] *om.* Br
whiche] whice Har¹; they Br   stirers and] *om.* Br   good] god Kk
Bo   11 as] *om.* Kk Har⁴   is] y Br   oþer] toþer CP   13 it] selfe
add. Har²   14 so] *om.* Br   it is] *om.* Kk Har² Bo Pw   aȝens-] aȝeyn-
Kk Har² Har⁴ Bo Pw CP Br   use] *om.* Br   15 custume] customed
Har⁴; custumable vse Br   16 deuocioun] fervowre Bo   aȝens] aȝen
Har⁴ CP Br; agaynste Bo Pw   so] *om.* Bo Pw   17 aȝens] aȝen Har⁴
CP Br; agaynste Bo Pw   godly] goodely Kk Har² Har⁴ Pw   18 &] *om.*
Br   aȝens] agaynste Bo Pw; ayen Br   19 wickidnes] so *add.* Bo Pw
hem] *om.* Kk Har² Bo Pw; tho vertues Br   20 þink] þaim *add.* Har²; on
add. Bo   as] a Bo Pw   21 þis] *om.* Har²   22 And] so *add.* Har⁴   þus]
thys Br   on] yn Br   23 hertes] herte Har⁴ CP Br   iuel] ille Har² Bo;
that *add.* Br   it] *om.* Har² Bo Pw   is] *om.* Br   -more] *om.* Har⁴ CP Br

of oure owne spirite; bot þe consent to þe þouȝt, whatsoeuer it be,
þat is euermore oure. Iesu graunt us his grace to consent to þe good
and aȝeinstonde þe iuel. Amen.

1 be] good or evyll *add.* Bo   2 is] þe speche of our owne spyrite *add.* Br
-more] *om.* Bo Pw   oure] oures Kk Har²; of our owne spyrite Bo
Pw; lord *add.* Br   his grace] *om.* Har⁴   his] *om.* CP Br   3 and] to
add. Har²   aȝein-] agaynste- Bo   iuel] ille Har²; for hys mykelle merecy
add. Har²

THE LATIN SOURCES OF *DEONISE HID DIUINITE**

DE MYSTICA THEOLOGIA

CAPITULUM I

(*H.D.* 2/14–27)

COMPRESBYTERO Timotheo, Dionysius presbyter salutem.—Trinitas supersubstantialis et superdea et superbona, inspectrix divinae sapientiae Christianorum, dirige nos ad mysticorum Eloquiorum superignotum et supersplendentem et summum verticem, ubi simplicia
5 et absoluta et inconversibilia Theologiae mysteria cooperta sunt secundum supersplendentem occulte docti silentii caliginem, in obscurissimo superclarissimum supersplendere facientem, et in omnino impalpabili et invisibili superpulchris claritatibus superimplentem non habentes oculos mentes.
10 Igitur ista mihi quidem sint oratione postulata.

(*H.D.* 2/31–5/24)

Tu autem, O amice Timothee, circa mysticas visiones forti contritione et sensus derelinque et intellectuales operationes, et omnia sensibilia et intelligibilia, et omnia non exsistentia et exsistentia; et

---

3 dirige nos] Gloss (col. 270): nos ad te elevando rege, ut perveniamus . . . ; *H.D.* 2/17: to drawe us up.   11 circa mysticas visiones] Par. (p. 454): ad hoc quod capax fias mysticarum contemplationum, quas in hoc libro docere intendo, sic cooperare radio divino; cf. Com. (f. 44ᵃ): non fit nisi ex magna gracia dei; Gloss (col. 272): sic cooperante divino radio; *H.D.* 2/31–32: what tyme . . . steryng of grace . . . beholdynges   11–12 forti contritione] Par. (p. 454): forti conatu mentis; Com. (f. 44ᵃ): forti contricione cum magno conatu mentis . . . animi magno vigore; *H.D.* 3/1: wiþ a stronge & a sleiȝ & a listi contricyon   12 sensus] Par. (p. 454): sensus et sensibilia; *H.D.* 3/2: bodely wittes . . . touching

---

* In the first three chapters the Middle English translator follows closely the Latin version of Johannes Sarracenus, in the last two chapters the Paraphrase of Vercellensis. The five basic chapters are here given in full, taken from *D. Dionysii Cartusiani Opera Omnia*, t. xvi (Tournai, 1902), pp. 471–4, 465, 468–9 respectively. But the indebtedness is complicated by the fact that the chapters based upon Sarracenus's version show the influence of the writings of Vercellensis, and similarly the chapters based on Vercellensis have occasional traces of the influence of Sarracenus. Where there appears to be evidence of conflation, the passage which might have been used is given below the full text. Of the works of Vercellensis, the Middle English translator draws most often from the Paraphrase, but sometimes he may have used the Commentary or the Gloss. See Introd., pp. xxxix, xlii–xliii. Quotations from the Commentary are taken from Brit. Mus. MS. Royal 8. G. iv, from the Gloss from *P.L.*, t. cxxii, cols. 267–84.

sicut est possibile, ignote consurge ad ejus unitionem qui est super
omnem substantiam et cognitionem. Etenim excessu tui ipsius et
omnium irretentibili et absoluto, munde ad supersubstantialem
divinarum tenebrarum radium, cuncta auferens et a cunctis absolutus, sursumageris.   5
    Vide autem ut nullus indoctorum ista audiat. Istos autem dico
qui in exsistentibus sunt formati, nihil super exsistentia supersubstantialiter esse opinantes, sed putantes scire ea quae secundum
ipsos est cognitione, eum qui ponit tenebras latibulum suum. Si autem
super istos sunt divinae doctrinae mysteriorum, quid dicat quidem 10
aliquis de magis indoctis, quicumque omnibus superpositam causam
et ex postremis in exsistentibus figurant, et nihil ipsam habere
dicunt super compositas ab ipsis impias et multiformes formationes?
    Oportet enim in ipsa, et omnes exsistentium ponere et affirmare
positiones, sicut omnium causa, et omnes ipsas magis proprie ne- 15
gare, sicut super omnia superexsistente; et non negationes oppositas
opinari esse affirmationibus, sed multo prius ipsam super priva-
tiones esse, quae est super omnem et ablationem et positionem.
    Ita igitur divinus Bartholomaeus dicit, et multam Theologiam esse
et minimam, et Evangelium latum et magnum, et rursus concisum: 20
ut mihi videtur, illud supernaturaliter intendens, quia et multorum
sermonum est bona omnium causa, et brevium dictionum simul et
irrationabilis, sicut neque rationem habens neque intellectum, propter
hoc quod omnibus ipsa supersubstantialiter est superposita, et solis
non velate et vere apparet his qui et immunda et munda transeunt, 25
et omnem omnium sanctarum extremitatum ascensum superveniunt,
et omnia divina lumina et sonos et sermones cœlestes derelinquunt, et
ad caliginem introeunt, ubi vere est, sicut Eloquia dicunt, qui est super
omnia.
    Etenim non simpliciter divinus Moyses mundari ipse primum 30

---

1 possibile] Par. (p. 454): tibi possibile; *H.D.* 3/9–10: possible . . .
vnderstonde   2–3 excessu tui ipsius . . . munde] Par. (pp. 454–5):
Quum enim te ipsum et omnia per mentis excessum nullo inferiori retina-
culo praepeditus transcenderis, ab omni concupiscentia et cura absolutus
et purgatus; cf. Gloss (col. 272): ita quod illorum amore non valeas retineri,
vel alias impediri, purgatus ab ultimis animae phantasiis tam spirituales
quam divinas operationes postponendo . . .; *H.D.* 3/12–16: þorou þe
ouerpassyng . . . knowyng   12 ex postremis in exsistentibus figurant]
Par. (p. 455): qui per idolatriae errorem figurant Deum . . . ex extremis
materiis, scilicet lapidibus et metallis, quae inferiora sunt animatis et
animalibus per naturam; *H.D.* 3/32–3: bi making of figures . . . stones
19 divinus Barth.] Par. (p. 455): B. Barth. apostolus; *H.D.* 4/12–13: þe
godliche Bertelmewe, þe Apostle of Criste   20 concisum] Par. (p. 455):
arctum esse et parvum; *H.D.* 4/15: streite & litil   21 quia et . . .] Par.
(p. 455): quod . . . designatur et tractatur; *H.D.* 4/16: where he seiþ þat . . .
23 neque rationem . . . intellectum] Par. (p. 455): neque ratione capitur
neque intellectu; *H.D.* 4/17–18: neiþer hauyng . . . comen to   28 Elo-
quia] Par. (p. 455): Scriptura; *H.D.* 4/25–26: þe Scripture

praecipitur, et rursus a non talibus segregari, et post omnem mun-
dationem audit multarum vocum buccinas, et videt lumina multa
cum fulgore emittentia mundos et multum effusos radios; postea a
multis segregatur, et cum electis sacerdotibus ad summitatem divi-
5 narum ascensionum pertingit: quamvis per haec quidem non fit
cum Deo, sed contemplatur non ipsum (invisibilis est enim), sed
locum ubi est. Hoc autem puto significare, divinissima visorum et
intellectorum esse subjectas quasdam rationes subjectorum omnia
excedenti, per quae praesentia ejus, quae est super omnem cogita-
10 tionem, monstratur intelligibilibus summitatibus sanctissimorum
locorum ejus superveniens. Tunc et ab ipsis absolvitur visis et videnti-
bus, et ad caliginem ignorantiae intrat, quae caligo vere est mystica:
in qua claudit omnes cognitivas susceptiones, et impalpabili omnino
et invisibili fit omnis exsistens ejus qui est super omnia, et nullius,
15 neque sui ipsius neque alterius; omnino autem ignoto vacatione
omnis cognitionis secundum melius unitus, et eo quod nihil cognoscit,
super mentem cognoscens.

CAPITULUM II

(*H.D.* 5/26–7/8)

Quomodo oportet et uniri et hymnos reponere omnium causae et
exsistenti super omnia

In hac superlucenti caligine fieri nos precamur, et per non videre et
per ignorare, videre et cognoscere eum qui est super omnem visionem
20 et cognitionem, in ipso non videre et non cognoscere; et supersubstantialem supersubstantialiter laudare per omnium exsistentium
ablationem: sicut ipsius naturae insigne facientes, auferentes prohibi-
tiones officientes mundae occulti visioni, et ipsam in se ipsa, ablatione
sola, occultam manifestantes pulchritudinem. Oportet autem, sicut
25 arbitror, ablationes laudare contrarie quam positiones. Etenim illas a
primis incipientes, et per media et ultima descendentes, ponebamus.
Hic autem ab ultimis ad principaliora ascensus facientes, et per media
rursus ad extrema, omnia auferimus, ut revelate cognoscamus illam
ignorantiam ab omnibus noscibilibus in omnibus exsistentibus circum-
30 velatam, et supersubstantialem illam videamus caliginem ab omni
lumine in exsistentibus occultatam.

1 a non talibus] Par. (p. 455): ab immundis; *H.D.* 4/29: fro occasyon of
fyling. 22–24 sicut . . . pulchritudinem] Par. (p. 458): sicut artifices
facientes aliquam imaginem de qualibet materia inanimata, sculpendo vel
incidendo auferunt exteriores partes ipsius materiae, quae occultant et
cooperiunt et videri prohibent illam puram imaginem quae naturaliter
et potentialiter est interius, et per solam ablationem talium offendi-
culorum, sine aliqua additione, manifestantes imaginis pulchritudinem in
propria specie, quae prius latebat in occulto; *H.D.* 5/33–6/31

CAPITULUM III

(*H.D.* 7/10–8/35)

Quae sint affirmativae theologiae, quae negativae

Igitur in Theologicis quidem Hypotyposibus maxime propria affirmativae theologiae laudavimus: quomodo divina et bona natura singularis dicitur, quomodo trina; quae secundum ipsam dicta paternitas et filiatio, quid vult monstrare Spiritus theologia; quomodo ex immateriali et simplici bono, in corde manentia bonitatis pullulaverunt 5 lumina, et quomodo a mansione in ipso et in se ipsis et in se invicem coaeterna pullulatione permanserunt ingressibilia; quomodo supersubstantialis Jesus humanae naturae veritatibus substantia factus est: et quaecumque alia ab Eloquiis expressa in Theologicis hypotyposibus laudantur. In libro autem de *Divinis nominibus*, quomodo 10 bonus nominatur, quomodo exsistens, quomodo vita et sapientia et virtus, et quaecumque alia intelligibilis sunt Dei nominationis. In Symbolica autem Theologia, quae sunt a sensibilibus ad divina Dei nominationes: quae sunt divinae formae, quae figurae divinae et partes, et instrumenta; quae divina loca, et qui ornatus; qui furores, 15 quae tristitiae et insaniae, quae ebrietates et crapulae; quae juramenta, et quae maledictiones; qui somni, et quae vigilationes; et quaecumque aliae sanctae formationes compositae sunt symbolicae deiformationis.

Et te arbitror conspexisse quomodo plurium sermonum sunt 20 ultima quam prima. Etenim oportebat theologicas hypotyposes et divinorum nominum reserationem, pauciorum sermonum esse quam symbolicam theologiam: quoniam quantum ad superius respicimus, tantum sermones conspectibus intelligibilium contrahuntur; quemadmodum et nunc in caliginem quae est super 25 mentem introeuntes, non sermonum brevitatem, sed irrationabilitatem perfectam et imprudentiam inveniemus. Et ibi quidem a superiori ad extrema descendens sermo, secundum quantitatem descensus ad proportionalem dilatabatur multitudinem. Nunc autem ab inferioribus ad supremum ascendens, secundum mensuram 30 ascensionis contrahitur; et post omnem ascensionem, totus sine voce erit, et totus unietur ineffabili. Dicis autem: Quare totaliter a primo ponentes divinas positiones, ab ultimis inchoamus divinam ablationem? Quoniam hoc quod est super omnem positionem ponentes, a magis ipsi cognato suppositivam affirmationem oportebat ponere; 35

25 quemadmodum et nunc] Par. (p. 464): Unde et in praesenti libro; *H.D.* 8/12: As it is now here in þis book   27 ibi] Par. (p. 464): Et in praedictis quidem libris; *H.D.* 8/15: And in alle þe oþer bookes   32–98/4 Dicis... intelligitur] Par. (p. 464): Forte autem quaeris quae sit ratio quare positiones incipimus a dignioribus, et ablationes ab inferioribus. Haec autem est ratio: quia quando volumus per positionem designare Deum, qui est super omnem positionem, congruit ut ipsi digniora et magis ei propinqua

illud autem quod est super omnem ablationem auferentes, a magis distantibus ab ipso auferre. Annon magis est vita et bonitas, quam aer et lapis? et magis non est crapula et non insania, quam non dicitur neque intelligitur?

CAPITULUM IV

(*H.D.* 9/1–21)

Quod nihil sensibilium est, qui est omnis sensibilis causa secundum excessum

5 Primo ergo a remotissimis incipientes, auferimus a Deo non substantiatum, aut non ens, quod remotius est his quae tantum sunt, nec vivunt; [et non vivens, quod remotius est his quae sunt et vivunt; et non sentiens, quod remotius est his quae sunt, vivunt et sentiunt;] et carens ratione et mente, quod remotius est his quae sunt
10 et vivunt, et ratiocinantur atque intelligunt. Deinde removemus ab eo omne corporeum, vel omnia corpora, vel corporea accidentia, ut est figura, forma, qualitas, quantitas, pondus, localitas, visibilitas, sensuum tangibilitas et activa et passiva, inordinationem carnalis concupiscentiae, aut complexionem turbidam materialis passionis.
15 Et removemus ab eo invaletudinem subjectam casibus sensibilibus, et luminis indigentiam, et generationem et corruptionem, aut divisionem, aut passibilitatem, et fluxum temporalem. Neque enim Deus est aliquid istorum, aut in se habet etiam aliquid sensibilium.

CAPITULUM V

(*H.D.* 9/23–10/23)

Quod nihil intelligibilium est, qui est omnis intelligibilis causa secundum excessum

Iterum etiam incipientes negationes ab altioribus, dicimus quod omni-
20 um causa neque est anima, neque mens; neque habet phantasiam

attribuamus principalius; quando vero Deum volumus designare per ablationem, primo congruit ab eo illa auferre quae magis ab ipso videntur distare. Verbi gratia: propinquius et congruentius ei attribuitur vita vel bonitas, quam aer aut lapis; aut congruentia evidentiori removetur ab eo crapula et insania, quam dici vel intelligi; *H.D.* 8/22–34: Bot happiliche . . . vnderstondyng

Title] *From the version of Sarracenus; the rest is the Paraphrase of Vercellensis* 7–9 et non vivens . . . sentiunt] *Omitted in the version of Paraphrase used. The emendation was suggested by that of McCann, p. 277. See above, p. xxxix.*

Title] *From the version of Sarracenus; the rest is the Paraphrase of Vercellensis* 19 incipientes] Sar. (p. 474): ascendentes; *H.D.* 9/25: ascendyng & begynnyng

inferiorem aut superiorem, neque opinionem, neque rationem, neque intellectum; neque est ratio, neque intellectus; neque dicitur, neque intelligitur. Et ut decurramus per media ad extrema, neque est numerus, neque ordo, neque magnitudo, neque parvitas, neque aequalitas, neque similitudo, neque dissimilitudo; neque stat, neque 5 movetur. Et ut ad summa per quaedam media revertamur, et in summis negationes terminemus, neque virtutem habet, neque est virtus, neque lumen; neque vivit, neque vita est; neque substantia est, neque aevum, neque tempus; neque etiam intelligibiliter tangibilis secundum essentiam suam, neque scientia, neque veritas, neque 10 regnum, neque sapientia, neque unum, neque unitas, neque bonitas, neque deitas; neque spiritus secundum quod nos intelligimus spiritum, neque filiatio, neque paternitas, neque aliquid aliud plene cognitum a nobis vel ab aliquo exsistente, scilicet homine puro vel angelo. Sed neque Deus est aliquid non exsistentium, aut aliquid exsistentium; 15 neque exsistentia ipsum cognoscunt secundum quod ipse est, neque ipse cognoscit ea secundum quod ipsa sunt in se ipsis, sed secundum quod sunt in Verbo. Neque est ipsius rationalis investigatio, neque nomen, neque cognitio; neque ipse est tenebrae a lumine deficientes, neque est lumen intelligibile, neque est error, neque veritas. Et 20 omnino nulla est ipsius aut positio aut ablatio; sed quum aliqua quaecumque sub ipsa sunt, ponimus vel negando auferimus, ipsum neque ponimus neque auferimus, quoniam et super omnem positionem est perfecta et unica omnium causa, et super omnem ablationem est excessus ipsius ab omnibus absoluti et super omnia eminentis. 25

6 movetur] Sar. (p. 474): movetur, neque silentium agit; *H.D.* 10/1: moueþ, ne he holdeþ no sylence   11–12 bonitas, neque deitas] Sar. (p. 475): deitas aut bonitas; *H.D.* 10/7: Godheed, or goodnes   19–20 neque ipse . . . intelligibile] Sar. (p. 475): neque tenebrae, neque lumen; *H.D.* 10/14: ne he is derknes, ne he is liȝt

It must also be noted that in this chapter the Middle English translator agrees with Sarracenus in omitting: 98/19–20 omnium causa, 99/10 secundum essentiam suam, 14 scilicet homine puro vel angelo.

APPENDIX B

Editor's Foreword

A Ladder of Foure Ronges is a Middle English translation of *Scala Paradisi* (or *Scala Claustralium*), now attributed to the ninth Prior of the Grande Chartreuse, Guigo II, and thought to have been written shortly before 1150.* This Middle English version has been comprehensively treated elsewhere,† in an account of the manuscripts, its treatment of the Latin source, its style. It is extant in three fifteenth-century manuscripts, Ff. vi. 33 in the University Library, Cambridge (F),‡ Douce 322 in the Bodleian Library (D), Harleian 1706 in the British Museum (H). In all three manuscripts the title is the same. The Cambridge MS. has, in addition, the running title of 'The Laddyr of Cloystrerys', and the Douce MS. ends with 'Explicit *Scala Celi*'.

The text given in full here is from F, with a few suggested emendations from the other manuscripts, where F appears obviously inferior. All three manuscripts have been fully collated and closely compared with the Latin. They appear to fall into two groups, with the number of suspect unique readings in F far fewer than the variant readings obviously inferior in which D and H agree against F. The footnotes indicate where D and H agree against F, but it was considered unprofitable to quote here all the unique readings in D and H.

f. 115ᵃ A LADDER OF FOURE RONGES BY THE WHICH MEN MOWE WELE CLYME TO HEVEN

    ·As I was occupied on a day in bodyly traueyle and thouȝt on gostly werkys that were nedefulle to Goddis seruauntys, foure gostly werkes
5 comme soon to my mynde, that is to sey:—lesson, meditacion, orison, and contemplacion. This is the ladder of cloysterers, & of
f. 115ᵇ oþere Goddis lovers, | by the which they clymbe from eerth into

    1 which] ladder *add.*   3 on²] of   7 from] the *add.*   into] vnto

---

* See A. Wilmart, *Auteurs spirituels et textes dévots du Moyen Age latin* (Paris, 1932), pp. 230–40. The Latin treatise is printed with the title *Scala Paradisi* among the works of St. Augustine in *P.L.*, t. xl (cols. 997–1004), and with the title *Scala Claustralium* among the works of St. Bernard in *P.L.*, t. clxxxiv (cols. 475–84). A modernized version of the Middle English treatise exists in pamphlet form, edited by Abbot Justin McCann, and printed and published by the Benedictines of Stanbrook Abbey, Worcester, 1953.

† P. Hodgson,'*A Ladder of Foure Ronges by the whiche Men Mowe Wele Clyme to Heven*. A Study of the Prose Style of a Middle English Translation', *M.L.R.*, vol. xliv (Oct. 1949), pp. 465–75.

‡ This manuscript is described in the Introduction, pp. xiv–xv.

heuyn. This is a longe laddir and a meruelous thouȝe it haue but foure
stavis, for the oon ende stondith on the grounde and the other ende
thrillyth the clowdys and shewith to the clymber heuenly pryvetees.

This is the ladder that Jacob sawe, as Genesis tellith, þat stode
vpon the erthe & rawȝt into heuyn, by the whiche he sawe angellis of 5
heuyn goyng vpward & downward, and God lenyng to the ladder. By
goyng vp & downe of these angellis is vndirstonde that the angellis of
hevyn gladyn vs with many gostly comfortis & bere vp oure prayers to
oure Lorde in heuyn there he sittyth on hye, & brynge from hym to vs
desires of oure hertys, as it may be prouid by Danyel. By the lenyng 10
of God to this laddir is vndirstond þat he is euere redye to help
alle tho that by thes iv staves of this | ladder wylle clymbe wisely, f. 116ᵃ
ne thar hym drede no snaperyng ther suche a laddyr wolle trewly
helpe hym.

Vndirstonde nowe what the iv stavis of this laddyr be ich bi 15
themself. Lesson is a besy lokyng vpon Holy Writte with intencion of
the wille and in the witte. Meditacion is a studious inserchyng with
the mynde to knowe that ere was hydde thurwe wischyng of propir
skylle. Prayer is a devoute desiryng of the hert for to gete that
that is good & to fordoo þat is eville. Cóntemplacion is a risyng of 20
hert into God that tastith sumdele of heuenly swettnesse & savourith.
Lesson sekyth, meditacion fyndith, orison askith, contemplacion
felith. *Vnde querite & accipietis; pulsate et aperietur vobis.* That is to
sey: 'Sekyth, & ȝe schal fynde; knocke, and the gatys shalle be
openyd vnto yowe.' That is: sekyth redyng, and ȝe shalle fynde holy 25
meditacion | thynkyng; and knocke prayeng, and the gatys shal be f. 116ᵇ
openyd to yowe to haue the entre throgh heuenly contemplacion to
fele that ȝe desire. Lesson puttyth as it were hole mete to þe mouth;
meditacion chewith & brekith it; prayere fyndith savoure; contemplacion is the likyng swettnes that so myche comfortith. Lesson is 30
withouteforth in the barke; meditacion is withynforth in the pythe;
orison is in the desyreful askyng; and contemplacion is in the delyȝt of
the grete swettnes. Lesson is in the first grounde that gothe before &
ledyth furth into meditacion; meditacion sekith bisily, and ay with
a depe thouȝt gravith & dyggyth depe as he wenyth to fynde that 35
tresoure; but for he may not wende ther-to by hymself, than he
sendith vs into prayer that is myȝtful and stronge. And so anone

2 stavis] stakes   3 to] *om.*   7 of] and   is] to *add.*   9
in] of   vs] the *add.*   10 as ... Danyel] *om.*   lenyng] louyng
11 this] the   12 wylle] *om.*   clymbe wisely] *trs.*   13 thar] dare
hym] hem   17 in the witte] the inwytte   18 ere] cryste   20 &]
for *add.*   fordoo] do awey   þat] that *add.*   21 -dele] and
sauereth *add.*   & savourith] *om.*   23 accipietis] inuenietis   23–
24 That ... sey] *om.*   25 vnto] to   fynde] with *add.*   26 gatys]
yate   28 ȝe] *om.*   31 is] *om.*   32 is]*om.*   is] *om.*   33
in] *om.*   be-] to-   34 in-] *om.*   meditacion] he *add.* F   ay] alwey
35 as] and   wenyth] wende   37 in-] *om.*

prayer styeth vp to God, and there he fyndith the tresoure that he so |
f. 117ª feruently desiryth, that is the swettnes & likyng of contemplacion.
And than commyth contemplacion & ӡildyth the trauayle of the other
thre thurwe a swete heuenly dewyng, that the sowle drynkith in
5 lykyng & in ioye.

The first degre is of begynners, the second of profiteris, the thridde
of hem that be devoute, the fourth of hem þat be holy & blissid of
God. Thes foure degrees be so bounde togedir, and ich of hem
seruyth so togedere to other, that the first as lesson & meditacion
10 helpith litel or nouӡte withoute tho that be folwyng as prayer &
contemplacion. Also withoute the two former [men] wynne late the
two latter. What helpith to spende thy tyme in lesson, redyng or
herkenyng of the dedys of holy Faderys, but if we them breke or
chewe thurwe meditacion, and drawe oute sumwhat & swalwe it and
15 send it to the hert, so þat we may fynde & by them vndirstonde oure
f. 117ᵇ owne defautys, | and aftir such knowyng þat we infors vs so warly to
werke þat we may wynne to þe vertuys that in them were? But howe
may we thus thinke or beware that no false thouӡt ne vnclene make
vs not in meditacion passe the bondes stabillid by oure holy Faderys,
20 but if we first eyther of heryng or in redyng be lawfully lernyd? Also
what helpith a man thouӡe he se thorogh meditacion what is [to] doo,
but if he throgh helpe of prayer & of Goddis grace doo that in him is to
wynne & to holde that he in meditacion hath founde, and vndirstonde that þat were to doo to þe sowle hele? For as the apostil
25 Jacob sayth: 'Alle good ӡiftys and alle perfeccion cummyth from
above from the fadir of liӡtes', wythoute whose helpe we be vnmyӡty
to doo eny good.

But the good þat is in vs, if there eny be, he dooth it in vs, but
f. 118ª not withoute vs, for as | Powle sayth: *Cooperatores Dei sumus.* That is,
30 we be Goddis helperis to oure good; that ys, we opyn oure hertis
when he sendith vs goodis of his grace, and doo þat in vs is to kepe &
to holde it. But for we may doo nothyng hym to paye, ne to oure
soule hele but with his grace, therfor it is nedefulle to speke of Goddis
grace sumwhat in this litelle boke.
35 Thou shalt vndirstonde that ther be thre gracys of God.

The first grace is a comoun grace ӡeven of God to alle creaturys.
And this is Goddis help that he thorughe his goodnes sondirly to alle
creaturys ӡevyth aftir their kynde that they may stere & fele, and

1 to] vnto 2 &] the *add.* 7 of³] with 9 togedere] *om.*
11 men] D H; may F late] to *add.* 12 two] *om.* helpith] hit *add.*
13 herkenyng] lystynyng of] *om.* if] *om.* 17 them] hym
18 or] and 19 not] *om.* bondes] boundys 21 helpith] hit *add.*
to] D H; *om.* F 22 if] *om.* grace] to *add.* F 24 þat] *om.*
to²] *om.* 25 Jacob] *om.* 27 to . . . good] any good dede to do
29 Powle sayth] seyth the Apostylle 30 hertis] hert 31 sendith
vs] *trs.* 33 -for] I holde *add.* is] *om.* speke] somwhat *add.*
Goddis] hys 34 sumwhat] *om.* boke] Therfore *add.*

withoute his grace they may noþing doo, neyther in their kynde laste
ne indure. For as þoue seest that riȝt as watyr, whan it is hote
thorohe strength of the fyre and if the fyre be drawyn from it, it
turnyth oute of his hete, & kyndely it waxeth colde: ryȝt so | it is of f. 118ᵇ
yche creature, as Seynt Austyn wittnessith. For as alle creatures are & 5
be made of nouȝt, but if they by his grace be susteyned & kepte, soon
they wille turne to nouȝt. That vndirstode wele Seynt Powle whan he
sayd: *Gracia Dei sum id quod sum*; as if he seyd: 'That I am, that I
haue lyfe, that I may se, fele, or goo, or stonde, alle is of Goddis grace.'

Another grace ther is of God, and this is more specialle. And this 10
grace offerith God oonly to man, take it if he wille. And this grace
stondith alwey at the gatys of oure hert, & knockith vpon oure fre
wille for to haue entre; as it sayth in the *Boke of Pryvites*:—'Lo, I
stonde at the dore & knocke. Whosoeuere herith my voice & openyth
þe gatis to me, I shalle entre into hym, & I shal sowpe with hym & 15
he with me.' Beholde here, man, the gentilnes of oure Lorde that
proferyth | hymself so mekely of his mercifulle grace. And this grace f. 119ᵃ
is callid the grace of Goddys fre ȝifte to man. It behouyth that men
receyve this grace whan God sendith it, and ordeyn hym thurwe
helpe of this seconde grace þat he may be worthy to receyve the 20
ȝifte of the Holy Gost, that steryth a man to good & callyth hym fro
eville.

Thou shalt vnderstond that to the hele of mannys sowle ii þingis
be nedefulle: the first is grace, of þe which nowe laste is spoke,
and the tothir is free wille. Withoute thes ii no creature of man may 25
comme to hele of sowle for owȝt þat in hym is. For nowther helpyth
fre wille wythoute grace, ne grace withoute fre wille helpyng &
assentyng. This wittnessith Seynt Austyn where he sayth: *Qui
creauit te sine te non iustificabit te sine te*. That is to sey: 'He that made
the withoute the', that is, withoute helpe of | the, 'he shal not make 30 f. 119ᵇ
the ryȝtwyse withoute help of the.' And thouȝe the fre wille of man
may not make grace in man, netheles he may doo that in hym is—caste
oute the olde dowe, which is the olde corruptible synne þat withdrawith man from grace, and so make hym redy þat he may receyve
this grace. As þou seest þat þou mayst not thurwe myȝt of thi self 35
make the hows liȝt, ȝit þou maist opyn the wyndowe & lette the sunne

2 ne indure] *om.*   riȝt as] *om.*   whan it] that   3 the]
om.   if] *om.*   4 it] *om.*   waxeth] becommeth   5 yche] euery
are &] *om.*   6 nouȝt] so *add.*   by] thorow   kepte] holdyn
7 turne] worthe   8 if] that *add.*   9 haue lyfe] lyue   or] *om.*
alle is] thys I haue   10 this] that   13–17 Lo . . . grace] *om.*
17 grace] *om.*   18 It behouyth] *om.*   men] man   20 the] thys
21 good] god   25 no . . . man] none   26 comme] wynne   to
. . . sowle] *om.*   is] to hele of soule   27 wythoute] thys *add.*   ne] nor
thys   31 withoute] the *add.*   ne-] neuer-   32–4 caste . . . grace] *om.*
36 make . . . liȝt] lyght the house   ȝit] neuertheles

yn to shewe his liȝt; and if þou close thyn yene aȝenst the sonne, who
is to blame if þoue se noute? And if þou wilt not opyn thi mouth to
take mete, þou playnyst the wrongfully, if þou haue hungyr. God
sayth to the: 'Take kepe, if þou wilt opyn thy mouth I wille fylle it.'
5 That is to mene: 'Opyn thi hert to me, and I wille fylle it of my grace.'
And therfor man is gretly to blame þat hathe not this grace, for Seynt
f. 120ª Austyn seyth: 'Man | wantyth not the grace for God ȝevyth it hym
not.' That is thus to vndirstonde: man dooth not that in hym ys to
receyve it, for if he dyd that in hym were, the grace of God wold lyȝt
10 in hym to dwelle with hym. Therfor seyth Seynt Austyn: *Deus ingenti
liberalitate replet omnes creaturas pro captu earum.* That is to sey: God
thurwe his grete fredom, so fre and so large he is that he fillith alle
creatures aftir that they are able to receyve. Therfor if man to this
grace that steryth & callyth wil opyn the ȝatys of his hert and with
15 his fre wille graunte it to entre frely he wylle dwelle holly with hym
and make hym to kache in werke he is his trewe fere. And therfor
seyth the apostyl: *Gracia Dei in me vacua non fuit.* That is: 'The grace
of God was not voyd in me.' No more it was, for he schewyd in his
f. 120ᵇ vttyr werkys that the grace of God wrouȝt | in hym. Vttirly so he doth
20 with alle tho that he makith his dwellyng with, for he may not
be ydille, for he must nedys doo the werkys wherfor the Fadyr of
hevyn hym sent. Of this grace spekith Seynt Austyn and sayth thus:
'This grace to me is euere redye, if he fynde me redy. Whither euere
so I weend, he levith me not, but if I leve hym first.'
25 God he is as felawe in half getyng in werkes of God, and doothe
with vs as a felawe that wille wynnyng haue. He ȝevith his grace, and
we oure werkes, as merchauntys to sette wynnyng þat fallith to them.
And wondirly he chalengyth the lovyng & the worship to haue for his
part of man, but we as fals wretchis benemme hym frawdabylly. And
30 we wene that we wynne alle, and we lese alle, for we doo iniury &
fraude, we ȝevyn oure love to the feend and oure worshipe to the
f. 121ª worlde & to the flessh, and so oure love ys | withdrawe from oure
gracious partenere. As John seith in his Epistil: *Nolite diligere mun-*

1 shewe his liȝt] lyghten   and] *om.*   close] loke   2 se] hit *add.*
3 the] *om.*   4 kepe] hede   mouth] to take mete and
add.   5 to mene] *om.*   6 for] as *add.*   7 Austyn] Anselme
grace] of god *add.*   it hym] *trs.*   8 not] but for man resceueth
hit nat *add.*   That . . . vndirstonde] *om.*   man] and   9
of God] *om.*   10 with hym] *om.*   seyth] *om.*   Austyn] seyth *add.*
11 to sey] *om.*   12 grete] grace   13 that] that *add.*   are] be
receyve] And *add.*   15 to] *om.*   dwelle] *om.*   hym] dwelle
add.   16 kache] kythe   werke] that *add.*   his] *om.*   And] *om.*
18 was] ys   19 vttyr] bytter   21 doo] to   22 hym] hath *add.*
23 he] hit   23-4 Whither . . . so] whereeuer   24 he] hit   if]
om.   hym] hit   25 he] *om.*   God] when we hem do *add.*   26
a] *om.*   felawe] doth *add.*   wille wynnyng] *trs.*   27 sette] a *add.*
29 of man] *om.*   hym frawdabylly] hys part   30 we] *om.*
30-105/10 for we . . . willfully] *om.*

dum neque ea que in mundo sunt. That is to sey: 'Nylle ȝe love tho
thynges that be in þe worlde.' Whosoeuere love the worlde, the
charite of the Fadir is not in hym, for alle that ys in the worlde is
covetise of flesshe and covetise of the eye and pryde of lyfe, which is
not of the Fadir but of the worlde. And the worlde shalle passe, and 5
covetise of hit. Thes thinges be biloved contrarie to the councellis of
oure Lorde God and partener. And we defraude hym of his parte
that he bouȝt with so grete price, that is with the blode of the
vndefyled Lambe, Crist Ihesu. We depart oureself from the blisse of
oure Lorde willfully, lyke as the hownde dyd that bare a chese by a 10
watyr syde, and as he lokyd in the watyr he sawe a shadwe of the
chese, and he openyd his mouth to take | it, and it fel from hym. And f. 121ᵇ
so he loste that he hadde, and that he desirid to haue hadde. Therfor
sayth God to such peple by Isay the prophete: *Gloriam meam alteri
non dabo.* That is: 'My lovynge & my worshipe I shalle ȝeve to none 15
oþere but to them, that is to sey that be my trewe seruauntys.' Be thou
than, man, to God as a trewe feer, & lette hym haue his parte.

The thridde grace is more specialle, for this is not ȝeven to alle
men, but oonly to them þat opyn the ȝatys of ther hert, and make her
fre wylle redy to receyve this grace that is before-sayd. This grace is 20
the ȝifte of the Holy Goste þat steryth men to doo good werkes. This
grace God ȝevith to man ther thurwe to wynne hym mede. Wythoute
this grace nothyng is medefulle that we doo. This grace risith of thre:
the first grace þat is frely ȝevyn þat steryth to fre wylle; the tothir is
the wylle assen|tyng; and the thridde is God makyng & ȝevyng this 25 f. 122ᵃ
grace. This grace is tokenyng of specialle love of God to them that
he sendyth hit. This grace makyth a man pacient in alle angrys
& mekely to suffyr losse of goodis, losse of worldly frendis, bodily
harmys, sekenesse, & penaunce for fordone synnes withoute grutch-
yng of hert. This makith a man to contynue in goodnes; this makith 30
to beware of eville & to knowe alle good. This God ȝevyth here to a
man as an eernest of the endles blisse if he wolle holde it. Therfor by
this grace spekith the angelle in the *Boke of Priuetees* thus: *Tene quod
habes.* That is: 'Holde that þou haste.' As if he sayd: 'If thou wylt
haue that ioy that is eendlees, holde faste that grace that God hath 35
sent to the, for this grace makith wey to blisse.'

But God wolle that we praye for this blissid grace, and he wolle
þat we opyn the | ȝatys of oure hert aȝens his commyng, and þat is f. 122ᵇ
that we assent with oure fre wille to receyue his grace. This consent

---

10 lyke] *om.*   11 in] into   12 and it . . . hym] *om.*   14 peple]
om.   15 shalle] wylle   16 but . . . seruauntys] *om.*   17
man] *om.*   19 them] tho   21 doo] *om.*   24 first] ys *add.*
25 this] hys   26 tokenyng] tokyn   29 fordone] theyr done
synnes] synne   30 to contynue . . . makith] *om.*   31 a] *om.*
32 the] *om.*   36 to] *om.*   this] the   37 for] after
blissid] *om.*   wolle] wolde   38 opyn] opened   39 consent] assent

askid Crist Ihesu of the woman·Samaritan with whom he spake at the
welle, as she stode there to drawe watyr, to whom oure Lorde Ihesu
sayde: 'Goo þoue, & clepe thy husbond'; as if he had sayd: 'I wille
ȝeve to the of my grace as þou wilt assente with thi propir wille.' Also
5 he askid prayer of her whan he sayd: 'If þou knewist the ȝifte of God,
and what he is that seyth to the "ȝeve me drynk", perauenture þou
woldist aske of hym, and he wolde ȝeve to the qwyke watyr.' Whan
þe woman herde thes wordys of Ihesu, anone she thouȝt in her hert
that good it were & nedeful to drynke of this precious qwyke watyr
10 that Cryst spake of. And anone with feruente desyre she ȝafe hyr to
prayer for to haue of this watyr, and seyd: 'Lorde, ȝeve þou me this
f. 123ᵃ watyr.' See | nowe howe heryng of Cristes worde, & folwyng theron
meditacion with depe thouȝt of hert sterid her to pray aftir this watyr.
Howe shuld she a be so besy to pray but if meditacion of hir hert
15 had steryd hir þerto? Or what shulde the former thouȝt of meditacion
haue brouȝt to hir, but if the prayer folwyng that she desired had wonne
it of Cryst?

If thou wylt than that thi meditacion be medefulle, it behouyth
than that thi deuocion of prayer folwe, thurwe which þou maist wynn
20 to swettnes of contemplacion. Thurwe this than mayst þou vndirstonde þat lesson withoute meditacion ys ydille; meditacion withoute
prayer is wythoute effecte; but prayer with deuocion wynnyth to contemplacion.

To wynne to the hye steyre of contemplacion withoute prayer, it
25 were wondyr or myracle. The power of Almyȝty God is eendles, and
f. 123ᵇ his mercy above alle his werkys. Other whyle he | reysith of the hard
stonys Abraham sonnys, whan he tho that be hard as stonys in
wykidnes movith & steryth to love God. And so as ho sayth: 'He
ȝevyth the oxe by the horne', that is, whan he not callid offeryth his
30 grace, and, neuere sowȝt ne desired, he ioyneth hymself vnto them.
If we rede that it is befalle thus to eny, as to Seynt Powle & suche
other, neuerethelesse we shuld not tempte God & trowe that God wolle
so doo to vs lyeng in synne. But we shulde doo þat fallyth to vs—

---

1 Crist Ihesu] god   2 Ihesu] *om.*   3 Goo þoue &] *om.*
clepe] calle   4 to] *om.*   as] yef   7 and] yef   to]
om.   qwyke watyr] water of lyfe   8 þe] thys   Ihesu] god
thouȝt] caste   9 qwyke watyr] water of lyfe   10 Cryst]
god   And] *om.*   desyre] to haue of thys water *add.*   11 for . . .
watyr] *om.*   þou me] me of   12 Cristes] goddys   14 she] we
besy] for *add.*   hir] *om.*   15 former] for   16 the] *om.*   17
Cryst] god   19 than] *om.*   24 withoute] helpe of *add.*   25 wondyr]
-fulle *add.*   Almyȝty God] *trs.*   26 mercy] ys *add.*   27 sonnys]
chyldren   he] *om.*   stonys] stone   27–8 in wykidnes] and euylle
28 movith] eggeth   30 neuere] neyther   he ioyneth] yete the
vnto] into   them] hym   31 to²] *om.*   &] to *add.*   32 other]
what so they were *add.*   shuld] shullen   33 so doo] *trs.*   shulde]
shalle

rede and sette depely oure hertys on Goddys holy lawe, and hertly
praye hym þat he helpe oure febylnes and that he wolde with the
eyen of his mercy see oure wretchidnes; and alwey holde oureself
vnworthy and wretchis. Be we euere vntrusty of oure sylf, and lene
we on hym with hertly love, makyng oure mone to hym, for to that 5
blissid Lorde is the cure of oure sowlys. As Petir sayth: *Omnem sollici-*
tudinem nostram proicien|tes in eum quoniam ipsi cura est de nobis. f. 124ᵃ
And therfore he comfortith vs & sayth: *Petite & accipietis.* That is:
'Traveyle ȝe with holy loue aftir my grace, and þoue, man, shalt haue
that þou desiryst.' This grace men muste wynne with strength.   10

Loo, nowe I haue ȝowe tolde of the propirtees and þe fowre degrees
of the fowre stavys of this wondirfulle laddyr. Blissyd be thoo alle
þat levyn vanitees & spende ther tyme & occupacion in thes councellys,
and tho that alle sellyn, & byen the felde wheryn lyeth the preciouse
passyng tresoure of swetnesse. As oure Lorde sayth: *Vacate & videte* 15
quam suauis est Dominus. That is: 'Beþinke yowe vttyrly and see
howe swete God our Sauyoure is.' Thus men shuld clyme by this
laddyr from gre to gre, from steyer to steyer, & from vertue to vertue,
euere tyl he see God of goddys in Syon, that is in the blisse of hevyn.

In Mathewe Cryste sayth thus: *Beati mundo corde, quoniam ipsi* 20
Deum videbunt. Lo, this is a litel worde, but it is of mych vertue,
swetnes, & of grete effecte, & makith wey to lyfe. Whan man with
eerys bodily this litel worde heryth, & with gostly eyen of his hert
hath seen it, he spekith to his soule and sayth: 'It semyth that þis
worde may make wey to God. I wille', he sayth, 'assaye in my hert & 25
fynde with wissyng of hym howe I may vndirstond and wynne to this
clennesse, for rych thyng it is, and sothly it makith hem þat haue it to
wynne the blisse of hevyn. And Cryst hymself byhotyth hem þat they
schal see God, þe which syght oonly is fulfillyng of alle ioye to alle
that be the freendys of God.'   30

Whan man this lesson hath redde or herde: *Beati mundo / corde* f. 124ᵇ
quoniam ipsi Deum videbunt—that is to sey: 'Blyssid are they
that be clene in hert for thei shal see God'—he begynnyth to chewe it
& breke it with skylle or reśon, and sekith besily howe he may comme

1 and] or   hertys] herte   2 the] *om.*   3 wretchidnes] wykednes
4 and²] but   5 we] alle   5–7 for . . . *nobis*] *om.*   8 And] *om.*
he . . . sayth] seyth he to vs   is] to sey *add.*   9 ȝe] *om.*   man]
om.   11 ȝowe] *om.*   tolde] sundyrly *add.*   of] *om.*   12 thoo alle]
trs.   13 &²] her *add.*   councellys] *om.*   14 tho . . . alle] D H; alle
tho that F   the²] here   15 of . . . sayth] *om.*   16 That] Thys
yowe] the   17 men shuld] shulle men   18 gre] D H; grees F
19 euere] alle wey   he] they   20 In . . . thus] In lesson I herde
rede thys   21 this] there   vertue] *om.*   22 to] vnto   Whan]
a *add.*   23 eerys bodily] *trs.*   26 fynde] founde   wissyng] wysshyng
this] hys   27 sothly] sely   it] that   28 Cryst] god   29 God]
heuen   30 that . . . god] goddys frendys   31 redde or] *om.*
32 to sey] *om.*   are] be   they] tho   33 in] of   34 skylle or] hys
and sekith] *om.*

to this clennesse that is so precious & so my3ty that it makith the
havers to se God. Than gothe meditacion & enserchith qwyckly, and
fyndith sothly þat is. He saith not blissid be thoo that be of clene body,
but þat be of clene herte, for it is not ynow3e for to haue handys clene
5 from eville dede but if the herte withyn be clene of thou3tis. Therfor
askith Dauid in the sawter there he sayth: *Quis ascendet in montem
Domini aut quis stabit in loco sancto eius?* And there furthwyth it is
answeryd thus: *Innocens manibus & mundo corde.* This is to sey:
'Who shalle clymbe or ascende into the hylle of God' that is in hevyn,
f. 125ᵃ 10 'or who shalle stonde in that holy stede', that is, there to | se God in
his Godhed? The Holy Goste in Dauid sayth & answerith: 'Thoo þat
noon evylle doo with her handys, and be clene of hert wythyn.' 3it in
meditacion he thynkith depely howe þe forsayde prophete Dauid,
Goddis derlyng, feruently prayeth aftir this clennesse there he sayth:
15 *Cor mundum crea in me, Deus.* 'Lorde', he seyth, 'make in me a clene
hert.' And also he sayth: *Iniquitatem si aspexi in corde meo, non
exaudiet Dominus deprecacionem meam.* That is to say: 'If I knowe eny
wickidnes in my hert, God wolle not here my prayer.' He bethinkith
hym 3ete of the holy man, Job, howe ferefulle he was that he were not
20 fyllid with fowle thou3t, whan he sayde: *Pepigi fedus cum oculis
meis ne cogitarem de virgine.* That is: 'I haue made couinaunt with
myn eyen that I shulde not thynke of a woman or of a virgyn.' Loo,
f. 125ᵇ howe streytly that holy man refreyned hymself, þat shytt his | eyen
that he shulde see no vanitees, that he as vnwitty cast not his eyen on
25 that thyng þat my3te make aftir fowle love to ryse & to fordoo the
clennesse of the hert.

Whan he is þus ferde to lese thurwe vayn si3te this clennes, he
begynnyth to taste the grete mede that risith therof that is so de-
lectable, so ioyful, to se the glorious face of God, that fayrest is befor
30 alle tho þat euere were—not lothly, grysly, & dedly, as oure dedly
synnes hym made, but goodly, graciously, & lovely, and crownyd alle
with ioy & clothid alle with blisse, as his Fadyr hym clothid at his
rysyng. He thynkith that in this fayryst si3t shal be alle the perfeccion
of ioy, of the which the prophete sayde: *Saciabor cum apparuerit
35 gloria tua.* That is: 'Lord, I shal be fulfilled of alle manere ioye whan
thou shewyst thi gloryous face to me', and forsoth not ere. Than whan

---

3 of clene] *trs.*   4 of clene] *trs.*   5 of] foule *add.*   7–8 And . . . *corde*]
om.   8 This . . . sey] That ys   9 clymbe] vp *add.*   or ascende] *om.*   into]
to   the] hygh *add.*   is] to sey shalle com *add.*   in] to   10 or] and
God] hym   11 The . . . in] *om.*   sayth—answerith] *trs.*   12 her] *om.*
15 he seyth] *om.*   make] thow *add.*   16 *meo*] *om.*   17
deprecacionem meam] *om.*   to say] *om.*   I] see or *add.*   19
ferefulle] feerde   21 haue] *om.*   22 not] *om.*   a] no   or . . .
virgyn] *om.*   23 that] the   24 eyen] eye   28 risith therof] *trs.*
29 the] that   30 &] ne   dedly] waryed   32 clothid¹ ᵃⁿᵈ²] clad
33 fayryst] sely   34 of] alle *add.*   35 manere] of *add.*   36 ere] or
whan] that *add.*

he seeth that so myche swettnesse com|myth of so litelle a worde, f. 126ᵃ
howe mych a fyre kendelyth of so litelle a sparkille as þat is—*Beati*
mundo corde : ' Blissid be the clene of herte '—he betith it oute hote as it
is, and drawyth it oute on length & brede. Whan the sowle of a
glowyng bronde of this fyre is enflaumyd & so ravisshed in desire to 5
that thyng that is as the sothfast mede to the clennes of herte, that is,
God for to se, than the alabastyr boxe with swete oyntment begynnyth for to breke, and sone anone he felyth the swete smellys comme.
But not with tastyng, but as it were with smellyng he vndirstondith
the swete savoure, and ioyfulle it were to fele this swettnes. Sothly as 10
it seeth in the menyng therof, sych sekynge men may fynde.

But what schal man doo that desireth this levyng to fele, & fyndith
not by hymself howe he it may haue ? For the more þat a man sus-
teyneth his meditacion theron, the more of | mornynge he fyndith, for f. 126ᵇ
that he fyndyth not the swettnes of the clennes of herte. Meditacion 15
hym [s]hewyth, but not hym ȝeuith, for neyther thurwe redyng ne
thurwe thynkyng of meditacion cummyth man to felyng of this
swetnes, but thurwe the ȝifte þat cummyth from above. For evyr to
rede and be in meditacion is comon both to goode & to eville ; for the
philosopherys thurwe prevyng of ther skylle founde what thyng was 20
the goodnes of God, but for they knewe God & his goodnes, and lovid
hym not ne worshipped as God, therfor they were vnworthy to haue
this swettnes & the lykyng of God that shuld haue rysyn of þat
knowyng, and therfor God withhelde it from them as fro vnworthy.
And herewyth alle worthidyn to nouȝt. That studye of mannys witte 25
ȝafe not them the spirite of wysdom, that gostly ȝeuyth wytte &
savoure to that sowle that he cummyth to, | and steryth hem with f. 127ᵃ
lykyng, and furtheryth hem with gostly ioy̆e. And this oonly is gostly
ioye and ȝifte of Gode, & doctryne to his chosyn disciples. This witte
lernyth nothyng but grace that cummyth from above. To this witte 30
it is not to opyn the eere but the herte. This witte is hidde from wyse
men of the worlde, & shewid & openyd to lowe & meke sothly to
vndirstande & fele.

Grete myȝt risith than of mekenes that is worthy to conceyve &

1 that] *om.*   2 kendelyth] quekeneth   sparkille] sparke   3 of]
om.   oute] *om.*   4 on] of   length] breede   &] on *add.*
brede] length   a] *om.*   5 so] hit ys *add.*   6 the²] *om.*
7 boxe] *om.*   with] the *add.*   9 vnderstondith] the swete smelles
he vnderstandeth *add.*   11 seeth] seyth   12 fyndith] the *add.*
13 it may] *trs.*   a] *om.*   13–14 susteyneth] fasteneth   15 the²] *om.*   16
shewyth] D H ; chewyth F   17 this] hys   18 the] *om.*   19 meditacion]
meditacions   is] *om.*   to²] *om.*   20 prevyng] ledyng   skylle]
reson   23 this] that   the] that   24 fro] for   25 worthidyn]
worden   26 not] to *add.*   27 savoure] fauoure   hem] here *add.*
28 oonly] allone   is] the *add.*   28–9 gostly . . . and] *om.*   29
doctryne] lore   30 lernyth] techeth   32 the] thys   to]
the *add.*   meke] And *add.*   33 vndirstande—fele] *trs.*   34 risith
than] *trs.*

wynne þat thurwe witte of man may not be lernyd, ne with bodily
ere herde, ne wyth tunge tolde. This witte hath God holdyn oonly to
his chosun, þat alle resonable creatures knowe & vndirstonde that
ther is a maistyr techyng & redyng in heuyn, that techith sothfast
5 wysdom & lore to his chosyn scolers, and thurwe his grace lyʒtenyth
hem withyn, and makith hem to knowe and fele that no worldly witte
f. 127ᵇ may wynne to. | Thoue mayst se if þoue wilte beholde a symple olde
pore woman that is pore of witte, that neyther sothly can sey the
Pater Noster ne the Crede, such likyng wille haue in so litel a while,
10 so in sely moornyng the hert al tomeltyth, þat withoute terys &
moornyngys may she not praye. Who, wenyst thou, techith hir thus
to praye ? Not witte of this worlde, but grace from above. Howe a pore
sely man þat so dul of witt is, that lyveth by his swynke, thouʒe he
shulde lese his hedde he cowde not bryng to an eende a reson, to this
15 lore & to this wysedom as perfiʒtly may wynne therto as the wisest in
a londe, whatsoeuere he be; and he doo that in hym is, whatsoeuere
he be. Sothly he may wele be callid a maistyr ouere alle other that this
name beryth, that vnwytty so kan teche wysdom withoute wittys to
fele & vndirstonde that thurwe no witte of this worlde men may reche
f. 128ᵃ 20 to, so þat | man doo that therto fallyth, and bowe the ere of his herte
to lysten that lore. This wisdom is oonly the ʒifte of God that he hath
holdyn to hymself to ʒeve to thoo that he wille, as the office to
cristyn children God hathe ʒeve to many, but the powere in bapteme
to forʒeve synne he hath holdyn oonly to hymself. Therfor Seynt
25 John sayth: 'Here is he that baptisith soothly'—þat is to sey, verily
forʒevith synne. Thus may we say by hym that is oure God, he that
ʒevith wysdom to fele & to taste howe swete he ys. Many ther be that
haue grace of worde, but this wisdome is ʒeven but to fewe. That God
ʒevith to whom he wylle and whan he wylle.
30   Thanne whan man s[ee]th þat to þe knowyng ne to the felyng of this
wisdome he may not comme ne reche thurwe hymself, and the more
he traveylyth thedyr to thynke, the more he seeth the Godhede what
f. 128ᵇ he dothe: | than he seeth that his myʒte ne his witte be nouʒte, and
begynnyth to knowe hymself, and, as a pore wretche & nedefulle,
35 lowyth hymself & fallith down mekely with a lowe hert to pray, &

2 holdyn oonly] *trs.*   3 resonable] skylfulle   knowe] wete   5
lore] oonly *add.*   thurwe] though   7 to] thys *add.*   8 the] *om.*
11 moornyngys] syghynges   12 praye] do   a pore] *trs.*   13 þat
. . . is] *om.*   lyveth] lyfed   swynke] that so dulle of wytte ys that
add. 14–15 to . . . &] *om.*   15 to] of   wysedom] and to thys loore *add.*
15–16 therto . . . be] *om.*   16 and] so that   is] as the wysest of a londe
add.   17 he²] thys   18 -oute] oure   20 to] therto   that] that *add.*
the] hys   23 bapteme] for *add.*   25 sayth] by hymself *add.*   bap-
tisith] crysteneth   to sey, verily] that sothly   26 oure God] *om.*   27
ther be that] *om.*   30 man] men   seeth] sayth F   31 comme ne reche]
teche   more] that *add.*   32 he] thereaboute *add.*   thynke] clymbe
33 seeth] seyth   be] ys   34 and] *om.*   35 lowyth] loueth   -self] *om.*

sayth: 'Lorde, þou that wylt not be seen but of tho that are clene of
hert, I haue doo that in me is, redde & deply thouȝt and inserchid
what it is and in what manere I myȝt beste comme to this clennes
that I myȝt sumdele knowe the. Lorde, I haue souȝte and thouȝt with
alle my pore herte; and, Lorde, in my meditacion the fyre of desire 5
kyndelyth for to knowe the, not oonly the bytter barke withoute, but
in felyng & tastyng in my sowle. Lorde, this worthynes I aske not for
me, for I am wretchid & synfulle, and most vnworthy of alle other.
But as myche, Lorde, as a whelpe etyth of the crummys that falle
from the borde of the lorde, of the heritage | that is for to cumme 10 f. 129ª
oo drope I aske of that heuenly ioye to comforte my thristy sowle þat
brennyth in love-longyng to the.' Wyth thes and other suche desyres
the herte is inflaumed. God is callid & prayed as dere spowse to comme
to the moornyng sowle that langurith in love.

What dooth God than whose helpe ys euere vpon the ryȝtwys, and 15
his eere at her prayer? He abidyth not tylle the prayer be fully
eendyd, but he percyth in the myddis of the brennyng desire of that
thirsty sowle, and wyth a deerne halywey of heuenly swetnes softyth
þe sowle and comfortyth it, and makith it so oueretaken wyth likyng
and ioye that alle erthly thyng it forȝetyth as in that stounde, and 20
makith it to lese on a wondyr wyse, as if it were ded, from knowyng of
hymself. And as in flessly werkys man is so oueerecomme that he lesyth
the ledyng of reson and so becummyth alle flessly, | ryȝt so in the f. 129ᵇ
steyer of contemplacion the flesshly steryngys of man are so fordoon
þat þe flesche in nothyng aȝensayth the spirite, but is become alle 25
gostely.

But, Lorde, by what thynge may men knowe whan þoue thus doost,
and what is the tokyn of thy commyng, whethir sighynges & teerys be
massengers of this likyng and this comforte? And if it so be, it semyth
wondyr. It semyth not commynly that comfort acordith with 30
syghyngys and ioy with terys. And it semyth þei shuld not be callid
terys, but an heuynly dewyng that cummyth from above, that
wetyth withoute & clensith withyn the sowle, as it fallith in the
sacrament of baptyme. The [vttyr] wasshyng of terys withoute
betokenyth the inere waschyng. They are [sely] terys, thurwe the 35
which vttyr waschynge the ynere spottys are fordoon, & fyre of synne

1 are] be	3 in] on(e)	this] hys	4 sum- . . . the] the
knowe sumdele	6 kyndelyth] kyndeled	7 &] in *add.*	Lorde]
And	9 as myche] *om.*	10 the²] hys	11 I aske] *om.*
16 tylle] to	17 percyth] preaseth	the] a-	of²] to	18 haly-
wey] halowyng	19 ouere-] euer	21 on] apon	if] *om.*	were ded]
trs.	22 hym-] hem	23 the²] thys hygh	24 are] be	27
thus] thys	28 tokyn] tokenyng	29 and] of *add.*	30 that
. . . acordith] ouer alle accorde comforth	31 And] *om.*	þei] hit
33 clensith] closeth	34 vttyr] D H; watyr F	35 are] bene
sely] D H; sothly F	36 are] be	&] the *add.*	synne]
synnes			

f. 130ᵃ is qwenchid. Blissid | are tho that thus wepen, for Cryste sayth
by them that they shalle lawȝe. In thes terys the sowle knowlechith
God his trewe spowse. This is thi solas that thy lovynge spowse ȝeue to
the syghyngys mengyd with teerys. But, dereworthi Lorde, syth thes
5 syghynges and thes teerys are so swete that comme of thi mouyng,
& lykyng of grete ioye, what ioy, Lorde, and cumforte shulle thi
lovers & thi chosyn haue of the whan they shalle knowe the & see the
suche as þou art ? But wherto of thyng þat is so hydde & so vnknown
to vs make we spech to othir to vndirstonde, syth none may vndir-
10 stonde it but they that haue felte it, as tho þat God hath sent to a ioy
& a lykyng of hym as to taast here what kyns he is and shal be in
swettnes to his lovers withoutyn ende ? For alle þat men rede & may
here in bokes þat owen to be radde, vnsauery it is, but if the hert it
vnderstond. |

f. 130ᵇ 15   Nowe, my sowle, longe we haue drawe þis worde in length. Me
thynkyth it is good & mery to vs to be here with Petyr & John for to
haue myrth & ioye with oure spowse, and make if we may oure
dwellyng here with hym. It is no nede iii howses to make, for oon is
ynouȝe to herborowe vs alle, in the which we may togedyr be and haue
20 oure talkyng in myrthis in mene.

    But what sayth oure Lorde ? 'Lette me go', he sayth, 'for the lyȝte
of the morwtyde is here.' The lyȝt & the comforte þat þou desiryst,
þou hast it. Aftir the blissyng ys ȝevyn, and senuys in the leendes
ben dryed and dedde, and the name of Iacob to Israel is turnyd, anone
25 the spowse that [by the with] gelows lovys was desyred, glydith awey,
& withdrawith that swettnes that he in contemplacion to his lover
sent, and he neuere the latter with hym is thurwe dereworthy grace &

f. 131ᵃ demenyng of wylle, as wyth his | dereworthy spowse. Therfor drede
the not that he hath forsake the, thouȝe he for a litelle while with-
30 drawith hym fro the, for alle this he doth for to helpe the and oonly
for thi good. This commyng & this partyng is wynnyng to the, and
wote þoue wele þat therthurwe gretely þou wynnyst. He cummyth to
the, and he partyth fro the. He cummyth to thi comfort; he partyth
fro the that þoue be the more ware that þou as the vnwytty for that
35 comfort and lykyng trowe not that þou were prevy wyth hym, and
wene that he sendythe it to the for thy holy lyfe, and therthurwe
sete goodly by thiself, and so anone þou lepyst into pryde.

    Also if thi spowse were euere with the þou woldyst sette the lyȝter
of hym. And if this likyng & this comfort þat þoue dyuerse tymes

1 is] *om.* are] be Cryste] god   2 knowlechith] knoweth   3 his]
hyr   4 thes] the   5 are] be   6 of] the *add.*   10 felte]
fylled   11 hym] self *add.*   12 &] or   13 if] *om.*   13–14 it
vnderstond] *trs.*   15 worde] worlde   in] on   19 the] *om.*   21 Lorde]
spouse   25 by the with] the with D H ; ȝevyth F   29 with-] *om.*
30 fro the] *om.*   for²] *om.*   32 wote] wete   wynnyst] wenyst
33–4 He . . . the] *om.*   34 as the] hast   35 trowe] thow *add.*
37 sete] late   þou] *om.*   38 sette] lete

takyst and felyst were eueremore lastyng, þou woldyst wene that it
were of kynde and not of grace. | Therfore wete thou forsoth þat this f. 131^b
grace & this comforte God thi dere spouse ȝeuith whan he wylle and to
whom he wylle, not as heritage to haue it in this lyfe, for it is sayde in
Olde Englisshe: 'Ouere mych felashipe makith oþerwhile men to be 5
dispised.' Therfor he departyth fro the that his longe dwellyng with
the make hym not vnworthy to the, and that þoue whan he is departyd
fro the desyre hym & moorn aftyr hym the more hertly, and seke hym
the qwycklyer þat with more grace þoue may fynde hym. And if it so
were that oure spouse the lykyng that [he] to his loveris sendith in con- 10
templacion lete hem haue it here at her wille, such likyng they wolde
haue theryn that the lesse they wolde desyre to the grete likyng that is
to comme in hevyn, þat shalle leste with ioyfulle lyfe withouten ende.
Therfor they shullyn not trowe of this exyle þat they ar cast yn her
penaunce for to doo that it were hevyn | that is a place of wo. Ther- 15 f. 132^a
for nowe our spowse commythe and nowe he wendith; nowe he
bryngyth comforte and nowe he wythdrawith it & levyth vs in oure
febylnes to knowe what we be; and letyth vs sumdele fele howe swete
he is, but or we may hym fele fully, he wythdrawith hym.

So doth God Almyȝty to his loveris in contemplacion as a tauerner 20
that good wyne hathe to selle dooth to good drynkeris þat wolle drynke
wele of his wyne & largely spende. Wele he knowith what they be there
he seeth hem in the strete. Pryvely he wendyth and rowndith hem in
the eere & seyth to them that he hath a clarete, and þat alle fyne for
ther owyn mouth. He tollyth hem to howse & ȝevyth hem a taast. 25
Sone whanne they haue tastyd therof and that they thynke the drynke
good & gretly to ther plesauns, than they drynke dayly & nyȝtly, and
the more they drynke, the more the[y] may. Suche lykyng they | haue f. 132^b
of that drynke that of none other wyne they thynke, but oonly for
to drynke þeir fylle and to haue of this drynke alle their wylle. And 30
so they spende that they haue, and syth they spende or lene to wedde
surcotte or hode & alle that they may, for to drynke with lykyng whiles
that them it good thynkith. Thus it faryth sumtyme by Goddis
loveris that from þe tyme that they hadde tastyd of this pyment, that
is of the swettnesse of God, such lykyng þei founde theryn that as 35

1 euere-] alwey more] *om.*   3 spouse] specyally *add.*   4 heritage]
euer *add.*   5 -shipe] -red   oþerwhile men] *trs.*   6 his] ys
8 the²] *om.*   9 fynde hym] *trs.*   10 he] D H; *om.* F   13
comme] to the *add.*   14 -for] that *add.*   this] the   ar] be
15 a] *om.*   place] stede   16 nowe] *om.*   spowse] nowe he *add.*   19
fele fully] *trs.*   22 his] thys   there] where   23 in] by   strete]
walkyng *add.*   rowndith] rouneth   24 them] hym   that] *om.*
25 a] to   26 therof and that] *om.*   27 gretly . . . than]
swete   dayly & nyȝtly] ouer nyght they drynkyn ouer day   and]
om.   29 none other wyne] nought elles   oonly] *om.*   30–1 And so] *om.*
31 spende or] *om.*   to wedde] *om.*   32 &] or   alle . . . may]
other necessaryes   33 that . . . thynkith] hem good thynke

drunkyn men they did spende that they hadde and ȝafe themself to
fastyng and to wakyng & to other penauns doyng. And whan they
hadde no more to spende they leyde their weddys, as apostelys,
martyrys, & maydenys ȝounge of ȝeris dyd in their tyme. Summe ȝafe
5　their bodyes to brenne in fyre, summe lete her hedys of to be smytte,
summe ȝafe her pappys corvyn from ther breestys, summe ȝaf |
f. 133ᵃ　ther skyn drawn from the flessh, and somme their bodyes wyth
wylde horsys to be drawe. And alle that they dyd they sette it at
nouȝt for the desyre of that lastyng wele that they desired fully to
10　haue in the lyfe that is withouten eende. But this likyng is here
ȝeven but for to taste, but alle tho that desyre fully to haue it, them
behovith to folowe Crist fote by fote, and evyn lyke steryn hym wyth
their lovys, as these drynkeris the tavernarys doon. Therfor whan
God eny gostly lykyng to thy sowle sendyth, thynke that God
15　spekyth to the, & rownyth in thyn eere, & sayth: 'Haue nowe this
litelle, and taste howe swete I am. But yf þou wylt fully fele that
thou ofte hast tastyd, renne aftyr me and folowe the savoure of myn
oyntementys. Heve vp thyn hert to me there I am syttyng on the
ryȝt half of my Fadyr, and ther shalt thou se me, not as in a myrroure,
f. 133ᵇ 20　but þou shalt | se me face to face. And than þou shalt fully haue at thy
wylle that ioye that þoue hast tastyd euere wythouten ende. And that
ioye or lykyng noon shalle the reve or take fro.'
　　But ho so wylle in contemplacion of this lykyng taste & clyme to the
steyre þat stondithe so high, hym behouyth to be Jacob here in this lyfe,
25　that is, hym behouyth to doo þat this name spellyth, that is holde
vndir fote alle worldly welth. Alle folye & synnes trede vndyr fote, for
the more that a man vndyr his fote castyth, it helpyth hym the more
on hyȝhe to clymbe or to reche. And than shalle his name to Israel be
turnyd, that ys in Englysshe: 'God he shalle se'; thurwe whiche syȝt
30　he shalle be fulfyllyd of that lykyng that alle othir passythe wythoute
comparison. Of this Iacob in the Boke of Genesis it tellith the angel
f. 134ᵃ　wyth Jacob wrestyllyd, and longe | stroglyde wyth maystry hym to
haue. But Jacob as the myȝty stalworthely wythstode, and the
maistry wan. Whan the angel sawe þat he myȝt no more, he towchid

　　1 they . . . spende] dispendyd　2 fastyng—wakyng] *trs.*　to] *om.*　3–4
apostelys, martyrys] martires and aposteles　5 in] the *add.*　6
pappys] to be *add.*　7 drawn] ryuen　8 it] alle *add.*　9 the] *om.*
10 the] that　11 taste] trust　　desyre] that *add.*　　it] *om.*
12 to] *om.*　Crist] god　by] after　evyn] euer　13 the tavern-
arys] in tauerne　14 to] in　15 spekyth] *om.*　the] speketh *add.*
& sayth] that I nowe say　17 ofte] *om.*　18 Heve] haue　19 half]
syde　shalt] sothely *add.*　20 me . . . to face] my face・　fully haue]
trs.　21 that] the　22 or] and that　the reve] *trs.*　or take fro] *om.*
23 this] thy　24 hym] he　Jacob] Jacobs　here] heyre　25 hym] he
this] the　26 welth] wele　Alle] and　26–7 for . . . more] forthermore
27 his] the　28 clymbe or to] *om.*　30 alle] *om.*　32 wrestyllyd]
and strofe *add.*　　maystry hym] *trs.*　　34 sawe] see　þat] *om.*

the hyppe of Jacob, and the synewis dryed, and euere aftyr that
tyme he haltyd on the oon foote, and aftir þat the foote was hym
benome, fro Jacob to Israel his 'hame was turnyde. By this Jacob
is vndirstonde man þat in contemplacion is lyfte on hygh. Than he
stroglyth with the angelle and stryvith whan he traueylith wyth alle 5
his myȝt God for to knowe. But than at the laste is the angelle ouere-
comme & vndyrcaste, whan man thurwe a depe thouȝt in a love-
longynge to knowe what God is and to fele in contemplacion, and that
he desirethe, conceyvith and felyth in his sowle of this swettnesse, and
so is ouertakyn on the lykyng of hym that alle the wele of this worlde 10
he settyth it at nouȝte. But | what is it to meen that whan the angelle f. 134ᵇ
sawe that he was ouerecome he towchyd Jacob vpon the hyppe and
the synewis dryed ? For myȝtful God that alle may, whan he to his
loverys sendith his grace that they thurwe his grace sothly may
knowe that alle flesshly desyres and oþer vnthewys that be senewys 15
are vndirstonde, he them fordothe & makyth hem drye as they dedde
were. And they that byfore vpon two fete ȝede and that wolde haue
lykyng in God & in þe world bothe, aftyr that they in contemplacion
swetnes haue founde, that oon foote in ther love is hool and in the
tother they halte, for worldly love qwenchyth in them, & wexeth alle 20
drye. The love of God is hool & sownde, and euere lyke stronge more
& more. Whoso on this fote stallworthly stondyth may no woo of this
worlde hyme ouerecaste. By a fote in Holy Wrytte is love vndirstond.

But euere, thou Goddys louer, be þoue waker and | ware, and f. 135ᵃ
vndirstond in what wyse he wythdrawith hym fro the, thy dere- 25
worthy spouse. Wete þoue wele forsoth he withdrawith hym not from
the thouȝe þou se hym not euere alyke. He seeth the for he is fulle of
eyen before & behynde. Thou mayst nothynge from hym hyde. He
hath on the his spyes sett that they wayten by day & by nyȝt howe
thou the beryst whyle thy spowse ys from the. They be sette to 30
bewrey the, yf they may take the, or eny countenauns or tokyn fynde
in the to eny vnthewys. Gelows ys thy spouse of the. If þoue eny other
love take or to eny other semlaunt make, soon he wyl forsake the and
turne hym from the, and wythholde hym tyl that þou trewly love hym,
for he wylle no lemman haue in meene. He will alle haue, or alle 35
leve. He wille haue here alle thy love if þou in blisse wylt be his fere.
Deliciouse is thy spowse, ful nobyl and ful fayre before alle tho that

3 benome] and *add.* F   5 stroglyth] *om.*   the] *om.*   angelle] aungelles;
strogeleth *add.*   6 the] *om.*   9 this] hys   10 on] in   11 it¹ ᵃⁿᵈ ²] *om.*
that] thereafter telleth *add.*   12 sawe] see   12–13 and . . . dryed]
&c.   15 that] *om.*   senewys] senewed   16 are] been   hem]
to   17 vpon] on   and] *om.*   19 in the] on that   23 is
love] *trs.*   24 þoue] *om.*   26 þoue] *om.*   not] ferre *add.*
27 thouȝe] yef   seeth] seyth   the for] therfor   28 eyen] bothe *add.*
30 sette] for *add.*   31 may] ouer- *add.*   33 wyl] the *add.*   the] *om.*
35 meene] men   will] wolde   36 wille] wolde   here] *om.*
love] here *add.*   fere] broke he ys nat but hit be bought dere *add.*

f. 135ᵇ euere | were borne of modyr. Therfor he wylle nothynge but honest and
fayre. If he se eny thynge in the of evylle soon he turnyth from the
his precious siȝt, as he that none vnclennesse may suffyr or se.
Therfor if þou desire of thy spowse lykyng to haue, and with hym
5 myrthys to haue at wylle, shamefast & chaste must þoue be. But be
thou euere ware, whatsoeuere þou be, that aftyr thou art reysid in contemplacion so hyghe this swettnes for to fele þat the thynkith for
lykynge that þou clyppyst thi spowse with myrthys in hevyn, that þou
fro the hyest steyer falle not downward to helle, that þou aftyr that
10 siȝt of God turne the not to wanton werkes ne flessly lustys.

But syth it is so that meditacion of mannys herte þat is rauischid
on high with gostly lykyng, as in contemplacion Goddys loverys, mowe
fele the febylnes of the flesche that euere drawith downward thurwe
f. 136ᵃ his | hevy charge wylle not suffyr that the lykyng be fully fyllid, ne
15 the bryȝtnesse of the sothfast lyȝte he wylle not see, therfor syth hym
behouyth fro so hygh stey thurwe charge of the flessh downwarde to
falle, good it is into summe of the degrees by the whiche vpward he
clymyd, warely and softely so that he hurt hym not, his cummyng
down to make, and anone reste hym in oon, and efte in another, aftyr
20 his fre wylle steryth hym, or stede or tyme it forgith. And as nygh
art þou God as þou the hygher clymedyst fro the first degre.

But foure inchesonys ther be that other while drawyn downwarde
fro thes degrees. The first is nede that here may not be lettyd. The
secunde is lovely werke and honest. The thride is febylnes of kynde.
25 The ivth ys vanyte of this worlde. The first harmythe not ; the secunde
may be sufferyd ; the thride is wretchide ; the fourth ys worthy
f. 136ᵇ penaunce to thole, | and namely to hem that the hyghest steyer of this
laddyr haue clymyd, and of this dereworthy lykyng wysely haue felyd,
and bifore other of that heuenly swettnes haue tastyd, that fro so
30 hygh fredom lyȝte so lowe into thraldom of this worlde, her lykyng
to haue theryn. And there they trowyd hony had be they fynde bytter
galle. Weelawey, bytter chafer men may this calle, for bettyr it were
of God no knowyng haue than aftir the knowyng of hym to lyve and
goo abacke.

---

1 he] *om.*   nothynge . . . and] nat ye but   4 and] betwene hys
armes swetely to be clepyd (clypped H) and *add.*   5 at wylle] *om.*   -fast]
-fulle   6 -euere] *om.*   in] to *add.*   7 thynkith] *om.*   9 hyest]
hygher   that²] sely *add.*   10 turne . . . lustys] to noon wanton
werkes ne flesshly lustys to turne   13 the²] *om.*   14 fully]
ful-   15 he] *om.*   not] he *add.*   16 hygh] a *add.*   stey]
steyre   18 clymyd] clymes   18–19 cummyng down] lyghtenyng
19 efte] anone   20 nygh] nere   21 þou] to *add.*   clymedyst]
clymbest   fro] for   22 drawyn downwarde] *trs.*   24 secunde]
other   27 thole] suffre   that] to *add.*   this] that   30
lyȝte] lyghtned to   into] to the   her] *om.*   31 And] *om.*   trowyd]
hopyd   hony had be] eny were   33 knowyng] to *add.*   34 goo]
styrte

What defens haue they as anemst God for ther synne? As who
shulde saye 'None'. For God may with hem riȝtfully mote & say:
'What shulde I doo to the and I haue it doon? Whan þoue were
nouȝt than made I the. And aftyr thou synnyd & made thiself þralle
that were free, than with the price of myself out of thraldom I 5
bouȝte the. And aftir, wyth the synfulle of this worlde þou ran, and I
from them | the cauȝte, and before other ȝaf the my grace, for I wolde f. 137ᵃ
that thou wer pryvy to me. And whan I wolde a made my dwellyng
wyth the, thou shytte me oute as fremyd from the, and whan men
spokyn my wordys to the, lightly þou castidyst them byhynde the, 10
and folowdist the vanytees of the worlde & the lykyng of the flesshe.'

But, dereworthy Lorde, swete freende, wyse councelour, & so
stronge an helper, vnwitty and vncely is he that castyth the, so
myldefulle & so nedefulle, fro his herte. A, welaway, howe balefulle a
change is this, oure maker, oure lover, and that alle is, and nought is 15
þat goode is withoute hym, whan we cast hym from vs, & fowle
thouȝtys and evylle drawe vnto vs, and that pryvy abydyng of the
Holy Gost that is in mannys sowle, that a while before was lustyng
in heuenly myrthe, so soon shalle be cast to wyckyd thouȝtys and to
vanite, and ther as wer the hote | foote steppys of thy spouse to bryng 20 f. 137ᵇ
in on hem lecherous desyres. It is not semely that tho eerys that riȝt
nowe herde thes wordys þat be not lefulle men to speke to bowe hem
to vayn talys & to bakbytyng; and the eyen þat ryȝt nowe with
holy terys were baptisid anone ouereturnyde to se vanytees; and
the tunge þat a litel before with lovyng & praysyng & other love 25
boonys or peticionys hath tillyd hir spouse to hyr bowre, & brouȝte
hym to hir chambre to clyppe & to kysse hym swetely, and nowe to
haue hir myrthys by oon & by oon turnyd into vanite & to fowle
speche, to waryyng & to forsweryng & to other ianglyng.

But wolde God for his pyte that alle suche vnthewys & alle that 30
were to myslyke were putte awey from vs, and if it so were that we in
eny of hem dyd falle or snapyr, sone turne aȝen to oure trewe leche,
that helyth the seke and cum|fortyth the sory of herte. To hym f. 138ᵃ
hertly we praye that he vs helpe to doo awey from vs alle evilles that
myȝt vs lette hym for to love. Amen. 35

1 as anemst] ayenst 1–2 As . . . none] *om.* 2 mote] mete
5 were] so *add.* 5–6 I bouȝte] *trs.* 6 of] in 7 the cauȝte]
rediled the for] And 8 a made] make 11 lykyng]
lykynges the] thy 12–13 so . . . helper] helpe so stronge 14
-fulle] -fully -fulle] -fully howe] so a] *om.* 15 is this]
om. maker] and *add.* 17 abydyng] beddyng 18 in] *om.*
21 hem] hym desyres] ne *add.* 24 turnyde] torne 25
be-] to- 26 or peticionys] *om.* 27 -ly] *om.* nowe] *om.*
28 myrthys] I mene *add.* by²] *om.* into] to & to] *om.*
31 were] bene to] the *add.* were putte awey] fer be it] *om.* were]
betyde 32 hem] thyse dyd] *om.* falle—snapyr] *trs.* sone turne]
turne we vs sone 34 to] and that we 35 myȝt vs] *trs.* for] *om.*

NOTES

DEONISE HID DIUINITE

2/1. There is no title in the manuscripts, but both describe thus the translation which follows of the *De Mystica Theologia* of the pseudo-Dionysius the Areopagite.

Dionysius, whom the author of *The Cloud of Unknowing* claims as his chief teacher, exercised a preponderant influence on the development of medieval thought both in the Eastern and the Western Church. His works were widely known in the sixth century, and from the ninth century to the Renaissance might be said to have helped greatly to fashion the thought of almost all the outstanding thinkers. Four treatises (*Divine Names, Mystical Theology, Celestial Hierarchy, Ecclesiastical Hierarchy*—to give the English translations of their titles) and at least ten epistles are generally attributed to him, and in the course of these extant writings claim is made to six more works (*Theological Institutions, Symbolic Theology, Of the Soul, Of Divine Justice, Divine Songs, The Objects of Intellect and Sense*), though if these works were ever written, they were subsequently lost. In *Divine Names*, iii. 2, *Celestial Hierarchy*, ix. 3, Epistles VII and X are apostolic references which support Dionysius's profession of being St. Paul's Athenian convert of A.D. 54. (See Acts xvii. 22–34.) The Timothy to whom *Mystical Theology* was addressed was supposedly St. Paul's companion. But the identity and the date of the author of these treatises are still a matter of controversy. The conclusions of two German scholars, J. Stiglmayr and H. Koch, have, however, been widely accepted. Though Dionysius's authenticity was barely disputed before the early fifteenth century, it seems highly probable that in his works there is one of the most momentous impostures of history. A weight of internal evidence indicates that Dionysius was probably a Syrian of the late fifth or early sixth century. He draws from the *De Malorum Subsistentia* of Proclus († c. 485), and though no source is named, passages abound in his extant works reminiscent of the writings of Clement of Alexandria, Origen, St. Cyril of Jerusalem, St. Basil, St. Gregory Nazianzus, St. Gregory of Nyssa, St. John Chrysostom, St. Cyril of Alexandria, and he shows knowledge of such comparatively late developments in church discipline as the introduction of the Creed into the Mass (A.D. c. 476).

The writings of Dionysius first became prominent in A.D. 533 when, at the Council of Constantinople, the supporters of Severus, accepting their authenticity, appealed to them in support of Monophysite teaching. Leontius of Byzantium, the most celebrated adversary of this heresy, refuted the Monophysites by basing his arguments, too, on Dionysius. German scholarship has tried to identify Timothy with Petrus of Caesarea, who was a close disciple of Severus, and the Hierotheus, who is cited in the *Divine Names*, with a fifth-century Syrian mystic, Stephen bar Sudaili. Once Dionysius had appeared in recorded history, there is ample testimony to the remarkable and immediate spread of his fame. His works were early translated from Greek into Syrian and Arabic. Commentaries were written in the sixth century by John of Scythopolis, in the seventh century by Maximus. Pope Gregory the Great referred to him as 'antiquus et venerabilis pater '. At the Lateran Council of 649 Pope Martin I pronounced his works most orthodox.

Dionysian treatises became generally known in the West after 827, when the Byzantine emperor, Michael the Stammerer, sent a copy of the works of Dionysius to Louis the Pious. From an early date St. Paul's Athenian convert had been identified with the St. Denis of France, and the Dionysian treatises were sent to Hilduin, the Abbot of St. Denys, who authorized the first translation of them from Greek into Latin, with the help of Greek collaborators. The first important translation, however, was that of John Scotus Erigena, an Irishman at the court of Charles the Bald, who made a new translation into Latin *c.* 858. He translated all four treatises and ten epistles, and also commented upon some of them, but his work was received with suspicion in orthodox circles, and at the best regarded as a barbarous and obscure paraphrase which itself required interpretation. From the twelfth century onwards there was a series of translations and commentaries, each commentary elaborating upon earlier work. Among outstanding Dionysian scholars were Hugh of St. Victor († 1141), John Sarracenus who dedicated a translation of the *Mystical Theology* to Odo of Taverny, Abbot of St. Denys 1162–9, Thomas, Abbot of St. Andrew's, Vercelli (†1246), Robert Grosseteste (†1255). St. Bonaventura based some of his central mystical doctrines upon Dionysian teaching; it has been calculated that St. Thomas Aquinas in his works quotes from or refers to Dionysius no fewer than 1,702 times.

2/5. **mad minde** : See *Cloud*, 125/10–15: '& herfore it was þat Seynte Denis seyde: " Þe moste goodly knowyng of God is þat, þe whiche is knowyn bi vnknowyng. " & trewly, whoso wil loke Denis bookes, he schal fynde þat his wordes wilen cleerly aferme al þat I haue seyde or schal sey, fro þe biginnyng of þis tretis to þe ende. '

2/9, 10. **nakid lettre, sentence**: See Introduction, pp. xxxix–xl. The basic Latin texts of Johannes Sarracenus and Vercellensis are given in Appendix A, with footnotes to indicate how the Middle English translator departed from his immediate source.

2/11. **Abbot of Seinte Victore**: i.e. Thomas, Abbot of St. Andrew's, Vercelli, known generally as 'Vercellensis', who was a Canon Regular of the Congregation of St. Victor.

2/13. **Seinte Deonise Preier**: This prayer contains in brief the central teaching of the *Mystical Theology*, and also clearly exemplifies some of the characteristic difficulties of abstruseness and concentrated thought which faced the Middle English translator. The prayer is for ableness to be raised by grace to a mystic knowledge of God in contemplation. In the state for which the soul yearns, God imparts knowledge of Himself directly, and the soul, in an ecstasy of mind, knows by intuition, not through any activity of reason or senses. In a state of simplicity, which is one of the greatest possible concentration, the normal faculties of knowing are stilled, and the mind is consequently dark in a state of not-knowing. Paradoxically, however, this state is one of transcendent light, for in a way ineffable and incomprehensible, the soul is filled with divine illumination.

2/14–16. **Þou . . . Good**: Erigena, Sarracenus, and Vercellensis all agree with Dionysius in invoking the Trinity, and in the epithets Vercellensis sees a reference to the three Persons of the Trinity. In its address to Eternal Wisdom, the Middle English version is appropriate, since the prayer is for the infusion of the supernatural knowledge of God; but in its attempt to express more than the Dionysian phrase it is admittedly clumsy. The associations of the Middle English version, however, are rich and deep, through the blend of Christianity and Neoplatonism. The Middle English translation invokes in effect the Word of God (cf. John i. 1–4) and the wisdom which 'reacheth from one end to another mightily, and sweetly doth she order all things' (Wisd. of Sol. viii. 1). In the development of the theme lies the influence of Neoplatonic thought. According to this, the first emanation from the One is Mind (*Νοῦς*). The highest circle of being is the world of Ideas, the universal principle, archetype, and pattern after which our world of things is framed. The first manifestation of God is the act by which He thinks the pattern of things. God's knowledge of things exists before and is the cause of the existence of all things. As Erigena says: 'God does not know things because they are. They are because He knows [i.e. thinks] them.' God is therefore the 'Firstheed', the source of all being. Another Platonic line of thought is that God is also the Good, which by the overflowing of goodness creates and sustains all things in being. Hence 'souereyn Good'.

The language is strained and loaded in this passage to convey this concentrated wealth of meaning. The epithet 'souereyn', used repeatedly to translate the Latin *super*, expresses the transcendency of God whose activity is transcendently different from that of created beings, and entirely above human understanding. 'Firstheed' = First Cause. Here an existing word is used in a special sense. Wyclif used it in the ordinary sense of 'position of being first'. 'Þe souereyn Goddesse' appears to be a reference to the Eternal Wisdom and an echo of the Wisdom of Solomon. The Latin epithet *superdea* qualifies *Trinitas* in Sarracenus, but the Middle English writer has changed the invocation, and is more likely to have changed the adjectives into nouns than to have misunderstood the Latin.

2/16–17. **inliche beholder . . . Cristen men**: The wisdom of Christians through which God is known is drawn from the Holy Scriptures, which are inspired by the Holy Ghost. God has not only given this spiritual knowledge and confirmed it, but also by the gift of grace through the Holy Ghost the Christian may participate in it. 'Beholder' is the Middle English equivalent of *inspector* (Scotus), *inspectrix* (Sarracenus, Vercellensis). Denis à Rickel (*D. Dionysii Cartusiani Opera Omnia* (Tournai, 1902), t. xvi, p. 447) explains it as 'approbator et cognitor, dator et confirmator'. (This edition will henceforth be referred to as Denis à Rickel.) Vercellensis expounds 'godliche maad wisdome of Cristen men' as 'optima portio Mariae' (Denis à Rickel, p. 454). A description of this wisdom is to be found in *The Cloud*, chs. 16–22.

2/17. **to drawe us up**: H. E. Allen, *The Book of Margery Kempe* (London, 1940), comments on the use of 'draw' to express the divine action on the soul in her notes to 11/24, 223/37. Most of the Latin translations of this passage and commentaries consulted have *dirige nos*, 'guide us'. The Gloss, however, contains both the ideas of grace and elevation. See Appendix A.

2/17–18. **in an acordyng abilnes**: Not in the Latin. Cf. *Divine Names*, I. i (C. Rolt, *Dionysius the Areopagite* (London, 1920), p. 52. Henceforth this edition, which contains an English translation direct from the Greek, is referred to as Rolt): 'Divine things are revealed unto each created spirit in proportion to its powers, and in this measure is perception granted through the workings of the Divine goodness . . .'

2/18–19. **souereyn-vnknowen . . . spekynges**: Cf. *Cloud*, 47/11–12: 'Þe

souereynest wisdom of his Godheed lappid in þe derk wordes of his Man-
heed.' The Scriptures are divinely illumined, and their truth exceeds our
natural knowledge, but it is expressed obliquely and hidden in parables lest
it dazzle men, who can no more contemplate absolute truth with the human
mind than they can the sun with the human eye. (Cf. Matt. xiii. 11 sqq.)
The image 'heiȝt' anticipates the account of Moses's meeting with God on
Mount Sinai described at 4/27–5/24, drawn ultimately from Exod. xix,
xxiv.

2/21. **wisest silence**: Cf. Gloss (270): 'a verborum velaminibus abso-
lutae.'

2/22. **schine . . . derkyst**: The prayer is for the direct infusion of supernatural knowledge in mystic union. The darkness is of the finite conditioned
mind unable to comprehend the infinite. The idea that God inhabits the
darkness is common in the Bible, e.g. Ps. (Vulgate) xcvi. 2, xvii. 12. But
illumination is possible in this darkness, for through it man may participate
in the life of God who is light, 'and in Him is no darkness at all'. 1 John
i. 5; cf. 1 Pet. ii. 9, 2 Cor. iv. 6.

2/23. **inuisible & vngropable**: i.e. not able to be perceived by the intelligence, the reason, and the senses. 'ungropable' translates the Latin
impalpabili, and is most probably a word coined by the Middle English
translator. The only reference in *O.E.D.* belongs to 1558—'like wind
ungropable'.

2/25. **wiþ affeccyon**: Not in the Latin. Cf. 3/16–17, 5/15. The Middle
English translator is most probably influenced by the interpretation of
Vercellensis in transforming the teaching of Dionysius and making the
mystic effort definitely an act of love. See note to 5/15. Cf. *Cloud*, 33/11:
'For whi loue may reche to God in þis liif, bot not knowing'; *Stirings*,
71/22–26.

2/26. **abouen mynde**: According to the classification of the faculties
of the soul in *The Cloud*, ch. 63, 116/6–9, Mind comprehends all the conscious activities of the soul: 'Minde is clepid a principal myȝte, for it
conteneþ in it goostly not only alle þe oþer miȝtes, bot þerto alle þo
þinges in þe whiche þei worchen.' The Middle English author follows
Benjamin Minor in his classification of two principal powers, reason and
will, and two secondary powers, imagination and sensuality. The act of
union described here takes place in a higher cognitive faculty than any
contained in mind. Dionysius himself does not stress this higher cognitive
faculty, but describes rather a union of the human spirit to the Divinity,
which gives a supreme illumination. The influence on the Middle English is
probably again that of Vercellensis. Cf. Commentary (f. 43ª): 'alium &
incomparabiliter profundiorem modum cognoscendi deum . . . non minus
excedit intellectum quam intellectus racionem . . . scintilla synderesis
que sola unibitur Spiritui Diuino . . . Istud sapiencie negocium sensus
ymaginacionis, racionis, intellectus tam practici quam theorici usus &
officia suspendit & excludit omnem intellectum & omne intelligibile
& ens.'

2/31–32. **by þe steryng of grace**: Here, as throughout *The Cloud*, the
Middle English author insists upon the need for grace to call one to the
mystical exercise he is describing. He is following Vercellensis rather than
Sarracenus. See Appendix.

2/32. **actueel**: The Middle English translator here and below, 3/1, with
stronger emphasis than in Sarracenus, stresses the fact that contemplation

is a state of high activity. That is, it is not one of physical and mental immobility such as is found among eastern mystics or among the Quietists. Possibly here again he is following Vercellensis. See Appendix.

2/32. blynde beholdynges: i.e. the contemplation of souls 'not hauyng iȝen of mynde' 2/24. Sarracenus has 'mysticas visiones'; Commentary (f. 44ᵃ): 'illas sapiencie contemplaciones'; Gloss (272): 'secretas contemplationes'. The Middle English is less vague and more suggestive in its vigorous paradox, which is a favourite in *Priue Counseling*, e.g. 139/12, 143/22, 144/1, 147/17, 24, 151/25. The repeated use of the epithet 'blind', often in close association with 'naked', to describe the activity which is the central theme of this author's teaching, is indeed one of the most recognizable marks of his style. Cf. 'blynde felyng', *Cloud*, 73/2, 5, 136/3, *Priue Counseling*, 140/4, 141/24–25, 143/10, 145/17–18, 152/10–11, 155/28, 156/6; 'blinde beyng', *Priue Counseling* 146/26–27, 147/9, 12, 157/1, 8; 'blinde stering', *Cloud*, 22/18, *Stirings*, 76/6, cf. 72/25–26.

The only reference comparable to this use of 'beholding' in *O.E.D.* is from Coverdale (1540): 'Sweet contemplation & beholding of God's almightiness.' Cf. *Hid Diuinite*, 5/7.

3/1. sleiȝ, listi: These appear to be a Middle English addition, and are both epithets characteristic of the treatises attributable to the author of *The Cloud*. Cf. *Priue Counseling* 145/3: 'þis listi sleiȝ(t) worching', *Cloud*, 47/15. They are to be interpreted as 'wise' and 'eager', the latter the very antithesis of 'listless'. The contrition they describe is fuller than mere sorrow for sins. They imply an eager love-longing for God, and a strong sense of the personal unworthiness which separates the soul from him. Cf. *Cloud*, ch. 16. The adverb 'listely' occurs in *Preier*, 57/14, *Stirings*, 75/3, 76/18, *Cloud*, 26/9, 87/7, 16, *Priue Counseling*, 144/27 with the same rather specialized meaning. Both adjective and adverb are first recorded in *O.E.D.* from *Prompt. Parv.* (*c.* 1440) as equivalents to Latin *delectabilis*, *delectabiliter* respectively. The corresponding noun 'listines', which is not in *O.E.D.*, occurs in *Cloud*, 8/18, *Priue Counseling*, 139/13, 148/11, 23.

3/7–9. þat ben now . . . not now: An unusual and rather clumsy expansion of the Latin, which has 'non exsistentia et exsistentia', but one which is easily intelligible compared with the highly philosophical explanation of the Commentary, f. 44ᵃ.

3/9–10. to me . . . vnderstonde: The Middle English is more personal than its sources. See Appendix.

3/10. in þis grace: Not in Sarracenus, or Vercellensis.

3/11. to be onid: Cf. 2 Cor. iii. 18 (A.V.): 'But we all, with open face beholding as in a glass the glory of the Lord, are changed into the same image from glory to glory, even as by the Spirit of the Lord.' Vercellensis here explains in both the Commentary and the Gloss where this union takes place. Commentary, f. 44ᵃ: 'per affectionem principalem, super intellectum eleuatam.' See note to 2/26.

3/12. substaunces: Kk here agrees with the Latin versions of Erigena, Sarracenus, and Vercellensis in the use of the singular. No emendation has been made, however, for the reading of Har¹ does make sense, and the Middle English text is not always an exact translation. Cf. Milton, *Paradise Lost*, v. 408: 'Intelligential substances'; ibid, viii. 109: 'corporeal substances'. 'Substaunces' can be used in the philosophical sense to denote 'beings'. It is admitted, however, that in the present context the singular 'substaunce' is closer to the frequently expressed Dionysian thought.

Cf. *Divine Names*, vii. 3 (Rolt, p. 151): 'He cannot be perceived by the mind or the senses and is not a particular Being'; v. 8 (Rolt, pp. 139–40): 'He *is* all things as being the Cause of them all, and as holding together and anticipating in Himself all the beginnings and all the fulfilments of all things; and He is above them all in that He, anterior to their existence, super-essentially transcends them all.'

3/13–16. ouerpassyng . . . knowyng: Here the Middle English translator enlarges upon the version of Sarracenus. Though the Middle English account of the condition of the mind is much simpler, it was probably inspired by the expansion of Vercellensis. See Appendix.

The exact sense of 'ouerpassyng' (= Latin *excessus* here and in 10/21–22) is not given in *O.E.D.*

3/16. abouen mynde in affeccioun: See notes to 2/25, 26.

3/17. souereyn . . . derknes: A close translation of Sarracenus: 'ad supersubstantialem divinarum tenebrarum radium.' Vercellensis is here more explicit: 'ad superclarissimum lumen occultissimae Deitatis', Gloss (272), Commentary (f. 44^b). The use of the word 'beme' recalls the passage in *The Cloud*, 62/14–17, which describes the supernatural illumination which at times rewards the contemplative on earth: 'Þan wil he sumtyme parauenture seend oute a beme of goostly liȝt, peersyng þis cloude of vnknowyng þat is bitwix þee and hym, & schewe þee sum of his priuete, þe whiche man may not, ne kan not, speke.' The context in *Hid Diuinite*, however, suggests 'radiance' rather than a single ray, the fullness of uncreated light, with a strong paradox comparable with that in 2/18–24. The sense of 'outstreaming radiance' may well be read into 'beme'. Cf. *Preier* 54/7–8. Bede uses 'columna lucis' (*Ecclesiastical History*, III. xi) to describe a stream of light rising from a saint's body, which Alfred translates 'swylce sunne beam'. In the Old English *Exodus* the fiery pillar is 'wuldres beam', 'byrnende beam'.

3/19–20. Beware . . . þinges: Cf. *Cloud*, Prologue, pp. 1–3. Such a warning is frequent in mystical writings.

3/20–35. Þees men . . . wittes: Following the Commentary, the Middle English version is here considerably expanded. The 'vnwise men' are the natural philosophers, the 'more vnwise', those with anthropomorphic beliefs and idolaters. These are limited in their knowledge to what their senses and intellectual faculties can apprehend.

3/24. maad . . . place: Ps. xvii. 12. The reference here and elsewhere is to the Vulgate, unless it is otherwise stated.

3/25. after hemself: i.e. according to their own natural understanding.

3/25. þe prophete: An emendation has been made to the reading of Kk, since the prophet has not been previously mentioned. The phrase is not in Erigena or Sarracenus. The Paraphrase of Vercellensis refers to Job xxviii. 20–21, but many similar passages occur in the Books of the Prophets, e.g. Isaiah lxiv. 4.

3/32. last and þe leest worþi: Ultimately based on Genesis and Plato, the Dionysian scale of being between nothingness and the transcendent Godhead rises from existence, through life, feeling, reason, to spirit.

3/35. fantastik ymagynatyue wittes: Latin *phantasia* and *imaginatio* are both terms of scholastic psychology. *Phantasia* (lit. 'a making visible') is the term for a mental apprehension of an object of perception, or the faculty by which this is performed. *Imaginatio* is the 'faculty of the mind by which are formed images or concepts of external objects not present to the senses'. (See *O.E.D.* Fantasy, Imagination.) It is possible that in this passage the two epithets are both used in their technical sense, but, because of the disparaging tone of the passage, 'fantastik' has been glossed with its transferred meaning of 'delusive'.

4/2. **for to see**: Not in the Latin. The phrase is explained by 4/9: 'in siȝt of byleue'.

4/4–5. **& more miȝtely**: Not in the Latin.

4/5 sqq. **to denye alle þees being þinges . . .**: This is the doctrine of the *Via Negativa* which is found already in the second century in the works of Clement of Alexandria, and which receives its fullest expression in the Dionysian writings. St. Thomas Aquinas states it succinctly in the *Summa Theologica*, I. iii, introd.: 'We cannot know what God is, but rather what He is not.'

4/9. **in syȝt of byleue**: Not in the Latin.

4/12. **þe godliche Bertelmewe**: This reference has not yet been traced. Nothing is known of any genuine writing of St. Bartholomew the Apostle. It is possible that this might be an invention of Dionysius to support his own claim to apostolic environment. Yet, if the words of Hierotheus quoted in *Divine Names* are indeed the work of the Syrian mystic, Stephen bar Sudaili (see Rolt, p. 1), Dionysius may be quoting from an actual pseudonymous writing. Though the name Bartholomew was not a favourite one to attach to pseudepigraphic works, there are still traces of writings bearing it. An apocryphal gospel attributed to St. Bartholomew was mentioned by St. Jerome and also condemned by a Council held at Rome in the episcopate of Gelasius. See *The Apocryphal New Testament*, translated by M. R. James (Oxford, 1953), pp. 166–86.

4/13. **Cristes deuinitee**: Latin *theologiam*; Rolt, p. 193: 'the subject-matter of the Divine Science.'

4/13–14. **moche . . . leest**: i.e. Many words are needed when it is spoken of with the mouth, one word when it is described in the mind, and that 'ineffable'.

4/14–15. **brode and moche . . . streite & litil**: The Gospel is long in words when it is written, read, or taught, and it is wide in its subject-matter with its history and parables; but the limited mind can but narrowly understand its mysteries.

4/16. **good**: This epithet reflects the Platonic term, the Good, for the one ultimate reality.

4/17–19. **boþe . . . þinges**: A close translation which, through its syntax, is both difficult and ambiguous. One is tempted to understand from the Middle English that St. Bartholomew had neither 'resoun ne vnderstondyng' with the which God 'miȝt be comen to', an interpretation applying the thought of the Gloss (273–4): 'Deus, qui est bonorum omnium causa, multis sermonibus designatur, et item paucissimis, ideo quia nec ratione capitur, nec intellectu comprehenditur, et ideo verbo non exprimitur, quia omnibus supersubstantialiter superponitur.'

4/21–22. **boþe . . . þinges**: i.e. pass beyond all distinctions to a simple unity.

4/24. **liȝtes . . . wordes**: i.e. divine enlightenment through supernatural gifts such as visions and locutions. The contemplative must not rest content with spiritual gifts, but be detached even from them. He must pass from the state of Illumination to that of Union. In the following passage the

mystic way is clearly described, with its three commonly accepted stages
of (1) Purgation, (2) Illumination, (3) Union.

4/25. wiþ affeccioun: See notes to 2/25, 26.

4/25. where verely he is: i.e. in His essential being.

4/27. Ensaumple: St. Clement of Alexandria (†A.D. 217) used the same
parallel in *Stromatum*, II. ii; v. xi (*P.G.* viii. 936–7; ix. 109): 'The nearer we
get to Him, the more do we perceive that He is above all our thoughts.
Hence, in order to contemplate Him and see Him we must, like Moses,
enter into the darkness of the cloud; that is to say, we must get rid of all
the thoughts we have of Him as unworthy of Him, and regard with the
eyes of faith the supreme Being who infinitely surpasses all our conceptions of Him.' (Quoted from P. Pourrat, *Christian Spirituality* (London,
1922), vol. i, p. 69.

4/27–28. mildest of men: Not in the Latin.

4/28–29. & also in hys puple: Exod. xix. 10, 14, but not in the Latin.

4/33. multitude of þis puple: Cf. Gloss (274): 'multifaria opinione
materiali.'

4/33. preestes: Cf. Gloss (274): 'cum principalibus affectionibus.' See
5/16 where the meaning appears to be 'his cognitive powers working on
their highest human level'.

5/1. þe hiȝenes . . . assenciouns: The Middle English version adds its
own simple and intelligible gloss.

5/2–3. be . . . grace: Not in the Latin.

5/3–4. as . . . deuinitee: Not in the Latin.

5/5. iȝe: i.e. of the natural understanding.

5/7–8. hiȝest . . . resons: Cf. 5/1; *Divine Names* (Rolt, p. 194): 'the
divinest and the highest of the things perceived by the eyes of the body
or the mind are but the symbolic language of things subordinate to Him
who Himself transcendeth them all.' Naming these highest manifestations
of the Godhead is the nearest that one can reach to positive statement,
but there still remains the distinction between the finite created mind and
the ultimate nature of the Infinite. The reason is 'in subieccioun' because
it is unable to comprehend the transcendent One from which these manifestations proceed. It is possible, however, that the Middle English translator, with his characteristic broadening and simplifying of subject-matter,
meant to include all supernatural revelations and physical phenomena of
rapture and delight which can be experienced but not understood.

5/8. as þe lady . . . maydens: Cf. *Priue Counseling*, 145/1–2; Ps. cxxii. 2.
The simile is not in the Latin.

5/15. syngulertee of affeccioun: Not in Sarracenus. Vercellensis in the
Paraphrase (Denis à Rickel, p. 455) here has the supplementary interpretation: 'per unitionem dilectionis, quae effectiva est verae cognitionis, unitur
Deo intellectualiter ignoto, cognitione multo meliori quam sit cognitio
intellectualis.' See 2/25-26 and notes. The only reference for the meaning
'singleness' in *O.E.D.* before 1640 is accordant: Rolle, Psalter iv. 10:
'syngularite is halden in haly men, for þai sett all þaire hert to luf anly a
god.'

5/16. departid . . . preestes: The Middle English, in simpler statement than
that of Sarracenus, refers back to 4/33. See note to 4/33.

5/17. derknes of vnknowyng: Richard of St. Victor, *Benjamin Major*, iv.
22, referring to this allegory, has 'nubes ignorantiae', which might have
given the title to *The Cloud of Unknowing*. It must be noted, however, that

Vercellensis in his Commentary on this passage (f. 45[b]) has: 'intrans in nubem condensam qua oculi eius tenebrantur . . . medium nebule.' 'Unknowing' is used characteristically by this author to express the idea which is basic in the Dionysian teaching on contemplation, and which can best be translated into modern English as 'ceasing to know'. The actual word is to be found in the *Prick of Conscience* and in Wyclif's writing, but with the ordinary sense of 'ignorance'. The earliest reference for the meaning of the verb *to unknow*, 'to cease to know' is taken from Sidney's *Arcadia* (*c.* 1586).

5/18. **schittiþ**: Kk schyneþ. The reading of Har[1] here appears to be superior, though Erigena has *relucet*. Cf. Sarracenus and Vercellensis *claudit*.

5/18. **knowable knowing**: i.e. the apprehensions of his understanding.

5/32–6/31. **þis ensaumple . . . proef**: Erigena and Sarracenus have in this passage abbreviated the image of the original Greek. Cf. Rolt, p. 195: 'like as men who, carving a statue out of marble, remove all the impediments that hinder the clear perceptive of the latent image and by this mere removal display the hidden statue itself in its hidden beauty.' Vercellensis expands this passage both in the Paraphrase and the Gloss. See Appendix. The Middle English translator has added more again, introducing the technical details of carving and the close explanation of the analogy.

The illustration was used by Plotinus, *Ennead*, i. 6. 9: 'Withdraw into yourself, and if you do not find yourself beautiful as yet, do as does the sculptor of a statue . . . cut away all that is excessive, straighten all that is crooked, bring light to all that is shadowed . . . do not cease until there shall shine out on you the Godlike Splendour, until you see the Final Goodness surely established in the stainless Shrine.' (Quoted from *The Mystical Theology of Dionysius the Areopagite*, published by the Shrine of Wisdom (London, 1923), p. 8.)

6/11. **so contrary a kynde**: A. B. Sharpe, *Mysticism. Its true Nature and Value* (London, 1910), p. 214 note, comments that this analogy 'expresses very precisely the attitude of mysticism towards the immanence of God, though it cannot be pressed as an illustration of the nature of immanence. The statue is revealed by abstracting superfluous material, as God is made known by abstracting all that is not God. But the residuum, which is the statue, is of the same nature as the abstracted superfluity; whereas the abstraction of what is natural leaves only the supernatural, or divine.'

6/13–14. **in itself . . . free**: Cf. *Priue Counseling*, 136/16–23: 'þof it be so þat alle þinges ben in hym bi cause & bi beyng & he be in alle þinges here cause & here being, ʒit in himself only he is his owne cause & his owne being. For as noþing may be wiþoutyn him, so may he not be wiþoutyn himself. He is being boþe to himself & to alle. & in þat he is only departid from alle þat he is being boþe of hymself & of alle; & in þat he is one in alle & alle in him þat alle þinges han her beinges in him & he is being of alle.'

6/14–17. **wiþinne . . . forþe**: Following on the statement of God's transcendence, here is a full statement of the immanence of God in all things.

6/20. **couerhid**: The more difficult reading of Har[1] has been retained, since it may be an unusual compound word, though it is most probably a form of 'couerid'.

6/22. **conielid . . . kumbros clog**: Cf. *Cloud*, 63/21–22: 'þis combros cloude of vnknowyng bitwix him & God'; 73/17: 'synne, þus conielyd in a lumpe.'

6/30–31. **maner . . . proef**: i.e. in a rapturous experience which they cannot communicate. Cf. Dante, *Paradiso* i, ll. 4–9:

> Nel ciel che più della sua luce prende
> fu' io; e vidi cose che ridire
> nè sa nè può qual di lassù discende;
> perchè, appressando sè al suo disire,
> nostro intelletto si profonda tanto,
> che retro la memoria non può ire.

(Temple Classics, London, 1936)

Cf. also *Ennead*, vi. 9, 10.

6/34. **settyng oure affermynges**: This passage is expounded more fully in the following chapter. Though the thought is, as usual, expressed simply in the Middle English, there obviously lies behind this passage the Neoplatonic theory of Emanations which Dionysius developed more fully in the *Divine Names*

6/34. **begynnen at þe moost worþi**: The way of affirmation asserts that God is immanent in all things, since by His continued activity of creation He holds all things in being. Dionysius would work downwards from the most universal conception to the most particular, because the most universal is the closest to the One.

7/2–5. **begynnyn at þe leest . . . awey**: In the way of negation there is an updrawing and indrawing of the consciousness as it passes from the most particular to the universal.

7/4–5. **foulden . . . awey**: This vigorous image is not in the Latin. Cf. *Cloud*, 28/10: 'þis entent lappid & foulden in o worde.'

7/6. **wallid aboute**: The solidness of the image is reminiscent of 'couerhid' 6/20, 'kumbros clog' 6/22. The Middle English translator possibly used a Latin version which read *circumvallatam*. The metaphor, however, is not Dionysian. Other manuscripts of Sarracenus have *circumvelatam*, the Paraphrase, p. 458, has 'latentem sub mysticis velis omnium exsistentium'; Rolt, p. 196: 'enwrapped'.

7/11. **oþer bookes**: See note to 2/1.

7/15. **synguleer**: 'unique'. The earliest example of this use in *O.E.D.* is taken from Latimer's Sermons (1555). See note to 67/24.

7/17–19. **liȝtes . . . hymself**: Cf. *Divine Names*, iv. 1 (Rolt, p. 87): 'For as our sun, through no choice or deliberation, but by the very fact of its existence, gives light to all those things which have any inherent power of sharing its illumination, even so the Good . . . sends forth upon all things according to their receptive powers, the rays of Its undivided Goodness. Through these all Spiritual Beings and faculties and activities . . . began.'

7/21. **vnpassyngliche**: This word, not in *O.E.D.*, corresponds to the Latin *inegressibilia*. In the act of creation the undifferentiated Godhead overflows into the realms of manifestations, but is still transcendent and undiminished in itself, like the sun, which, though light radiates from it, loses none of itself by the overflow. Though it is immanent in everything, holding everything in being, yet it cannot go forth from itself because it is the transcendent Unity containing all things. Cf. *Priue Counseling*, 136/18–23 quoted above.

7/22. **souereyn-substancyal Jheſu**: This refers to the Godhead of Our Lord, which is transcendent.

7/22–23. **maad . . . mankynde**: i.e. possesses a true human nature.

7/27. **Vertewe**: Probably 'Power' rather than 'Virtue'. See *Divine Names*, viii (Rolt, pp. 154 sqq.).

7/28–29. **Gadering of Deuine Sentence**: Latin *Symbolica Theologia*. This work is not extant. One cannot say for certain that it never existed, for Sarracenus in a unique reference just possibly informed Odo, Abbot of St. Denys, of his intention to translate it. See E. Bulhak, *Authenticité des Œuvres de Saint Denys l'Aréopagite* (Rome, 1938), pp. 246–7. One gathers from *Mystical Theology* that this work was an attempt to raise anthropomorphic conceptions of God to a higher spiritual level. The word 'sentence' is strained to bear an unusual signification. The central idea would appear to be that of 'meaning', and the Middle English title could, perhaps, be expanded to one such as 'A compilation of phrases used symbolically to describe God'. Its use recalls the title of Peter Lombard, 'Master of the Sentences', from his compilation of Patristic statements on questions of Christian doctrine. The earliest reference to *gadering*, 'compilation', in *O.E.D.* belongs to the sixteenth century.

7/30 sqq. **þe names . . .**: i.e. metaphorical descriptions drawn from the world of sense. The Middle English list follows the Latin of Sarracenus closely, and the Commentary (f. 46ᵇ) provides most of the following references, though some appear now rather far-fetched: *formae*, Phil. ii. 6; *figurae*, Song of Sol. i. 14–15, v. 10 sqq.; *partes*, Hos. xiii. 7; *instrumenta*, Amos vii. 8; *loca*, Ezek. iii. 12, Ps. xcvi. 2, ciii. 3; *ornatus*, Rev. i. 13; *furores*, Ps. vi. 1; *tristitiae*, Gen. vi. 6; *insaniae*, Hos. ix. 7, Mark iii. 21, 1 Cor. i. 25; *ebrietates et crapulae*, Ps. lxxvii. 71; *juramenta*, Ps. cix. 5; *maledictiones*, Gen. iii 14; *somni*, Ps. lxxvii. 71; *vigilationes*, Ps. cxx. 4, Jer. vii. 13.

8/7. **openyng**: Sarracenus *reserationem*, 'exposition'. The noun is not recorded with this sense in *O.E.D.*, but the verb is similarly used in medieval homiletic and devotional writings from the early thirteenth century, e.g. Trinity College Homilies, *Ancrene Riwle*, Rolle's Psalter, the 1382 Wycliffite translation of the Bible.

8/8. **in þe þrid book**: The precise reference is not in Sarracenus.

8/10–12. **þe wordes . . . vnderstondyng**: Sarracenus: 'sermones conspectibus intelligibilium contrahuntur'; Rolt, p. 198: 'our language becomes restricted to the compass of purely intellectual conceptions.' The farther away one moves from the perceptions of the senses or the imagination, the more difficult it is to give clear expression. This is one of the very few passages where the Middle English does not keep close to the Latin.

8/14. **madnes & a parfite vnresonabiltee**: The Middle English translator is adding here to the thought of his original. Since the experience is incommunicable and the mystics will not profane it by the inadequate terms proper to earthly joy, they tend to describe it in terms which are fantastic, and which do not make sense to the reason. Hence the impossible creatures of the Book of Revelation, the paradoxes of negation of the Dionysian school.

8/19. **þe whiche . . . oþer**: Not in the Latin.

8/22–33. **Bot happiliche . . . woodnes**: This passage leaves Sarracenus, and closely follows Vercellensis. See Appendix. The version in the Gloss (280) is very close to the Paraphrase.

8/22–23, 24. **affirmatyue deuinitee, negatyue deuinitee**: i.e. statements that God is thus, or He is not thus.

8/34–35. **And ȝit . . . vnderstondyng**: Not in the Latin.

9/4 sqq. We put awey . . .: This chapter is drawn chiefly from the Paraphrase of Vercellensis. See Appendix.

9/6–7. And . . . leuen not: This emendation is needed to complete the sense of the passage. Though it is omitted in both Har¹ and Kk its omission can easily be explained as a scribal error of haplography in their common source.

9/25 sqq. Also we . . .: This chapter, like ch. IV, is chiefly drawn from the Paraphrase. See Appendix.

9/27. soule, ne aungel: i.e. 'rational soul, nor intuitive'. The angels are believed to have intuitive knowledge, whereas men know by discursive reasoning.

10/1. ne he spekiþ: Not in the Paraphrase or in Sarracenus, but cf. Gloss (282): 'non est volubilis'.

10/7. Godheed: The transcendent God is above all manifestations of Himself.

10/11–12. ne he knowiþ . . . in hym: The Commentary explains that 'the knowledge which God has of existing things is not gathered, as is ours, from their natures and forms, but he knows them by knowing himself, the eternal cause of all things'. (Abbot Justin McCann, *The Cloud of Unknowing* (London, 1952), p. 148 note.)

10/20–21. abouen alle . . . doyng awey: The end of the *via negativa* is thus positive, and the way is paradoxically one of affirmation. The denyings do not, in fact, reduce God to Nothing, but are the only possible guide to forming a conception of Him which is worthy of His unique existence and infinite majesty.

A TRETYSE OF ÞE STODYE OF WYSDOME ÞAT MEN CLEPEN BENIAMYN

12/1–2. Title: The variant titles in the different manuscripts are descriptive of the contents of the treatise rather than a direct translation of the title of the Latin source, which is known today as *Benjamin Minor*, with the subtitle: *De praeparatione animi ad contemplationem*. In accordance with the medieval habit of interpreting Scripture allegorically, Benjamin in this work typifies contemplation, and the treatise is called *Benjamin Minor* to distinguish it from a longer work on contemplation by the same author, which is known as *Benjamin Major*. These Latin works will be referred to as *Ben. Maj.* and *Ben. Min.*

12/3. a greet clerk: Together with St. Bernard and St. Bonaventura, Richard of St. Victor is acknowledged as one of the chief influences on the course of European mysticism. Dante based the mystical psychology of the *Paradiso* on *Ben. Maj.*, and referred to his master (*Par.* x. 131) as: 'Richard who in contemplation was more than a man.' Richard is thought to have been a native of Scotland or England, but the exact place and date of his birth are unknown. He died in 1173. Some details of his career are available. He was professed at the famous Abbey of St. Victor, the House of the Augustinian Canons near Paris, sometime before 1140, and there he became a pupil of one of the great doctors and mystics of the Middle Ages, Hugh of St. Victor, who died in 1141. Richard adopted his teacher's principles and methods, and continued his work of systematizing the mystical theology of the Church according to the methods of medieval allegory. Richard's career was entirely monastic; chosen as sub-prior in 1159, he subsequently rose to be prior. His written work, which is considerable, falls into three kinds—dogmatic, mystical, and exegetical. Eight editions of it have already appeared—in Venice, 1506 (incomplete) and 1592, Paris, 1518 and 1550, Lyons, 1534, Cologne, 1621, Rouen, 1650, and lastly it was edited by Migne, whose text of *Benjamin Minor* (*P.L.* cxcvi, Paris, 1855) has been used here for comparison with the Middle English treatise.

12/4–14/7. two . . . þristy: This introduction to the treatise appears to be no more than a brief digest of the Latin, composed almost entirely of a close translation of selected key phrases in the source.

12/6. reson . . . affeccioun: The earliest example in *O.E.D.* of the use of *affection*, 'feeling', as opposed to *reason* is from Trevisa's translation of Barth. *De P.R.* (1398).

12/6. affeccioun or wille: The two words of the reading of Group A are not usually synonymous in English, but cf. *Ben. Min.* iii. 3: 'affectio, qua diligamus, . . . ex affectione desideria sancta.' The identification is further supported by *Cloud*, 116/17–21, where the same dichotomy of loving and choosing is implied in will.

12/8. goostly wittes: Cf. *Ben. Min.* iv. 4: 'Rachelis est meditari, contemplari, discernere, intelligere.'

12/12. By Jacob: This didactic emphasis is not in the Latin, which is less explicit.

13/8–9. wiþoutyn ymaginacioun . . . fele: The Middle English translator here omits Richard's theory of knowledge, which is fundamental to his thought. Cf. *Ben. Min.* v. 4: 'ad invisibilium cognitionem nunquam ratio assurgeret, nisi ei ancilla sua, imaginatio videlicet, rerum visibilium formam repraesentaret. Per rerum enim visibilium speciem surgit ad rerum invisibilium cognitionem.'

13/10. vnkunnyngly: So Har[1] Kk Har[2] Ar Har[5] W, but *inportunably* F, *vncouenabeli* R G, *enconuenyently* Pw; *Ben. Min.* vi. 5: 'tanta importunitate.' 'uncouenable' is used to translate *importuna* in Chaucer's translation of Boethius, and 'uncouenabli' occurs in the 1382 Wycliffite Bible.

13/17–18. þe luste of fleschly, kyndly, & wordly delices: The author's characteristic use of triplets is here well exemplified. Cf. *Ben. Min.* vi. 5, 'gaudium est voluptatis.'

14/1 sqq. And perfore . . .: The illustration from personal experience, the figure, and the explanation describing Jacob, his two wives, their hand-maidens, and all their children, are not in the Latin.

14/4. concupiscence: Not in the Latin, but the word is used by Rolle to express 'desire for the things of the world'.

14/8 sqq. The many variant readings in the passage are easily understandable as scribal errors. The order in Har[1]—Lia, Zelfa, Bala, Rachel—has little in its favour. The grouping, Lia—Zelfa—Rachel—Bala, repeats the order in which they have previously been listed; the grouping, Lia—Bala—Zelfa—Rachel, is in accordance with the sequence of events described in the following chapters.

16/11–12. ordeind . . . vnmesurid: Group B retains the order of the Latin.

17/1 sqq. How þe Vertewe Of Drede . . .: This chapter is a close and full translation of *Ben. Min.* viii. 6–7.

17/3. psalme: Ps. cx.

17/11. verrely: *Ben. Min.* viii. 6: 'Quodammodo'.

17/13–18/1. **God . . . meeknes:** Gen. xxix. 32.

18/3–4. **by rewardyng of pite:** *Ben. Min.* viii. 7: 'per respectum pietatis', i.e. by a return look of mercy.

18/5 sqq. **How Sorow . . .:** Much of this chapter follows the Latin closely, though the order of the thoughts is sometimes reversed.

18/9–10. **Oure Lorde . . . dispite:** Gen. xxix. 33. Lia's cry, which is parallel to that in the preceding chapter, is not in the Latin.

18/11–14. **heryng; for . . . coumforted:** A different reason for the name is given in the Latin, where it is linked with the fiftieth psalm: 'Cor contritum et humiliatum, Deus, non despicies.'

18/13–14. **Blessed . . .:** Matt. v. 5.

18/15–16. **Þus witnessiþ . . . Scripture:** The reference, possibly to Ezech. xxxiii. 14–15, or xviii. 27, is not in the Latin.

19/1. **haþ conpunccioun of teres:** *Ben. Min.* ix. 7: 'in fletu compungitur', lit. 'is pricked into weeping'. Rolle uses the abstract noun 'compunccioun' in Ps. xxxi.

19/5 sqq. **How Hope . . .:** As far as it goes, the translation follows the thought of cap. x of the Latin closely, though the Middle English expression is more succinct.

19/9. **clepid . . . doyng to:** *Ben. Min.* x. 7: ' *additus*, vel *additio* vocatur.' According to *O.E.D.*, 'do to' occurs in the Saxon Leechdoms (*c.* 1000) and in Wyclif's *Sel. Wks.* iii. 70.

20/2. **psalme:** Ps. xciii. 19.

20/8. **homlynes:** *Ben. Min.* xi. 8: 'familiaritas'. The English noun is used by Rolle, Wyclif, and Chaucer. See note to 21/8–10.

20/10–11. **not only . . . comyng:** *Ben. Min.* xi. 8: 'haec se sentiat ab illo saepius visitari, et ex ejus adventu non tantum jam consolari, imo aliquoties quodam ineffabili gaudio repleri.' The reading of Group A has the characteristic balance of this Middle English author's style, but Group B retains the threefold climactic thought of the Latin.

20/13–14. **Now . . . me:** Gen. xxix. 34.

21/3–15. **Lya . . . good:** This is a very free and greatly abridged adaptation of the thought of caps. xi–xii of the Latin.

21/3–4. **Now . . . Lorde:** Gen. xxix. 35: 'Modo confitebor Domino', 'Now will I praise the Lord.' In fourteenth-century versions of the Psalms and in the *Prymer* (see *O.E.D.* SHRIVE), *schrive* is used to translate *confiteri* of the Vulgate, with the meaning 'to ascribe praise and glory to God'. The more common meaning of the verb, derived from O.E. *scrífan*, 'to allot, to impose penance', was 'to make one's confession and receive absolution and penance'. The Latin treatise in this context lays far greater stress than the Middle English version on the need to confess one's own iniquity as well as the goodness of God, of which aspect the translation makes only brief mention (21/11–12).

21/4. **clepid schrift:** *Ben. Min.* xi. 8: 'id est *confitens*.'

21/8–10. **so swete . . . homly:** *Ben. Min.* xii. 8: 'O quam bonus, quam benignus, o quam suavis, quam dulcis, o quam amandus, quantum amplectendus, quam totus admirabilis, quam totus desiderabilis!' The Middle English is suggested by the Latin list, but does not follow it exactly. Many of the epithets selected are characteristic of fourteenth-century English devotional writers. The idea of the courtesy of God was a typical Franciscan conception; God is our courteous Lord, and would have His creatures like Him in this. Dame Julian of Norwich elaborated the idea, and also combined the epithet with 'homely', another of her favourite adjectives. See *Revelations of Divine Love*, ed. R. Hudleston (London, 1927), p. 20: 'it is the most joy that may be ... that he that is highest and mightiest, noblest and worthiest, is lowest and meekest, homeliest and most courteous.'

21/10–11. þer leuiþ ... homly vnto hym: cf. 21/4–5. Neither passage is in the Latin. This stress on the offering of love rather than on the thought of sin, wherein the Middle English has a different emphasis from the Latin, is comparable with certain passages in *The Cloud*, e.g. ch. 16.

21/14. oft-tymes: e.g. Ps. cv. 1, cvii. 3, cviii. 30–31, xxxiii. 2.

22/2. saluacion ... perfeccioun: The distinction is not in the Latin.

22/3–4. enflaumyd ... reson: This is highly characteristic of the thought of Richard of St. Victor, but it does not occur in this context in the Latin.

22/7–24/11. þus ... soule: Most of this section closely renders the Latin of sentences taken from different chapters of *Ben. Min.*, but with no attempt to draw from consecutive passages. So 22/7–16 is taken from cap. xiii. 10, 23/1–17 from cap. xiv. 10, 23/17–19 from cap. xviii. 12, 24/4–7 from cap. xix. 13. Most of the remaining part of this chapter is almost independent of the Latin, and where the same Biblical quotations or interpretations of proper names are introduced, they occur in a different context. A great deal of the subject-matter of the Latin is here omitted.

22/7 was borne: *Ben. Min.* xiii. 10: 'Nato itaque Juda.' The unique reading of Har¹ has been emended to the reading of the rest.

23/16. fayre ymagynacioun: *Ben. Min.* xiv. 10: 'imaginaria . . . pulchritudine.' The earliest reference in *O.E.D.* to the meaning 'result of the process of imagination, mental image' belongs to 1450.

25/4. dome: *Ben. Min.* xix. 13: '*judicium.*'

25/5. Dan ... folk: Gen. xlix, 16.

25/14. I ... Lya: Gen. xxx. 8.

25/15. clepid ... lyknes: *Ben. Min.* xxii. 16: '*comparatio* vel *conversio* interpretatur.'

25/18–26/1. an hert ... fairheed: Gen. xlix. 21.

26/2–4. We seyen ... heuen: Not in the Latin.

26/5 sqq. How þe Vertewes ...: In this chapter there is great abridgement of the thought of caps. xxv, xxvi, xxvii, xxxiii of the Latin. Caps. xxviii–xxx are not at all represented, caps. xxxi–xxxii are reduced to 29/8–10. Yet where the Latin is followed, the Middle English text keeps closely to it.

26/11–16. And þus ... felyng: Not in the Latin.

27/10 Happely: *Ben. Min.* xxv. 17: '*Feliciter*'. Gen. xxx. 11.

27/12–14. For whi ... loue: Not in the Latin.

27/15. þis ... blis: Gen. xxx. 13.

27/17–28/2. For whi ... affeccioun: Not in the Latin.

28/9–11. Moche pees ... pyne þerof: The Middle English is much more vivid than the Latin. *Ben. Min.* xxvi. 18: 'Quanta enim putas pax cordis est, vel tranquillitas, nulla hujus mundi oblectamenta concupiscere, nulla ejus adversa formidare?'

28/15–16. þe jangelyng ... inrennyng of veyne þouȝtes: *Ben. Min.* xxvii. 19: 'imaginationis evagatio quae fit per inutiles cogitationes.' The Middle English free rendering is again more vivid. The only reference to 'inrennyng' in *O.E.D.* before the nineteenth century is the Wycliffite use of it in Ps. xc. 6 to translate Latin *incursus*.

29/11. pees: *Ben. Min.* xxxiii. 23: 'sui'.

29/13. horribilite: *Ben. Min.* xxxiii. 23: 'terrore'. Har¹ has a characteristic alliterative pattern.

29/14. cherischiþ: *Ben. Min.* xxxiii. 23: 'demulcet', soothes, caresses.

30/1. parte: The readings of all the manuscripts would here appear to be corrupt and without sense. *broder* is better than *fader*, but cannot be correct since Asser himself typifies 'patience'. The Latin text, however, elucidates the problem (23): 'Sed Aser hosti suo facile illudit, dum partem tuetur, alta patientiae rupe munitam conspicit.' It seems likely that the common ancestor of all the extant manuscripts had *fader*, either because of a meta-thesized form in the manuscript of the Latin text, or a misreading of *partem* as *patrem*. Kk contains an unsuccessful attempt at emendation. For once, the present edition offers an emendation different from the reading of any of the extant manuscripts.

30/9 sqq. How Ioy . . .: This chapter is a very free and greatly abridged adaptation of cap. xxxvi. Caps. xxxvii and xxxviii are omitted from the Middle English, cap. xxxix is barely drawn upon.

30/10. proueþ: *Ben. Min.* xxxvi. 25: 'experiatur'. Here the reading of Group A is closer to the Latin than that of Group B.

30/11. hiӡe pees . . . wit: Phil. iv. 7.

30/13–16. For trewly . . . affeccioun: The Middle English translator, in characteristic explanatory style, concentrates upon the state of the con-templative, whereas the Latin expounds the theme of 'deliciae spirituales'.

30/18. clepid mede: *Ben. Min.* xxxvi. 26: '*merces* interpretatur'. Gen. xxx. 18.

31/4–5. God . . . children: Lia's cry, parallel to those when the other children were born, is not in the Latin.

31/5–10. And so . . . heuen: This personal reference is not in the Latin.

31/7–8. ese . . . disese: The manuscripts of Group A appear all to have some scribal error of omission. To complete the sense conveyed by the interpretation of Gad and Asser, the reading of Har¹ has here been emended partly to the reading of Kk Har², with an additional phrase from Group B.

31/9. erles: A favourite word in the writings of the author of *The Cloud* (e.g. *Cloud*, 15/9, 90/20, *Stirings*, 76/20) to denote the anticipation of heavenly sweetness granted to contemplatives while still living on earth. It translates the Latin *arrha*. Cf. Hugh of St. Victor's *De Arrha Animae*.

31/11. Jacob seide . . .: Gen. xlix. 14.

31/12. bitwix þe teermes: *Ben. Min.* xxxviii. 27: '*inter terminos.*'

32/8, 9. deedlynes, vndeedlynes: *Ben Min.* xxxix. 28: 'morientium terram, viventium terram.' The Middle English writer prefers abstract nouns common in the native tradition of devotional literature. *vndeedlynes* is used for 'immortality' in Old English homilies, *deedlynes* is to be found in the *Ancrene Riwle*.

32/14. Þus I trowe . . .: This development is not in the Latin.

32/15–16. Who . . . body: Rom. vii. 24.

32/16–33/1. I coueyte . . . Criste: Phil. i. 23.

33/6 sqq. How Parfite Hate . . .: This chapter contains a free and greatly simplified expression of the thought of caps. xl–xliv of the Latin, with many long omissions. The teaching in the Middle English version is more direct, and explains the allegory of the Latin rather than reproduces it.

33/12–14. For þe felyng . . . harmyng: Not in the Latin.

34/5. Wraþþes . . . not synne: Ps. iv. 5. Reference is made to this verse in Ephes. iv. 26, where the wording is closer to that in the present context than is the original phrase in the psalm. *Ben. Min.* xl. 29:, '*Irascimini, et nolite peccare.*'

34/14–35/1. Wiþ parfite hateredyn . . . hem: Ps. cxxxviii. 22.

35/1–2. had . . . wey: Ps. cxviii. 104.

35/13. a dwellyng . . . strengþe: *Ben. Min.* xl. 29: '*habitaculum fortitudinis.*'

35/14. Lya seide . . .: Not in the Latin.

35/14–15. My housbonde . . . me: Gen. xxx. 20.

36/3 sqq. How Ordeinde Schame . . .: Cap. xlv is followed very closely and fully.

36/6–8. Ȝif . . . us: 1 John i. 8.

36/8–9. Seinte Austyne . . . synne: This reference to St. Augustine, which is not in the Latin source, is possibly to one of the writings against the Pelagians, e.g. Epistola clvii, Ad Hilarium (*P.L.* xxxiii. 674).

37/9–16. þink . . . heuen: An independent working out of a theme suggested by caps. xlvi and xlvii. 34–35. Cf. *Cloud*, 101/7–12.

39/1–4, & þan . . . before: Not in the Latin.

40/2. profite: The exact meaning, 'proficiency', is not given in *O.E.D.* where the only comparable reference is from *A.Y.L.I.* (1600). Rolle and Wyclif both used the noun with the sense of 'benefit'. Cf. *Cloud*, 71/18: 'vnto hem þat ben biginners & profiters—bot not to hem þat be parfite', where 'profiters' is obviously used with the technical sense of the Latin *proficientes*. A similar use of the verb is illustrated in *O.E.D.* from the works of Rolle and Wyclif. Cf. *Cloud*, 15/13.

40/2. seerly: *Ben. Min.* lxvii. 48: 'unaquaque'.

40/4. vsen us in: cf. 42/11, 45/13. The earliest reference in *O.E.D.* to this particular construction with this sense belongs to 1534.

41/3–5. betir . . . victories: *Ben. Min.* lxvii. 48: '*Quia melior est vir prudens viro forti* (Prov. xvi). *Vir enim prudens loquitur victorias, et qui cum consilio cuncta agit, in aeternum non poenitebit* (Prov. xxi).'

41/4. betyr . . . strengþe: Not in the Latin. A favourite proverb in Middle English, which is quoted in *The Cloud*, 87/6–7, *Freier*, 58/2, Laȝamon's *Brut*, 17210, *Owl and Nightingale*, 172–3, and elsewhere. A similar thought is expressed in *The Ancrene Riwle*, ed. M. Day (E.E.T.S. o.s. 225, London, 1952), p. 120.

42/2–4. And al . . . liknes: Not in the Latin.

42/3–4. þe ymage & þe liknes: Gen. i. 26–27.

43/5–7. as a mirour . . .: The image is in the Latin, but not the Middle English explanation of it.

43/9 sqq. kandil . . .: The candle image is not in the Latin text consulted.

43/17–44/3. a maner of sonnebeme . . . be tymes: The image of illumination occurs in *Ben. Min.* lxxii. 52: 'quaedam divini luminis claritas interlucere, et immensus quidam insolitae visionis radius, oculis ejus apparere.' The Middle English text, however, is more reminiscent of *The Cloud* than of the Latin text, e.g. *Cloud*, 62/14–18. See note to *Hid Diuinite*, 3/17.

44/3. þis siȝt . . . be tymes: Not in the Latin. The insistence on the transitory nature of illumination is characteristic of the teaching of the author of *The Cloud* (e.g. ch. 75), as indeed of that of most of the great western mystics.

44/7–8. Lorde . . . herte: Ps. iv. 7. *Ben. Min.* lxxii. 52: '*Signatum est super nos lumen vultus tui, Domine, dedisti laetitiam in corde meo.*'

44/8–12. þe liȝt . . . Beniamyn: Not in the Latin.

44/16. **bittyr . . . hony**: This vivid simile is not in the Latin.

45/4. **iche desire on desire**: *Ben. Min.* lxxiii. 52: 'desiderium suum quotidianis incrementis acrius inflammat.'

45/6. **Rachel diȝeþ**: Gen. xxxv. 18.

45/14 sqq. **lerne þee þerin . . .**: The Christocentric conclusion is a Middle English modification. The Latin has 'verum bonum' as the object to be loved. The act of recollection through devotion to the Holy Name of Jesus is reminiscent of Rolle and his followers. The devotion was common in fourteenth-century English literature, and its development can be traced from the writings of St. Anselm, St. Bernard, and especially from the hymn *Jesu dulcis memoria*, now thought to have been composed by an Englishman. See A. Wilmart, *Le 'Jubilus' dit de Saint Bernard* (Rome, 1944), p. 222.

46/2-3. **Lorde . . . chirches**: Ps. xxv. 12.

46/12-13. **Ibi . . . excessu**: Ps. lxvii. 28.

A PISTLE OF PREIER

48/7. **diȝe . . . preier**: What follows is an individual application of an exhortation common in the Middle Ages of the uncertainty of life and the value of meditations upon death. Cf. St. Gregory, *Morals on Job*, xiii, cap. xxix. 33 (*P.L.* lxxv. 1032).

49/2-3. **so þfastnes . . . God**: Cf. *Summa Theologica*, 1, q. xvi. a. 6.

49/4-5. **moment . . . iȝe**: Cf. *The Pricke of Conscience*, ed. R. Morris (Berlin, 1863), ll. 5650-1:

> A moment of tyme es nan othir thyng,
> Bot a short space als of a eghe twynklyng.

49/6. **psalme**: Ps. xlvi. 8.

49/8-10. **anoþer psalme . . .**: Ps. cx. 10. Cf. *Stodye of Wysdome*, 17/3-4.

49/9. **is drede**: The reading of all the manuscripts, 17/4, proves that the unique reading of Har[1] here need not show a scribal error of omission.

49/11-12. **for drede**: Here the reading of Har[1] CP can be strongly defended as being superior to that of the rest. The original reading of Kk lends further support. The beginning of the sentence with its paradox and its pointed antithesis, *sekir stonding . . . drede of sinking*, is characteristic of this author's incisive style, and the use of Antanaclasis in the repetition of the same word in a different sense, more strongly emphasizes the contrast.

49/12. **ouer moche heuines**: This is the beginning of another common theme. Cf. *Ancrene Riwle*, p. 150: 'vor ase seint gregorie seið. . . . Timor sine spe.' degenerat in desperationem.'

49/12-13. **perfore . . . foloweþ**: Cf. St. Augustine, *De Quantit. Anim.* 73 (*P.L.* xxxii. 1075).

49/17. **accept**: Cf. Wycliffite Bible (1382), 2 Cor. vi. 2: 'In tyme accept, or wel plesynge.' (*O.E.D.*)

49/20-21. **lawfulich . . . confession**: Frequently in the works attributable to the author of *The Cloud* there is this insistence upon the importance of institutional religion as the background to the exercises he is recommending. Cf. *Cloud*, 10/3, 43/21-22.

50/1. **þe prophete seiþ**: Despite the reference in Har[1] to Ps. xxxvi, the quotation here may be from Ps. xxxiii. 23.

50/11. **sekir staf**: Cf. St. Gregory of Nyssa, *De Vita Moysis* (*P.G.* xliv. 358). The same image occurs in a similar context in Hilton's *Scale of Perfection*, ed. Dom M. Noetinger (London, 1927), p. 47: 'For he that cannot run lightly by ghostly prayer, for his feet of knowing and loving be sick for sin, he needeth to have a sure staff to hold him by.'

50/13–14. **hiʒe mount of perfeccioun**: Cf. *Priue Counseling*, 155/2–3.

51/5–7. **deuocioun . . . God**: Cf. *Summa Theologica*, ii. ii, q. lxxxii. a. 1: 'Devotio nihil aliud esse videtur quam voluntas quaedam prompte tradendi se ad ea, quae pertinent ad Dei famulatum.'

51/10. **swiftlich & gladliche**: Cf. *Vitis Mystica, inter op. S. Bernardi*, c. xix (*P.L.* clxxxiv. 674–5).

51/14. **bodiliche penance . . .**: The value of bodily exercises and their use in prayer is a common theme in the writings of the author of *The Cloud*. The greater part of *Discrecioun of Stirings* is a development of the thought in this passage.

52/18. **licned to a tre**: The tree image is common both in patristic writings and in religious treatises of the later Middle Ages. Cf. Hugh of St. Victor, *De Arca Noe Morali*, iii, cap. 1, ix, x (*P.L.* clxxvi. 647, 655). Similar teaching occurs in Cassian, *Coll.* xi, caps. xi–xiii (*P.L.* xlix. 861–7); *Summa Theologica*, ii. ii, q. xix. a. 7, ad 2; q. xxvii. a. 3, ad 3. Cf. also *Bonum Est* (*Minor Works of Walter Hilton*, ed. D. Jones (London, 1929), p. 204), which is based on St. Augustine's *Enarr. in Ps.* xci. 13.

53/8. **chast loue**: The definition is given later, 55/7–13. Cf. *Cloud* 93/21–24; *Priue Counseling*, 169/17 sqq. Cf. St. Bernard, *De Diligendo Deo*, x (*P.L.* clxxxii. 991): 'O amor sanctus et castus! O dulcis et suavis affectio! O pura et defaecata intentio voluntatis!'

53/21. **what**: The unique reading of Har[1] has been emended to the reading of the rest of the manuscripts which preserves the balance of alliterating consonants, and has greater variety.

54/5–8. **touched . . . liʒt**: Cf. *Stodye of Wysdome*, 12/10–12; *Cloud*, 17/4–5.

54/7–8. **beme . . . God**: This is a favourite image in St. Gregory's works. Cf. *Hom. in Ezech.* ii. v. 18 (*P.L.* lxxvi. 995). See note to 3/17.

54/16. **pointe . . . prik**: The *O.E.D.* does not record this as a common alliterative phrase. The figurative use of the two nouns in close association occurs repeatedly in the writings attributable to the author of *The Cloud*. Cf. *Priue Counseling*, 135/11, 141/11, *Stirings*, 72/5–6, 10, 13, 73/1. The earliest reference to the meaning 'target' for *prik* is taken from the Wycliffite Bible of 1382, 1 Sam. xx. 20. In 54/16 Har[1] alone retains the usual order of these two images.

55/14. **þi**: Har[1] CP have the more personal reading.

55/25–56/1. **vnnoumerable . . . oure**: Cf. *Cloud*, 22/6–10: 'it is bot a sodeyn steryng, & as it were vnauisid, speedly springing unto God as sparcle fro þe cole. & it is merueylous to noumbre þe sterynges þat may be in one oure wrouʒt in a soule þat is disposid to þis werk.'

56/12–14. **what maner . . . wile**: Cf. *Cloud*, ch. 8.

56/15–16. **Qui . . . illo**: 1 Cor. vi. 17.

56/17–18. **o sperit . . . kynde**: This is common teaching. Cf. St. Bernard's *Sermo lxxi*, 10 (*P.L.* clxxxiii. 1126); *Eight Chapters* (*Minor Works of Walter Hilton*), pp. 103–4.

56/19. **bot**: The reading of Har[1] has here been emended to that of the rest of the manuscripts, since the addition not only helps to point the antithesis, but also completes the rhythmical balance of the sentence.

56/21. **mariage**: Dom Cuthbert Butler, *Western Mysticism* (London, 1927), pp. 160 sqq., comments on the considerable place held in the literature of mysticism by the image of spiritual marriage as an allegory of the relationship between God and the soul in the highest stage of mystical contemplation. St. Bernard fully developed the image in his *Sermons on the Canticles*. 'The idea that Jesus Christ . . . is the Bridegroom, and the devout soul the Bride of the Canticle goes back to Origen, and became acclimatized in the West by the translations of his Commentary on the Canticle made by Jerome and Rufinus.' It is found in an accentuated form in Richard of St. Victor's *De Quatuor Gradibus Violentae Charitatis*. The first to 'give utterance to the realities of the mystical experience in terms of a sublimated human love was the austerely intellectual Plotinus (*Ennead*, VI. ix. 9), so little is such imagery in itself liable to suspicion of erotic sensuousness'.

56/25. **Book of Songes**: Song of Sol. ii. 16.

57/1. **glewe**: The image is used by Richard of St. Victor in *De Gradibus Charitatis*, iv (*P.L.* cxcvi. 1204).

57/14. **sodenly, listely, & likingly**: Cf. *Priue Counseling*, 144/27: 'sodenly, listely, & gracyously.'

57/16. **þe hiȝe king of heuen**: CP comments in the margin: 'nouȝt here in erþe, for it is departid fro þe rote of þe tre; ne in þe eir, for it is departid from þe bodi & þe bowes; but vp an heigh at his lord in heuene, þidir þow presentist it.'

57/23–24. **ete . . . bark**: This is a common figure in Middle English religious prose. Cf. *Cloud*, 107/15–18; *Scale of Perfection*, pp. 22, 33; *Mirror of Simple Souls* (London, 1927), pp. 13, 14.

58/2. **Betir . . . strengþe**: See note to 41/4.

58/8. **sodeyn . . . menes**: Cf. Cassian, *Coll.* xiv, cap. ii (*P.L.* xlix. 955).

58/12. **aungel messenger**: i.e. Guardian Angel.

58/17–22. **For as a man . . . þerto**: Cf. *Cloud*, 90/17–19: 'for God wil be seruid wiþ body & wiþ soule, boþe togeders, as seemly is, & rewarde man his mede in blis boþe in body & in soule.'

A PISTLE OF DISCRECIOUN OF STIRINGS

62/15–16. **þe kinde . . . consentyng**: The phraseology is reminiscent of *Priue Counseling*, 163/12–164/6.

62/20–21. **passing . . . degre**: Cf. the criterion of 'comoun custum of kynde & degre, eelde & conpleccyon' in 'þinges leueful & actyue', *Priue Counseling*, 162/22–23.

63/5–6. **to be only**: It is possible that *to* in Har[1] CP is not a scribal error of addition, influenced by the preceding gerundial infinitive, but an example of a gerundial infinitive used after an auxiliary verb. See Kellner, *Historical Outlines of English Syntax* (London, 1924), p. 248.

63/23. **of þe apostle**: 1 Cor. ii. 11.

64/4–7. **For . . . risinges**: Cf. *Stodye of Wysdome*, 40/16–41/2.

64/7 sqq. **For riȝt as amonge . . .**: The same image of the sea occurs in *Priue Counseling*, 167/14–168/2.

64/18–23. **londe of stabelnes . . . soule**: This is reminiscent of *Ben. Min.* xxxviii. 27: 'Haec est illa vere beata terra, mentis videlicet stabilitas tranquilla, quando mens in seipsa tota colligitur, et in uno aeternitatis desiderio immobiliter figitur.'

64/24. seiþ þus: Jas. i. 12. The same quotation is introduced in *Ben. Min.* xxvi. 18.

65/24. þe toretes . . . lices: This description has commonly been considered to be that of the crown of France or Scotland, and illustrations in French histories certainly show Charles V wearing a crown that corresponds to·this description. This has been used as evidence that the author of this treatise had lived in one of these countries. But apart from the fact that the whole symbolism of the passage may have been borrowed from some French writer, the description may even possibly be that of the English crown. According to W. Jones, *Crowns and Coronations* (London, 1883), p. 471: 'The introduction of the fleur-de-lys by our English monarchs, and the alteration from . . . an indefinite number to three, extends from Edward III . . . .' According to the *Encyclopaedia Britannica*, the shape of the English crown from William the Conqueror to Henry IV would agree with this description. Dom Noetinger, however, *Le Nuage de l'Inconnaissance* (Tours, 1925), pp. 291–2, maintains that here is a description of a French crown. 'Il est vrai qu'à partir de la guerre de Cent ans, les rois d'Angleterre, se prétendant rois de France, avaient introduit les fleurs de lis dans leur couronne; mais il ne semble pas qu'elles y aient jamais figuré seules, comme dans la couronne dont il s'agit ici.'

The earliest reference in *O.E.D.* to 'turrets' of a crown belongs to 1610.

66/12. bataile: Cf. *Stodye of Wysdome*, 44/5: 'þe batayle of þis deedly liif.'

66/18–19. meekly . . . Lorde: Cf. *Priue Counseling*, 167/13–14: 'suffre meekly & abide paciently þe wille of oure Lorde.'

67/23–24. experte in singuler leuyng: *singuler* would appear here to be a technical term connected with the contemplative life, unrecorded with this sense in *O.E.D.* Cf. *Cloud*, 14/12: 'degre & maner of leuing, þe whiche hiȝt Synguleer'; 15/1 'þe singuler fourme of leuyng', and note to *Cloud*, 14/13. R. Rolle, *Form of Living* (*English Writings*, ed. H. E. Allen, Oxford, 1931), p. 105, uses the word in a technical sense to denote the highest degree of love. The meaning 'solitary' is described as rare in *O.E.D.*, and the only example quoted before 1728 is from the 1382 Wycliffite Bible, Mark iv. 10: 'whenne he was singuler, or by hymsilf.'

singuler and the related *syngulertee(s)*, *syngulerly*, are favourite words with this author, and he uses them in various senses, which sometimes anticipate by centuries the date of usage cited in *O.E.D.* See note to 5/15, 7/15. In 'singulere abite' 70/16, 'singulere fastyng' 62/4, 15, 'singulere doynges' 67/9–10, 'singulere sterings' 67/20, the sense is that to be found in Rolle and Wyclif, viz. 'in contrast to the general'. There is the implication herein of 'oddness' too, but the earliest reference to this meaning in *O.E.D.* belongs to the seventeenth century. The first reference to 'singularity' = 'difference from others in order to render oneself conspicuous or to attract attention', which appears to be the signification of 86/12, belongs to 1502. The earliest parallel to the use in *Priue Counseling*, 160/10, with the meaning of 'individual judgment', belongs to 1622. The use of the adverb in these treatises is comparable with that quoted from *c.* 1430, but the use in *Priue Counseling*, 160/19, is not noted before 1669.

67/29–31. perilous . . . wyle: Cf. *Priue Counseling*, 160/17–18:' it is þe perilousest purpose þat may be, a ȝong man to folow þe feersnes of his desire vnrewlid bi counseil.'

68/13. streite: The unique reading of Har¹ has been emended to the reading of the rest, which retains the usual epithet (cf. 62/9, 63/3, 74/25) and preserves the alliteration. Yet cf. 68/17.

69/3–4. **wiþinne . . . wittes**: Cf. *Cloud*, 91/1–4: 'som beþ not comyng fro wiþoutyn into þe body bi þe wyndowes of oure wittys, bot fro wiþinne, risyng & spryngyng of habundaunce of goostly gladnes, & of trewe deuocion in þe spirit.' Cf. also *Priue Counseling*, 165/22–25.

69/6. **Mors . . . fenestras**: Jer. ix. 21: 'Quia ascendit mors per fenestras nostras.'

69/12. **Aungel of Grete Counseile**: Isa. ix. 6, in the versions of the Septuagint and the Vetus Itala.

70/13–71/4. The vehemence of this attack on ascetic devotions voluntarily undertaken without the calling of grace or the discipline of a rule, or penance (76/15–16), is startling. Yet cf. *A. Riwle*, pp. 2, 3; *Scale of Perfection*, ii, ch. 19.

70/20–21. **midday deuel**: Cf. Ps. xc. 6; also *Ancrene Riwle*, p. 100: 'Dauid cleopeð hine Demonium meridianum . þet is briht schininde deouel . ant seinte powel cleopeð hine angelum lucis . þet is engel of lihte.'

70/25. **witnes of Poule**: 2 Cor. iii. 17.

71/5–6. **corious beholdyng & seching**: The phraseology is reminiscent both of *The Cloud* and *Priue Counseling*.

71/26. **wille . . . herte**: Cf. *Cloud*, 94/20–21: 'I mene not in þi bodily herte, bot in þi goostly herte, þe whiche is þi wil.'

71/26. **þee**: Har¹ CP preserve here a dative of interest, a more archaic construction than that in the other manuscripts.

72/3. **lesing**: This may be the present participle of the Middle English verb developed from either OE. *lesan*, 'to release', or OE. *lesan*, 'to glean'. In this context, the former derivation gives the wider meaning. God is to be released or separated in the mind from all thought connected with bodily exercises of devotion. If the second interpretation is accepted, *lesing* is parallel to and almost synonymous with *seking*. There is no record of a figurative use of *lese*, v. 'to glean' in *O.E.D.*, but such a use is quite likely in Middle English; cf. *E. E. Allit. P.* A 9'54: 'In þat oþer (Jerusalem) is noȝt bot pes to glene.' (*O.E.D.*)

72/4. **clene . . . trewe**: Though Kk Har² Pw have these words in an order which is more customary than the order of Har¹ CP in religious literature, and which would therefore be more familiar to the scribe, yet the reading of Har¹ CP does make sense, and, moreover, is more suggestive than that of the other group, especially when the teaching of *The Cloud* is remembered. In view of what follows, the significance of 'clene wille' may resemble that of the characteristic 'nakid entent'. See *Cloud*, note to 17/2.

72/10–11. **God . . . þe pointe of þin herte**: See note to 54/16. It is not wholly satisfying to gloss *pointe* simply as 'target'. The collocations of this word in works attributable to this author suggest a more subtle depth of meaning. This passage is associable with *Stirings*, 73/15–16, *Priue Counseling*, 140/6–7, 143/9–10. Cf. 'þe first poynt of þi spirit, þe whiche is þi beyng' (140/6–7). Through the 'blind' feeling and offering of one's own being, the 'perfeccioun of onheed' is brought about between God and the soul. The following image of the 'sharp dart' here suggests a deliberate word-play, with threefold suggestion of sharp-pointedness, intention, and the unitive faculty of the soul.

72/12–13. **blinde . . . loue**: Cf. *Cloud*, 26/11–12: 'smyte apon þat þicke cloude of vnknowyng wiþ a scharp darte of longing loue.'

72/14. **Book of Loue**: Song of Sol. iv. 9.

72/19. I3en . . . loue: Cf. Richard of St. Victor, *Explic. in Cant.*, cap. xxvii; *De Gradibus Charit.* iii (*P.L.* cxcvi. 484–5; 1203); (?) St. Bernard, *Tract. De Charitate*, cap. iii (*P.L.* clxxxiv. 592).

73/3. **reson ransakiþ & sekiþ**: The phraseology is again reminiscent of *The Cloud* and *Priue Counseling*.

73/11. **þe apostle**: Cf. 1 Cor. i. 26, vii. 20; Eph. iv. 1.

73/15. **Mary, Martha sister**: Like Origen, St. Augustine, St. Gregory, St. Thomas Aquinas, Hugh and Richard of St. Victor, and many others, the author of *The Cloud* and its related treatises interprets the story of Martha and Mary in terms of the active and contemplative lives. Cf. *Cloud*, chs. 8, 17–21. His exegesis is based upon the common tradition, which developed from the interpretation of St. Augustine in his *Sermones ciii, civ, clxix, clxxix, cclv* (*P.L.* xxxviii).

73/16–17. **For . . . nesessarie**: Luke x. 42; cf. *Cloud*, 52/13–23; 52/25–55/6.

75/8–19. **For . . . discrecioun**: Cf. *Cloud*, 80/24–81/8.

75/18. **mistely**: Cf. *Priue Counseling*, 144/25. The *O.E.D.* does not clearly recognize the meaning: 'mystically, spiritually', which is obvious in these passages, but gives the definition: 'in a misty manner'. *O.E.D.* does suggest, however, in connexion with a quotation from *The Pricke of Conscience* (l. 4364: In þe appocalipse apparty Es sayd þus ful mistyly') that the adverb is connected not with the usual adj. *misty*, but with a second adj. of the same form, which has acquired the meaning 'spiritual, mystical' by form-association with Latin *mysticus*. The *O.E.D.* also clearly distinguishes between *mist* 'cloud' and *mist* 'spiritual things', but provides only thin evidence for the existence of the second meaning.

76/6. **blinde stering of loue**: The same phrase occurs in *Cloud*, 22/18. See note on *blynde*, 2/32 above.

A TRETIS OF DISCRESCYON OF SPIRITES

80/1. There is no justification for emending che title. Cf. the Wycliffite Bible of 1382, 1 Cor. xii. 10: 'To another (is 3ouun) discrescioun, or verrey knowynge, of spiritis.' (*O.E.D.*) The Latin source has *discretio*. This treatise is closer in subject-matter to the common homiletic tradition than the previous works; yet, though much of it closely follows the thought of two of St. Bernard's *Sermones de Diversis* (viz. xxiii and xxiv, *P.L.* clxxxiii. 600–3), it will also be seen to contain traces of the highly individual thought and expression of the author of *The Cloud*.

80/2–83/12. **For-þi . . . soule**: A close translation of *Sermo xxiii*. 2, 3 (600–2).

80/4. **not . . . spirites**: 1 John iv. 1–6.

80/6. **þat souniþ . . . herte**: Not in the Latin.

80/9. **seiþ . . . Dauid**: Ps. lxxxiv. 9.

80/11. **anoþer prophete**: Zech. i. 9–21.

80/12. **psalme**: Ps. lxxvii. 49.

80/14. **where he seiþ**: Col. ii. 18.

80/15. **blowyn**: Latin *inflatos*. Cf. Wycliffite 1 Cor. iv. 19: 'The word of hem that ben blowun with pride.' (*O.E.D.*)

80/15–81/4. **þer . . . Goost**: Cf. 1 Cor. ii. 12: 'Nos autem non spiritum hujus mundi accepimus, sed Spiritum qui ex Deo est.' Cf. also 1 Thess. i. 2–9.

81/6–7. **seruauntes . . . helle**: More precise than the Latin: 'satellites maligni illius principis tenebrarum.'

81/7. **lorde**: Cf. *Priue Counseling*, 149/1–2: 'þe feend & his fautours, þe woreld & þi flessche.'

81/10–11. **lede . . . soule**: The Middle English translates the Latin metaphor into a more positive and direct statement. Cf. Latin: 'sanguinem sitiunt . . . animarum.'

81/13 sqq. **For euermore . . .**: What follows is a commonplace in religious teaching. Cf. *Ancrene Riwle*, p. 87: 'vre wiþerwines beoð þreo . þe ueond . þe world . & ure owune vleshs ꝛ̣ . . . lihtliche ne mei me nout oþerhule icnowen hwuc of þeos þreo weorreð him . uor euerichon helpeð oþer . þauh þe ueond kundeliche eggeð us to atternesse . as to prude . to ouerhowe . to onde . & to wreððe . & to hore attri kundles . . . þet flesh put propremen touward swetnesse . & touward eise . & toward softnesse . ant te world bit mon ȝiscen wordes weole & wunne & wurschipe . . . .'

81/17. **smiteþ**: Latin *pulsat*. Cf. 92/22; *Stirings*, 75/25–26.

81/18. **softe cloþing, of lecherie**: Not in the Latin.

82/2. **as we . . . grace**: Not in the Latin.

82/3–9. **of veyne ioye . . . siȝte of hymself**: An independent development from the Latin, which has 'cum autem . . . de ambitione saeculi, de jactantia et arrogantia, caeterisque similibus cogitatio vana versatur in cordibus nostris'.

82/14–16. **ouþer by grace . . . wiþdrawen**: This passage, strongly reminiscent of *The Cloud* in its metaphor and phraseology, is an independent interpretation of the Latin: 'satellitibus istis terga vertentibus.' The use of a spiritual stratagem ('goostly sleiȝt') is a frequent theme in *The Cloud*, e.g. 66/13–67/14, 128/18. With the violent metaphor in 'stifly . . . fote' cf. *Cloud*, 22/20, 66/5, though the image is a common one, to be found, for example, in St. Gregory, *Morals* (*P.L.* lxxv. i, § 37 (544), iv, § 42 (657)), Richard of St. Victor, *Ben. Maj.* i. 8.

82/18. **lyon rennyng felly**: Cf. 1 Pet. v. 8.

82/18. **to asaile . . . soules**: Latin: 'adversus nos'.

83/1–3. **murmuryng . . . sorow**: Latin: 'ad iram, ad impatientiam, ad invidiam, ad amaritudinem animi provocamur.'

83/2. **malencoly**: This denotes the condition of having too much black bile, one of the four chief fluids or cardinal humours of the ancient and medieval physiologists. Its prominent symptoms are sullenness and propensity to causeless and violent anger.

83/8. **it makiþ . . . us**: A penetrating psychological observation not in the Latin.

83/12–85/15. **No doute . . . of alle**: Not in the Latin.

84/6–7. **lusty . . . list**: The use of *paronomasia* (*adnominatio*) to sharpen the distinction between self-indulgent appetite and eager spiritual longing is typical of this author's pointed style. So *lusty* 84/6, *lustly* 84/10, contrast with *list of deuocioun* 84/7, 15. See note to 3/1.

84/9–10. **contemplacioun . . . heuen**: Cf. *Priue Counseling*, 144/27–145/2 and note.

84/10 sqq. **for whoso . . .**: This is common teaching. Cf. *Ancrene Riwle*, pp. 64–65.

85/1. **liuely . . . louely**: The association of these two epithets, with *paronomasia* here used for emphasis, is to be found elsewhere in the works of this author. Cf. *Priue Counseling*, 146/16.

85/1–2. **good . . . self**: Cf. *Priue Counseling*, 138/28, 139/6–7.

85/2. **psalme**: Cf. Ps. cxxxi. 13, lxxv. 3.

85/4 sqq. **Syon is as moche . . .**: Cf. St. Augustine, *Enar. in Ps. lxiv* (*P.L.* xxxvi. 774); *Scale of Perfection*, p. 245: 'Jerusalem is as much as to say a sight of peace, and betokeneth contemplation in perfect love of God. For contemplation is naught else but a sight of God, which is very peace.'

85/7. **þe prophete**: Dom Noetinger, op. cit., p. 317 note, refers to Isa. lxvi. 2, explaining: 'La Vulgate porte: *ad quem respiciam, nisi ad pauperculum et contritum spiritu*; mais la "Version antique" lisait: *super quem respiciam, nisi humilem et quietum*. Quant à la forme employée ici . . . elle était · bien connue des Pères (cf. Sabatier, *Bibliorum sacrorum latinae versiones antiquae*, t. ii (1751), p. 634), et se trouve plusieurs fois citée par S. Bernard, à qui notre auteur l'a sans doute empruntée.'

85/11. **þe hiȝest . . . contemplacion**: Cf. *Priue Counseling*, 163/9–10.

85/16–86/9. **And it is . . . sclaundre**: A slightly expanded translation from *Sermo xxiv* (603).

85/16–17. **ful needful . . . deseites**: Latin: 'Sed hujus specialiter astutias nosse necesse est, hujus cogitationes non expedit ignorare.' *doelful* has been glossed with its usual fourteenth-century meaning of 'bringing sorrow'. It seems possible, however, that it is here an early example of the word meaning 'crafty', which is described in *O.E.D.* as appearing first in the seventeenth century. Cf. *doles* 86/21, which seems to be an adaptation from Latin *dolus*, though the earliest record of this word in *O.E.D.* belongs to 1563.

85/18. **aungel of liȝt**: The idea is taken from 2 Cor. xi. 14: 'ipse enim Satanas transfigurat se in angelum lucis.' Stories illustrative of Satan's activities 'are one of the commonplaces of early monasticism, witness Cassian and Palladius'. (*Western Mysticism*, p. 187, note.)

86/1. **schewiþ**: Latin *spargit*. Though *O.E.D.* gives some fifteenth-century spellings of the verb 'to sow' with initial *sch*-, it seems likely that the common ancestor of all the known manuscripts had here a scribal error of *schewiþ* 'shows', anticipating *schewing* below.

86/1–2. **seem . . . schewing**: Not in the Latin.

86/2. **steriþ . . . holines**: A similar detailed account of the temptations when the devil transforms himself into an angel of light is to be found in Rolle's *Form of Living*, ch. 2 (pp. 90–92). Here, however, and in *The Cloud*, there is particular awareness of the insidiousness of the temptations. Cf. *Cloud*, 102/7–17.

86/2–10. **singuleer holines . . . singulertees**: An expanded version of the Latin: 'Suadet enim nonnullis singularia jejunia quaedam, unde caeteri scandalizentur; non quia jejunium diligat, sed quia scandalo delectetur.'

86/3. **wering**: The epithet is not required. Cf. *Ancrene Riwle*, p. 3: 'Of weriunge. of liggunge. of vres. of beoden.'

86/10–21. **For . . . doles**: Not in the Latin. See note to 85/16–17.

86/22–88/2. **Bot . . . deuil**: A greatly expanded version of *Sermo xxiii*. 4 (602).

87/2–4. **brouȝt . . . itself**: A rhetorical elaboration of the Latin: 'servus illi addictus, in suam ipsius perniciem.'

87/5–8. **And þis . . . froward**: Not in the Latin.

87/10–12. **bringiþ . . . oþer**: Latin: 'aut voluptuosas, aut vanas, aut amaras pariat cogitationes.'

87/19–21. **concent . . . enemye**: Latin: 'resiste viriliter'.

87/19–20. **meek þee . . . miȝtly wiþstonde**: This paradox is reminiscent of *The Cloud*, 67/10–11: 'þis meeknes deserueþ to haue God himself miȝtely descendyng.'

88/2–92/4. **Schriue . . . same good**: Not in the Latin.

88/8–9. **for oft-tymes . . . errour**: Cf. *Preier*, 52/8.

88/13. **counsel**: The sense of 'spiritual adviser, father confessor' is not in *O.E.D.* where the only reference to a single person before 1647 is taken from Chaucer's *Knight's Tale*, l. 289: 'I . . . tolde thee my wo As to my conseil & to my brother sworn.'

90/16–18. **by soche . . . liiftyme**: Cf. *Cloud*, 46/5–14.

92/4 sqq. **For as ofte . . .**: This returns to *Sermo xxiii*. 5 (602).

92/5–7. **chastite . . . charite**: The list is only partly suggested by the Latin, which has: 'super castigando corpore, humiliando corde, servanda unitate [*alias*, virtute patientiae], et charitate fratribus exhibenda, seu caeteris virtutibus acquirendis, conservandis, amplificandis.'

92/8–93/3. **þat is to sey . . . Amen**: This is independent of the Latin.

92/9. **aungelles . . . trewe techers**: Cf. Wycliffite Gal. iv. 14: 'ȝe resceyueden me as an aungel of God.' (*O.E.D.*)

GLOSSARY

abyde *pr. 3 pl. subj.* submit to *D.* 66/19; **abideþ** *imp. pl.* endure *D.* 73/13.

abiding *n.* submissive awaiting *P.* 49/3.

abil, able *adj.* capable *S.* 91/14; liable *D.* 67/8.

abilnes, abel- *n.* capability *H.D.* 2/18; fitness *D.* 63/20; propensity *D.* 67/12; potentiality *D.* 67/28; capacity *S.* 91/1.

abite *n.* dress *D.* 70/16.

aboundingly *adv.* plentifully *D.* 66/19.

absteyne (hym) from *v. refl.* withhold (himself) from *B.* 28/18.

abstynence *n.* self-restraint *B.* 27/2.

accept *adj.* acceptable *P.* 49/17.

acceptacioun *n.* acceptance *P.* 50/18.

acomptyd *pp.* counted *B.* 16/13.

acordaunce *n.* conformity *P.* 56/14.

acordeþ to *pr. 3 s.* is proper to *H.D.* 5/3; agrees with *P.* 51/9.

acordyng *adj.* fitting *H.D.* 2/17; appropriate *H.D.* 8/31.

actueel, actuele *adj.* active *H.D.* 2/32; *D.* 75/10.

affeccioun *n.* feeling (as opposed to reason) *B.* 12/7; inclination, bent *P.* 50/6; love *P.* 50/25; *pl.* feelings *B.* 38/2.

afferme *v.* confirm *H.D.* 2/8; aver *H.D.* 4/2.

af(f)erming *adj.* affirmative, positive *H.D.* 7/10, 12.

afferminges *n.pl.* positive statements *H.D.* 6/33.

affermingly, affermyngliche *adv.* positively *H.D.* 10/16, 7/25.

affirmatyue *see* **deuenite.**

after (þat) *conj.* according as *H.D.* 10/7; *prep.* following the nature of *H.D.* 7/16; in proportion to *H.D.* 8/16; according to *B.* 41/1.

aȝeinstonde *v.* withstand, resist *S.* 83/10; **aȝenstonde** *pr. 2 s. subj.* *S.* 89/6.

aȝens *prep.* against *B.* 34/3.

aȝenstonding *n.* withstanding *S.* 88/8; **not aȝenstonding** *prep.* notwithstanding *S.* 83/18.

aȝensward *adv.* conversely *D.* 73/22; on the other hand, *S.* 88/9.

al, alle *adv.* entirely *H.D.* 8/20; just, exactly *P.* 51/25.

algates *adv.* wholly *H.D.* 5/18; somehow *H.D.* 6/7; always *H.D.* 8/6.

als, as: whan . . . als sone *trans. of Latin* quoties . . . toties 24/8–9.

amendement *n.* correction *B.* 36/13; reparation *P.* 48/15.

and *conj.* if *B.* 37/5.

apely *adj.* apelike *D.* 68/22.

aperte *adj.* plain *S.* 86/17; *in aperte,* openly *D.* 77/6.

apertly, apeertly *adv.* plainly *S.* 89/20, 80/14.

as anemste *prep.* as regards *B.* 34/12.

ascencioun, ass- *n.* ascent *H.D.* 8/19; **assenciouns** *pl.* ways of ascending *H.D.* 4/22.

assoilid *pp.* absolved, released *H.D.* 5/11.

at *prep.* from *B.* 41/14; according to *D.* 62/3.

atempereely *adv.* temperately *B.* 26/17.

attemperaunce *n.* moderation *B.* 28/4.

attemperid *pp.* controlled *B.* 27/4.

auȝt *pt. 3 s. (impers. with preceding dat.* us), (we) ought *B.* 34/12.

auisement *n.* deliberation *B.* 37/6; advice *D.* 67/30.

auoidyng *pr. p.* voiding, emptying *H.D.* 5/22.

auowe *n.* vow *D.* 70/21.

aworde *adj.* aware *S.* 88/16. *Not in* O.E.D.

bak *n.*: *torne þe bak,* turn round *B.* 30/6.

beable *adj.* capable of existing *H.D.* 4/10. *Not in* O.E.D.

beforetyme *adv.* previously *P.* 49/19.

behetyng *n.* promise *B.* 30/1.

beholde *v.* comprehend *H.D.* 4/16; consider *B.* 17/7. **beholden (to)** *pr. 1 pl.* consider *H.D.* 8/10.

beholder *n.* supervisor *H.D.* 2/16. *See note.*

beholding *n.* regard *P.* 54/16; sight *D.* 66/2; contemplation *D.* 72/6; **beholdynges** *pl.* acts of contemplation *H.D.* 2/32, 5/7; *see note* *to* 2/32; kinds of sight, *B.* 14/15; *to oure beholdynges*, as far as our perception is concerned *H.D.* 8/11.

behote *v.* promise, *P.* 49/2.

behouiþ *pr. 3 s. (impers.)* is necessary *H.D.* 6/32.

beyng *adj.* existing *H.D.* 3/23.

beynges *n.pl.* existences *H.D.* 4/2.

beme *n.* radiance *H.D.* 3/17. *See note.*

bemene *v.* signify *B.* 16/5.

bere *v.* bear *B.* 22/9; **bere (us),** behave *S.* 83/4.

besy *adj.* busy, engrossed *B.* 14/4.

besily, besyli *adv.* earnestly, attentively *B.* 17/6, 29/2.

besines *n.* activity *S.* 81/19; pains, exertion *S.* 82/11.

bewar (wiþ) *imp. 2 s.* beware (against) *D.* 67/32.

bi *prep.* about *P.* 52/15.

byleue, beleue *n.* faith *H.D.* 4/9, *S.* 80/8.

bileue (to) *v.* believe *S.* 80 /4.

bitwix *prep.* between *B.* 20/9.

bleendid, blent *pp.* blinded *D.* 70/20, *B.* 17/11.

bles *v.* praise, adore *B.* 46/3.

blis *n.* joy, blessedness *B.* 27/9.

blissidheed *n.* blessedness *B.* 27/16.

blowyn *pp.* puffed up *S.* 80/15.

bodely, bodiliche *adj.* bodily, physical *H.D.* 6/4, *P.* 51/14.

body *n.* trunk (of tree) *P.* 52/21. *(Earliest reference to this use in O.E.D. 1523.)*

bodyn *pp.* bidden *H.D.* 4/28.

boistous *adj.* gross, crude *H.D.* 6/11.

borionid oute *pt. 3 pl.* burgeoned, burst forth *H.D.* 7/18. *Translates Latin* pullulaverunt.

borionyng *n.* burgeoning *H.D.* 7/21.

bot, but *adv.* only *D.* 62/16; *bot onliche* only *H.D.* 6/31; *conj.* unless *B.* 29/2; *prep.* except *H.D.* 6/30.

bowes *n.pl.* boughs *P.* 52/21.

brast *pt. 3 s. subj.* burst, broke *P.* 53/20.

brenne *v.* burn *S.* 81/19.

certein(e) *adj.* sure *P.* 50/8; particular *P.* 55/9; *a certein tyme*, for some time *P.* 53/2.

certes *adv.* assuredly *D.* 68/18.

charge *n.* burden *B.* 32/1.

charge *v.* attach importance to *P.* 52/9; accuse *S.* 90/13; **charging** *pr. p.* indicting *S.* 89/15.

chast(e) *adj.* pure, single *P.* 53/8, 54/24.

chaunses *n. pl.* happenings *H.D.* 9/17.

cheef *adj.* chief, principal *P.* 56/3; *n. P.* 55/18.

cherischiþ *pr. 3 s.* gladdens, encourages *B.* 29/14.

chese *imp. s.* choose *D.* 71/8.

chesing *n.* choosing *D.* 72/3.

chirche *n.* church *B.* 45/14.

cleer, clere *adj.* clear *H.D.* 6/4; bright, pure *P.* 54/7; plain *D.* 64/19.

cleerte *n.* brightness, clearness *B.* 43/16.

clene *adj.* clean *H.D.* 3/14; pure *H.D.* 4/22; clear, bright *H.D.* 4/32.

clennes *n.* purity *S.* 83/19.

clepe *v.* call *B.* 45/13.

cleping *n.* calling, vocation *D.* 73/12.

clergie *n.* scholarship *D.* 69/21.

clerk *n.* scholar *B.* 12/3.

cloþe *n.* garment *B.* 37/7.

colour *n.* *vnder c. of,* under the alleged authority of *D.* 70/22.

com (to) *v.* attain *H.D.* 6/4; **c. abouen** *pr. 3 pl.* transcend *H.D.* 4/22; **comen to** *pp.* reached *H.D.* 4/18.

combrance *n.* clogging, entanglement *S.* 92/1.

comende *v.* praise *P.* 52/9.

comonly, comounly *adv.* commonly, generally *D.* 68/8; in the common way *D.* 75/21.

comounyng *n.* conversing *D.* 68/15.

companous *adj.* in company *D.* 63/7, 73/20. *Not in* O.E.D.

concyence *n.* inmost thought *B.* 29/5; conscience, moral sense, *P.* 49/20.

concupiscence *n.* lust *H.D.* 9/16; desire for the things of this world *B.* 14/4.

confusion *n.* *in grete confusion of,* to the great discomfiture of *D.* 63/11.

conielid *pp.* congealed, consolidated *H.D.* 6/22.

connyng *n.* wisdom, intelligence *P.* 49/19.

conplexion *n.* disturbance, complication *H.D.* 9/16, *troublid con- plexion* = *Latin* inordinationem.

conseite *n.* understanding *P.* 59/9; opinion *D.* 63/17.

consentes *n. pl.* acquiescence *D.* 67/22.

contemplacioun *n.* religious medita- tion *B.* 23/3; = si3t of God *B.* 42/13, 45/10. *See note to* 85/4 sqq.

contenaunce *n.* look *S.* 83/6.

continouaunce *n.* perseverance *D.* 67/24.

contrary *adj.* extremely unlike *H.D.* 6/11.

contrariing (vnto) *pr. p.* counter- acting *H.D.* 6/27.

contrey, cuntre *n.* district *D.* 68/12, 16.

coroun *n.* crown *D.* 65/2.

corumpid *adj.* corrupt *H.D.* 6/19.

costomable, customable *adj.* habi- tual *S.* 92/12, 87/6.

costum *adj.* customary *S.* 88/2.

counsel, counseyl, counseile *n.* counsel, direction *B.* 41/1, 11; advice *D.* 69/11; (spiritual) ad- viser *S.* 88/13 counselles *pl.* purposes, intentions *B.* 12/8.

cours *n.* þe *cours of kynde*, ordinary procedure of nature *D.* 62/20.

couerhid *pp.* hidden with a cover *H.D.* 6/20. *See note.*

couetyse *n.* covetousness *S.* 81/15.

craft(e) *n.* skill *H.D.* 6/1, 6.

crokid *adj.* perverted, *D.* 70/21.

cuntre, *see* contrey.

cursid *adj.* damned *S.* 81/6.

custumed *pp.* practised habitually *B.* 40/1.

dampne *v.* condemn *B.* 29/8.

daunger *n.* subjection *S.* 87/3.

deceyuiþ *pr. 3 s.* overcomes *B.* 29/17. *Translates Latin* illudit. 'destroys'.

deceyte, disseite *n.* deception *B.* 42/1, *D.* 67/6; *pl.* deseites *S.* 85/17, disceites *S.* 86/18.

declaracioun *n.* exposition, *P.* 52/12.

declare *v.* explain *H.D.* 2/10; prove *S.* 81/1.

declaring *n.* explanation *P.* 52/14.

ded(e) *n.* action *B.* 34/7; act *S.* 86/8; *in dede*, in fact *P.* 48/20.

deedly *adj.* mortal *B.* 32/1; deadly *P.* 56/23.

deedlynes *n.* mortality *B.* 32/8.

deeþ *n.* death *P.* 50/7.

defaile *v.* fail *D.* 74/5; fall short *D.* 72/21.

defautes *n. pl.* defects *S.* 86/5.

defoulid *pp.* defiled, corrupted *S.* 83/17.

degre *n.* stage *B.* 21/5; state *D.* 62/21; rank *S.* 82/6.

delaied *pp.* deferred *B.* 19/11.

delaiing *n.* delay *B.* 45/5.

delices *n. pl.* delights *B.* 13/18.

deme *v.* judge *B.* 25/5; think *H.D.* 8/5; *for demyng of*, as a precaution against being thought *D.* 62/10.

deming *n.* judgement, criticism *S.* 87/12.

deniinges *n. pl.* negations *H.D.* 6/33.

deniingly *adv.* by negation, *H.D.* 10/16.

departe *v.* separate, *P.* 53/6.

dere *adj.* dear, precious *S.* 85/2.

dere *n.* harm *S.* 85/19.

derke *adj.* dark, hard to understand *H.D.* 2/19.

derknes *n.* darkness *H.D.* 2/20.

deseert *n.* deserving *B.* 44/18.

determinid *pp.* judged *S.* 86/16.

deuely *adj.* devilish *S.* 90/5.

deuelnes *n.* devilish conduct *S.* 90/8.

deuenite, deuinytee, deuinite(e) *n.* Theology *P.* 55/21, *H.D.* 2/19; divinity, Godhead *H.D.* 4/13; *affirmatyue deuinitee*, positive statements made about God *H.D.* 8/22–23; *negatyue deuinitee*, negative statements made about God *H.D.* 8/23–24.

deuyne *adj.* divine, leading to God *H.D.* 6/10.

deuisid *adj.* distinct *D.* 70/10.

deweliche *adv.* rightly, as is due *P.* 50/23.

dietyng *n.* taking of daily food *D.* 62/4.

di3e *v.* die *P.* 48/7.

discrecioun, discrescyon *n.* discre- tion, discrimination *B.* 39/5, *S.* 80/1.

discrete *adj.* discriminating *B.* 27/4, *S.* 80/3.

diseese, disese *n.* absence of ease, dis- comfort *B.* 29/16, 27/5.

diseyuable *adj.* deceptive *B.* 23/17.

dispite *n.* contempt *B.* 18/10.

disposicioun *n.* temperament *D.* 63/19; *pl.* inclinations *D.* 63/25.

dissolucioun *n.* dissoluteness *B.* 38/16.

diuerse *adj.* different *B.* 13/13.

diuersite *n.* variety, *D.* 64/11; **diuersitees** *pl.* unlikenesses *H.D.* 6/25.

do(o) *v.* do *D.* 71/5; *done up*, raised *H.D.* 5/27; *done to*, added *B.* 19/12.

doctour *n.* Doctor (*title applied to leading Schoolmen of medieval philosophy*) *P.* 51/6.

doelful *adj.* sorrow-bringing *S.* 85/17.

doyng n. action *P.* 51/14; *doyng to*, addition *B.* 19/9; *doyng awey*, negation *H.D.* 4/9; *doinges awey*, *pl. H.D.* 9/25–26.

doles *n. pl.* deceits, wiles *S.* 86/21.

dome *n.* judgement *B.* 25/4.

domesman *n.* judge *B.* 17/9.

drawe *v.* draw, lead *P.* 54/17; **draweþ nere**, *translates Latin* adheret *P.* 56/16.

drede, dreed *n.* fear *B.* 17/3, 4.

drede *v.* fear *B.* 29/1.

dreuen *pp.* driven *H.D.* 6/17.

dronken *adj.* intoxicated *B.* 13/2.

dronkenesses *n. pl.* drunkennesses *H.D.* 8/1.

drounyd *pp.* drowned *B.* 28/10.

eelde *n.* age *H.D.* 10/4.

eend *pr. 1 pl. subj.* end *H.D.* 10/2.

eende *n.* aim *D.* 69/25; *pl.* extremities *H.D.* 4/23.

eendeles, eendles *adj.* endless *B.* 31/2, *D.* 65/7.

eerþe, *see* **erþe.**

eft *adv.* again *S.* 88/19.

eftsones *adv.* again *H.D.* 4/14; afterwards *B.* 21/17.

eggen *pr. 3 pl.* set on edge *P.* 57/22.

eiþer *adj.* (*with pl. n.*) both *P.* 58/21.

elles, ellys *adv.* else, otherwise *B.* 16/5, 37/11; **elles þat**, *quasi-conj.* so long as *P.* 55/12.

encresing *n.* increase *P.* 55/8.

enditing *n.* setting down *H.D.* 8/15.

enflaumyd, enflawmyd *pp.* inflamed, burning *B.* 22/3, 45/8.

enforceþ *pr. 3 s.* urges *B.* 33/3; *refl.* forces himself *B.* 40/12.

enioinyng *n.* prescription *D.* 76/16.

enournementes *n. pl.* adornments *H.D.* 7/33.

ensaumple *n.* example *H.D.* 4/27.

ensaumpled *pp.* exemplified *D.* 64/13.

ensclaundre *pr. 3 pl.* bring scandal upon *S.* 86/13.

entent *n.* intention *H.D.* 5/34.

enuirouneþ *pr. 3 s.* encircles *D.* 66/1.

er *conj.* before *H.D.* 6/3.

eres *n. pl.* ears *B.* 13/10; **eren** *D.* 69/5.

erles *n.* foretaste *B.* 31/13; *in erles of*, as a foretaste of *B.* 31/9.

erþe, eerþe *n.* ground, earth *P.* 52/20, *S.* 84/11.

eschewe *v.* avoid, shun *B.* 41/17.

ese *n.* ease, comfort *B.* 29/16; *þe most ese*, the easiest *D.* 71/4–5.

etyngly *adv.* whilst eating *D.* 72/2. *Not in* O.E.D.

euen- *adj.* equal *H.D.* 7/21; fellow- *B.* 34/11.

euen *adv.* just; *euen up*, straight up *D.* 66/5.

euenheed *n.* equality *H.D.* 9/31.

euenyd *pp.* made equal *B.* 25/8.

euydence *n.* obviousness *H.D.* 8/32; *by euydence þat*, through the instance that *D.* 68/11.

experte *adj.* experienced *P.* 55/20.

expositour *n.* expounder *H.D.* 2/11.

fader *n.* Father *B.* 12/5.

faderheed *n.* Fatherhood *H.D.* 7/16.

fage *pr. 2 s. subj.* beguile *P.* 48/18.

faile *n.* *wiþoutyn faile*, for certain *B.* 30/5.

faile (of) *v.* fall short (of) *D.* 72/13; pass away *D.* 74/4.

fairheed *n.* Beauty *H.D.* 6/29.

falle *v.* fall *B.* 36/11; occur *D.* 69/11; **falliþ (to)** appertain (to) *B.* 22/2; *impers.* (it) happens *B.* 32/11; *falleþ for to be*, befalls *B.* 35/11.

fals *adj.* false *B.* 29/9.

fantasie *n.* mental faculty of sensuous perception *H.D.* 9/27; *pl.* images *B.* 13/13.

fantastik *adj.* delusive *H.D.* 3/35. *See note*; represented in the mind *H.D.* 6/22.

fast *adv.* unshakeably *D.* 63/19; *as fast*, immediately *S.* 83/8.

fastliche *adv.* steadfastly *H.D.* 4/8.

fautours *n. pl.* supporters *S.* 86/16.

febely *adv.* inefficiently *P.* 48/3.

feend(e) fende *n.* fiend, devil *S.* 81/7, 16, 87/2.

feerþe *adj.* fourth *B.* 21/2.

feinid *adj.* deceptive *P.* 48/9; *pp.* pretended *D.* 70/22.

feinyng *n.* deception *P.* 48/7.

felle *adj.* fierce, cruel *S.* 81/16.

felly *adv.* fiercely, savagely *S.* 82/18.

fer *adv.* far, *moost fer*, furthest *H.D.* 8/30.

feriþ *pr. 3 s.* terrifies *B.* 29/13.

ferþer *adj.* more remote *H.D.* 9/6.

fyling *n.* defilement *H.D.* 4/29.

filþe *n.* defilement, corruption *S.* 84/5.

firstheed *n.* First Cause *H.D.* 2/15.

flateryng *n.* flattery *B.* 38/15.

fleschly *adj.* fleshly, carnal *H.D.* 3/14; unregenerate *B.* 23/2.

floure-de-lices *n. pl.* fleurs-de-lis *D.* 65/24.

flowyng *n.* flux, succession of changes *H.D.* 9/19.

folden *pp.* enclosed *P.* 48/17.

foles *n. pl.* fools *S.* 86/12.

for *prep.* in spite of *B.* 13/11.

forbede *pr. 3 s. subj.* forbid *P.* 48/18.

forby *prep.* in comparison with *B.* 44/16.

forcostoumid *pp.* too accustomed *S.* 91/13. *Not in* O.E.D.

fore *prep.* for *P.* 53/13.

forȝetyng *n.* forgetting *B.* 46/7.

forȝeuenes *n.* forgiveness *B.* 19/8.

formaciouns *n. pl.* productions *H.D.* 3/34.

forsake *pr. 2 s. subj.* withdraw from *H.D.* 3/1.

forseide *adj.* aforesaid *H.D.* 3/23.

forþ(e) *adv.* onwards, henceforth *B.* 20/8; *so forþ(e)*, then in regular sequence *H.D.* 7/1; and similarly *D.* 71/19; *as fer forþ*, to such an extent *B.* 46/7.

forþering *pr. p.* furthering, promoting *D.* 70/2.

for-þi *conj.* therefore *B.* 17/3; *for-þi þat*, because *H.D.* 2/5.

forþink *v.* repent, regret *B.* 41/3.

foulden *pr. 1 pl.* fold *H.D.* 7/4.

foule *adj.* wicked *B.* 13/15; grievous *B.* 40/15.

fouler *comp. adv.* more grievously *B.* 40/14.

fourme *n.* form *H.D.* 3/15.

freel *adj.* frail, weak *D.* 74/19.

freelte *n.* frailty, weakness *B.* 46/8.

freend, frende *n.* friend *H.D.* 2/31, *P.* 48/2.

frenesiees *n. pl.* frenzies, ragings *H.D.* 7/33; *translates Latin* furores.

fro *prep.* from *H.D.* 3/14; fro þat *conj.* from the time that *B.* 30/5.

frute *n.* fruit *B.* 26/14.

ful(le) *adj.* full, complete *P.* 49/17,

D. 63/22; *ful list*, free inclination *D.* 71/10; *adv.* fully *P.* 48/6; *at þe fulle*, fully *P.* 52/4.

fulfille *pr. 2 s. subj.* carry out *B.* 46/2; **fulfillyng** *pr. p.* filling to the full *H.D.* 2/23.

gadering *n.* compilation *H.D.* 7/28. *See* sentence.

gaderid, *see* sentence.

gaderist *pt. 2 s.* gathered, should gather *P.* 56/11; *gadered on one*, collected together *P.* 53/16.

galle *n.* gall *B.* 44/16.

gendriþ *pr. 3 s.* begets *S.* 87/9.

gete *v.* get, acquire *B.* 23/11; **getyn** *pp.* begotten, conceived *B.* 16/3.

gladid *pp.* gladdened *B.* 20/4.

glewe *n.* glue *P.* 57/1.

glose *pr. 2 s. subj.* flatter, cajole *P.* 57/7.

glosyng *n.* cajolery *B.* 38/15.

glotenye *n.* gluttony *H.D.* 8/33; **gloteniees** *pl. translates Latin* crapulae *H.D.* 8/2.

godheed *n.* Godhead *B.* 45/9.

godly, godlich(e) *adj.* pertaining to God, divine *B.* 44/2, *H.D.* 3/17; godly, saintly *H.D.* 4/12, 27, *S.* 92/17; *adv.* divinely *H.D.* 2/16.

goodes *n. pl.* good things *B.* 22/1; things *B.* 32/10.

goodly *adv.* in a proper manner, excellently *D.* 64/22; conveniently *S.* 82/2.

goostheed *n.* state of Spirit *H.D.* 7/17. *Not in* O.E.D.

goostly, goostliche, gostly *adj.* spiritual, mental *H.D.* 3/3; in the spirit *P.* 50/23; spiritual *B.* 38/14.

gracious *adj.* with the help of divine grace *H.D.* 6/27.

gracyously *adv.* through grace *P.* 58/10.

graunt *pr. 3 s. subj.* grant, give *S.* 93/2; **graunted** *pt. 3 s.* admitted *D.* 68/14.

gredy *adj.* greedy, eager *D.* 67/12.

greet, grete *adj.* great *H.D.* 6/24, *P.* 49/23; *sup.* grettest *H.D.* 5/33.

greetnes *n.* greatness, magnitude *H.D.* 9/30.

grucching *n.* grumbling *S.* 83/1.

gruchid *pp.* discontented, complaining *B.* 28/11.

ȝe *adv.* yea *H.D.* 4/11.

ȝeue *v.* give *B.* 44/4; *pp.* ȝeuen *P.* 58/14; ȝouen *B.* 44/8.
ȝit *adv.* yet *H.D.* 3/7; still *H.D.* 3/19; moreover *H.D.* 6/31.
ȝong(e) *adj.* young *B.* 46/14, *D.* 67/6.
ȝouen, *see* ȝeue.
ȝow *refl. pron.* yourselves *D.* 70/21.

han, *see* haue.
hande, honde *n.* hand, side *D.* 71/7; *taken on hande,* undertaken *D.* 67/1.
happely, happiliche *adv.* happily *B.* 27/10; perchance *H.D.* 8/22.
hardnes *n.* difficulty, obscurity *H.D.* 2/10.
harmyng *n.* injury *B.* 33/14.
hateredyn, hatereden *n.* hatred *B.* 33/8, 11.
haue *v.* (*refl.*) behave *H.D.* 6/9; *pr. 3 pl.* han have *H.D.* 3/21.
hede *n.* notice *B.* 19/15.
heed *n.* head *D.* 66/1.
heelful, *see* heleful.
heiȝ, hiȝe, hie *adj.* high *H.D.* 4/6, 6/10, *P.* 54/15.
heilich *adv.* loftily *P.* 54/4.
hele *n.* salvation *S.* 86/18.
heleful, heelful *adj.* salutary *B.* 44/13, *S.* 92/4.
helply, helpliche *adj.* helpful *P.* 59/10, 52/2.
helpe *n.* salvation, well-being *D.* 64/18.
herdesay *n.* hearsay, report *D.* 68/21.
herfore *adv.* for this reason *B.* 35/13.
hert *n.* hart *B.* 25/18.
hert(e) *n.* heart *H.D.* 7/17, *B.* 29/13.
hertly, hertlich *adv.* earnestly *P.* 57/6, 59/13.
hete *n.* ardour *P.* 56/22.
hetyng *n.* promising *B.* 29/14. *See* hiȝt.
heuily *adv.* with anger *S.* 83/4.
heuynes *n.* torpor, dullness *B.* 25/2; despondency *P.* 49/12; heuinesses *pl.* griefs, *translates Latin* tristitiae *H.D.* 7/33.
hid *adj.* mystical *H.D.* 5/18, 6/27; hid *pp.* hidden *H.D.* 6/23.
hiȝe, *see* heiȝ.
hiȝt *pp.* promised *D.* 65/2. *See* hetyng.
hir, *see* sche.

hold(e) *v.* keep *B.* 23/12, *D.* 77/1; holden *pp.* held, considered *S.* 82/4; holdeþ oute, keeps out *B.* 29/16; holde (þee) by, adhere to *D.* 70/6; holde silence, maintain silence *D.* 76/24.
hole *adj.* whole *H.D.* 6/7; undistracted *D.* 75/12.
holyliche *adj.* holy-like, having the appearance of being holy *D.* 70/23.
holpen *pp.* helped *H.D.* 5/2.
homly *adj.* homely, intimate *B.* 21/10; *adv.* simply *B.* 21/11.
homlynes *n.* intimacy *B.* 20/8.
hony *n.* honey, *B.* 44/16.
horribilite *n.* horribleness, terror *B.* 29/13.
houso *adv.* however *D.* 68/25.

iche *adj.* each *B.* 12/14.
ierarchies *n. pl.* hierarchies *H.D.* 7/13.
iȝe *n.* eye *H.D.* 5/5; *pl.* iȝen *H.D.* 2/24.
ilke *adj.* same *B.* 41/17.
ymagyn (of) *pr. 1 pl.* imagine, conceive of *B.* 26/4.
ymaginacioun, ymaginacyon *n.* imagination *H.D.* 6/6, *B.* 13/3; mental image *B.* 23/16.
ymagynatyue *adj.* = working by means of mental images *H.D.* 3/35.
inclusid *adj.* enclosed *H.D.* 6/14.
inliche *adj.* inward, in the spirit *H.D.* 2/16.
inordynacioun *n.* irregularity, excess *H.D.* 9/16.
inow *adj.* enough *B.* 22/2.
inparfite *adj.* imperfect *P.* 50/15.
inrennyng *n.* incursion *B.* 28/16.
into *prep.* up to *P.* 51/17.
yuel *adj.* evil *B.* 13/13.
iuels *n. pl.* evils *B.* 17/7.

jangelyng *n.* jabber, babbling *B.* 26/12.
jangler *n.* babbler *B.* 13/1.
ioie (in) *v.* rejoice (in) *B.* 40/8.

kepe *n.* care *P.* 57/8; heed *D.* 74/13.
kynde *n.* nature *H.D.* 6/13; sort *H.D.* 6/11; species *B.* 35/9; natural quality *B.* 36/1; natural constitution *D.* 62/16.
kynd(e)ly *adj.* natural *H.D.* 3/14, *B.* 13/18.

kynne *n.* kindred, lineage *S.* 82/5.
kirnel *n.* kernel *P.* 57/23.
knaues *n. gen. s.* menial's *P.* 53/4.
knittyngly *adv.* generally *H.D.*
10/15. *Not in* O.E.D. *Translates*
Latin omnino.
knowable *adj.* knowable, that may
be known *H.D.* 3/21; that may
know *H.D.* 7/6. *This sense is not*
in O.E.D.
knowe *v.* know *H.D.* 5/28; **not**
knowe, *simple negative infinitive*
used substantivally = act of not
knowing *H.D.* 5/29.
knowing *n.* knowledge *H.D.* 5/18;
pl. B. 22/13.
kumbros, koumbrous *adj.* cumbrous,
obstructive *H.D.* 6/22, 24.
kun *v.* know how to *B.* 40/3; *pr. 3*
pl. are able *H.D.* 3/30.
kunnyng *n.* knowledge *H.D.* 10/6.
See **connyng.**

last *n.* lowest *H.D.* 7/3.
lastyng *pr. p. used absolutely,* while
. . . continues *S.* 84/3.
late *v.* allow, let *D.* 64/3; *imp. s.*
behave *D.* 73/7; *lat be,* cease from
D. 73/7.
latter *adv.* later *B.* 27/3.
lawfulich, lawfuly *adv.* in accordance
with the practice enjoined *P.*
49/20, *D.* 70/1.
ledde *pp.* led *D.* 62/21.
leder *n.* leader *D.* 69/20.
leef *n.* leaf, page *S.* 90/22.
le(e)st *sup. adj.* least *H.D.* 4/14, *P.*
53/23.
lemman *n.* lover *D.* 72/18.
lene (to) *v.* rely (upon) *D.* 63/18;
lenid vnto, desired after *D.* 75/3.
lenger *compar. adv.* longer *P.* 48/11.
lere *v.* learn *B.* 36/12; *lered hym,*
taught himself *B.* 42/15.
lerne *v.* learn *B.* 26/17; **le(e)rnid** *pp.*
taught *B.* 42/12, *S.* 80/12.
lerner *n.* teacher *D.* 69/20.
les *adv.* less *B.* 27/13.
lesid *pp.* released *B.* 33/1.
lesing *n.* lie *P.* 49/1.
lesing *pr. p.* releasing, separating *D.*
72/3. *See note.*
lepir, *see* **liper.**
letters *n. pl.* hindrances *H.D.* 6/26.
lettyng *pr. p.* hindering *H.D.* 6/9.
leue *n.* leave, permission *D.* 71/9.
leue *v.* leave *P.* 59/9; **leuiþ** *pr. 3 s.*

remains *B.* 21/10; **left** *pt. 3 s.* left
off *B.* 21/17.
leuer *comp. adv.* rather *P.* 51/13.
leuyng *n.* life *D.* 75/17.
leuiþ *pr. 3 s.* lives *H.D.* 10/4; *pt. 2 s.*
leuedist *P.* 49/23.
lewid *adj.* ignorant *D.* 69/18.
liche (to) *adj.* like *B.* 25/16.
licne *pr. 1 s.* compare *P.* 55/1.
licnes, liknes *n.* likeness, similitude
H.D. 9/31, *B.* 42/4; compara-
bility, *translates Latin* comparatio
B. 25/15; form, appearance *S.*
85/18; *at þe licnes of,* according to
the metaphor of *D.* 64/17.
liʒe *n.* lie *P.* 57/7.
lyʒtenyng *pr. p.* shedding spiritual
light upon *B.* 42/7.
liʒtly *adv.* easily *D.* 63/11; quickly
D. 68/4.
liking *adj.* pleasant, delightful *P.*
53/20; *n.* pleasure *B.* 24/12.
likingly *adv.* pleasantly *P.* 57/15.
lynyng *n.* alignment *H.D.* 6/2.
list *n.* craft, cunning *B.* 41/4, *P.*
58/2.
list *n.* pleasure, inclination *D.* 71/10,
S. 84/7.
listi *adj.* ready, eager *H.D.* 3/1;
listely *adv.* with eager longing *P.*
57/14, *D.* 75/3, 76/18.
liper, lepir *adj.* evil *B.* 41/4, *P.* 58/2.
liuely *adj.* necessary to life *S.* 85/1.
loke *v.* see, examine *D.* 71/6; consider *S.* 90/20; *imp.* make sure
S. 88/13; **lokyþ** *pr. 3 s.* looks *B.*
23/6; *lokest after,* concern yourself
with *P.* 55/12; *loke þat þou rise,*
Latin consurge *H.D.* 3/10.
londe *n.* land *D.* 64/10.
longeþ *pr. 3 s.* belongs *D.* 75/22.
losable *adj.* in danger of damnation
S. 84/4. *Earliest reference in*
O.E.D. *1611, and this sense not*
recorded.
losse *n.* perdition *S.* 81/10.
loued *n.* beloved *P.* 56/26.
louely, loueliche *adj.* loving *B.*
21/9, *P.* 51/11; *adv.* lovingly *D.*
76/18.
lowe *adv.* humbly *D.* 66/12.
lust(e) *n.* pleasure *B.* 13/17; appetite
B. 26/15.
lusty *adj.* lustful *S.* 84/6.
lustly, *adv.* with inordinate desire
S. 84/10.

mayden *n.* maid-servant *B.* 12/14.

maister *n.* master *S.* 82/16.

makiþ *pr. 3 s.* composes, writes *B.* 12/4.

malencoly *n.* melancholy, ill-temper *S.* 83/2. *See note.*

maner *n.* manner, way *H.D.* 3/11; kind *B.* 20/8; (*without following* of) kind of *H.D.* 3/12; *on a maner,* in some degree *B.* 20/9.

manyfold(e) *adj.* varied *H.D.* 3/34; many *D.* 64/15.

mater *n.* occasion *B.* 30/2; subject *D.* 63/17.

material *adj.* physical, bodily *H.D.* 9/17.

mede *n.* reward *B.* 30/18.

medeful, meedful *adj.* profitable *P.* 51/18, 20.

medel (þee of) *v.* concern (thyself with) *D.* 74/19; **medelid** *pp.* mingled *P.* 51/3; combined *P.* 55/17.

meek, meke *v.* humble, abase *P.* 57/10; submit *D.* 67/18; **mekyd** *pp.* made humble *B.* 18/16.

meeknes *n.* abasement *B.* 18/1.

meenyng, menyng *n.* meaning *D.* 68/23; intention *D.* 72/10.

mene *adj.* common to both *P.* 58/21.

mene *n.* mean, intermediary *P.* 55/22; method, means *D.* 75/7; way *S.* 89/17; **me(e)nes** *pl.* means *P.* 50/4, *D.* 69/25; *by* (*þe*) *menes, bi som menes,* through the (some) intermediate stages *H.D.* 7/3, 9/30, 10/2.

mengid *adj.* mixed *P.* 58/17.

merk *v.* characterize *H.D.* 8/25; **merkyd** *pp.* marked *B.* 44/7. *Translates Latin* signatum.

mesure *n.* after þe mesure of, in proportion to *H.D.* 8/18–19; *oute of mesure,* out of proportion *B.* 40/13.

mesuryng, *n.* measurement *H.D.* 6/2.

mete *n.* food *B.* 28/4.

middes *n.* middle *H.D.* 6/3.

miȝt(e) *n.* strength *B.* 21/10; power *B.* 40/13; *pl.* faculties *H.D.* 5/12.

miȝt(e)ly *adv.* strongly, emphatically *H.D.* 4/5; with great power *D.* 64/21; vigorously *S.* 87/20.

miȝti *adj.* mighty, powerful *P.* 53/15.

mynde *n.* mind *H.D.* 2/24; consciousness *B.* 23/6; memory *P.* 54/9; thought *D.* 75/10; *mad minde,* mentioned *H.D.* 2/5; *abouen mynde,* in ecstasy *H.D.* 6/28.

mirour *n.* mirror *B.* 43/5; exemplar *D.* 74/5.

misreule *v.* rule badly *S.* 89/15.

mistely *adv.* mystically *D.* 75/18. *See note.*

moche, mochel *adj.* much, great *H.D.* 4/13, *B.* 38/10; *adv.* much *B.* 22/15; in-so-mochil, to such an extent *B.* 20/10.

mochilnes *n.* multitude *B.* 20/2.

mo(o) *comp. adj.* more *H.D.* 8/6, *B.* 30/2.

moder *n.* mother *B.* 17/13.

most *pr. 3 s.* must *H.D.* 4/1.

moste *n.* greatest things *H.D.* 7/3.

moten *pr. 1 pl.* must *H.D.* 6/12.

mow(e), mowen *pr. 3 pl.* may *H.D.* 3/4, 6, *B.* 36/12.

multyplieþ *pr. 3 s.* increases *B.* 45/3.

multitude *n.* copiousness *H.D.* 8/17; magnitude *B.* 45/8.

nakid *adj.* bare, unglossed *H.D.* 2/9; absolute *H.D.* 6/13; mere *P.* 51/18; stripped *S.* 91/12.

namely *adv.* especially *D.* 62/21.

napeles *adv.* notwithstanding *H.D.* 4/20.

ne *adv.* (*preceding verb*), not *H.D.* 9/20; *expletive B.* 43/1.

nedelynges *adv.* of necessity *H.D.* 10/19.

nediþ *pr. 3 s.* is necessary *B.* 18/6; him nedeþ *impers. with dat.* he needs *B.* 32/10.

needfulnes *n.* want, need *H.D.* 9/18.

negatyue, *see* deuenite.

nice *adj.* foolish *S.* 90/16.

niȝ(e) *adv.* more niȝ *comp.* nearer *H.D.* 8/31; moost niȝe *sup. H.D.* 8/28.

niȝhond *adv.* almost *B.* 23/1, 32/9.

no *adv.* not *S.* 89/4.

noble *n.* = *an English gold coin, first minted by Edward III, and having the current value of 6s. 8d. D.* 66/22.

noȝt, *see* nouȝt.

noye *n.* distress *D.* 65/10.

noresching *n.* nourishing, strengthening *D.* 70/18.

not-beyng *adj.* non-existent *H.D.* 10/9.

noþing *adv.* in no way *H.D.* 4/1.
not-vnderstondable *adj.* incomprehensible *H.D.* 10/21.
nouȝt *adv.* not *H.D.* 5/28; *n.* nothing *B.* 23/5; noȝt *P.* 55/11; *of nouȝt,* to no purpose *B.* 13/7; *doþ for nouȝt,* acts in vain *B.* 42/13; nouȝtes *adv. gen.* of no worth *P.* 52/3.
nowise, *see* wise.
nowþer ... ne *conj.* neither ... nor *B.* 28/10–11.

o, oo *adj.* one *P.* 56/17, *B.* 32/11; *on n.* singleness *H.D.* 10/6.
occasyon *n.* opportunity *H.D.* 4/29; cause *P.* 59/16.
of *adv.* off *P.* 57/24.
of *prep.* by *H.D.* 3/35; from *H.D.* 6/1; with *B.* 31/15; for *P.* 49/17; concerning *D.* 62/3.
oft *adv.* often *B.* 40/5, 42/1; *comp.* ofter *P.* 57/14.
oft-tyme *adv.* often *B.* 36/10; oft(e)-tymes *B.* 13/12, *P.* 52/4.
on *prep.* in *B.* 28/8.
on, *see* o.
onheed, oonheed *n.* oneness, unity *H.D.* 7/19, *P.* 56/21; oneheed concord *B.* 46/5.
onid *pp.* united, made one *H.D.* 3/11, *P.* 58/20.
only *adj.* mere *H.D.* 3/30.
only, onlich(e), oonly *adv.* only *H.D.* 6/31, *P.* 51/15; alone *H.D.* 6/30, *D.* 62/5.
onlines *n.* solitude *D.* 62/20.
open *adj.* revealed *H.D.* 4/20; clear, obvious *B.* 41/6.
openyng *n.* exposition *H.D.* 8/7.
opinion *n.* opinion *H.D.* 9/27; *han opinion, haue it in opinyon,* believe *H.D.* 3/22, 4/7.
or *prep.* before *B.* 28/14.
ordeynd(e), ordeined *adj.* well-ordered *B.* 12/9, 16/9; *pp.* destined *B.* 36/11; directed *P.* 59/4.
ordinaunce *n.* practice enjoined *P.* 49/20.
oþer *pron.* another *H.D.* 6/5.
ouerlappid *pp.* wrapped up in *H.D.* 6/20.
ouerleide *pp.* overlaid *H.D.* 6/20.
ouerpassyng *n.* going beyond *H.D.* 3/13; transcendency *H.D.* 10/22. *Translates Latin* excessus.
ouȝt(e), owȝt *n.* anything *B.* 13/11,

S. 83/6; *ouȝt bot,* except *B.* 19/7, 26/17.
oure *n.* hour *B.* 18/14.
oure *possess. pron.* ours *S.* 93/2.
ouþer *adv.* either *P.* 59/7; *ouþer ... or,* either ... or *B.* 29/6–7.
outrageous *adj.* excessive, immoderate *B.* 38/15, 16.
owe, *see* owne.
owne *adj.* own *S.* 89/19; owe *S.* 89/19; *þe owne,* its own *D.* 67/19.

pacyence *n.* calm endurance *B.* 27/7; long-suffering *B.* 29/17.
parauenture *adv.* perchance *D.* 63/8.
parfite *adj.* perfect *H.D.* 8/14; *adv.* parfytely *B.* 29/1.
party(e) *n.* part *P.* 52/19, 20; *a party,* a little, somewhat *B.* 16/1; *in party,* partly, a little *P.* 53/1; *on o partye,* on one side *B.* 17/7; partiees *pl. H.D.* 7/32.
passeþ *pr. 3 s.* transcends *B.* 30/11; *passen abouen,* transcend *H.D.* 4/21; passing *quasi-prep.* beyond the limit of *P.* 53/24.
passibilitee *n.* passingness, change, *H.D.* 9/19.
passing *adj.* extreme *D.* 76/19. *See* passeþ.
peyne *n.* sufferings of hell *B.* 22/5; pain *P.* 55/8.
perfeccioun *n.* highest state of holiness attainable by man *B.* 22/2; highest degree *B.* 39/14.
pesible *adj.* gentle *D.* 64/9.
pesid *pp.* reduced to tranquillity *B.* 30/10.
pyne *n.* torment (of hell) *B.* 18/8.
pine *v.* pain, distress *D.* 75/26.
pinful *adj.* painful, distressing, *D.* 76/18.
pleinly *adv.* clearly *P.* 50/22; fully *D.* 70/2; entirely *S.* 87/8.
pleseþ (to) *pr. 3 s.* is pleasing (to) *P.* 51/23.
point(e) *n.* object, aim *P.* 54/16, *D.* 72/5. *See notes to* 54/16, 72/10.
ponyschid *pp.* punished *B.* 27/7. *Translates Latin* affligatur.
pouert *n.* poverty *S.* 92/6.
preise, -yn *v.* praise, glorify *H.D.* 6/28; pronounce, declare *H.D.* 5/30, 7/26.
preisyng *n.* = affirmation of the glorious attributes of God *H.D.* 7/14.
prese *pr. 3 pl.* press, strive *S.* 91/2.

presume (of) *v.* presume, over-confidently expect *B.* 19/16; *presume on hymself*, set himself up *B.* 36/6; takes too much upon himself *B.* 40/12.

pricke, prik *n.* object *D.* 72/6; target *D.* 72/13; goad *D.* 75/26.

pryue *adj.* secret, mysterious *H.D.* 2/19; private *D.* 63/24.

priueliche *adv.* mystically *H.D.* 7/7.

priuetees *n. pl.* mysteries, profundities *H.D.* 3/26.

proces *n.* bi *proces of tymes*, in the course of time *H.D.* 9/19.

proef, profe, proue *n.* experience *H.D.* 6/31; actual trial *P.* 50/24; result *P.* 51/4, *D.* 75/8; demonstration *S.* 89/13.

profite *n.* proficiency *B.* 40/2.

profiteþ *pr. 3 s.* advances *B.* 42/3.

profre *imp. s.* put *B.* 43/14; **profren** (hem) *pr. 3 pl.* offer (themselves) *D.* 72/5.

propirly *adv.* appropriately *H.D.* 4/4.

propirte *n.* right to the possession *P.* 58/9.

propre *adj.* individual *H.D.* 3/15.

proueþ *pr. 3 pl.* experience *H.D.* 6/30; **prouen** *pr. 3 pl.* prove, demonstrate *S.* 80/8; **proue** *pr. 3 s. subj.* let . . . put to the proof *P.* 51/7; **prouid** *pp.* established *B.* 13/15; tested *D.* 65/2.

pullid *pp.* picked *P.* 57/21.

puple *n.* people *H.D.* 4/29.

purchase *v.* acquire, gain *H.D.* 2/26.

put (aȝeyn) *v.* drive (back) *B.* 29/9; *put awey*, remove *H.D.* 9/4; dispel *S.* 82/1-2; *put doune*, repress *B.* 24/4.

quantite(e) *n.* size *H.D.* 5/33; amount, magnitude *H.D.* 8/16, *P.* 51/25.

queintise *n.* cunning *S.* 82/15.

queintly *adv.* cunningly *S.* 82/16.

ransakiþ *pr. 3 s.* searches thoroughly *D.* 73/3.

raþer *adv. þe raþer*, the more quickly *P.* 48/8.

rauesching *n.* ecstasy *B.* 46/14.

rauische *v.* transport *P.* 58/24.

rechelesnes *n.* recklessness, negligence *P.* 49/18.

rechest *pr. 2 s.* carest *P.* 55/11;

What þar reche . . .? What does it matter . . .? *S.* 87/16.

rede *pr. 1 s.* counsel, advise *B.* 43/1; *imp. s.* reed read *P.* 59/15; *pp.* red *B.* 16/4.

redy *adj.* ready, willing *P.* 51/8; **redier** *comp.* quicker *P.* 50/4; **rediest** *sup.* quickest *B.* 41/1, *not in* O.E.D.

rediliche *adv.* quickly *P.* 50/6.

rediliche *adv.* wisely *S.* 85/20.

refreyne *pr. 3 s. subj.* restrain *B.* 26/15.

refresching *n.* refreshment *P.* 55/10.

reyse *v.* raise, uplift *B.* 24/6.

relesing *n.* release *P.* 55/7.

remedye *n. do remedye*, make amendment *B.* 41/14.

remena(u)nt *n.* remainder *D.* 71/19, 73/23.

remowe *pr. 1 pl.* remove *H.D.* 9/13.

renne *v.* run *S.* 90/17.

rere up *v.* rouse up *B.* 24/3.

resceyte *n.* reception *S.* 91/5.

resonable *adj.* reasonable, of the intellectual powers *B.* 28/7.

reso(u)n *n.* reason *H.D.* 4/18, 9/11; *pl.* exercises of reason *H.D.* 5/8; *is no reson*, is not agreeable to reason *P.* 57/22-23.

reule *n.* principle, guide *P.* 54/22.

reule *v.* govern *P.* 48/3; **rewlyd** *pp.* ruled, guided *B.* 41/1.

rewardyng *n.* (return) look *B.* 18/3. *Translates Latin* respectum.

rewme *n.* realm *B.* 37/11.

riȝt *adj.* correct *H.D.* 6/2; good, virtuous *B.* 12/8; *adv.* just, exactly *B.* 12/9; *þorow riȝt*, appropriately *B.* 17/10.

riȝtyd *pp.* put right, amended *B.* 36/12.

ruyde, rude *adj.* unlearned, inexperienced *B.* 23/2; ignorant *D.* 63/17.

saaf *adj.* saved *B.* 18/15.

sauelich(e) *adv.* safely *P.* 48/12, 59/9.

scaterst *pr. 2 s.* distract, dissipate *D.* 75/13.

schal *pr. 1 pl.* shall *B.* 41/14; *pr. 1 pl.* schul *H.D.* 3/27; *pr. 3 pl.* scholen *B.* 15/1; *pt. 2 s.* schuldest *D.* 71/13; *pt. 3 pl.* schold, schuld *D.* 68/8, *P.* 51/10.

schame *v. impers., þee wolde schame*, you would be ashamed *B.* 37/9.

schap *n*. shape *H.D.* 9/14.

schap(e) (þee) *imp. 2 s.* prepare to *P.* 53/5–6, 55/14.

scharply *adv*. vigilantly *P.* 59/16; sternly *D.* 67/20.

sche *pron. f. s.* she *B.* 13/11; scho *B.* 25/17; *acc*. hir, 13/12.

scheteþ *pr. 3 s.* shoots *D.* 73/2; *pp*. schotte *S.* 86/17.

schewe *v*. show, *H.D.* 6/5.

schittiþ *pr. 3 s.* shuts off *H.D.* 5/18; *pp*. schit (oute) *H.D.* 6/15.

scho, *see* sche.

schortyng *n*. cutting down, defect *H.D.* 8/14.

schote *n*. shot *D.* 72/12.

schotte, *see* scheteþ.

schrift *n*. confession *B.* 21/4. *See note to* 21/3–4.

schriue *v*. confess, ascribe praise and glory *B.* 21/3; schreuyn *pp*. absolved, shriven *S.* 88/14.

sclaundre *n*. slander, scandal *S.* 86/9.

scole *n*. school *D.* 64/6.

seable *adj*. visible *B.* 23/6.

seching *n*. seeking *D.* 71/6. *See* seek.

seek (at) *v*. ask for . . . (from) *B.* 41/14.

seeknes *n*. sickness *S.* 82/18.

seerly *adv*. separately *B.* 40/2.

seeþ *n*. satisfaction, amends *P.* 49/17.

sei, seie, seyn *v*. say *S.* 85/4, *P.* 52/14, *B.*16/3; *pr. 3 s.* seiþ *H.D.* 4/13; seyde *pp*. described *H.D.* 9/28; told *B.* 38/1.

sekir *adj*. sure, certain *P.* 49/11.

sekirly, sikyrly *adv*. surely, certainly *B.* 36/5, 44/14; sekerly *D.* 65/9; sekirliche *P.* 50/13.

self *adj. self fairheed*, very (i.e. absolute) beauty *H.D.* 6/29; *þe self feend*, the devil himself *S.* 83/11; same *H.D.* 6/29; himself *B.* 34/11.

sely *adj*. poor, helpless *D.* 64/10.

selynes *n*. blessedness *B.* 27/11.

semely *adj*. fitting, appropriate *B.* 26/11.

sensibilitee *n*. capability of feeling by the senses *H.D.* 9/15.

sensible *adj*. perceptible by senses *H.D.* 6/21, 7/30; that can be felt *P.* 54/6; considerable *P.* 59/1.

sensualite *n.* = part of the nature of man concerned with the senses *B.* 13/4.

sentence *n*. opinion, gist (of book) *H.D.* 2/7, 10; sentence *B.* 18/13; Gadering of Deuine Sentence *translates Latin title* Symbolica Theologia *H.D.* 7/28–29; Gaderid Book of Deuine Sentence *H.D.* 8/8–9.

sere *adj*. separate *P.* 56/18; various *D.* 73/4.

seriauntes *n. pl.* sergeants, servitors *S.* 81/6.

seruage *n*. servitude, slavery *S.* 87/3.

set(te) *v*. attribute, affirm *H.D.* 4/1; fix *B.* 23/3; setteþ *pr. 3 s.* puts *H.D.* 5/10; sette þee to, apply thyself to *D.* 76/2; sette *pt. 1 s.* planted *P.* 56/11; set *pp*. set down *H.D.* 7/14.

settyng *n*. affirming *H.D.* 8/25; *pl*. positive attributions *H.D.* 4/2.

siȝingly *adv*. with sighing *S.* 87/21.

signe *n*. gesture *S.* 83/6.

siȝt *n*. sight, seeing *H.D.* 6/4; *translates Latin* visionis *B.* 17/13, *Latin* consideratio *B.* 24/5, *Latin* speculatio *B.* 24/7.

synguleer, singuler(e) *adj*. unique *H.D.* 7/15; special, extraordinary *D.* 62/4, 63/2, *see note to* 67/24.

syngulertee *n*. singleness *H.D.* 5/15; singule(e)rtees, *pl*. singularities *D.* 70/21, *S.* 86/10, 12.

syngulerly *adv*. especially *B.* 39/11.

siþ *conj*. since *P.* 50/3.

siþen *conj*. since *H.D.* 3/25.

skyle *n*. reason *H.D.* 4/12.

sleckyn *v*. slake, quench *B.* 13/17.

slee *v*. slay *S.* 86/17.

sley, sleiȝ *adj*. knowing, wise *B.* 41/3, *H.D.* 3/1, 6/27.

sleiȝt *n*. wisdom *H.D.* 6/26; activity, *translates Latin* industria, *B.* 44/18; sleiȝtes *pl*. stratagems *P.* 58/2.

slepinges *n. pl.* sleepings, slumbers *H.D.* 8/2.

slewþe *n*. sloth *B.* 25/2.

so *conj. so þat*, provided that *P.* 49/16.

sodeyn *adj*. sudden *P.* 58/8; sodeyner *comp*. quicker, swifter *H.D.* 8/19.

sodenly *adv*. suddenly *P.* 56/1.

softe *adj*. pleasant *D.* 64/9; soft *S.* 81/18; softer *comp*. pleasanter *B.* 44/13.

softely *adv.* gently *D.* 75/24.
sogestion *n.* suggestion, incitement *S.* 87/9; *pl.* promptings *B.* 24/4.
soget (vnto) *adj.* subject (to) *H.D.* 9/17.
somdele *adv.* in some measure *B.* 42/18.
sondrid *pp.* divided, distracted *D.* 73/2.
sone *adv.* soon *B.* 20/1; **sonner** *comp.* earlier *B.* 27/3.
sone *n.* son *B.* 17/6; *pl.* **sons** *B.* 16/4, **sones** *B.* 16/7.
sonheed *n.* Sonhood *H.D.* 7/16.
sonnebeme *n.* sunbeam *B.* 43/17.
sore *adv.* sorely, exceedingly *D.* 75/25; **sorer** *comp. B.* 13/19.
sorouful *adj.* sorrow-bringing *D.* 70/20.
soþ *adj.* true *P.* 48/20.
soþfast *adj.* true *B.* 21/1.
soþfastly *adv.* truly, veritably *S.* 88/5.
soþfastnes *n.* truth *B.* 36/7.
souereyn *adj.* supreme *B.* 31/10, *D.* 70/24; potent, efficacious *P.* 51/20. *This word is used to translate Latin super- in Hid Diuinite,* e.g. *s. schinyng,* exceeding all light = supersplendentem, superlucenti 2/20, 5/27; *s. substancyal,* above all existence that one can understand = supersubstantialis 2/15, 5/31, 7/7; *s. substancyaly* = supersubstantialiter 3/22–3, 5/30; *s. vnknowen,* exceeding all knowledge = superignotum 2/18.
souereynli, -liche *adv.* in a surpassing (transcendent) manner. *See* **souereyn.** *s. fulfillyng* = superimplentem *H.D.* 2/23; *s. for to schine* = supersplendere 2/21; *s. set* = superposita, 3/31.
soule *n.* 'anima', rational soul *H.D.* 9/27; soul, spiritual part of man *B.* 40/10.
sounde *adj.* solid *H.D.* 5/33.
sounes *n. pl.* sounds *H.D.* 4/24.
souniþ *pr. 3 s.* sounds, speaks *S.* 80/6.
speche *n.* speech *S.* 80/7; *speches of fairheed,* goodly words *B.* 26/1.
specyal *adj.* particular *P.* 48/15.
spede *pr. 2 s. subj.* bring to an end *P.* 48/8; **sped** (of) *pp.* successful in getting *D.* 73/10.
speedful *adj.* profitable, helpful *B.* 24/1.

spekingly *adv.* eloquently *D.* 72/1. *Earliest reference to this form in* O.E.D. *1633.*
spousid *pp.* united in marriage *B.* 12/11.
stabelnes *n.* stability, immunity from destruction *D.* 64/18.
statute *n.* ordinance *D.* 70/13.
stede, steed *n.* place *B.* 30/8, *S.* 85/3; *to ȝeue stede,* to yield *D.* 67/5.
steedlynes *n.* local existence *H.D.* 9/15. *Not in* O.E.D.
steryng *n.* prompting *H.D.* 2/32; stirring, inward movement of feeling *P.* 51/1.
steriþ *pr. 3 s.* incites, prompts *B.* 34/7. *See* stire.
stifly *adv.* steadfastly *D.* 73/13.
stille *adj.* silent *D.* 62/9.
stille *adv.* ever *H.D.* 7/21.
stille *v.* silence *B.* 13/12.
stire *v.* stir, prompt *D.* 75/24. *See* steriþ.
stirer *n.* prompter, inciter *S.* 90/6.
stok *n.* block of wood *H.D.* 5/33; **stockes** *pl.* stocks *H.D.* 3/33.
stonde *v.* stand *B.* 37/10; depend *P.* 51/25; **stondeþ**, *pr. 3 s.* consists *P.* 50/24.
stonding *n.* standing *P.* 49/11.
stonding *pr. p.* (*used absolutely*), it being the case *P.* 49/19.
streite *adj.* narrow, restricted *H.D.* 4/15; strict *D.* 74/25; **maken streite,** contract *H.D.* 8/11, **maad streite,** contracted 8/20.
streitly, -liche *adv.* strictly *D.* 62/9; severely *P.* 57/19.
streitnes *n.* rigour, severity *D.* 76/17.
streng *n.* strength *B.* 27/5.
strengþing *pr. p.* strengthening *B.* 35/16.
stressing *pr. p.* constraining *P.* 57/19.
study, studie *n.* thought *B.* 45/1; study *B.* 12/4.
studieþ (after) *pr. 3 s.* directs efforts towards *B.* 22/16.
substaunce *n.* essential nature *H.D.* 7/19; separate created being *H.D.* 7/22; *pl.* separate being things *H.D.* 3/12; kinds of matter *H.D.* 6/21; substances, essential parts *P.* 58/17.
sufficyently *adv.* adequately *B.* 40/3.
suffringly *adv.* with patient endurance *D.* 65/1.

taast *n.* taste, slight experience *B.* 31/2.
taastyng *n.* faculty of taste *H.D.* 3/2.
take *v.* *take apon him*, presume *P.* 48/10–11; *take to*, assume to be against, *S.* 83/8; *toke to hem*, adopted *B.* 12/14; **take** *pp.* taken *D.* 74/8.
taried *pp.* hindered, kept back *D.* 62/7.
teermes *n.pl.* limits *H.D.* 4/23.
tyl *prep.* until *B.* 21/16.
tymes *be tymes*, now and then *B.* 44/3.
to, tone *þe tone, þe to*, the one *B.* 24/2, *D.* 62/6.
to *prep.* for *P.* 56/12.
togeders, togedir *adv.* together *H.D.* 7/4, *D.* 65/5.
tokyn *n.* sign *B.* 21/12.
toretes *n. pl.* turrets *D.* 65/24.
torne *pr. 1 pl. subj.* turn *H.D.* 10/1; *torne þe bak*, turn round *B.* 30/6; *pr. 3 s.* **turne**þ *B.* 18/15.
toþer *þe toþer*, the other *B.* 24/2–3.
touchid *pp.* mentioned *H.D.* 8/9; affected *P.* 54/5.
touching *n.* contact *H.D.* 10/5.
touching *prep.* with respect to *P.* 48/2, *D.* 68/6.
trace *v.* trace, search out *D.* 72/20; **trasid** *pp.* discovered *D.* 71/25.
trasing *n.* searching out *D.* 72/6.
trauayle *n.* labour *B.* 33/15.
trauayliþ *pr. 3 s.* labours *B.* 35/17.
trewþ(e) *n.* truth *H.D.* 10/6, *S.* 88/9; *pl.* **trewþes** *H.D.* 7/23.
trist *n.* trust, faith *P.* 51/12, *D.* 67/2.
tristen *pr. 3 pl.* believe *P.* 50/2.
troublid *adj.* wild, disordered *H.D.* 9/16.
trumpes *n. pl.* trumpets *H.D.* 4/30.

þan, see **þen.**
þan(ne) *adv.* then *B.* 43/14, 16.
þei *pron. nom. pl.* they *B.* 27/2; *acc.* hem *H.D.* 2/26; *dat.* hem *H.D.* 6/28; hemself *dat. pl.* themselves *H.D.* 3/35; *possess. adj.* here *H.D.* 3/19; **þeire** *B.* 13/6.
þen *conj.* than *H.D.* 8/19; *first . . . þan of*, first before *B.* 23/9–10.
þenk *v.* think *D.* 74/14; *imp. s.* **þink** *D.* 74/15.
þer(e) *adv.* where *B.* 25/16; **þerafter** accordingly, in like proportion *B.* 33/14; **þerfro(o)** from it *D.*

75/14, *S.* 83/11; **þerof**, with it *B.* 14/6; **þerto**, moreover *D.* 71/3.
þicke, þik *adj.* plentiful *S.* 89/2; thick *H.D.* 6/24.
þink *v.* consider *B.* 17/8.
þirst, þrist *n.* thirst *B.* 13/17, 26/15.
þof *conj.* though *H.D.* 3/7; *þof al*, although *B.* 23/10.
þoo *demonstr. adj.* those *H.D.* 2/24.
þorou, þorow *prep.* through *H.D.* 3/12, *B.* 12/7.
þrid *adj.* third *H.D.* 8/8.
þristy *adj.* thirsty *B.* 13/2.
þristeþ *pr. 3 s.* thirsts *B.* 13/19.

unacording *adj.* unsuitable, inappropriate *P.* 59/11.
vnbigonne *adj.* unbegun, eternal *H.D.* 2/14.
vndeedly *adj.* immortal *B.* 32/7.
vndeedlynes *n.* immortality *B.* 32/9.
vnderloute *adj.* subservient *B.* 26/13.
vnderstondable *adj.* able to understand, intellectual, *translates Latin* intellectuales *H.D.* 3/3; that can be understood, intelligible *H.D.* 6/21; which the understanding frames *H.D.* 7/27; *vnderstondable þinges*, mental qualities *H.D.* 9/26.
vnderstondyng *n.* understanding *H.D.* 4/18; interpretation *D.* 65/13; **vnderstondynges** *pl.* faculties of understanding *H.D.* 5/10.
vnesy *adj.* hard, unpleasant *B.* 27/1.
vngropable *adj.* impalpable, intangible *H.D.* 2/23.
vnknowe *v.* be ignorant of *S.* 85/17.
vnknowyng, vnknouing *n.* not knowing, ceasing to know *H.D.* 5/28; ignorance *S.* 88/8.
vnkunnyngly *adv.* ignorantly *B.* 13/10.
vnleueful *adj.* unlawful *B.* 24/8.
vnlicnes *n.* dissimilitude *H.D.* 9/31.
vnmaad *adj.* uncreated *H.D.* 6/13.
vnmesurid *adj.* unrestrained *B.* 16/12. *Earliest reference in* O.E.D. 1820.
vnmiʒtfulnes *n.* impotence *H.D.* 9/17.
vnnoum(m)erable *adj.* innumerable *H.D.* 6/20, 25.
vnordeynd(e) *adj.* uncontrolled *B.* 16/6, 38/3.
vnpassyngliche *adv.* = 'without departing from itself', unchange-

ably, *translates Latin* inegressibilia *H.D.* 7/21. *Not in* O.E.D.

vnresonabiltee *n.* irrationality *H.D.* 8/14. *Not in* O.E.D.

vnseable *adj.* invisible *B.* 23/3.

vnspekable *adj.* ineffable *H.D.* 8/21.

vntemprid *adj.* unrestrained *B.* 38/16.

vn-vnderstondabely *adv.* in a way not to be understood *H.D.* 10/22. *Not in* O.E.D.

vnwise *adj.* untaught, unitiated *H.D.* 3/19.

uprising *n.* resurrection *P.* 58/20.

vse *n.* habit, practice *S.* 92/12.

vse (þee) *v. refl.* accustom (yourself) by practice (in) *B.* 45/13, 40/4, 42/11. *See note to* 40/4.

vtter *adj. vtter man* outward man *D.* 70/13.

vanitees *n. pl.* profitless things *B.* 23/17.

veyne *adj.* unprofitable *B.* 28/16.

verely, -liche, verrely *adv.* truly *H.D.* 4/20, 5/17, *B.* 17/11.

verrey *adj.* true *B.* 41/8.

vertewe, verteue *n.* power *H.D.* 7/27, 10/3, *D.* 66/1; *pl.* virtues, moral qualities *B.* 14/12.

voide *v.* remove *H.D.* 6/8; dismiss *D.* 75/6.

vouche-saaf *v.* condescend *B.* 44/4; *pr. 3 s.* vucheþ-saaf *B.* 20/5.

waking *n.* keeping vigil *P.* 51/22; *pl.* wakings *H.D.* 8/3.

wakiþ *pr. 3 s.* watches *B.* 29/10.

wallid (aboute) *pp.* enclosed *H.D.* 7/6.

wantonnes *n.* unruliness, extravagance *B.* 38/16.

warnes *n.* cautiousness, vigilance *B.* 38/6, 40/6.

wawes *n. pl.* waves *D.* 64/8.

waxeþ *pr. 3 s.* grows *B.* 18/6.

weders *n. pl.* weather *D.* 64/9.

weike *adj.* weak *P.* 58/1.

weyknes *n.* weakness *B.* 41/13.

wel(e) *adv.* well *B.* 17/12; much *D.* 73/2.

wenen *pr. 3 pl.* think *H.D.* 3/23.

were *n.* perplexity *D.* 62/6.

wering *n.* wearing (a special habit) *S.* 86/3; *scharp weryng*, wearing haircloth *P.* 51/22.

werk *n.* work, exercise *H.D.* 6/12.

wetyn, wite(n) *v.* know, be known *B.*

28/13, 29/4, *D.* 74/14; *pr. 1 s.* wite *P.* 59/10; *pr. 2 s.* wost(e) *H.D.* 3/11, 6/3; *pr. 3 s.* wote *B.* 23/1; *imp. 2 s.* wite *B.* 37/3; *pt. 2 s. subj.* wist *D.* 73/7.

whereþorou *adv.* whereby, by means of which *S.* 91/16.

wheþer *interrogative particle introducing question B.* 36/5; *pron.* which of the two *B.* 27/11.

whi *adv.* why; *for whi*, = Latin *etenim*, for, because *H.D.* 6/33.

whiles (þat) *conj.* while *B.* 18/6, 32/10.

who *pron.* who; *as who*, as if one *D.* 65/13.

wiȝt *n.* weight *H.D.* 9/15.

wiȝt *n.* creature *S.* 85/18.

wyl, wile, wille *n.* intent *B.* 37/6; *pl. B.* 24/6; will, faculty directed to conscious and intentional action *P.* 51/6, *B.* 24/15; = affection *B.* 12/6.

wyl(e) *pr. 3 s.* wills, desires *P.* 58/4, *D.* 72/8; wol(e) *pr. 3 s.* will *P.* 59/2, 3; *pr. 1 pl.* wolen *H.D.* 8/25; wolde *pt. 1 s.* desire *P.* 52/6.

wilful *adj.* voluntary *S.* 92/6.

wilne *v.* desire *D.* 76/19.

wynn(e) (to) *v.* attain (to) *B.* 39/14; come (to) *P.* 49/15.

wise *n.* way *B.* 28/8; *nowise*, in no way *P.* 53/14.

wisse *pr. 3 s. subj.* guide *D.* 69/14.

wit, witte *n.* understanding *B.* 30/11; reason *B.* 53/13; *pl.* senses *H.D.* 3/2; mind *D.* 71/6; *natureel wit*, natural intelligence *H.D.* 6/3; *goostly wittes*, intellectual faculties *H.D.* 3/3; spiritual ways of perception, *translates Latin* spirituales sensus *B.* 12/8.

witen, *see* wetyn.

wiþinne-forþ *adv.* within *H.D.* 3/6.

wiþouten *adv.* outside *B.* 29/15.

wiþoutyn, -owten *prep.* outside *H.D.* 5/34; without *P.* 56/8.

without-forþe *adv.* without *H.D.* 3/5.

witnes *n.* testimony *D.* 67/22.

witnes *v.* testify, furnish proof *D.* 75/8.

witty *adj.* wise *P.* 53/15.

wittirly *adv.* truly *B.* 43/15.

wode *n.* wood *H.D.* 6/2.

wolde, *see* wyle.

wole, wolen, *see* wyle.

wonder *n. no wonder þof*, (it is) not

surprising if *B.* 39/11; *what wonder þof,* is it surprising if *B.* 39/13.

wonyng *n.* dwelling *D.* 62/5; *wonyng stede,* dwelling-place *B.* 30/8.

wonyng *pr. p.* remaining *H.D.* 3/19.

woodnes *n.* madness *H.D.* 8/33; fury, mania, *translates Latin* furorem *B.* 38/17; **woodnesses** *pl.* frenzies, *translates Latin* insaniae *H.D.* 8/1.

worche *v.* work *P.* 58/14.

worching *adj.* active *H.D.* 5/12.

worching *n.* working *P.* 48/16; **worchinges** *pl.* activities *H.D.* 3/4.

worde *n.* utterance *B.* 32/15.

wordly *adj.* worldly *H.D.* 3/14.

worschepid *pp.* honoured *S.* 84/11.

worschip *n.* honour *S.* 81/15.

worschipful *adj.* worthy of honour *S.* 82/8.

worþelich *adv.* worthily, with real desert *P.* 52/5.

worþi *adj.* good *P.* 53/15.

worþines *n.* excellence *B.* 26/4.

wote, *see* **wetyn.**

wrappes *2 imp. pl.* be wroth *B.* 34/5.

wretin *pp.* written *H.D.* 2/6.